Invisible Crises

Critical Studies in Communication
and in the Cultural Industries
Herbert I. Schiller, Series Editor

INVISIBLE CRISES

———

*What Conglomerate Control
of Media Means
for America and the World*

edited by

GEORGE GERBNER
HAMID MOWLANA
HERBERT I. SCHILLER

WestviewPress

A Division of HarperCollinsPublishers

Critical Studies in Communication and in the Cultural Industries

Copyright © 1996 by Westview Press, A Division of HarperCollins Publishers, Inc.

Published in 1996 in the United States of America by Westview Press, 5500 Central Avenue, Boulder, Colorado 80301-2877, and in the United Kingdom by Westview Press, 12 Hid's Copse Road, Cumnor Hill, Oxford OX2 9JJ

A CIP catalog record for this book is available from the Library of Congress.
ISBN 0-8133-2071-2.   ISBN 0-8133-2072-0 (pbk.)

The paper used in this publication meets the requirements of the American National Standard for Permanence of Paper for Printed Library Materials Z39.48–1984.

10   9   8   7   6   5   4   3   2

Contents

PART FOUR
GLOBAL FAULT LINES

PART FIVE
THE NEW TYRANNIES

Introduction

GEORGE GERBNER, HAMID MOWLANA,
AND HERBERT I. SCHILLER

We see around us a profound unease and the crumbling of the vision of a good society. Bombarded by eruptions of surface consequences (often presented as unique events stripped of historical context), people are bewildered, fearful, angry, and cynical.

The collapse of the Soviet Union and Eastern European governments ushered in not a rebirth of hope but a rebirth of greed and a series of power grabs resulting in new tyrannies and civil wars. Civil wars rage at home too, disguised as wars on crime, drugs, youth violence, and immigrants.

We have come to the end of the illusion that the post–World War II order can realize the expectations that greeted it or justify as Cold War necessities the repression that dominated it. The new political shifts, touted in media cover stories—with unintended irony—as a "revolution," mark a turn to deeper, more deeply disguised, and thus even more critical delusions.

The crisis in the West may be less visible but is no less serious than the collapse and its aftermath in the East. And, as in the East, it represents not just the corrosion of the democratic process but the corruption of the democratic idea itself. How else can we permit and even promote practices that drug, hurt, poison, and kill thousands every day? Media formulas that dehumanize and stigmatize? Cults of violence that desensitize, terrorize, and brutalize?

How else can we build theme parks and palaces of commerce but conceal the growing siege mentality of our cities, the drift toward ecological suicide, the silent crumbling of our infrastructure, the widening resource gaps and the most glaring inequalities in the industrial world? How else can we accept total control of communication, technocratic fantasies of an information superhighway, or destructive global fault lines and new transnational tyrannies as "free market" benefits?

Even the language we speak has been corrupted by the uses to which it is put. Not only *revolution* but words such as *democracy, freedom, justice, capitalism, socialism, liberalism,* and even that misbegotten *media* have been twisted out of shape to serve strange purposes of powerful users. Of course, one of these words is *crisis* itself.

In his chapter "Global Drug Scourge" in this volume, Stephen E. Flynn explains why "crisis" is difficult to define. "The word has become so much a part of popular parlance," he writes, "that on any given day we are likely to hear people speaking of their identity crises, midlife crises, and crises in their families." The mass media have "considerable power to identify, substantiate, bypass, or create crises." Flynn then defines an "invisible crisis" as a situation in which "the objective reality that new developments are undermining the stability of a system or subsystem is ignored or denied and no new initiatives are considered in response."

"Crisis" comes from the Greek *krinein,* to judge, whence *krisis,* the decisive moment, the time for judgment. It is in that sense that we are using the word in this book. We explore and expose some realities that have been ignored or denied either because they are all-pervasive or because their full disclosure is unacceptable to the systems they threaten.

The crises explored in this book are all connected. They range from the local to the global and from the concrete and specific to the ideological. Any classification, such as evident in the part headings of this volume, is a somewhat arbitrary device of convenience. It may be suggestive but also somewhat misleading. The whole is not only larger than the sum of its parts. It adds up to more than the crisis of a system; it adds up to the crisis of vision.

Invisible crises can be the results of natural processes, such as the environment or an apparently dormant volcano, that do not reveal their threat to the casual observer until it is too late. Or they can be social realities that are either hidden from sight or submerged in the flood of distractions an advanced communication and information system can discharge into the mainstream of the common cultural environment.

A crisis so pervasive that it escapes vision is hidden behind the irony of the transformation of "media" from a plural noun to its singular use. Media used to denote plurality—of senses, modes, institutions, ideologies, and perspectives. But, for all practical purposes, the media mainstream has coalesced into a seamless, integrated cultural environment that has pervaded our world while it drifted out of democratic reach. Converging technologies fill the mainstream with a single perspective to which there is no equivalent challenge.

We begin this book with the race toward total control of that media mainstream. Ben H. Bagdikian projects a "Brave New World Minus 400" in which channels proliferate while ownership consolidates and alternatives vanish. In "Information Deprivation in an Information-Rich Society," Herbert I. Schiller describes how the most powerful suppressors of free speech hide behind the shield of the First Amendment. "The Hidden Side of Television Violence" by George Gerbner illuminates other aspects of control such as the demonstration of power and global marketing. And in "Speaking Volumes: The Book Publishing Oligopoly and Its Cultural Consequences," Leah F. Binder explores some implications of the transformation of what has been the most diversified part of culture.

Part 2 projects trendy technocratic fantasies—and their antidote. Rick Crawford in "Computer-Assisted Crises" sounds a wake-up call before the "information superhighway" becomes a super highway robbery of most public and private communication. Nicholas Johnson's warning about the theology of the marketplace applied to communication closes this section with "Freedom, Fun, and Fundamentals: Defining Digital Progress in a Democratic Society."

The narrowing of vision blots out the gaps of class and race that divide us and tear us apart, the theme of Part 3. Stanley Meisler recounts his experience in "Writing About Poverty in the Age of Plenty." Rosalyn Baxandall and Elizabeth Ewen report on "Race Relations in the Suburbs." And Jerry Mander tells the story of "National Amnesia, Cultural Darwinism, and the Pursuit of Power, or What Americans Don't Know About Indians."

Other gaps open up global fault lines, traced in Part 4. One of these is gender-based, seen by Sue Curry Jansen in "Beaches Without Bases" as worldwide power plays fueling wars and media blackouts. Johan Galtung exposes "The New World Intellectual Order" of cosmology, epistemology, and style. "Whose Whispers Are in the Gallery?" asks Erskine B. Childers as he observes the dangers of media colonialism spreading ignorance and disinformation. The conflict between the nation-state system and communities based along lines of faith, tradition, and values is explored by Hamid Mowlana in "The Crisis of Political Legitimacy and the Muslim World." A dangerous and destructive fault line running across all borders and providing new opportunities for repression is the mass displacement and migration of people, discussed by Nancy Snow in "The Crisis in Mobility."

The hardships and sacrifices once justified by Marxist regimes as investment in the future are now imposed by the new tyrannies of environmental degradation and international banking, monetary, and trade practices, the focus in Part 5. In "Let Them Eat Pollution," John Bellamy Foster argues that the global system of capitalist production and distribution is ecologically, economically, politically, and morally unsustainable. Jill Hills demonstrates in "The Silent War: Debt and Africa" that the invisible "debt crisis" is really a food crisis, a health crisis, an education crisis, a deindustrialization crisis, an environmental crisis, an export crisis, a crisis of sovereignty, a crisis of political influence in world affairs, and a crisis for survival in a world system becoming ever more racist and undemocratic. In "Global Drug Scourge: The Hidden Story," Stephen E. Flynn describes how the illicit drug trade further compounds the misery of the many and the profits of a few.

Invisible crises include those hidden or obscured and the dark side of those very much in the limelight. The new frontier of the struggle for vision and for access to visibility is thus the mainstream of the cultural frontier that now pervades every home. It is our hope that the chapters in this volume will help to alert, energize, and mobilize citizens on that frontier.

PART ONE

TOTAL CONTROL

1

Brave New World Minus 400

BEN H. BAGDIKIAN

Sixty years ago, Aldous Huxley published his novel *Brave New World,* a nightmare vision of the twenty-fifth century when whole populaces would be conditioned and controlled by high technology in the hands of a central power. We may be moving toward that chilling vision far faster than even Huxley imagined.

Although the mass media have properly kept our eyes glued to the dismal results of centralized control by political dictators, such as Hitler and Stalin, they remain virtually silent about the contemporary threat—the same kind of nightmare of mass conformity envisioned by Huxley but this time created by a family of powerful private corporations and four hundred years before Huxley's twenty-fifth-century prediction.

A few combinations of high-tech corporations already are organizing to inundate the world populations with what comes to them as second nature, making maximum profits through their closely held control of the coming world cultural and informational systems. Second nature also is their goal—to shape the global message with a view to creating mass conditioning of the young and the old on every continent. If that sounds alarmist, one need only look on the track record of the mass media operators in the United States, which is the model for replication around the world.

Though today's American commercial television is the early model, it is primitive compared with the new technology that will soon provide vastly more powerful mechanisms of interactive television, computers, and high-capacity channels not just in the United States but around the globe. If there is a replication worldwide, as there seems to be today, of the sad archmodel of commercial television in the United States, the world will be flooded with a seamless culture of destructive consumerism, the basic source of media profits.

The same system, once consolidated, will use its access to the massed public to do what its operators have done in the United States. They remain almost silent about the social problem of their tight control of the country's mainstream printed and broadcast news. That news contains little about the alternatives available to the public beyond the media corporation's own agenda. If the standard news stresses anything on public policy in broadcasting and print, it stresses statements by sympathetic spokespersons pushing media goals.

In politics, the same standard news highlights and supports politicians who favor the corporate policies. It all but buries news about any political leader who tries to promote alternatives closer to the needs of the general public and who tries to enlarge democratic participation by the citizenry in corporate communications policies.

Narrow corporate control of our mass communications goes far beyond the already grim uniformity of what comes out of our television sets. The goal of the media giants is not limited to their desire to control mass communications and its content. It is also to maximize profits by conditioning the world to buy compulsively and in most cases unwisely. And to do that, they have developed techniques that grip public attention with constant violence and high-speed graphics that deny the viewer time to reflect on the message just heard. This approach sells goods. But it also infects news about everything, including politics. What those techniques have done to the American electoral democracy—punishing with obscurity any politician who does not meet the media's demand for superficial photo footage or sound bites—should be evidence enough of the alarming political consequences.

In the United States, there has been steady perversion of the basic Communications Act of 1934 declaration that the airwaves are the property of the public, to be used for the public interest. The legislation, still theoretically the basic law, required that commercial users ascertain problems and issues in their communities and with those results produce noncommercial programs and give competing civic groups fair access on those issues as a condition of renewing their broadcast licenses. But as the power of commercial broadcasters grew, so did their influence within government. Those legal requirements have either been repealed or ignored. For a citizen or citizen group to challenge successfully a delinquent community broadcaster has been made almost impossible.

The history of the cable industry has been the same. Originally, operators were granted their monopoly in 98 percent of all cities by competing for the degree to which the community at large could have noncommercial access for community programs. Once in place, the cable industry's power produced deregulation of cable, tossing out the public service requirements with lowered quality of service to cable users and ever higher charges.

Politicians quickly discovered that once out, the genie of unrestrained corporate power could not easily be put back into the bottle. Without legally mandated free public service, corporate control by television and cable operators has meant their exclusive control over how each politician is presented—or never presented—to the public in news and in other images. The high monopolistic profit levels of the industry produced large campaign contributions to congenial politicians that spoke louder than the voices of voters and civic groups asking for access to *their* systems.

Now that commercial broadcasters and cable operators have protected themselves from effective public challenge, there has been steady escalation of the cheapest entertainment to mass produce and fix attention: violence, gratuitous sex, the international disgrace of what the commercial operators call "children's television," and wildly irresponsible consumerism that is economically and environmentally destructive. If the global reenactment of that sad history is to be prevented, effective action is needed before the major corporate players have firmly established the world system on their own terms.

The emerging systems begin with extremely high-capacity technology that can bring hundreds of channels to each household. At present the concentration is on fiber optics, but other high-capacity techniques are on the horizon. A fast-moving amalgam is being made today of the new channels with computerized television screens and the global corporations that own or control most of the entertainment archives (records, films, film production companies, and scientific and scholarly journals of the world). The current systems already use communications satellites in space that permit feeding of these channels to every part of the world.

There is never any certainty or precision in predictions of social consequences of new technology. There is always a tendency to regard new technology as having within the machinery some dues ex machina that foreordains the machine's future uses in ways originally seen by the machine's innovators. Henry Ford thought his Model T would merely provide fast mechanical transportation, but the automobile did more than make horse-drawn vehicles and blacksmiths obsolete. Ford's machine transformed all of modern life, the shape of its cities and the occupational patterns of the population, the nature of the air we breathe, and even the sex life of the young.

So it is possible that the next century will bring neither the corporate rosy view of limitless channels full of enriching and diverse information and entertainment nor the forbidding picture of a world inundated with the sanctity of soda pop, cosmetics, cigarettes, and the cultural-political power of the world's largest corporations. But the history of commercial mass communications so far cannot be ignored, nor can we overlook the genetic compulsions of the corporations that created that history and now have growing control of the future.

If a global repetition is to be prevented, there is little time to waste. By mid-1993, combinations of large corporations already were forming to control the new multimedia. One preliminary set of partners, for example, included Time Warner, the largest media company in the world; Tele-Communications, Inc., the largest cable company in the United States; and Microsoft Corporation, the largest manufacturer of software for computers.

Time Warner appears repeatedly in other big corporate combines that would seem to be competitors but in fact have interlocked hands with the dominant giants in a variety of combinations. One reason is that corporations like Time Warner are dominant in almost every branch of the media, such as having archives of existing programs and control of facilities to produce new ones. Time Warner is also the second largest cable company and is dominant in magazines, books, and records. In short, the interlocked world of giants of the present communications scene leaves little opening for new, smaller entries that could dilute the power of the giants and therefore their oligopoly over global information.

Although the United States offers the prime model in the world of mass communications controlled by a few corporations, the same trend exists in western Europe and Japan. The large multinational corporations in those countries are already ensconced in their national economies—and expanding internationally.

The present models in the developed world offer no comfort for democratic communications. In the United States, the system virtually ignores and resists central needs of society—easy access for citizens and citizen groups; a democratic electoral system in which voters hear and see a fair sampling of alternative candidates, parties, and issues not sponsored by the wealthy; and a retreat from converting the world population into a global mass of compulsive consumers and polluters of the planet.

Tentative steps by nonprofit civic groups call for national and international reservation of the new systems for mainly noncommercial uses that include education, access by a wide spectrum of individuals and civic groups, activity by broadly diverse political and social movements, and restrictions on advertising and advertiser-controlled programming. But those forces need strengthening and more popular support if they are to counter the economic and political power of the corporations now shaping the new systems. And they need support for efforts to break into the present resistance of our mass media to let their ideas reach a large public.

The American model is supported by advertising that precludes creation of other kinds of programming and socializes populations to become neurotic in their need to buy advertised commodities. The harmful social effects are intensified because television is effective in using our culture's artful conditioning of people to spend their money on marginal or harmful goods that are sold most effectively by emotional associations made in seconds. Most of our mass advertising provides little or no useful product information.

Furthermore, it has generated mass spending on goods such as cosmetics, cigarettes, beer, soft drinks, and patent medicines completely out of proportion to the rational use of national income. Public attention is diverted from society's central needs, including public education, health care, democratic economics, and other human and national activities central to a decent modern civilization. Those core needs of our society have no profit-motive commercials seen on our television screens day in and day out. These central constructive institutions of society are not included in the rapid-fire, twenty-four-hour drumbeat of commercial persuasion on television because they provide no immediate cash profit for the communications industry and its advertising clients.

The new systems will have vast numbers of channels—as many as five hundred. But the large numbers are misleading as a measure of the diversity of their uses. The channels will be controlled by a few conglomerate firms. The firms are in the business of selling commercial time to advertisers who will insist on or support only those programs that will be ferociously competitive for instant attention. All commercially supported channels use the established techniques to dissuade a user from switching to another channel—endless scenes of violence and other aggressive melodrama, gratuitous sex, split-second cuts on a busy screen, all designed to keep a viewer glued to that channel and not shift to one that may have a competitive ad. That competition is already fierce with the existence of thirty channels in major cities today. The present void of effective public policy means that multiplying channels will simply multiply the uniform and destructive content that already dominates American commercial television.

Ordinary commercial television and cable already represent the ability to decide how the image of politicians and public issues will be displayed—or, worse for a politician, not to be displayed at all. As a result, those with central control of mass communications have an overwhelming pattern of getting what they want in regulatory and legislative action from government bodies.

Part of concentrated media power is the ability to keep out of the news the social dysfunctions of the present system. The same power is used to accentuate the arguments of the industry for making governments conform to its wishes. The sad history of the evolution of official policies on mass communications in the United States is full of episodes in which the industry publicized its rhetorical promises of public service but engaged in quiet moves behind the scenes to do the opposite.

In addition to framing the public agenda on all issues, including communications policy, the industry giants use powerful law firms, influential lobbyists, and heavy campaign contributions to frustrate large-scale public protests by citizen groups and educators. Public objection to violence on television has been massive and growing steadily for decades. But except for honeyed words and brief pauses in the escalation, the level remains bloody and pervasive because violence grips attention for the interposed commercials and sells well abroad because it requires no translation. A bloody body and an exploding automobile need no words anywhere in the world. Even if violent programs may not be the top moneymakers in the United States, they still make enough money in this country and do well in the multilanguage international world. They can eventually condition otherwise nonviolent foreign mass media as they have done in this country.

The new systems not only will carry entertainment television and cable but also will greatly expand other informational services that already exist on a smaller scale—home and office access to huge banks of data useful in business, the professions, scholarly research, and personal pursuits of subject matter of interest to ordinary people. But as the system is structured today, these will cost the consumer per use. Business and industrial users of such electronic data usually can deduct the charges as a business expense; individual users seldom can. And it is a given in marketplace economics that the tighter the control of a product by a few firms, the higher the prices and the lower the quality of services.

"Free" television may well disappear in time, replaced by fee-per-viewing, as with cable and large home storage of digitized programs that can be used in the home at times of the individual's choosing. Those who can afford the fee-per-use arrangement and be trained on how to use the system will be at an advantage in gaining education, finding good jobs, and obtaining detailed information on politics and occupations.

(I put "free" in quotation marks because the hidden costs of "free" television are not small—the consumer must pay for the elaborate equipment to receive programs and pay the added cost that advertising places on the consumer goods sold through expensive television commercials. It is not a small hidden cost but is borne by most American households because once the hidden cost is met, the TV set can be baby-sitter and a substitute for tickets for personal attendance at real events like the theater and sports. That enables the household to recoup some costs, but it further isolates people from community contact with fellow citizens.)

Free access to information is already a problem in the world of libraries. Much that was once in print to be read in a library without charge is now produced in databases accessed by computer, and most of these services are commercially owned and charge a fee per use. For libraries, already economically starved, it presents a terrible dilemma to dilute a basic democratic institution, the free public library, with the anathema of fee per use.

An increasing amount of strictly public information for which taxpayers have paid, such as the census and many other governmental surveys, is quickly disappearing into the databases of private corporations that charge for access to that information and whose public propaganda urges the government to stop issuing its own data "because it competes with private industry."

The impact of the growing proportion of information available only at a fee per use will create further social stratification in our society. The information "haves" versus "have-nots" already represent a social problem in the United States, including in schooling: On the one hand are students who have home computers and family funds for pursuit in depth in commercial databases; on the other are students, now a majority, who have neither the computers nor the money to subscribe to a database. The new complex fee systems and enlarged capacity of computer users intensify the social disparities between children in poor school districts with inadequate civic services in poor neighborhoods and children in more affluent districts who have better education facilities and access to superior information. Consequently, informational haves and have-nots become social, economic, and political haves and have-nots. That, in turn, makes for an ominous growth of large-scale alienation and civic instability within societies, already too evident in the United States.

There is little time left for action to prevent repetition of the social errors of the past. Action must be taken now on the emerging communications while they are still in the process of technical and corporate formation. A few major corporations control the technology, design, and construction of the systems. They have tied up access to the archives of existing programs and facilities for creating new ones. They control public access to the system. The history of mass communications is that once a mass system is in place, it is almost impossible to alter it or to dislodge the control by their designers and owners.

Action needs to be taken not only within nations but also internationally. Each communications satellite can transmit messages over large portions of the globe, ignoring national boundaries. Just as even the tightest dictatorship in the twentieth century could not prevent citizens from receiving information by shortwave radio, a positive result, it will be impossible for national regulatory bodies to represent public need in what is transmitted from international satellites in space, a negative result. Most of what is commercially transmitted is controlled by multinational corporations that find it easy to resist even the few strictly national attempts to prevent monopoly and denial of public access on a worldwide basis. The new systems make boundaries of the individual nations less significant but also transmit distinctive cultures.

Major access by the citizenry to communications has to be raised to the level of a new world right. The present worldwide fervor for what is called "the free market system" permits private commercial power to dislodge any attempt to integrate serious public, noncommercial needs into mass communications, and that kills contrary public voices. Commercial operators like to reject public intrusion by raising the image of dictatorships that have used mass communications for totalitarian political control. They do not mention the ills that have befallen the American electoral process that depends largely on wealth to buy commercial political time, and they do not contrast their private system with the BBC and other quasi-national bodies that have demonstrated that mass communications can serve the best interests of the whole public without becoming the propaganda arm of any particular regime or party.

A generation ago, Marshall McLuhan popularized the idea of television creating a "global village." The peoples of the world, no longer separated by different languages and cultures, would be drawn together in the universality of images that need no words and ideas but are transmitted dramatically by nonverbal graphics. The concept implied a more peaceful, fruitful era in empathetic global human relations. But that is not what the twentieth-century model has been. The twenty-first-century model is in danger of being built not on the unity of a humanistic global village but on the commercial unity of Coca-Cola and Liggett &

Myers, of bloody bodies and exploding automobiles, of wasteful consumption and the socialization of the world's infants to an adoption of violence and aggression as the prime methods of conducting human relations.

Unless there is organized public intervention, the mass media of the twenty-first century will not represent a parliament of the people but the organizing of masses of children and adults everywhere, including in the Third World, into an electronic shopping mall devoted to the culture of wasteful and ultimately fatal use of the planet's natural resources and a diminishing of the human spirit.

2

Information Deprivation in an Information-Rich Society

HERBERT I. SCHILLER

An all-embracing structural transformation of the past fifty years has been the ascendance of corporate power and the corresponding decline of government authority over key areas of national economic, political, and social life. This has occurred in all industrialized as well as less developed economies, though with considerable variability from one country to another.

In the United States, where this change is most fully developed, it is also less evident because of the continuing though declining global hegemonic role of the American state. This requires a huge military, intelligence, and police apparatus to monitor and discipline the far-flung territories as well as a potentially disaffected domestic public. This vast apparatus, now being reluctantly downsized, still confers great power on the state. The trend, however, has been to extend private decisionmaking at the expense of governmental authority.

In the increasingly central spheres of communication and information, the shift from state to private power is especially marked and observable. Here, too, however, exceptional conditions conceal the full dimensions of the transfer of authority. Not least is the capability of the private informational machine to withhold the evidence of its own primacy and activity. Additionally, there is the continuing barrage, issuing from the same source, of an *information glut* and the burdens of living in an *information society*. This clamor serves to divert attention from the very real but largely invisible deficit of socially necessary information. More about this is presented later.

What are the effects of the enormous extension of private power in the informational sphere? They can be appreciated best, perhaps, by considering what has been happening to individual expression, and how this is explained.

Historically, the threat to individual expression has been seen to come from an arbitrary state. This view is embodied in the U.S. Constitution, in which free speech is explicitly protected against governmental power and its potential for abuse. And so it has been for centuries: states limiting and suppressing individual expression, and individuals and social movements struggling to reduce and overcome censorial power.

Now a new condition exists, though it is barely acknowledged. What distinguishes this era is that the main threat to free expression has shifted from government to private corporate power. This does not imply that the state has lost its taste for controlling individual expression. It means instead that a more pervasive force has emerged that now constitutes a stronger and active threat to such expression.

Today, the power of huge, private economic enterprises is extended across national and international boundaries, influencing and directing economic resource decisions, political choices, and the production and dissemination of messages and images. The American economy is now hostage to a relatively small number of giant private companies, with interlocking connections, that set the national agenda.

This power is particularly characteristic of the communication and information sector in which the national cultural-media agenda is provided by a very small and declining number of integrated private combines.[1] This development has deeply eroded free individual expression, a vital element of a democratic society.

At the same time, the new private information power centers strive actively and, to date, successfully to persuade the public that their corporate message and image-making activity are a daily exercise in individual free expression. This effort relies heavily on a century-old Supreme Court ruling that the corporation is an individual. It follows from this extravagant interpretation that the threat to individual expression can come only from the state.

How this logic works is exemplified in a full-page advertisement in the *New York Times* (February 11, 1993, p. A–11) in which the Freedom Forum Foundation approvingly quoted the view of the late Supreme Court Justice Thurgood Marshall: "If the First Amendment means anything," Marshall wrote, "it means that a state has no business telling a man, sitting alone in his own house, what books he may read or what films he may watch. Our whole constitutional heritage rebels at the thought of giving government the power to control men's minds." And so it does!

What readers of the ad may not know is that the Freedom Forum is the creation of the Gannett Corporation, one of the nation's largest media combines, owner of a countrywide chain of papers as well as the national newspaper *USA Today.* The Gannett enterprise fits precisely the definition of a media conglomerate, heavily dependent on corporate advertising revenues and disseminating carefully processed material to millions of readers and viewers. In quoting Marshall's cautionary words, Gannett through the Freedom Forum was identifying its powerful, nationally expressed voice as individual expression. At the same time, it was deflecting attention from its oversized influence on popular opinion and shifting the nation's focus to the older and familiar concern, state control of expression.

Yet where once there was justified fear of government control and censorship of speech, today there is a new form of censorship, structurally pervasive, grounded in private, concentrated control of the media, and generally undetectable in a direct and personal sense. Marshall's words, were they to include the new reality, could well be recast: If the First Amendment means anything, it means that a media combine has no business telling individuals, sitting alone in their homes, what books they may read or what films they may watch. Our whole constitutional heritage rebels at the thought of giving giant information corporations the power to control people's minds.

There is more than enough justification for this reformulation of traditional free speech doctrine. What American voices, other than corporate ones, can afford to pay half a million dollars or more for a thirty-second commercial on national television? Elder statesman George Kennan reflected: "As things stand today, without advertising presumably very little of the communications industry would survive."[2]

Given these economic realities, much of the space in the American cultural house has been appropriated for corporate messages. This has become literally so. Atlanta, for example, is seriously considering renaming some of its streets and parks with corporate logos—"Coca-Cola Boulevard [and] Georgia Pacific Park"—to raise funds.[3]

Corporate speech has become a dominant discourse, nationally and internationally. It has also changed dramatically the context in which the concepts of freedom of speech, a free press, and democratic expression have to be considered. Whereas the corporate voice booms across the land, individual expression, at best, trickles through tiny, constricted public circuits. This has allowed the effective right to free speech to be transferred from individuals to billion-dollar companies that, in effect, monopolize public communication.[4]

Corporate influence now penetrates almost every social space. One of its earliest and continuing efforts has been to shake off or at least greatly reduce the relatively modest restraints imposed on its economic and social decisionmaking. These limitations derived from the populist and reform movements of the late nineteenth century and the devastating impact of the Great Depression in the 1930s.

The rapacious behavior of the industrial monopolies that emerged after the Civil War and the social misery that accompanied the economic crisis of sixty years ago compelled the political leadership of those times to produce a variety of protective social measures. These included social security, bank and financial regulations, communication and transport rules, and labor's right to organize. The upsurge of the civil rights, feminist, and antiwar movements in the 1960s introduced additional social protections. Undeniably, these also interfered with the freedom of corporations to ignore such matters.

Since the end of World War II, and especially during the past twenty-five years, corporate power has countered these developments with intensive and largely successful efforts. It has pressed to have the machinery of socially responsible supervision removed, a shift that goes under the name of deregulation. It has led the campaign to privatize a variety of activities and functions formerly under public administration. And in a related move, it has sought to extend market relationships to new spheres of rapidly growing economic activity, such as information management.

Deregulation, privatization, and the expansion of market relationships have affected all corners of the economy. In this chapter I consider only the impact on the national information condition, not the peripheral area. The generation and provision of information and entertainment and the technology that makes this influence possible are among the most dynamic elements in the economy. How these are put together affect profoundly the character of the national information condition. The hope is always that they will constitute the basis for an informed population and a democratic social order.

In fact, when the effects of privatization, deregulation, and expanded market relationships are added to the corporate near-monopoly on public communication channels, a deep though not generally visible erosion in the national information infrastructure can be detected. In *The Age of Missing Information*, Bill McKibben reflected on the loss of understanding of nature and its ways:

> I've tried to describe some of the information that the modern world—the TV world—is missing. Information about the physical limits of a finite world. About sufficiency and need, about proper scale and real time, about the sensual pleasure of exertion and exposure to the elements, about the human need for community and for solid, real skills."[5]

McKibben is calling attention to a real loss. But here I am examining another kind of missing information. It is a consequence of the warped social institutional environment.

The spectacularly improved means of producing, organizing, and disseminating information has transformed industrial, political, and cultural practices and processes. Manufacturing, elections, and creative efforts are increasingly dependent on informational inputs. This has conferred great value on some categories of information. The production and sale of information have become major sites of profit making. What had been in large measure a social good has been transformed into a commodity for sale.

Wherever potentially profitable information is produced, the drive for its commercialization now rapidly follows. In the scientific sector, for example, research findings have become a source of intense effort to gain competitive advantage. Profit-seeking ventures now penetrate the core of many major universities and threaten to undermine the openness of the scholarly community.

Science, the publication of the American Association for the Advancement of Science (AAAS), increasingly publishes accounts of distinguished scientists engaged in deal making, organizing their own companies, or selling their findings to existing enterprises. A typical report observed: "In many areas of biology these days it's hard to find a researcher who doesn't hold biotech equity [in a for-profit company]."[6]

The University of Miami's vice president for research voiced concern over this condition: "As money becomes less and less available, more people are going to be compromising their principles, compromising their time. . . . We can get to the point at some stage in this process where we're not research universities any longer but fee-for-service corporations—hired guns."[7]

No less emphatic in his disapproval of these developments has been Derek Bok. In his final president's report to Harvard's Board of Overseers, as reported in the *Chronicle of Higher Education,* he identified "the commercialization of universities as [perhaps] the most severe threat facing higher education." Harvard's former president said: "[Universities] appear less and less as a charitable institution seeking truth and serving students and more and more as a huge commercial operation that differs from corporations only because there are no shareholders and no dividends."[8]

This distinction, too, may be rapidly disappearing. The commercial incursion is not limited to universities. The single largest generator of new information, produced in pursuit of its public functions, is the U.S. government. Not surprisingly, the rich informational pool derived from governmentally undertaken and financed activity has been an early target for corporate takeover. Especially in the past fifteen years it has been enveloped in market relationships, its content commercialized, and its disposition privatized. Its widespread general availability, formerly underwritten by public taxation, has been progressively narrowed and subjected to the criterion of ability to pay.

What remains of government information is being steadily siphoned off into commercial products. The American Library Association called attention to this phenomenon early on and has continued to voice its concern. In the 1992 edition of its twelve-year-old chronology "Less Access to Less Information by and About the U.S. Government,"[9] it continued to document the multiplying efforts to restrict and commercialize government information.

The practice of selling governmental (or any) information, serves the corporate user well. Ordinary individual users go to the end of the dissemination queue. Profoundly antidemocratic in its effect, privatizing or selling information that once was considered public property has become a standard practice in recent years.

A subset of the wider phenomenon has been the behavior of political leaders who leave office. Although U.S. District Court Judge Charles A. Richey ruled in a 1975 decision that "[documents and other informational matter] . . . produced or kept by a public official in the administration and performance of the powers and duties of a public office belong to the government and may not be considered the property of the official,"[10] his ruling, to date, has been mostly ignored.

Nearly twenty years after the Richey ruling, the *New York Times* editorialized after the November 1992 elections: "Over the years, Presidents have managed to establish legal claim to their papers chiefly because they possessed them when they left office. Rather than fight with departing Presidents, Federal officials negotiated for limited access."[11] Under this perverse procedure, former President Nixon sued, and was upheld by a U.S. District Court of Appeals, for compensation for the White House tapes and papers that were seized when he was the subject of the Watergate scandal.[12]

Withholding public documentation for private gain is not limited to former presidents. Innumerable other former high governmental officials have gone off with their papers associated with their functions of presumably serving the nation. Cavalierly regarding public documents as private property, they have used the material for financial gain in the sale of personal memoirs and historical studies.

There is still another factor, in addition to greed, that has limited and misshapen what should be the public record in recent years. The Bush administration, for example, destroyed vital information to prevent it from coming into the possession of its successor. Federal archivists reported many computer tapes were missing from the White House computer record.[13]

Upon assuming office, the Clinton administration did nothing to preserve the Bush computer record and was excoriated by, once again, Judge Richey for its dilatory behavior: "This case has been one of avoidance of responsibility by the government bureaucracy."[14] The Clinton administration contested Richey's ruling, but it was upheld by the U.S. Court of Appeals for the District of Columbia.[15]

The commercialization and privatization of government and scientific information have led to a paradoxical situation. Unarguably, the trend has been of great benefit to affluent users who now have access to kinds and amounts of data that would have been unimaginable not many years ago. Commercialization therefore has been rewarding to private information providers and to their clients. For the rest of the population, the vast majority, the quality and the availability of information leave much to be desired. In the domain of general governmental information, the supply has been curtailed severely. In 1992 the American Library Association noted that "since 1982, one of every four of the Government's 16,000 publications has been eliminated."[16]

An additional encroachment on the public information supply has been the reluctance of the government, prior to the Clinton administration, to provide government information in electronic format to governmental depositories and other public users. Because the electronic format has become the dominant mode of data organization, lack of access to this material effectively excludes the public from the national information stockpile.

In June 1993 this need to supply government information in electronic formats to public depositories was recognized in passage of the Government Printing Office Electronic Enhancement Act of 1993 (Public Law 103-40) signed by President Clinton. Among other provisions, it provides direct electronic access to public information through an on-line system established at the Government Printing Office—free of charge through depository libraries and at the incremental cost of dissemination to others.

Contracting Out

There is more to the problem of making public information widely available than the obstacles raised by its commercialization, important as that is. The advance of privatization into more and more governmental activities has taken different forms. One of the most widespread, and the effects of which are still to be fully calculated, is what is called "contracting out" (or "outsourcing"). In this arrangement, government at any level—local, state, or national—makes deals to have some of its functions undertaken by private contractors.

Justified to the public as a significant money-saving strategy and as a means of reducing the role of government—a central tenet of conservative doctrine for a very long time and particularly pronounced in the Reagan years—contracting out has been a flourishing field in Washington and elsewhere around the country. It has been widely adopted for all kinds of what were once public services—fire protection, waste disposal, some elements of the judicial system, libraries, and even police functions. According to a statement of the U.S. General Accounting Office (GAO), "civilian agencies currently spend about $55 billion per year on contracts and have become increasingly dependent on contractors to help agencies manage and carry out their missions."[17] In some government agencies (e.g., the Department of Energy, the Environmental Protection Agency, and the National Aeronautics and Space Administration), "contractors are performing virtually all of the work."[18]

In addition to the colossal waste found to exist in the general practice of contracting out governmental information functions, there are closely related problems that seriously affect the national information supply and especially the needs of the general citizenry. The American Library Association described one of these: "The increased emergence of contractual agreements with commercial firms to disseminate information collected at taxpayer expense [has resulted in] higher user charges for government information and the proliferation of government information in electronic format only."[19] In each case, the individual ordinary user is disadvantaged.

Still more problematic is that when the information function is transferred from governmental oversight, criteria other than public interest may determine the formats, organization, and categories of the information produced. What may be of importance to the general user may be of little concern to large-scale commercial users. When the supply function is commercialized, the priority inevitably goes to the major paying customers. When this occurs, what may be missing is not even realized. If the collection and organization process is exclusionary at the outset, data absence may not be recognized. But deprivation, visible or not, exists.

The reliance on private firms to perform what once was the government's work via contracting out has grown markedly in recent years, in keeping with the conservative philosophy of abandoning the protective social role of government. The shift has had especially damaging effects on the public information supply. The Office of Management and Budget (OMB) noted that despite the huge sums involved in the private contracting sphere, information about the management of the projects was sorely lacking. Auditors were in short supply, and as of the end of 1992, $160 billion in contracts had not been audited. In short, no one knew how the taxpayers' money had been spent, although there were enough clues to indicate that the waste was staggering.[20]

Whether these trends will be reversed in the late 1990s remains to be seen, although the initial evidence is hardly reassuring. What can be safely said is that the damage to public information is severe, its full dimensions are still largely unknown, and its impact is likely to be long-lasting.

Contracting out governmental activities to private enterprise has created a vast black hole in information about the government's essential functions. Yet it is only part of the story of a growing deficiency in such information. When public business is transferred from government to private management, it is likely to become less visible to the public. This condition has been widened and institutionalized by the wave of deregulation that has swept the nation since the mid-1970s.

Deregulation

Deregulation of industry in the United States in fact predates the 1970s. It began to appear in limited ways as early as the Eisenhower era (1952–1960). The New Deal measures, initiated in the 1930s, began to be rolled back by a resurgent corporate sector enriched and reinvigorated by the massive military outlays required for waging World War II as well as by the immediate postwar recovery expenditures.

In this period, American big business concentrated its energies on consolidating its hold on the domestic economy and expanding into a wide-open European and global market. The regulations imposed in the Roosevelt era, though never acceptable to big business, were borne relatively easily while the economy grew rapidly at home and abroad. American products and services, filled the global shelves for two decades. The U.S. dollar was the global currency.

Relatively quickly, however, the western European and Japanese economies gained strength, and American business began to feel the bite of their competition into profitability. The immediate corporate reaction at home was to focus on regulation as the chief source of the problem. "By the late 1970s," two Washington observers reported, "complaints of excessive regulation had become management's all-purpose cop-out. Were profits too low? Blame regulation. Were prices too high? Blame regulation. Was American industry unable to compete with foreign competition? Blame regulation."21

Besides the ideological value in blaming regulation for the emerging business difficulties in the 1970s, substantial material objectives also were served. In the communication sector this was particularly evident. The English writer Jeremy Tunstall explained the growing pressure for deregulation as one means to preserve the U.S. world hegemonic position:

> Behind the loose deregulatory consensus lie the twin assumptions that communication is becoming the number one industry in the world, and that the traditional position of the U.S. as numero uno in all aspects of electronics, telecommunications, video, entertainment, computers, and information technology is being challenged. A central purpose [of deregulation of communications] is to maintain both communications and the U.S. as number one.22

Tunstall also observed that "American business had geared itself up much more systematically in the last decade [1970–1980] to influence politics" through lobbying and the use of the mass media.23

Tunstall's perceptions were well-grounded. With almost unlimited access to the domestic information system—in fact, it owned the system—American big business moved decisively, with the communication sector in the forefront, to rid itself of whatever rules it regarded as impediments to management autonomy and profit making.

First and foremost, aim was taken at the social functions of government that had been strengthened in the Roosevelt period and expanded in the brief Great Society years of Lyndon Johnson, which lasted only from the mid-1960s to the early 1970s. "The prime targets," two Washington reporters noted, "were those agencies that sought to protect consumers and workers and to improve the air, water and work place. They were the agencies, in effect, that tried to get industry off the backs of the people."24

Another target was the Federal Communications Commission (FCC) with its mandate to oversee the vital and powerful communication sector. It too had to be reined in, though anyone familiar with the industry-serving commission had to regard its alleged role as a protector of the public interest and a scourge of the broadcasters as a fantasy.

In any case, reducing or eliminating the social regulatory function over consumer and workplace protection and corporate communication practices meant also reducing or eliminating information available to the public about these crucial social spheres. When industry is relieved of its obligation to pay its share of taxes, control pollution, reduce toxic wastes, cease interfering with workplace rights of the labor force, provide adequate children's and public affairs TV programming, and engage in a host of other tasks inherent in democratic life, the data concerning these social undertakings either vanish or are never collected. In short, information vital to social well-being silently falls out of the national supply, its absence noted, if at all, only when some later potential user finds it no longer exists or never was generated.

Indicative of what now may be a pervasive condition is the experience of the Task Force on National Health Care Reform established in the first days of the Clinton administration. In formulating its proposals, the task force encountered an unexpected difficulty. It could not find basic data. The *New York Times* reported that the task force "discovered that the Government quit collecting state-by-state data on health spending a decade ago. The Federal Government tabulated health spending by state from 1966 through 1982, but has not compiled state data since then."[25]

What the *Times* account did not say is that this information gap originated with the many data discontinuances ordered by the Reagan White House in its zeal to cut out the social functions of government. Paradoxically, accompanying the shortfall of social welfare and human care information has been an enormously enlarged amount of custom-tailored information, priced for an upscale clientele and thereby available to commercial and corporate users or anyone who can afford to pay for it.

Information needs of the corporate sector, to the most minute and refined degree, are now satisfied instantaneously. What is occurring in the information sphere is of a piece with what can be observed in the economy at large. The social order is splitting into at least a two-tiered structure: one with a full and expanding range of social and economic amenities, the other with a declining share of both but also with a growing amount of junk food, junk entertainment, and junk information.

Finally, deregulation in the communication sphere, in addition to encouraging a more rapid concentration of facilities (radio, TV, press) in fewer and fewer hands, also enables the newer media, especially cable, to claim First Amendment rights. When and if these rights are conferred, the now heavily concentrated cable franchise owners (MCOs, multiple cable owners) will be able, among other benefits, to avoid their obligation to provide public access channels in the communities they serve. Their argument is that they are being deprived of their free speech if government insists that they make some of their channels available for public purposes. This is a development to watch for in the time ahead.

In sum, the past fifty years have brought phenomenal growth of corporate power deployed across the social and economic landscape. The expansion of this power has relied heavily on three far-reaching structural changes in the institutional infrastructure: deregulation of economic activity, privatization of functions once public, and commercialization of activities once social.

Taken together and applied to the now central sector of communication and information, these processes are profoundly altering the informational condition and the democratic character of American society. The corporate voice is the loudest in the land. Vast new assemblages of information are produced but are available mainly to those who can afford their costs. The collection of socially vital information has been neglected wherever it has not been entirely eliminated.

These developments have been maturing over many decades, but the tempo has accelerated in the past fifteen or so years. With commercialization continuing to enfold the social and scientific realm, today's communication policies become tomorrow's visible crisis. Video dial tones and interactive media notwithstanding, the informational condition is social. It cannot be satisfactorily managed or improved either with technological instrumentation or individualistic and private custodianship. A new approach is needed.

NOTES

1. Ben Bagdikian, *The Media Monopoly,* 4th ed. (Boston: Beacon, 1993).

2. George Kennan, *Around the Cragged Hill* (New York: W. W. Norton, 1993), p. 167.

3. Peter Applebome, "Adman in Atlanta Tries to Sell City," *New York Times,* February 9, 1993, p. A-8.

4. Kennan, *Around the Cragged Hill,* p. 167.

5. Bill McKibben, *The Age of Missing Information* (New York: Random House, 1992), p. 236.

6. Marcia Barinaga, "Confusion on the Cutting Edge," *Science* 257 (July 31, 1992):616–619. See also "Hughes' Tough Stand on Industry Ties," *Science* 259 (February 12, 1993):884–889.

7. Anthony De Palma, "Universities' Reliance on Companies Raises Vexing Questions in Research," *New York Times,* March 17, 1993, p. B-8.

8. Liz McMillen, "Quest for Profits May Damage Basic Values of Universities, Harvard's Bok Warns," *Chronicle of Higher Education* 37 no. 32 (April 24, 1991):1.

9. American Library Association, "Less Access to Less Information by and About the U.S. Government" (Washington, D.C., December 1992).

10. For discussion of Richard M. Nixon v. Arthur F. Sampson, see "Government Records Are Public Property," *New York Times,* June 2, 1993, p. A-13.

11. "Richard Nixon's Unjust Demand," *New York Times,* November 19, 1992, editorial.

12. "Court Says Nixon Must Be Compensated for Tapes," *New York Times,* November 18, 1992.

13. John O'Neil, "Bush Tapes Lost, U.S. Archivists Say," *New York Times,* March 14, 1993, p. 16.

14. "Judge Calls Administration Lax on Predecessors' Computer Records," *New York Times,* June 9, 1993, p. 8.

15. Neil A. Lewis, "Government Told to Save Messages Sent by Computer," *New York Times,* August 14, 1993, p. 1.

16. American Library Association, "Less Access."

17. Statement of J. Dexter Peach before the Subcommittee on Oversight and Investigations, Committee on Energy and Commerce, House of Representatives, December 3, 1992; GAO report, "Federal Contracting," GAO/T-RCED-93-2.

18. Keith Schneider, "U.S. Lack of Supervision Encouraged Waste in Contracts," *New York Times*, December 2, 1992, p. 1.

19. American Library Association, "Less Access."

20. Schneider, "U.S. Lack of Supervision."

21. Susan Tolchin and Martin Tolchin, *Dismantling America* (Boston: Houghton Mifflin, 1983), pp. 4–5.

22. Jeremy Tunstall, *Communication Deregulation* (Oxford: Basil Blackwell, 1986), p. 7.

23. Ibid., p. 12.

24. Tolchin and Tolchin, *Dismantling America*, pp. 39–40.

25. Robert Pear, "Health Data Sought by Clinton Is No Longer Collected," *New York Times*, March 1, 1993, p. A-13.

3

The Hidden Side of Television Violence

GEORGE GERBNER

Humankind may have had more bloodthirsty eras but none as filled with *images* of violence as the present. We are entertained with an average of five violent scenes per hour in prime time and between two and three murders a night. One out of every four or five news stories features violence, precluding any chance of balanced reporting. The prime-time overkill has been consistent for the nearly thirty years our Cultural Indicators (CI) research project has been tracking violence in television drama.[1]

Almost as regular have been periodic media "debates" about television violence. The most recent peaked in 1993 with the usual charade that begins with legislative posturing and ends with a contrite industry response (such as the appointment of "monitors") that leaves policy essentially unchanged.

The reason is that the media-violence debate addresses the wrong questions. The usual questions—Does television violence incite real-life violence? and Isn't that what viewers really want?—are symptoms rather than diagnostic tools of the problem. They obscure, falsify, and even trivialize the issues involved.

Media undoubtedly contribute in major, if not exclusive, ways to the creation of a culture of violence that has now invaded every home. But whatever real-life violence media directly incite (and estimates suggest at most 5 percent), its full cost and significance is far greater.

Media violence must be understood as a complex scenario and an indicator of social relationships. It has both utility and consequences other than those usually considered in most public discussion. And it is driven by forces other than free expression and audience demand.

An earlier version of this chapter was published as "Television Violence: The Power and the Peril," pp. 547–557 in Gail Dines and Jean M. Humez, eds., *Gender, Race, and Class in Media: A Critical Text-Reader* (Sage Publications, 1995). Copyright © 1995 by Sage Publications, Inc. Reprinted by permission of Sage Publications, Inc.

Whatever else it does, violence in drama and news demonstrates power. It portrays victims as well as victimizers. It intimidates as well as incites. It paralyzes as well as triggers action. It defines majority might and minority risk. It shows one's place in the pecking order that runs society.

Besides being a projection of (mostly white, male) power, television violence is but the tip of the iceberg of a massive underlying connection of program content to an industry dependent on global markets. This relationship has been obscured by trendy talk of multiple media and many channels.[2]

Television has been seen as one medium among many rather than as the mainstream of the cultural environment in which most children grow up and learn. Traditional regulatory and public-interest conceptions are based on the obsolete assumption that the number of media outlets determines freedom and diversity of content. Today, however, a handful of global conglomerates can own many outlets in all media, deny entry to new and alternative perspectives, and homogenize content.

It is necessary, then, to preview the task of broadening a discourse that has gone on too long in a narrow and shallow groove. Violence on television is an integral part of a system of global marketing. It dominates an increasing share of the world's screens despite its relative lack of popularity in any country. Its consequences go far beyond inciting aggression. The system inhibits the portrayal of diverse dramatic approaches to conflict, depresses independent television production, deprives viewers of more popular choices, victimizes some and emboldens others, heightens general intimidation, and invites repressive postures by politicians that exploit the widespread insecurities the system itself generates.

The First Amendment to the U.S. Constitution forbade the only censors its authors knew—government—from interfering with the freedom of their press. Since then large conglomerates, virtual private governments, have imposed their formulas of overkill on media they own. Therefore, raising the issue of overkill directs attention to the hidden controls that in fact abridge creative freedom, dominate markets, and constrain democratic cultural policy.

Behind the problem of television violence is the critical issue of who makes cultural policy on whose behalf in the electronic age. The debate about violence creates an opportunity to move the larger cultural policy issue to center stage, where it has been in other democracies for some time. Thus, an analysis of the issue should include a review of the reasons and evidence for the social functions of the violence scenario and the structural basis for its profitability despite relatively low popularity.

The New Cultural Environment

A child today is born into a home in which television is on an average of over seven hours a day. For the first time in human history, most of the stories about people, life, and values are told not by parents, schools, churches, or others in the community who have something to tell but by distant conglomerates that have something to sell.

This shift is a radical change in the way we employ creative talent and shape the cultural environment. The roles we grow into and the ways others see us are no longer homemade, handcrafted, community-inspired. They are products of a complex integrated and globalized manufacturing and marketing system. Television violence is a central part of that system.

Of course, there is blood in fairy tales, gore in mythology, murder in Shakespeare. Not all violence is alike. Violence is a legitimate and even necessary cultural expression. Individually crafted, historically inspired, sparingly and selectively used expressions of symbolic violence can balance tragic costs against deadly compulsions. However, such tragic sense of life has been swamped by violence with happy endings produced on the dramatic assembly-line. This "happy violence" is cool, swift, painless, and often spectacular, designed not to upset but to deliver the audience to the next commercial in a mood to buy.

How people and life are represented in the new cultural environment is, of course, not only a question of numbers. Representation cultivates a sense of opportunities and life chances. It contributes to our conceptions of who we are and how we relate to others and the world. It helps define our strengths and vulnerabilities, our powers and our risks. No longer can family and community engender a sense of self and of values without the presence in the home of a tireless outside storyteller relating compelling tales about people, power, and peril.

On the whole, prime-time television presents a relatively small set of common themes, and violence pervades most of them.[3] The majority of network viewers have little choice of thematic context or cast of character types and virtually no chance of avoiding violence. Nor has the proliferation of channels led to greater diversity of actual viewing.[4] If anything, the dominant dramatic patterns penetrate more deeply into viewer choices through more outlets managed by fewer owners and conveying programs created by fewer creative sources.

Casting and Fate

Casting and fate in the world of television drama fit the violence scenario. Middle-class white male characters dominate in numbers and power. Women play one out of three characters. Young people constitute one-third and old one-fifth of their actual proportions of the population. Most other minorities are even more underrepresented. That cast sets the stage for stories of conflict, violence, and the projection of white male prime-of-life power. Most of those who are underrepresented are also those who, when portrayed, suffer the worst fate.

The moderate viewer of prime time sees every week an average of 21 criminals arrayed against an army of 41 public and private law enforcers. There are 14 doctors, 6 nurses, 6 lawyers, and 2 judges to handle them. An average of 150 acts of violence and about 15 murders entertain us and our children every week, and that does not count cartoons and the news. Those who watch over 3 hours a day (more than half the viewers) absorb much more.

About one out of three (31 percent) of all characters and more than half (52 percent) of major characters are involved in violence in any given week. The ratio of violence to victimization defines the price to be paid for committing violence. When one group can commit violence with relative impunity, the price it pays for violence is relatively low. When another group suffers more violence than it commits, the price is high.

In the total cast of prime-time characters, defined as all speaking parts regardless of the importance of the role, the average "risk ratio" (number of victims per 10 "violents," or perpetrators of violence) is 12. Violence is an effective victimizer—and characterizer.

Women, children, poorer and older people, and some other minorities pay a higher price for violence than do white males in the prime of life. The price paid in victims for every 10 violents is 15 for boys, 16 for girls, 17 for young women, 18.5 for lower-class characters, and over 20 for elderly characters.

Violence takes on an even more defining role for major characters. It involves more than half of all major characters (58 percent of men and 41 percent of women). Most likely to be involved either as perpetrators or victims or both are characters portrayed as mentally ill (84 percent), characters with mental or other disability (70 percent), young adult males (69 percent), and Latino Americans (64 percent). Children, lower-class, and mentally ill or otherwise disabled characters pay the highest price—13–16 victims for every 10 perpetrators.

Lethal victimization extends the pattern. About 5 percent of all characters and 10 percent of major characters are involved in killing. Being poor, old, Hispanic, or a woman of color means double trouble; they have a disproportionate chance of being killed and pay the highest relative price for taking another's life.

Researchers in the CI project have calculated a violence "pecking order" by ranking the risk ratios of the different groups. In general, women, children, young people, lower-class, disabled, and Asian Americans are at the bottom of the heap. When it comes to killing, older and Latino characters also pay a higher-than-average price. That is to say, hurting and killing by most majority groups extracts at most a tooth for a tooth. But minority groups tend to suffer greater symbolic reprisals for their transgressions.

What Are the Consequences?

These representations are not the sole or necessarily even the main determinants of what people think or do. But they are the most pervasive, inescapable, common, and policy-directed *contributions* to what messages large communities absorb over long periods of time. "Cultivation analysis" attempts to assess those "lessons." It explores whether those who spend more time with television are more likely than lighter viewers to perceive the real world in ways that reflect the most common and repetitive features of the television world.[5]

The systematic patterns observed in television content provide the basis for formulating questions about people's conceptions of social reality. Respondents in each sample are divided into those who watch the most television, those who watch a moderate amount, and those who watch the least. Cultivation is assessed by comparing patterns of responses in the three viewing groups (light, medium, and heavy) while controlling for important demographic and other characteristics.

Data from numerous large national probability surveys indicate that long-term regular exposure to television tends to make an independent contribution to the feeling of living in a mean and gloomy world. The "lessons" range from aggression to desensitization and to a sense of vulnerability and dependence.

The symbolic overkill takes its toll on all viewers, but heavy viewers are more likely than comparable groups of light viewers to overestimate one's chances of involvement in violence; to believe that one's neighborhood is unsafe; to state that fear of crime is a very serious personal problem; and to assume that crime is rising, regardless of the facts of the case. Heavy viewers are also more likely to have bought new locks, watchdogs, and guns "for protection." Heavier viewers in every subgroup (defined by education, age, income, gender, newspaper reading, neighborhood, and so on) express a greater sense of apprehension than do light viewers in the same groups.

Moreover, viewers who see members of their own group underrepresented but overvictimized seem to develop a greater sense of apprehension, mistrust, and alienation, what is called the "mean-world syndrome." Insecure, angry people may be prone to violence but are even more likely to be dependent on authority and susceptible to deceptively simple, strong, hard-line postures. They may accept and even welcome repressive measures such as more jails, capital punishment, harsher sentences—measures that have never reduced crime but never fail to get votes—if these promise to relieve their anxieties. That is the deeper dilemma of violence-laden television.

The Structural Basis of Television Violence

Formula-driven violence in entertainment and news is not an expression of freedom, viewer preference, or even crime statistics. The frequency of violence in the media seldom, if ever, reflects the actual occurrence of crime in a community. It is, rather, the product of a complex manufacturing and marketing machine.

Mergers, consolidation, conglomeratization, and globalization speed the machine. "Studios are clipping productions and consolidating operations, closing off gateways for newcomers," noted the trade paper *Variety* on the front page of its August 2, 1993, issue. The number of major studios declines while their share of domestic and global markets rises. Channels proliferate while investment in new talent drops, gateways close, and creative sources shrink.

Concentration brings streamlining of production, economies of scale, and emphasis on dramatic ingredients most suitable for aggressive international promotion. Having fewer buyers for their products forces program producers into deficit financing. Thus most producers cannot break even on the license fees they receive for domestic airings. They are forced into syndication and foreign sales to make a profit. They need a dramatic ingredient that requires no translation, "speaks action" in any language, and fits any culture. That ingredient is violence. (Sex is second but, ironically, it runs into more inhibitions and restrictions.)

Syndicators demand "action" (the code word for violence) because it "travels well around the world," said the producer of the film *Die Hard 2* (in which 264 were killed compared with 18 in *Die Hard 1*). "Everyone understands an action movie. If I tell a joke, you may not get it but if a bullet goes through the window, we all know how to hit the floor, no matter the language."[6]

Analysis shows that violence dominates U.S. exports. Researchers in the CI project compared 250 U.S. programs exported to ten countries with 111 programs shown in the United States during the same year. Violence was the main theme of 40 percent of home-shown and 49 percent of exported programs. Crime and action series constituted 17 percent of home-shown and 46 percent of exported programs.

The rationalization for the imbalance is that violence "sells." But what does it sell, to whom, and at what price? There is no evidence that, other factors being equal, violence per se is giving most viewers, countries, and citizens what they want. The most highly rated programs are usually not violent. The trade paper *Broadcasting and Cable* editorialized in 1993 that "the most popular programming is hardly violent as anyone with a passing knowledge of Nielsen ratings will tell you."[7] The editorial added that "action hours and movies have been the most popular exports for years"—that is, with the exporters, not the audiences. In other words, violence may help sell programs cheaply to broadcasters in many countries despite the dislike of their audiences. But television audiences do not buy programs, and advertisers, who do, pay for reaching the available audience at the least cost.

Data were compared from over 100 violent and the same number of nonviolent prime-time programs stored in the Cultural Indicators database. The average Nielsen rating of the violent sample was 11.1; for the nonviolent sample it was 13.8. The shares of viewing households in the violent and nonviolent samples were 18.9 and 22.5, respectively. The amount and consistency of violence in a series further increased the gap. Furthermore, the nonviolent sample was more highly rated than the violent sample for each of the five seasons studied.

However, despite their low average popularity, what violent programs lose on general domestic audiences they more than make up by grabbing younger viewers the advertisers want to reach and by extending their reach to the global market hungry for a cheap product. Even though these imports are typically also less popular abroad than quality shows produced at home, their extremely low cost compared with local production makes them attractive to the broadcasters who buy them.

Of course, some violent movies, videos, video games, and other spectacles do attract sizable audiences. But those audiences are small compared with the home audience for television. They are the selective retail buyers of what television dispenses wholesale. If only a small proportion of television viewers growing up with the violent overkill become addicted to it, they can make many movies and games spectacularly successful.

Public Response And Action

Most television viewers suffer the violence daily inflicted on them with diminishing tolerance. Organizations of creative workers in media, health professionals, law enforcement agencies, and virtually all other media-oriented professional and citizen groups have come out against "gratuitous" television violence. A March 1985 Harris survey showed that 78 percent disapproved of violence they saw on television. A Gallup poll of October 1990 found 79 percent in favor of "regulating" objectionable content in television. A Times-Mirror national poll in 1993 showed that Americans who said they were "personally bothered" by violence in entertainment shows jumped to 59 percent from 44 percent in 1983. Furthermore, 80 percent said entertainment violence was "harmful" to society, compared with 64 percent in 1983.

Local broadcasters, legally responsible for what goes on the air, also oppose the overkill and complain about loss of control. *Electronic Media* reported on August 2, 1993, the results of its own survey of 100 general managers across all regions and in all market sizes. Three out of four said there is too much needless violence on television; 57 percent would like to have "more input on program content decisions."

The Hollywood Caucus of Producers, Writers, and Directors, speaking for the creative community, said in a statement issued in August 1993: "We stand today at a point in time when the country's dissatisfaction with the quality of television is at an all-time high, while our own feelings of helplessness and lack of power, in not only choosing material that seeks to enrich, but also in our ability to execute to the best of our ability, is at an all-time low."

Far from reflecting creative freedom, the marketing of formula violence restricts freedom and chills originality. The violence formula is, in fact, a de facto censorship extending the dynamics of domination, intimidation, and repression domestically and globally. Much of the typical political and legislative response exploits the anxieties violence itself generates and offers remedies ranging from labeling and advisories to even more censorship.

There is a liberating alternative. It exists in various forms in most other democratic countries. It is public participation in making decisions about cultural investment and cultural policy. Independent grassroots citizen organization and action can provide the broad support needed for loosening the global marketing noose around the necks of producers, writers, directors, actors, and journalists.[8]

More freedom from violent and other inequitable and intimidating formulas, not more censorship, is the effective and acceptable way to increase diversity and reduce the dependence of program producers on the violence formula and to reduce television violence to its legitimate role and proportion. The role of Congress, if any, is to turn its antitrust and civil rights oversight on the centralized and globalized industrial structures and marketing strategies that impose violence on creative people and foist it on the children and adults of the world. It is high time to develop a vision of the right of children to be born into a reasonably free, fair, diverse, and nonthreatening cultural environment. It is time for citizen involvement in cultural decisions that shape our lives and the lives of our children.

NOTES

1. The study, called Cultural Indicators, is a database and an ongoing research project that relates recurrent features of the world of television to viewer conceptions of reality. Its cumulative computer archive contains observations on over 3,000 programs and 35,000 characters coded according to many thematic, demographic, and action categories.

2. George Gerbner, "'Miracles' of Communication Technology: Powerful Audiences, Diverse Choices, and Other Fairy Tales," in Janet Wasko, ed., *Illuminating the Blind Spots* (New York: Ablex, 1993).

3. L. Sun, "Limits of Selective Viewing: An Analysis of 'Diversity' in Dramatic Programming" (master's thesis, Annenberg School for Communication, University of Pennsylvania, Philadelphia, 1989).

4. M. Morgan and J. Shanahan, "Do VCRs Change the TV Picture? VCRs and the Cultivation Process," *American Behavioral Scientist* 35, no. 2 (1991):122–135.

5. M. Morgan and N. Signorielli, "Cultivation Analysis: Conceptualization and Methodology," in M. Morgan and N. Signorielli, eds., *Cultivation Analysis: New Directions in Media Effects Research* (Newbury Park, Calif.: Sage Publications, 1990), pp. 13–33.

6. Cited by Ken Auletta in "What Won't They Do," *New Yorker,* May 17, 1993.

7. *Broadcasting and Cable,* September 20, 1993, p. 66.

8. One such alternative is the Cultural Environment Movement. CEM is a nonprofit educational corporation, an umbrella coalition of independent media, professional, labor, religious, health-related, women's, and minority groups opposed to private corporate as well as government censorship. CEM is working for freedom from stereotyped formulas and for investing in a freer and more diverse cultural environment. It can be reached by writing to Cultural Environment Movement, P.O. Box 31847, Philadelphia, PA 19104.

4

Speaking Volumes: The Book Publishing Oligopoly and Its Cultural Consequences

LEAH F. BINDER

Poets and philosophers have expounded on the worthiness of the book since the printing press was invented. For any culture, the diversity and brilliance of its books symbolize and help regenerate the diversity and brilliance of its people. Books are an intellectual and literary heritage passed from one reader to the next, one generation to another. Some books are better than others, yet overall much of the pride and joy of a culture is preserved, described, and experienced in its books.

We are in danger of losing that heritage to an international oligopoly in which books are a poor stepcousin to other, more profitable products. The very qualities that make books special—physical durability over time, high-quality editorial standards, and good writing—are last priorities in the mass commercialization process. As a nation, we are blithely handing over our history, our creative heritage, our intellectual lifeblood, and the future of our most vulnerable, interesting new ideas to impersonal megacorporations that value them according to how well they play on Oprah.

During the boom times in publishing, the mid-1980s, I was employed in the marketing departments of three different publishers: Ballinger Publishing Company, a since-eliminated division of HarperCollins; Schocken Books, then an independent house and now part of Random House, and Pantheon Books, another Random House subsidiary. In my short career in publishing, I experienced firsthand the changes occurring in the publishing industry. I became concerned that although disturbing trends were well documented in the media and in literature, the implications of these events for the publishing, distribution, and availability of books were not. Yet there seemed to be a transformation in the way books for publication were selected, edited, presented, and made accessible to readers.

Beginning in the 1980s and continuing with opening of the European market, megacorporations like Bertelsmann and the one headed by Rupert Murdoch, with large holdings in media enterprises, began to acquire book publishers. They also bought up the means to maintain their position as cultural behemoths by purchasing printing and paper companies and expanding tie-ins between different forms of media.[1] Books are considered a low priority in the cultural environment created by these megacorporations, since book publishing is the least profitable among the media acquisitions.[2]

Further worldwide expansion of these companies in the future is a certainty; the European market, for instance, is the fastest growing market in the world, with an estimated growth potential of 75 percent in the 1990s.[3] This makes the market larger and faster growing than the U.S. market and creates incentives for further multinational expansion originating in the United States as well as Europe. Many governments have moved to protect their book publishers from cultural dominance by these megacorporations, rightfully fearing that native literature and intellectualism will be sidelined to make room for internationally produced best-sellers and other mass media products. Small local presses cannot compete with the printing and distribution economies of scale available to the large conglomerate, and as a result some governments have established policies to promote and support local book publishing to even the competitive playing field.[4]

However, Britain, Germany, and the United States, which are among the birthplace nations of the publishing conglomerates, have not for the most part advanced policy to protect their populations from the incursion of oligopolies. Yet being the birthplace of a megacorporation does not protect the public from corporate excesses. As a result of increasing governmental disenfranchisement from the book marketplace, the criteria used for selecting books for U.S. publication are increasingly dominated by demands of the mass marketplace, including the compatibility of books with the culture of the mass media. A self-help book that plays well on the talk show circuit is more likely to be published, promoted, and featured prominently in bookstores than a new novel by an unknown author. The novel *Schindler's List* was published with little attention and could rarely be found in the bookstore until Steven Spielberg's Oscar-winning film based on the novel came out. Public intervention to ensure competing criteria for publishing books is essential to prevent the coming era when good books are rare and the few that are published are accessible only to an elite population willing to pay a high cost.

People who work in publishing tend to love books and pooh-pooh the concept that the publishing industry is moving toward restricting the diversity of titles, censoring truly innovative or controversial ideas, and reducing the literary and intellectual power of the contents of books. Yet economic trends in the publishing industry portend just that, and despite good intentions individuals within the world of publishing are not immune to the incentives to stay the course. Authors are not unhappy with high advances, publishers do not resist higher paychecks, retailers will not forfeit a competitive edge by expanding their range of titles, and everyone else is riding the crest of the wave of the massification of book publishing. Without good public policy, market forces can squander the cultural environment as ferociously as a coal mining company can destroy the physical environment.

The U.S. Marketplace

A brief sketch of the U.S. book industry suggests problem areas. There are two broad categories of books explicitly defined in the U.S. marketplace and roughly equal in profitability: (1) trade books and (2) scholarly books and textbooks.[5] Trade books are sold in bookstores to the general public; scholarly books and textbooks are marketed to specific populations and generally sold through direct mail solicitation and targeted advertising. Scholarly books are fiction and nonfiction books with a limited readership or a specific appeal to a specific market. These are occasionally sold through bookstores but depend for the backbone of their sales on libraries and experts with interest in the topic. They are expensive to produce and have a low profit ratio.

Textbooks, in contrast, claim as much of a market share in the publishing world as trade books do. Because of the profit potential, most textbooks are now published by conglomerates constructed out of the mergers of several old independent textbook houses. Since textbooks are extremely expensive to produce and it takes considerable time for a new textbook to gain acceptance in the marketplace, only a few conglomerates with a track record are in the business. As a result, schools complain that they no longer have meaningful competitive options for textbooks in certain subject areas.[6] School districts and even states have banded together to demand editorial changes in textbooks, which has had problematic consequences including debates over the removal of information about evolution from history texts. Yet the objective should not be to construct the one or two volumes that everyone in the country can agree with but to have a sufficiently open publishing environment and diverse purchasing public that more than one book exists. There should be room in our culture for a cacophony of voices.

The contraction of product diversity is a classic outcome of an oligopoly, which tends to limit new initiatives and ultimately narrow the range of all products; the classic example is the airline industry eliminating airline service to small cities. The dominance of oligopolies in the publishing industry, which is problematic in the textbook industry, can similarly affect the diversity of books and public access to new ideas among the trade books, the books that are meant for a popular audience. This did not seem to be the case at first. In the 1980s, while publishing conglomerates swallowed every publisher in sight, there was also an explosion in the number of small presses from 12,000 in 1981 to 16,000 in 1984. These seemed to expand the range of books available to the public, since small presses are known for bringing to market the youngest of ideas and talents.[7] Yet there is evidence that the explosion in small presses ended abruptly with the recession in the early 1990s, when cash-hungry, debt-laden conglomerates were less tolerant.

The existence and health of small presses are predicated on the benevolence of competing publishing oligopolies, chain bookstores, taxpayers, and foundations. The small presses would not exist without concessions from their giant competitors and retailers and subsidies from library and school sales. Because conglomerate publishers and retailers are less likely to administer concessions and library and school budgets are dropping, small presses are having increasing difficulty staying afloat and getting their books into the marketplace. The top ten chain bookstores are themselves a retail oligopoly, accounting for 57 percent of the total annual retail sales of books in the United States[8] and featuring a per-bookstore inventory about one-quarter the size of independent booksellers.[9] Although independent booksellers will buy from anyone, most chains buy directly from the top fifty publishers only. Small presses must go through a distributor, which pays the small press as little as 35 percent of the book's cover price. The distributor sells to the chains, just as the big publishers do, at 60 percent of the book's cover price.

Some distributors are less draconian in their terms, and some chains will buy trade books directly from small presses on a limited basis. Moreover, many conglomerates help a few of the small presses by agreeing to distribute their books for a token cost. Yet since small presses cannot depend on bookstore sales alone, and only a few benefit from the benevolence of conglomerate distribution arrangements, small presses rely heavily on libraries and direct mail. In these two areas, the taxpayer has a role in subsidizing their operations, and the taxpayer has been less and less generous. Postage rates have made direct mail and shipping costs increasingly prohibitive, and libraries have steadily declining budgets. Moreover, the library squeeze is compounded by the fact that libraries pay much more for books than retailers, large-scale distributors, and national bookstore chains; whereas publishers discount books 20 percent for libraries, retailers get a 40 percent discount, and chains and distributors get 45–50 percent and sometimes more.

The volume discount obviously offers retailers a price advantage, but it should be noted that the library discount is not dependent on how many books libraries buy, and libraries are never rewarded for their most common purchasing advantage, the fact that they consistently purchase a large number of different titles from each publisher. The penalty libraries pay more than covers the added cost of shipping small numbers of a variety of titles; wholesale jobbers have no trouble earning profits by buying large quantities of a variety of books at the retail discount and then selling to libraries at the library discount.

As a result of consistent buying patterns covering a wide range of titles, libraries offer a foundation of support for nearly every book on a publisher's hardcover list, support that extends to the small presses. As book prices increase, libraries with already shrinking budgets are hardest hit because they pay more for books and tend to purchase the more expensive, more durable hardcover editions of books. As a result, taxpayer subsidies for libraries have an important advantage beyond offering free public access to books: They sustain small presses—and the new and diverse ideas they publish.

Libraries offer an additional advantage to the cultural environment: Librarian purchasers pay attention to peer reviews and care about the quality of editing. Librarians purchasing the book will have read good reviews of the book or will have a knowledgeable patron (such as a faculty member in a university library) making a good case for adding the book to the library's collection. Retailers and publishers, on the other hand, may devalue or bypass entirely the book reviewers, especially when they have a title that is truly "hot." Mass marketed romance novels and mysteries are rarely reviewed seriously yet will sell far more copies than more "distinguished" literature that is widely reviewed. As one marketing professional said on plans for bypassing book reviewers to publicize one of Tama Janowitz's books, "Tama is just too fabulous for the reviewers!"[10]

Joseph Turow pointed out that the different purchasing criteria used by retailers and libraries can have substantial implications for the style and substance of books that await readers.[11] Turow interviewed librarians and retailers of children's books and observed that retailers preferred books that "self-sold," usually series books with colorful illustrations. Librarians, on the other hand, chose books with quality reputations as gleaned from the independent review literature. The quality of a book's content was of lesser concern to the retailers, who were most interested in the point-of-sale appeal of the book. As a result, Turow observed that although bookstores and libraries may have similar clientele, they stocked different books.

What Turow did not comment on is the unequal influence libraries and retailers have over publishers. The dominance of bookstores in dictating publishers' marketing and acquisitions priorities is well known in publishing and has been documented.[12] Chain bookstores often make or break a book and start publishing trends through their purchasing habits.[13] To adhere to the needs of the retail marketplace, publishers spend more time designing and testing book covers than they did in the past, which has made art directors increasingly central to publishing operations. Yet if the surface appearance of the book is better, the quality of physical construction of the book—the materials used to bind pages and the acid content and weight of the paper—is shoddier.[14] Cheap construction is a common complaint of librarians who watch books deteriorate on the shelves. It is acceptable for bookstores, however, since they have no concern with the shelf life of returnable merchandise but a great deal of interest in the immediate aesthetic appeal of the book.

Mass Marketing of Books

Thus, if booksellers create market incentives for publishers to concentrate resources in a few, very popular titles, libraries create a limited counterincentive for publishers to produce a large variety of high-quality, hardcover titles as well. Yet currently American college students spend more on liquor annually than universities spend on library acquisitions and student scholarships combined.[15] The extent to which book prices increase and library budgets shrink could as a result have a direct impact not only on the range of books the public can access at the library but also on the variety and quality of books available overall in the marketplace.

Indeed, mass market potential has become a defining influence in the selection and availability of books in the United States. This was clear as early as the 1960s, when the first conglomerates were formed by multimedia companies CBS, RCA, and Times Mirror claiming they wanted the books to give them storylines for movies and television.[16] The books would help them gain access to the new and emerging mass audience. Today marketing and accounting executives have determinant authority in setting the criteria by which books will be selected and advances paid. Marketing is a common career ladder for individuals who want to become acquisitions editors or run publishing houses; copyediting is anachronistic in publishing.

Marketing campaigns for each book are decided long before a manuscript is ready, and often books are rushed through the editorial process in order to facilitate shipment to the bookstores on a convenient date. Bookstores do not usually select books by looking at the final product; they read the publisher's catalog about the book, listen to a salesperson who has rarely read the book either, and select based on a variety of criteria not usually related to whether the book is a good read or not. Catalog copy sometimes gives a synopsis of the book but always includes the more important information: number of copies in the first print, positive endorsements by celebrity influentials persuaded by the author to do so, information on whether and to whom first serial and bookclub rights sold, and a description of planned publicity and advertising efforts.

The marketing protocol favors books by and about celebrities and subjects of proven interest to the mass public. Since the book itself is usually unavailable at the time of purchase, famous endorsements and publicity potential make the best catalog copy and as a result earn the book optimal space on the retail shelves. The mass electronic marketplace, which creates and sustains the celebrity culture, thus has growing influence on which books achieve publication and how likely they are to reach readers.

Like all publicists, I pitched books by noncelebrity authors by relating the book to a news event or trend in the mass media. Because making a book timely and newsworthy was my job, I was given considerable latitude to set the publication date, which was understood by the media and booksellers to be a phony date for news coverage only. Thus, a book on nursing would be promoted with a publication date on Florence Nightingale's birthday. I dealt with a book only at its publication time, if at all. After that, much to the author's consternation, no effort was made to promote the book except to send it to a smattering of reviewers requesting a copy. This is because the mass marketplace values only what is new, and the mass marketplace sets the priorities for promotional efforts. This is another area in which libraries understand the value of books and publishers and retailers misuse it. The availability of a nonfiction book is our cultural hedge against having to reinvent the wheel when someone else two generations from now needs the information for some new purpose we cannot imagine today. Fiction and poetry are a different kind of gift to future generations, but they also have appeal far beyond the immediacy of the electronic worldview. Yet the current book marketplace renders each book passé after a few months, and without libraries books would be put out of print and lost forever before they were a year old. As Alfred Kazin said, "The marketplace has little room for a book that has a long life."[17]

Television and the media have an important influence in setting the criteria for book publishing, but other influences send publishers into the mass market. One of the most important defining characteristics of the trade publishing industry is the fact that retailers and wholesalers are permitted to return unsold books to the publisher at any time for any reason. Few industries offer such admirable terms to their customers. As a result of this policy, publishers monitor their warehouse inventory with a religious zeal. They lose sleep over the possibility of the worst-case scenario, the Jekyll and Hyde book: the book with high sales one day and high returns the next. As the Jekyll and Hyde scenario was described by Clarkson Potter,[18] the initial high sales deplete inventory, prompting the publisher to print more books. When the new shipment of books comes in, so do the returns from the first printing, resulting in an inventory disaster and wasted expenditures on a useless second printing.

Thus the accountants and marketing executives in publishing never read sales figures without studying the accompanying inventory reports; the two sets of numbers are literally of equal importance. Although book owners are often loath to throw away a book no matter how awful it is, publishers consider it a matter of integrity to do so. Books with numerous returns or without consistently high sales figures are put out of print and then destroyed or remaindered (sold at a discount) to avoid the possibility of high inventory. Excessive inventory is not tolerated long; even classics are put out of print if they fail to sell consistently. Publishers are the nation's busiest book burners.

As a result of this inventory issue, the most valuable and vaunted products of publishing houses are not books per se but the rights to publish books. Publishers will discard the books, but they will fight to the death for the rights. The physical book is a liability, a necessary evil in the warehouse; the rights to the book are on the other side of the balance sheet.[19] Publishers retain the rights to a book for a number of years regardless of whether they choose to keep the book in print or not; often an author will face the frustrating experience of being denied the rights to his or her out-of-print book. Publishers also sell rights, never physical books, to book clubs (which usually print books themselves), other publishing houses, television and movie producers, international publishers, and other kinds of media that create their own products out of the rights.

There is also a push to create new salable forms of "books" that are not paper-bound. Publishers are selling books on tape and entering the electronic age with CD-ROM discs and software programs. There is evidence that so far this tactic has not been as successful as conglomerates hoped, probably because the book marketplace wants books.[20]

Publishers also buy and sell rights to books yet to be written. Unlike in earlier days when authors usually wrote the book and publishers then paid for it, nowadays individuals almost always receive an advance for a proposed book.[21] Book advances, frequently negotiated by agents who are now major players in the publishing industry, contractually prohibit authors from publishing similar ideas in magazines or newspapers and making unauthorized public appearances to tout ideas they are planning to put in the book. Paperback, first serial, movie, and other rights to books are often sold by the publisher and are part of the package deal included in the author's advance.

Much has been made of the multimillion-dollar advances given to high-ticket authors.[22] Some observers argue that the high advances impede publishers' cash flow and limit their ability to sign a maximum number of less well known authors. Others argue that the high advances help improve the quality of a book and create an incentive for the author to deliver the manuscript in a timely fashion, which in turn improves the overall financial health of the publishing house.[23] Because of the increasingly high advances paid despite the recession, it is unlikely that the cash proceeds of best-sellers are being used to promote less well known titles.

Even though the publishing industry is a vocal opponent of media censorship, the policies surrounding advance book contracts place prior restraints on the speech and actions of authors who sign these contracts. Whatever the economically and legally defensible justification publishers have for invoking these restrictions, the restrictions are suppression of speech, and suppression of speech is censorship. This is a high-stakes gamble in which freedom of speech is but one more value on the table. Indeed, the author advance game has turned book publishing into a commodities futures market. This may be a good way to handle pork bellies; it is a risky and dangerous strategy for dealing with the nation's most treasured resources, its speech and its culture.

The preeminence of the rights to the book over the book itself is apparent from the internal hierarchical structure of publishing houses. For instance, among the lowest-paid workers in the publishing industry are the copyeditors; the highest-paid workers, some of them superstars, are the acquisitions editors who solicit and bargain book contracts. The implications of this fact formed the centerpiece of a famous investigation in the *New Republic* by Jacob Weisberg.[24] Weisberg provoked consternation in the publishing world when he pointed out that as a result of publishing's devaluation of the editorial process, books are increasingly long-winded, filled with grammatical, typographical, and factual errors, and poorly organized.

I experienced this firsthand when I wrote jacket copy for numerous books and found to my surprise that the acquisitions editors had rarely read the books themselves. Often only the beleaguered copyeditor whose desk and shelves were piled high with manuscripts had actually plowed through the books. Even she often sent manuscripts out-of-house to freelance editors, meaning that many of the books the company published had not been read by a single person on staff. This may have been an exception in publishing, but it is notable that jacket and catalog copy for books often describes only the beginning of the book—a hint that the jacket copywriter perhaps never got beyond those first few pages of the manuscript.

Conclusion

Thus, in the new publishing environment, the substance of the book is less relevant than the mass media coverage of it, and high sales for one title are more important than having a diverse and interesting selection of books. Books are becoming products for immediate consumption, as intangible, fleeting, and homogeneous as television programs. Chain retailers not only are restricting the number of titles available from their own bookstores but also are exercising their clout to restrict the number of titles that get published at all. Small presses that have depended on public support to survive in the marketplace are buckling under budget cuts to libraries and increasing postal rates.

The globalization and commercialization of the book marketplace have created unprecedented challenges to the integrity of national culture and the preservation of history and heritage. Libraries, foundations, and schools offer some challenge to the increasing dominance of mass market values. Yet the merger of publishers with conglomerates, the dominance of chain bookstores, the segregation of books into best-sellers and tiny sellers, and the overarching influence of celebrity appeal seem to have a defining influence on the definition and designation of books.

Our very speech and culture are at stake in the changing world of book publishing. Just as the public supports the arts and sets aside land for conservation, so should some part of the world of publishing be preserved by support for libraries, schools, literacy projects, and other programs to enhance public access to good books and maintain democratic control of our cultural heritage.

NOTES

1. R. A. Baensch, "Consolidation in Publishing and Allied Industries," in F. Kobrak and B. Luey, eds., *The Structure of International Publishing in the 1990s* (New Brunswick, N. J.: Transaction Publishers, 1992), p. 144.

2. "Book Conglomerates," *World Press Review* 37, no. 3 (June 1990):63.

3. P. Attenborough, "The Rebirth of European Publishing," in Kobrak and Luey, *The Structure of International Publishing,* p. 185.

4. B. Luey, "Introduction," in Kobrak and Luey, *The Structure of International Publishing,* p. 3.

5. For a detailed overview of categories within these two groups, see L. A. Coser, C. Kadushin, and W. W. Powell, *Books: The Culture and Commerce of Publishing* (New York: Basic Books, 1982).

6. Luey, "Introduction," p. 9.

7. J. Huenefeld, "Can Small Publishers Survive . . . and Who Cares?" in Kobrak and Luey, *The Structure of International Publishing,* p. 160.

8. Baensch, "Consolidation in Publishing," p. 145.

9. T. Solotaroff, "The Paperbacking of Publishing," *Nation* 253, no. 11 (October 7, 1991):300.

10. "Yuppie Lit: Publicize or Perish," *Time* 130, no. 7 (October 19, 1987):300.

11. J. Turow, "A Mass Communication Perspective on Book Publishing," *Journal of Popular Culture* 17 (Fall 1983):100.

12. T. Whiteside, *The Blockbuster Complex: Conglomerates, Show Business, and Book Publishing* (Middletown, Conn.: Wesleyan University Press, 1981), pp. 49–55.

13. Ibid., pp. 39–48.

14. C. N. Potter, *Who Does What and Why in Book Publishing* (New York: Birch Lane Press, 1990), pp. 208–209.

15. Luey, "Introduction," p. 9.

16. J. P. Dessauer, "Coming Full Circle at Macmillan: A Publishing Merger in Economic Perspective," in Kobrak and Luey, *The Structure of International Publishing,* p. 29.

17. "Yuppie Lit: Publicize or Perish," p. 79.

18. Potter, *Who Does What and Why,* pp. 208–221.

19. Ibid., p. 237.

20. "Book Conglomerates," p. 63.

21. Potter, *Who Does What and Why,* pp. 191–198.

22. See Whiteside, *The Blockbuster Complex,* p. 18.

23. Ibid., pp. 146–147.

24. J. Weisberg, "Rough Trade: The Sad Decline of American Publishing," *New Republic* 204, no. 24 (June 17, 1991):16.

PART TWO

TECHNOCRATIC FANTASIES

5

Computer-Assisted Crises

RICK CRAWFORD

New developments in computers and information technology are profoundly re-shaping American society. But if "technology is the engine of the future," who is in the driver's seat? Most people would prefer a future of individual freedom and autonomy, of responsible citizenship by which participatory democracy thrives and a reasonable degree of social justice and economic equity prevail. Yet all these basic social goods are threatened by the increasing concentration of information technology power in the hands of unaccountable institutions—both government agencies and private corporations—that currently are beyond democratic control. A 1990 Harris poll found 45 percent of the American public agreed that "technology has almost gotten out of control." But the poll neglected to probe further by asking "almost gotten out of *whose* control?" If we are to regain some control over our future, we need to begin asking questions about what forces are steering information technology, in which directions, and for whose purposes.

Every technology entails both costs and benefits. Because most technologies are advertised and sold as commodity products, their benefits need to be highly visible and concentrated in the hands of the purchaser. On the debit side, technologies that succeed in the marketplace tend to have costs that are relatively invisible and dispersed or "externalized" onto other people. The costs of information technology may be financial, but more often they are hidden in structural changes and take the form of surveillance, technological dependence without control, and altered ways of life—for example, speeded-up lifestyles or a more shallowly rooted existence.

A balanced journalistic story featuring a new technology ought to ask whether those who enjoy its benefits will bear their fair share of its costs. But balanced reporting on technology is rare. Because the popular press has long been saturated with Pollyannaish perspectives proclaiming technological "progress," I attempt in this chapter to remedy that imbalance. Through case studies of computer applications, I examine the ramifications of arguably unwise, and certainly undemocratic, control of technological "evolution." The dystopian visions presented here should not be considered inevitable outcomes. Rather, the struggle among various contending forces will determine where our futures will lie.

The case studies cover five major aspects of information technology: corporate computerization, surveillance and power, video games and consciousness, the political economy of encryption, and the information superhighway. But before I focus on these specific application areas, some background may be helpful to provide perspective and establish an analytical framework.

Society as a Technological Construct

Information technologies—computers and telecommunications—are shaking and restructuring the foundations of societies worldwide. Is technology our autonomous master, or is it our obedient servant? The computer is only the latest manifestation in a long line of technological evolution in which technological artifacts and techniques become adapted to meet the demands of their socioeconomic environments. Biological adaptation is a two-way process of coevolution: The environment shapes the organisms, and the organisms in turn alter the environment. Similarly, generations of technological evolution produce a series of constructed environments that in turn affect the human cultures enclosed within them.

But societies are not monolithic, and the coevolution of technology with society is strongly influenced by socioeconomic power relations. Various institutions impose significant strategic "selection pressures" that influence the research funding and regulatory environments of technological evolution. Large defense contractors exert such immense influence on the development of military infrastructure that they have earned the label "military-industrial complex." But multinational communications corporations also wield enormous power. The communications industries—cable TV and broadcasters, entertainment companies, computer makers, telephone companies, newspapers, and electronic publishers—made over $50 million in campaign contributions for U.S. federal elections during the decade that ended December 1993. These targeted sums generate significant leverage but are dwarfed by the communications industries' advertising budgets.

Public relations salvos promoting the latest technologies invariably advertise best-case scenarios. In 1988 the microcomputer industry alone spent over a billion dollars on advertising.[1] Any doubts about the "march of progress" are assailed as neo-Luddite. One explicitly anti-Luddite advertisement by IBM closed with the slogan "Smashing the clocks might destroy the mechanism of progress. But it will never delay tomorrow."[2] This was a rhetorical device designed to preempt genuine debate. The issue is not whether tomorrow should be delayed but rather what kind of world we want to live in tomorrow. Who decides how technology will structure the space and time of our daily life?

Even in an ostensibly free market, the dominant social groups and economic institutions influence the next generation of technological development by embedding their own (often unconscious) biases, value judgments, and social rules in the new technological designs. Other social strata then adapt their lifestyles to the constrained technological choices available in their new cultural environment. In this manner, the dominant socioeconomic power relations tend to be reproduced—and amplified—in the technological enclosures that arise to surround the lower social strata. "Relations of power, subsumed into the functioning of technology, become automatic and invisible."[3] Technology is thus a key strategic site in the struggle over socially and politically contested terrain.

The so-called information age and information superhighway are ideological constructs. They are outgrowths of the prevailing American ideology that claims the United States has transcended ideology; that it has outgrown false idols, and there is now no god but the market. The ideology of the information age is heavily intertwined with the myth of the benevolence of corporate technology or at least the inevitability of something called "progress."[4] But progress for which sectors of society, and at what cost?

The techno-ideology of social Darwinism that serves to justify an inequitable status quo is every bit as self-serving as was the divine right of kings in a previous era. Yet such ideological assumptions cause people to accept the inevitability of whatever is labeled by those in power as "technological progress." Neil Postman suggested that this tendency has allowed the idea of human progress to be replaced by the idea of technological progress. Many people are willing to sacrifice shared cultural values if they stand to benefit from some form of progress. Such benefits can include money, market share, cultural hegemony, and political power. In this context, it is important to bear in mind one fundamental economic dynamic of private-enterprise systems: Private firms can prosper by internalizing benefits and externalizing costs. The classic example is pollution: A community situated around a factory bears the externalized costs of the pollution produced, and the factory owner and the firm's customers internalize the benefits.

The privatization of public security exemplifies another dimension in which benefits are internalized and costs are externalized. In the United States, the social environment has deteriorated as the ratio of funds spent for public versus private security has plummeted. By 1989 the private security industry in the United States had revenues 50 percent greater than those of all public police forces combined.[5]

In the case of modern technology, those who succeed in internalizing benefits within machines prosper. Yet the resulting externalized costs—the pervasive, often deep, structural changes—typically are debited against our common social fabric and cultural environment. The modern corporation has evolved into an entity that functions to internalize rights and to externalize responsibilities.[6]

Architectures of Captivity: The Panopticon

Because of the ideological nature of hi-tech terms, they warrant oppositional de-codings such as "misinformation" or "myth-information age," "information super-hyped way," "snooper highway," or "super highway robbery." One myth in particular that may prove to be a fatal distraction is the notion—widely shared by computer-literate denizens of the cyberspace networks—that the only signifi-cant danger to society is the emergence of an oppressive centralized government. But the emergence of civil society may be threatened less by the iron fist of a pub-lic-sector Big Brother than by the velvet touch of invisible private-sector hands working to channel modern life into a digital panoptic enclosure.

The concept of a panoptic prison originated with Jeremy Bentham in 1791. The circular architecture of his Panopticon would consist of a central surveillance tower surrounded by a series of individual cells. Each cell was to be illuminated from the perimeter, thus backlighting the inmates. But the central tower would remain dark, so that the wardens inside could keep the inmates under constant surveillance without being seen themselves.

Panoptic surveillance techniques allow architectures of social control to be gen-eralized beyond what are nominally considered prisons. Today's new hi-tech Panopticon resembles a computerized virtual prison planet under construction on the information superhighway at great social cost. New digital techniques for remote surveillance and control have rendered physical enclosures, concentration camps, and chain gangs obsolete. The panoptic information enclosure is an in-terlacing mesh of digital networks designed to channel the flows of data and of economic and political power—a transnational effort to overlay the planet with a computerized surveillance grid.

The panoptic project is not the result of one vast conspiracy. Rather, it is dri-ven by the decades-old dynamics of technological evolution in the consumer marketing and national security sectors. The would-be wardens of the new Panopticon are drawn from the ranks of corporate interests, intelligence agencies, and military elites.

The power of panoptic architectures derives not only from data surveillance but also from techniques that classify, segment, and isolate the population. In Bentham's Panopticon, the inmates, isolated from communication with one an-other, would be reduced to the status of "solitary sequestered individuals. . . . Indulged with perfect liberty within the space allotted to him, in what worse way could he vent his rage, than by beating his head against the walls?"[7]

These passages chillingly foreshadow the much-vaunted "consumer choice" of modernity. As the public sphere erodes, the public space available for community fragments, leaving individuals isolated inside shrinking private spaces—corpo-rate-designed technological enclosures such as the automobile and the home en-tertainment center. While mentally confined within these cells, individuals are "indulged with perfect liberty" to choose among the commodities advertised as individual "solutions" to collective social problems. Segmented by psychographic class into virtual panoptic internment camps, citizens and consumers are bombarded with targeted images as symbolic substitutes for freedom and community, and the barrage thereby dissipates the forces available for genuine social change.

In what Michel Foucault called the "microphysics of power," the control of time is as significant as the control of space. The power of panoptic structures inheres in their ability to induce self-discipline by those under surveillance. The inmate "assumes responsibility for the constraints of power. . . . He becomes the instrument of his own subjection."[8] When most citizens consider it normal to return to their home entertainment centers after each day's "work furlough," it is clear that physical enclosures and chain gangs have been superseded by more economically efficient disciplinary instruments.

Thus, for citizens, "'free time' becomes increasingly subordinated to the 'labor' of consumption."[9] People literally spend their time trying to buy their freedom and happiness.[10] What is portrayed as individual freedom under the rubric of "consumer choice" is increasingly restricted to a constrained set of outcomes that pose no threat to the established order. This notion of the political economy of cultural power is essential for understanding the new modalities of communications power in the information age.[11]

The Media-Industrial Complex

In the post–Cold War era of low-intensity conflict, corporate technological power has outgrown the military-industrial complex. A new media-industrial complex is arising that uses control of information—and disinformation—as a more cost-effective means of fine-grained social control. As the "saturation bombing" tactics of mass marketing moved from the commercial to the political realm, modern corporate firepower evolved to extract precise intelligence data via panoptic consumer surveillance and then responded with surgically targeted commercial "smart bombs."

The American public is increasingly concerned about technological threats to personal privacy. The high visibility of this issue helps ensure the periodic mobilization of forces to defend against particularly egregious invasions of privacy (e.g., the Lotus Marketplace incident).[12] But a report to the Club of Rome suggested that the primary threats of the information age are not to personal privacy as traditionally perceived. "The real issue . . . is power gains of bureaucracies, both private and public, at the expense of individuals and the nonorganized sectors of society, by means of gathering information through direct observation and by means of intensive record keeping."[13]

Contrary to popular belief, the shift from centralized computing to distributed (and ubiquitous) computing entails a further increase in the concentration of power within the commercial sphere. These distributed tendrils of computerized surveillance and control are channels for what Foucault called the "capillary functioning of power." This fundamental shift in the balance of power between individuals and institutions is likely to remain an invisible crisis.

Computers and Corporate Impacts

Computers have played a major role in facilitating the transnationalization of corporate operations and the growth of centrally controlled regimes. According to the Business Roundtable, an organization composed of chief executive officers from the Fortune 500 companies, "Telecommunications is central to the operations of all multinational business activity. . . . The dependence of multinational corporations—whether they are pursuing intracorporate functions or providing services or both—upon international information transfer is steadily increasing."[14]

Electronic Banking

Transnational businesses are dependent on international computer networks for more than mere abstract data flow. Some data represent quite tangible promises to pay—electronic dollars. Each day, over $1 trillion flows through a perpetual-motion money-market machine known as CHIPS—the Clearing House Interbank Payments System—owned by a consortium of New York banks. That is $1 billion speeding through cyberspace every minute! The dollar volume on this private corporate network exceeds even that flowing through the network of the U.S. Federal Reserve banks.

Although the number of economic transactions made electronically constitutes only 2 percent of the total, compared with 85 percent that is mediated by "hard-copy" cash, the relationship is reversed when the total dollar amount is examined. Cash covers less than 1 percent of the dollar value exchanged; electronic transfers between computers account for more than 83 percent (the remainder is mostly in the form of checks and money orders).

The velocity of capital flow through cyberspace continues to accelerate. In 1980 the flow of electronic dollars per day was already twelve times greater than the total balances held in accounts at the U.S. Federal Reserve. By 1991 this daily dynamic flow had grown to fifty-five times the static base of bank reserves. This degree of electronic leverage is a crisis waiting to happen. It may be triggered by electrical breakdown, software bugs, human error, computer crime (by knowledgeable insiders), or some nonlinear dynamic coupling between different electronic financial markets.

The situation regarding foreign exchange transactions is similar: Less than 10 percent of total foreign exchange volume constitutes payments for goods and services. The balance of power between central banks and commercial currency traders was lost long before the waves of selling by speculators forced Britain and Italy to drop out of the European Community exchange rate mechanism in 1992. As Wall Street wizards conjure up new derivative financial instruments, the risk increases that computerized cross-market arbitrage strategies will destabilize the global electronic intermarket. The Wall Street tail is wagging the Main Street dog, but few can perceive the volatile ramifications of this dialing for data dollars.

Precisely because the corporate form of organization is so dependent on computers, the magnitude of corporate computing power dwarfs the computing power controlled by civil society. As just one example of corporate computing scale, the private telecommunications network operated by General Motors has 300,000 computer terminals and 250,000 telephones and carries over 1 billion transactions per year. Approximately half the volume of all transborder data flows is internal corporate communication carried on private networks. "As technology advances, the importance of national boundaries will decline and the communications network of the multinational corporation, developed in form by the banks, will have the potential to become the guiding force for the development of world political and economic policies."[15] Such disparities in power are driving fundamental social change.

Deskilling the Workforce

The phenomenon known as deskilling is a cumulative process whereby skills are "extracted" from humans via "knowledge engineering" and then replicated in (computerized) machines. Deskilling is not merely a copying of skills but results eventually in those skills dying out in the human workforce. The deskilling of workers is a product of corporate competition coupled with computerization. In a different institutional context, the competitive dynamic might instead have promoted different forms of computerization that favored increases in worker skills across the board.

Deskilling of clerks and blue-collar workers is nothing new, but there are powerful economic incentives to devalue human labor throughout the white-collar echelons as well. "In 1980, out of $600 billion spent on office personnel costs in the U.S., nearly 75% went to managers and professionals, with the balance going to the numerically superior clerical and secretarial workers."[16]

Work flows and job descriptions will continue to be restructured in order to coalesce tasks that can be accomplished more readily by technological capital than by human labor. For these tasks, technology will be both cheaper and smarter than labor. Whichever tasks meet this criterion will become fixed nodal points in the flow of work, because their functioning can be precisely specified. Driven by the imperative to rationalize work flow, the wave fronts of future task restructuring will conform to these technological fixed points and will preferentially erode the remaining human capital instead. The crux of the problem is that American business culture designs technological capital as a substitute for human capital rather than as a complement to it.

Deskilling is another example of internalizing benefits (i.e., profits for the corporation) in machines and externalizing costs (e.g., unemployment, anomie) onto society at large. Computers do not require wages, become fatigued, take leave to care for sick children, or go on strike. Thus, the dynamic of deskilling will act to shrink the information society's middle class, causing the knowledge gap between the info-rich and the info-poor to diverge further.

Even the narrow macroeconomic results of deskilling are detrimental: Products can be produced more cheaply, but increasing numbers of consumers—being unemployed workers—are no longer able to afford them. Some critics label this trend a deep structural crisis of industrial capitalism and advocate radical changes, such as a significantly shorter workweek or a guaranteed national income.

How can this crisis, too, remain invisible? It turns out that this is not a collective crisis of corporate capitalism but merely 80 million individual human crises! Neoclassical economists—true believers in Joseph Schumpeter's "long wave" theory of economic decline and technological innovation[17]—preach that just as the industrial revolution catalyzed a period of rapid growth, so too shall the information age enable a second coming of "Lite" growth. But perpetual growth on a finite planet is unsustainable.

Computer Simulations

Deskilling—the transfer of skills from workers to computers—might be viewed as an increasing "knowledge gap" between workers and computers. In this light, it may be understandable for deskilled workers to view computers as omniscient. After Joseph Weizenbaum constructed his ELIZA program in the 1970s to simulate a Rogerian psychotherapist, he was horrified that it fooled many ordinary people into thinking this trivially simple computer program truly "understood" them far better than any human therapist. But even psychologists were snared by the lure of computer-assisted therapy. Prominent therapists of the time expressed a desire to establish numerous computerized psychology clinics to make therapy available to the masses. "Several hundred patients an hour could be handled by a computer system designed for that purpose. The human therapist . . . would not be replaced, but would become a much more efficient man."[18]

Not only psychologists were attracted by the lure of a technological fix. Astronomer Carl Sagan wrote in a 1975 article in *Natural History:* "In a period when more and more people in our society seem to be in need of psychiatric counseling . . . I can imagine the development of a network of computer psychotherapeutic terminals something like arrays of large telephone booths, in which, for a few dollars a session, we would be able to talk with an attentive, tested, and largely non-directive psychotherapist."[19]

Why is it that more and more people in our society seem to "need" counseling? Perhaps computer-assisted psychotechnology is being called on to fix (or at least paper over) problems caused by the social and psychological externalities resulting from dependence on other forms of technology. If computers can heal minds, then surely they can harm them as well. Rather than embracing computer-assisted psychology as a cure for what the Trilateral Commission has called "democratic distemper,"[20] we should regard it as a highly problematic technology of social control: "If you are troubled, my child, enter our trademarked Tele-Confessional Booth. Open your heart and reveal your mind to Big Cyber Brother."

Economists have been fooled by computerized economic simulation models, including those of their own construction. In the debate over free trade and the North American Free Trade Agreement (NAFTA), most mainstream economists cited computer projections claiming that NAFTA would create thousands of new jobs in the United States. The computer simulations on which these NAFTA proponents rely are known as "computable general equilibrium" (CGE) models, and to make their analyses tractable, the neoclassical economists must make certain simplifying assumptions.

When simulating the impact of a trade agreement on labor, it seems absurd to assume a priori that capital is immobile, that full employment will prevail, that unit labor costs are identical in the United States and Mexico, that American consumers will prefer products made in America (even if they are more expensive), and that trade flows between the United States and Mexico will exactly balance. Yet a recent examination of ten prominent CGE models showed that nine of them included at least one of those unrealistic assumptions, and two models included all the assumptions.[21]

This situation bears a disturbing resemblance to computer-assisted intellectual dishonesty. Human beings have always been masters of self-deception, and hiding the essential basis of one's deception by embedding it in a computer program surely helps reduce what might otherwise become an intolerable burden of cognitive dissonance. Perhaps those early psychologists who foresaw computer programs bringing mental relief to overstressed humans were not so wrong after all.

Surveillance, Segmentation, Privacy, and Power

In June 1991, in response to a grand jury subpoena, Cincinnati Bell searched the dialing records of 650,000 residential customers to help Procter & Gamble identify employees suspected of leaking embarrassing company information to a reporter. The balance of power between individuals and institutions is terribly skewed when one company's "corporate privacy" outweighs the privacy rights of 650,000 households. A computerized database shifted the balance of power between workers and businesses: After winning the right to workers' compensation insurance, any worker injured on the job who has the temerity actually to file a claim will find his or her records entered in a national computerized blacklist. For a fee, employers can examine these files for employment applicants to weed out those they deem high risk.

When people object to computerized surveillance, it is usually because they feel it is an invasion of privacy. But the notion of privacy is bound up with the inviolability of individual dignity and autonomy. Both these attributes are inextricably linked to relations of power. Clearly, personal autonomy suffers when institutions compile information on one's past experiences and use that data to amplify their power to constrain one's future options. But the attribute of personal dignity likewise is vulnerable to the exercise of power—the power to define an individual.

The global Panopticon under construction as an "information snooper highway" is not a unified architecture with a single central tower. Instead, multiple central towers correspond to various institutions, including credit bureaus, insurance companies, media conglomerates, and government agencies. These towers may obscure wardens' views of the inmates, but that problem can be alleviated by the sharing or sale of surveillance data.

The wardens in the Panopticon towers utilize various digital data-gathering practices to track the behaviors of inmates. Many economic transactions generate long-lived electronic records that identify the parties involved in and the nature of those transactions. Such digital records carry information that may have predictive value regarding future economic transactions. Thus, a large secondary market has arisen to trade in this transaction-generated information (TGI).

Files of TGI on consumers permit institutions to define an individual—for example, as a poor credit risk or as a sucker for "Buy 2 get 1 free" sales ploys. The panoptic structures of modern life, coupled with fast interactive feedback mechanisms, also mean greater power for institutions to influence the self-definitions of individuals. Just as the media's control of news surveillance and distribution carries the power to define events as they happen and to impose those definitions on the public as "instant history," so too control of the panoptic surveillance grid increases institutions' power to impose self-images on the subjects of private life, thereby violating personal dignity as well as infringing on individual autonomy.

Information generated for one purpose can be linked with data gathered for another purpose to produce a data shadow that reveals more than the sum of its parts. Familiar examples include the use of medical information to deny employment and of census information to deny credit. Corporations use TGI to reduce their risks, thus increasing their probable profits. But from the individual's viewpoint, this is data-based discrimination. One's life chances may be circumscribed—not because of any crime one has committed—but merely because some aspect of one's digital persona resembles that of people who are on record (rightly or not) as high-risk parties in various business transactions. One may be blacklisted or redlined based not on past transgressions but on computerized predictions of future behavior.

The use of TGI data to deny options to targeted individuals is only one disturbing aspect of the secondary market in TGI; another is its use to extend "opportunities" to them. Correct TGI does have predictive value. Although few individuals exhibit behavior so invariant as to be deterministic, many businesses can profit handsomely from increasing the probability that they guessed right. And the more predictable is a person's behavior, the more power is transferred to businesses that can access records of the person's digital persona. Moreover, fine-grained surveillance data permit fine-tuned manipulation through psychographically targeted corporate communications. Economies of scale become significant. Even if a company has correctly inferred intimate details of an individual's psychological makeup, it is seldom worthwhile to invest staff resources in constructing a custom-designed communication to manipulate that one individual (unless the business involves high-stakes fraudulent telemarketing). But once hundreds or thousands of individuals can be lumped together in one psychographic class, susceptible to the same forms of manipulation, these techniques can generate a predictable, cost-effective revenue stream. Moreover, such methods of segmenting the population allow political organizations to conduct controlled experiments to hone their propaganda techniques.

Residential Power Line Surveillance

Many people are aware of telephone wiretapping. But few understand the potential for gathering covert intelligence via a form of "wiretapping" I call "real-time residential power line surveillance" (RRPLS).[22]

A primitive form of nonreal-time power line surveillance has been used for years by U.S. drug enforcement agents. By acquiring from local electric utility companies the billing records for the top residential electric power consumers, government agents can draw plausible inferences as to whether certain residences may be using banks of high-powered lights to cultivate indoor marijuana gardens. In the United States, a search warrant is not required to gather such data from an electric utility. U.S. law does not consider residential electric bills "private," just as residential telephone dialing records are not private.[23]

Innovative advances in computerization have given rise to "smart meters" that enormously increase the data-gathering ability of those engaged in residential power line surveillance. Indeed, RRPLS has joined the panoply of techniques that collectively constitute "dataveillance."[24]

Whereas primitive forms of power monitoring merely sampled one data point per month by checking the cumulative reading on the residential power meter, modern forms of RRPLS permit nearly continuous digital sampling. This allows watchers to develop a fine-grained profile of the occupants' electrical appliance usage. A computerized RRPLS device may be placed on-site with the occupants' knowledge and assent, or it may be hidden outside and surreptitiously attached to the power line feeding into the residence. This device records a log of both resistive power levels and reactive loads as a function of time. The RRPLS device can extract characteristic appliance "signatures" from the raw data. For example, existing RRPLS devices can identify whenever the sheets are thrown back from a water bed by detecting the duty cycles of the water bed heater.[25] RRPLS can infer that two people shared a shower by noting an unusually heavy load on the electric water heater and that two uses of the hair dryer followed.

RRPLS may sound like just another expensive hi-tech spy toy used, for example, only by the FBI against a few suspected terrorists. But we ignore the data-gathering incentives of the market at our peril. Several economic dynamics promote the widespread use of RRPLS for commercial purposes. In fact, utilities already have deployed RRPLS in pilot programs covering thousands of U.S. homes.[26]

One factor promoting computerization of residential power metering is the electric utilities' desire to reduce their costs by automating the job of reading residential meters. Thus, most of the RRPLS devices installed in the United States today use packet radio techniques to transmit their (your) data to the utility's billing department (or to whomever else may be monitoring those transmissions).

Another factor driving the proliferation of RRPLS is concern for the environmental impacts of energy use. The generating capacity needed by electric utilities is driven by peak power demand—the maximum power required at any one time. As an incentive to reduce peak power demand, some utilities already have deployed RRPLS monitors to homes so that customers using power during periods of peak demand (e.g., when many air conditioners are switched on during a hot summer afternoon) are charged higher prices. Thus, the laudable goal of equitably allocating the environmental costs of energy consumption is contributing to the spread of RRPLS techniques.

Once a utility company "owns" a profile of a household's appliance usage, marketing motives tend to propagate that information. Appliance companies might buy these data for use in targeting sales prospects more precisely. For example, field tests of a prototype RRPLS device detected a malfunctioning underground septic pump. The occupant was unaware of the urgent need for repair. Or the household RRPLS data might indicate that the occupants own an old-style washing machine, which suggests the possiblility of replacing it with a modern, energy-efficient washer. Or perhaps the household RRPLS appliance profile indicates its occupants use a microwave oven every weekday morning. Targeted direct mail might then send coupons or even free trial samples of new microwave breakfast foods.

A less benign result is that health insurance companies may pool the RRPLS data from thousands of policy holders, correlating health insurance claims with statistical appliance usage profiles. They may determine that, for unknown reasons (perhaps a more time-stressed lifestyle), morning microwave users constitute a high-risk group and may boost their insurance premiums accordingly. Those who spend too many nights tossing and turning on their water beds may experience a similar boost in car insurance rates.

Undoubtedly the greatest danger of widespread RRPLS is an invisible one: that utility companies will gradually degrade the norms of privacy as perceived by the public. Utility companies can buy off most of the uninformed populace by offering "surveillance subsidies"—discounts or rebates to those who permit the sale of their private data. These personal surveillance contracts may be cloaked in the rhetoric of "new improved services" and "consumer choice." But for a utility to obtain the genuinely informed consent of its customers would require the utility to undertake expensive campaigns to educate customers regarding the long-term social consequences of this panoptic surveillance. Given the conflict of interest inherent in such a scheme, it is clear that once again, the consent of the technological consumer will be manufactured rather than informed.[27]

Surveillance subsidies may become common in many transactions to induce individuals to communicate with corporations via interactive feedback. But as with advertising, it is the consumer who ultimately pays the price for these information subsidies. The net result will be the further monetarization of "inalienable" human rights into transferable corporate property rights.

Yet another economic factor contributing to the proliferation of RRPLS is the Smart House campaign being pushed by builders and the Electronics Industry Association. The Smart House concept envisions "electronic systems that allow household appliances such as televisions and dishwashers to communicate with each other."[28] One wonders what would motivate two such disparate appliances to speak with one other. Could the dishwasher perhaps tell the TV what brands of detergent and cookware the occupants used, and the TV could adjust its interactive advertising accordingly?

Another selling point of a Smart House retrofit is its reputed advantage in terms of home security, since its motion-sensing devices presumably could distinguish among occupants, invited guests, and unwelcome intruders. It is difficult to evaluate the degree to which fear of violence will lead to electronic fortification of existing homes via RRPLS, thereby locking its occupants in to perpetual surveillance as effectively as it locks intruders out. But in light of the thriving market in labor-intensive private security services, the growing disparities between well-to-do homeowners and the restless underclasses, and the existing movement by the upper classes to "fort up" in specially designed housing tracts, the wide acceptance of RRPLS for home security purposes is quite likely.

One final economic incentive promoting the technological evolution of RRPLS is the lure of profits from a high-speed national information network. It could cost tens of billions of dollars to install "on-ramps" (e.g., fiber optic cables) from every residence to the information superhighway. Yet utilities' profits from RRPLS could generate enough surplus cash flow to finance that construction. Through RRPLS, electric utilities "can sharply reduce the future costs of making power at the same time they are capitalizing the cost of building the great information superhighway."[29] Once again, corporations are poised to internalize profits by externalizing costs—in this case, the social costs of utility surveillance.

Fine-grained RRPLS monitoring of entire populations is not inevitable. Much of the tension between privacy interests and the need for incentives to reduce peak home energy consumption could be resolved by limiting the "intelligence" of smart RRPLS meters. But the level of RRPLS surveillance acceptable to consumers may artificially be boosted by surveillance subsidies. Given the corporate forces jockeying for position on the emerging information superhighway, electric utility surveillance subsidies are of particular concern at the present time. Panoptic RRPLS surveillance, once frozen into the architecture of the "snooper highway" as an embedded technological bias, would have pervasive and irreversible effects on any future cultural trajectory through the information age.

Monitoring in the Workplace

Computerized monitoring of clerical workers is commonplace. In America in 1990, 26 million employees had their work tracked electronically, and 10 million of those had their work evaluated—and their pay determined—based on computer-generated statistics. Airline reservation clerks are expected to arrange flight bookings within 106 seconds. If the customer asks too many questions, it increases the clerk's TATT (total average talk time), for which penalties can result. Directory assistance operators have twenty-nine seconds to handle a caller's request. Any pleasantries, such as saying "please" or "thank you," increase the operator's "handle time," and the incident is logged immediately in that employee's evaluation file.[30]

But life in the lower occupational strata was nasty, brutish, and short even before modern technologies. How has computing affected white-collar workers? An examination of twenty-five popular Macintosh programs—for electronic mail, network management, and integrated groupware applications—found that in the typical modern networked environment, every product allowed a network manager to "eavesdrop on virtually every aspect of your networked computing environment with or without your approval or even knowledge."[31] Nor are such capabilities unique to Macintosh network environments. An ad for networking software in *PC Week* magazine—clearly addressed to management—boasted that the product "Brings you a level of control never possible. You decide to look in on Sue's computer screen—Sue won't even know you're there. All from the comfort of your chair."[32] That chair may be in the adjacent office, or it may be halfway around the world, far from a corporate electronic sweatshop set up to exploit cheap labor.

To determine whether these surveillance capabilities were actually utilized, *Macworld* magazine conducted a survey of 300 CEOs and MIS (management information system) directors at firms of various sizes in different industries. In the survey, 22 percent of employers admitted they had searched the networked communications of employees, such as electronic mail, voice mail, or computer files. The figure rose to 30 percent for heads of larger companies (over 1,000 employees). Demonstrating the casual justification for this intrusive behavior, only 18 percent of the companies responding had written policies dealing with employees' electronic privacy.[33]

According to Cindia Cameron, a field organizer for Nine to Five, the National Association of Working Women, "Technology now allows employers to cross the line from monitoring the work to monitoring the worker."[34] In light of the publicity from the *Macworld* survey, might we expect any federal legislation to limit employee surveillance? Lawrence Fineran of the National Association of Manufacturers (NAM) spoke against any such regulations: "NAM opposes any legislation that will interfere with the ability of modern and future equipment that can assist domestic companies in their fight to remain competitive. Otherwise the U.S. may as well let the information age pass it by."[35] The rhetoric of "competitiveness" was invoked despite the fact that Japan and much of Europe long ago imposed tougher restrictions than were proposed in the Privacy for Consumers and Workers Act that failed to pass Congress during the Bush administration.

Economic competitiveness is a weapon used not only against government regulation but also against workers. Some workers find their computer screen will flash the message "You're not working as fast as the person next to you." Proponents argue that worker surveillance software is an improvement because it guarantees that workers' performance will be evaluated objectively. But such an analysis ignores the context of underlying power relations.

We might wonder whether workplace surveillance is destined to fulfill the intent of Bentham's 1791 Panopticon that "for the greatest proportion of time possible, each man should actually be under inspection." Or if that goal cannot be met, that "the persons to be inspected should always feel themselves as if under inspection" because "the greater chance there is, of a person's being at a given time actually under inspection, the more strong will be the persuasion—the more intense . . . the feeling he has of his being so."

Fortunately, in societies where some employers must fund worker health care costs, there is a countervailing economic incentive. A joint study conducted by the Communications Workers of America and researchers from the University of Wisconsin found that electronic monitoring on the job increases boredom, tension, anxiety, depression, anger, and fatigue.[36] These findings are consistent with earlier studies implicating electronic surveillance as "a major workplace stress factor—linked, in part, to the sense of powerlessness that monitored employees feel."

Intelligent Vehicle-Highway Systems

Proponents of "intelligent vehicle-highway systems" (IVHS) say that if computers are attached to all vehicles and their positions tracked precisely, traffic jams can be averted and air pollution reduced. By transforming highways into electronic toll roads, proponents hope to force drivers to internalize the environmental costs of automobile use that would otherwise be externalized.

A rudimentary form of IVHS is already operational during periods of peak traffic in Hong Kong. This system employs only surveillance, not control. A chip is installed in every car, and it responds automatically to queries from sensors installed along the roadways. In effect, certain streets are toll roads during peak traffic times. But rather than slow traffic further by physically collecting tolls, the IVHS toll system does this electronically. In a similar manner, vehicle speed and identification could be recorded, and speeding tickets could be mailed automatically to offenders.

A related technology presents similar prospects. The Teletrac vehicle-locator system employs a frequency-agile transmitter to announce vehicle location. Already in Los Angeles, it is charged, "the courts have been utterly promiscuous in allowing the police to clandestinely tag suspects' cars with these devices. It is not far-fetched to imagine a situation in a few years where everyone on probation, or entered in one of the criminal databases, will have to submit to some form of 24-hour electronic surveillance. We shall soon see police departments with the technology to put the equivalent of an electronic bracelet on entire social groups."[37]

Video Games and the Colonization of Consciousness

As arcades for video games have multiplied, video games themselves have moved into American homes, so that by 1993, Sega and Nintendo systems appeared in an estimated 50 million U.S. households. The $5.3 billion spent on video games in 1992 in America exceeded total ticket sales at movie theaters nationwide.[38] A single video game company, Nintendo, had higher after-tax profits than Apple Computer or Microsoft, higher than all Hollywood studios combined.

Video games are big not merely in terms of money but especially when measured in that scarcest of currencies, discretionary time. Estimates are that children in homes with video games spend on average between 1.5 and 2 hours per day hooked into them.

Consider Sega's "Night Trap" video game: This realistic, live-action CD-ROM product features bloodthirsty vampires dressed in black who stalk scantily clad teenage girls through a large house. The girls are portrayed as powerless to defend themselves. Unless rescued by the (male) player, they are caught by the vampires, who drill holes in their necks and hang them up on meat hooks.

Perhaps "Night Trap" is too complex as an object lesson, since it mixes male chauvinism with violence. A purer form of video game violence is Sega's "Mortal Kombat," which offers icing on the cake of gratuitous interactive violence: "At the climax of Mortal Kombat, after an opponent is beaten to the ground, the winner is invited to tear out the loser's bloody, beating heart, or snap off the loser's skull and pull the spine out of the body."[39] "Mortal Kombat" was America's top-grossing arcade game in 1992, and versions for home systems (both Nintendo and Sega) were propelled into the home video game market by a $10 million advertising budget.

Given society's agonizingly slow response to the crisis of television violence, those who sounded the alarm on that earlier crisis are watching the growth of video game violence with the horror usually reserved for watching a highway pileup develop in slow motion. Marsha Kinder, a professor at the University of Southern California, noted a big difference between video games and other media because the games actively engage children in violent acts: "It's worse than TV or a movie. It communicates the message that the only way to be empowered is through violence."[40] In terms of desensitization, actively participating in virtual violence is expected to have even stronger desensitizing effects than passively witnessing violence.

Educational Software

Video game proponents correctly point out that the genre is not monolithic. For example, many educational software applications masquerade as video games to pique students' interest. But even "purely" educational software has its problems. These include the perils of simulated reality, which frequently mislead even adult Ph.D.'s. How realistic are the rules and assumptions embedded in educational software? After "test-driving" an educational simulation, are children reminded that "Your mileage in the real world may differ"? Would such warnings be contradicted by the weight of (simulated) experiential evidence?

Perhaps the assumptions most deeply embedded in educational software are those of the Cartesian epistemology inherent in most notions of "problem solving." These Cartesian postulates include the highly problematic notions of data as objective, technology as value-neutral, and communication as a conduit between autonomous individuals who construct their own ideas. When computerized educational problem-solving software reduces the real world's degrees of freedom to those of the Cartesian worldview, this precludes creative solutions that redefine the problems in a larger (typically social) context. Cartesian software teaches students to approach situations as narrowly defined problems to be solved, not as circumstances to be comprehended by means of organizing principles animated by a set of values.

Education is a process of cultural transmission, and students often learn unintended lessons from teachers. What implicit lessons will instructional technology teach? It would seem that surveillance is one such lesson: In order for teachers to monitor students' progress, the instructional computer programs will track virtually all aspects of each interactive lesson. Thus, one impact of interactive computerized instruction will be the initiation of students into the socialization of surveillance.[41]

Prevailing notions of computer literacy are often thinly disguised economic ideology.[42] The rhetoric of "economic competitiveness" is used to prey upon parents' fears that their child will lose the "educational competitiveness" contest unless they purchase a home computer.

Despite all the hype from the computer industry, one should at least consider the possibility that computers are largely irrelevant to our educational problems. An International Assessment of Educational Progress survey ranked American students behind thirteen other countries in math and science proficiency, yet not one of those other countries used computer technology in the classroom.[43] The "digital convergence" of computers with video and telecommunications will not be confined solely to adults. Trends toward news as "infotainment"—already accelerating in TV broadcasting—undoubtedly will be replicated in educational software. Competition among educational video software makers can be expected to shrink the attention span of young people further and to reduce their tolerance for electronic spaces that are only sparsely action-packed. Thus, even if teachers rarely select a particular educational software package based on its superior electronic baby-sitting capabilities, it would seem that a Gresham's law of video games nevertheless may apply to the educational software market—in short, that the "tainment" crowds out the "info."

But even this volatile mixture of futuristic trends would be incomplete without factoring in advertising. Given the commercial convergence of movies, toys, clothes, breakfast foods, and video games, perhaps Teacher of the Year honors soon will be awarded to the Teenage Mutant Ninja Turtles. Think of the licensing fees to be reaped from every school district! If your child can read this, thank a cartoon character.

Pawns in a Panoptic Video Game?

The digital convergence of most importance involves the convergence of advertising and other forms of propaganda with interactive video or "virtual reality" (VR). Advertising modes that can gather data portend fine-tuned personalized manipulation rather than coarse-grained statistical manipulation of large population segments.

Although the power relationship between "info-producers" and "info-consumers" will be uneven enough as the corporate sector develops more detailed files of consumers' transactions, that power relationship will become utterly skewed if more citizens are induced to accept technology that incorporates involuntary input devices (IIDs). This conceptual family of apparatus represents the extreme pole of what has been called "extractive" information technology. Data are involuntarily extracted from the objects of surveillance, regardless of their wishes as subjects.

One tangible example of an IID is a system to scan viewers' pupils. Other involuntary input devices include galvanic skin response transducers and infrared blood capillary sensors. Such sensors are a logical extension of current trends in VR gear.

An earlier IID was the Nielsen passive peoplemeter, designed to scan viewers' faces and the pupils of their eyes. Image recognition software was intended to categorize facial expressions as a means of enabling instantaneous measurement of audience response to TV ads.[44] Today, with interactive multimedia, as soon as a frown is detected, an interactive ad might be "morphed" into alternative colors and scenes until the viewer once again displays a docile, contented, smiling face.

Supposedly, Nielsen's passive peoplemeter project was (temporarily) discontinued a few years ago because viewers were uncomfortable that the device knew when they were drowsing or talking to somebody rather than watching the tube. This unfortunate lack of social acceptance can be overcome by a suitably designed surveillance subsidy. The lure of VR technology is the ideal bait on the hook of interactive surveillance. Much existing VR gear depends on an opaque helmet worn by the subject and sensors attached to various body parts, so that when the subject physically moves, the VR scene can change accordingly to provide a convincing illusion. VR absolutely requires involuntary input devices.

Whereas current advertising provides an information subsidy, technology to implement the "pay-per-view" society would enable a market in which competing messages might carry negative prices—advertisers might "pay to be viewed." How could advertisers ensure that receivers actually watched their messages? Physiological surveillance technology—IIDs. Naturally, advertisers would demand the right to use real-time surveillance feedback to present their case in the most compelling manner possible. Encounters with such interactive, morph-able messages might literally be tests of wills, even if traditional hypnosis were illegal. Interactive ads, coupled with IIDs, constitute a giant leap in advertisers' ability to "get inside the mind of the consumer"—in a decidedly nonpassive manner.

The following VR (or video) game is represented in the format of a crude ASCII-driven video game coupled with a user-friendly interface that employs a pupil-scanning IID:

ENTER COMMAND> Shoot convenience store clerk. [Video of] Clerk, bleeding profusely, drops behind counter.

ENTER COMMAND> Take case from frozen foods locker. [Video of] A frosty case of Cyber-Suds beer.

ENTER COMMAND> Open case. Take out bottle. Open bottle. [Video of] Bottle being opened. [Audio track:] "Fizzz." [Video of] Refreshing beer foaming out. [Audio track:] "Ahhh."

ENTER COMMAND> Tell Bob, "It just doesn't get any better than this."

[Interactive software checks response to verify that Subject has properly memorized Product Slogan.] Bob agrees. [Video of] Something falling from the sky.

ENTER COMMAND> Look up. [Video of] The Swedish Bikini Team! [Video of] You and Bob partying with the Swedish Bikini Team. Bob smiles at you.

The girl fawning over Bob turns seductively toward the virtual camera and says [audio track]: "Cyber-Suds for Cyber Studs . . . it just doesn't get any better."

[Interactive software detects Subject's pupils straying to Bob's girl, who is blond. It dynamically reprograms the scene to switch the two girls and logs Subject's preference for blondes in its permanent files.]

Bob's girl, now fawning over you, says [audio track]: "I'd love to go for a nude swim with you, but your file shows you only bought three cases of Cyber-Suds last month. You can be a Real Cyber Stud Man by making your monthly Cyber-Suds Bikini Team Quota. Let's DO IT right now! Whip out your credit card . . . and then we can go skinnydipping."

ENTER COMMAND> Debit—5 cases Cyber-Suds beer

ENTER COMMAND> MasterCard 1349 1277 8652 1109

ENTER COMMAND> Authentication Code 3381 7047 5944

ENTER COMMAND> Give bottle to girl. [Video of] Girl thanking you gratefully as she opens the bottle. [Video of] Frothy beer foaming out. [Audio track accompaniment:] "Ahhh" as her bikini drops to the ground.

Naturally, such interactive applications would have contingency video and audio footage for those who learn to mix their sex with virtual violence.

Among young males, video games already serve as a significant source of self-identification and self-esteem. In the future, interactive video entertainment will be used to build brand-name identification and loyalty. Yesterday's consumers were willing to pay for the privilege of advertising a corporate logo on the clothing they wore in public spaces. Product placement and corporate logos on video game characters are already occurring in cyberspace.[45] Perhaps tomorrow's cyber-consumers can be manipulated not only into having their own VR character display a logo but also into killing VR characters who display competing logos. A variant of the Cyber-Suds game might offer "points" (exchangeable for merchandise or free replays) whenever one's VR alter ego encounters and kills an opponent wearing the wrong corporate logo. Today's youth gangs kill over patches of color on clothing. One can imagine hate groups using the power of interactive video feedback to indoctrinate youngsters in the benefits of ethnic cleansing.

Home video game systems provide extremely high video resolution, and VR gear promises to provide an even more realistic experience for technophiles of all ages. Except for the cybernaut's dream of connecting the human brain directly to computer interfaces, VR technology represents the culmination of the information revolution—the seamless replacement of warning signals from the natural environment by synthetic constructs. This ought to set many alarm bells to ringing. But we are told that ethics ought to transcend mere cultural relativism and be technologically relativist: "I think it is good to beware of looking at the future through the moral lens of the present. . . . In a world of tens of billions of people, perhaps cyberspace is a better place to keep most of the population happy, most of the time."[46]

This sketchy solution should come as a relief to the Trilateral Commission. But how might the governing elites be certain the populace would remain docile in their VR cocoons? Cybernetic social control would require sensing (surveillance) and precisely calibrated feedback—exactly those functions provided by interactive panoptic technologies. To maintain computerized social control over billions of cybernauts might seem expensive, but perhaps any resistance by the populace can be gradually degraded until people are willing to pay surveillance subsidies to ensure their own comfortable incarceration.

Intelligence Agencies and the Political Economy of Encryption

The metaphors of older communications technologies are extended to cyberspace, but many do not make that transition well. E-mail (electronic mail) is popularly conceived as sending a letter through the postal service. But a more accurate analogy is to a typewritten postcard. The distinction is crucial, since the contents of a postcard are visible to many mail handlers in the delivery system. Furthermore, a typewritten postcard carries no signature to authenticate its origin. Proponents of generalized e-mail surveillance argue that despite various laws, monitoring e-mail is legal, since experienced cyber-citizens should have no expectation of privacy.

Suffice it to say that with currently installed software, neither the confidentiality nor the authenticity of e-mail can be assured. Because e-mail monitoring is cheap and undetectable (unlike steaming open and then resealing postal envelopes), practices of eavesdropping and forgery should be considered widespread. A tapped telephone line is a closer analogy to e-mail.

To tap an individual's phone legally in the United States formerly required a search warrant and visible hardware. A government agent had to travel physically to a local telephone company's Central Office switch, attach alligator clips to a selected wire, and remain in the building, visible to telephone company management and employees alike. This labor-intensive process was eased somewhat by tape recorders. But even then, someone had to listen to those tapes and transcribe them before other observers could skim the contents quickly.

With e-mail, the balance of power between observer and subject has shifted. Once intercepted, the contents of e-mail are already transcribed and entered in a computer for easy keyword searching. Moreover, e-mail can be intercepted after transmission, since the recipient's host computer contains a copy. Thus, an agent can penetrate the system and copy the e-mail anytime before the recipient deletes it. And as Lieutenant Colonel Oliver North learned to his dismay, even if the recipient deletes the e-mail after reading it, redundancy programs installed on many host systems make backup copies of all data, which may persist indefinitely. Moreover, because the labor cost of cybersurveillance is so low, it enables a small organization (with immense computer resources) to surveil the digital communications of an entire population. Human labor is needed only after a particular suspect is singled out. Thus, there is the potential for "retroactive wiretapping" of an entire society.

How might a society defend itself against such a surveillance program? One tactic involves avoidance of a single uniform, easily tapped network. Instead, multiple overlapping local, regional, and national networks would be employed. Surveillance agents would then need to install many physical "wiretaps" to guarantee interception of all data flows. Another tactic is security through overload. If the volume of traffic is sufficiently large, the recording capabilities of the monitoring agents can be exceeded.

Curiously, descriptions of both tactics seem to characterize the evolution of the Internet, an international collection of over 20 million users on 2 million host computers connected via 16,000 networks in 60 countries (concentrated in the industrialized nations) that communicate in a manner best described as anarchic. Network topology evolves rapidly and is in a constant state of flux, factors that make it difficult even to measure the dimensions of the Internet. The number of networks connected to the Internet currently is doubling every year, and the volume of traffic on the Internet is expanding at the rate of 20 percent per month. If an agency is trying to keep all this under surveillance, the job must be a nightmare.

But to monitor such volume and complexity, it is not necessary to access the contents of each message. Instead, a discipline known as traffic analysis simplifies the task by recording only the addresses of e-mail senders and recipients (or those of telephone calls, for that matter). Clustering or block modeling algorithms can deduce shared interests among subgroups of communicators, identify leaders, and the like.[47] The surveillance potential is vast and once again alters the balance of power.

The ultimate solution to network surveillance is encryption, coupled with anonymous remailer systems to foil traffic analysis. If both the contents and the terminal addresses of messages are strongly encrypted, that should suffice to thwart any would-be surveillance agents. But what evidence indicates this concern with communications surveillance is more than simple paranoia?

A March 1992 proposal by the FBI would require all U.S. telecommunication companies to provide the FBI with a remote surveillance capability. The FBI argues that with new forms of digital telephony, it is becoming difficult or impossible for the agency to wiretap enemies of the people, such as organized crime figures and drug barons. Naturally, citizens would continue to receive full constitutional protections of due process; a search warrant based on probable cause would be required (except in cases of national security) before the FBI could initiate a remote digital wiretap.

"If you've done nothing wrong, you have nothing to worry about," we are told. "Don't you want to be protected from criminals?" Intelligence agencies raise the specter of hackers breaking into TRW's database and destroying citizens' credit ratings or breaking into hospital computer systems and interfering with the functioning of intensive-care equipment. In the ultimate irony, the threat of hacking is used to sell the public on the benefits of government telecom monitoring. If the scheme succeeds, all government-inspected e-mail may one day carry the tag "This e-mail has been monitored by the state to protect individual privacy." To develop this remote wiretapping capability would cost hundreds of millions of dollars. Who would absorb the cost? "Pass it on to the consumers," responds the FBI. "Either that or let the taxpayers foot the bill." But what about the social costs? The FBI has a habit of illegally wiretapping social activists, such as Rev. Martin Luther King Jr. With this proposal, as usual, the benefits would accrue to those in control of the technology—a government agency or transnational corporation. The external costs would appear in the social column as an immense debit in the categories of freedom, privacy, and personal autonomy.

This technology carries a similar risk to that of nuclear power: It must be safeguarded from misuse for generations. Just as stockpiled plutonium represents concentrated military power and thus must be guarded in perpetuity, so too centralized mass surveillance technology offers concentrated social power and presents a long-lived irresistible temptation—an attraction that eventually may prove fatal to democracy.

The FBI's proposal to achieve "universal surveillance for all" is opposed by many large corporations, since it would require every company PBX system to include a port allowing the FBI access to conduct remote surveillance. Thus, presumably armed with a search warrant, the FBI could intercept all communications traffic transiting a corporate site without ever visiting the site to physically tap into its PBX switch. Corporate interests are concerned that such a remote surveillance capability would be a security hole that could be exploited by competitors engaged in industrial espionage. The FBI's proposal seems ludicrous in light of encryption technology. Why bother to intercept communications if you are unable to decipher the language in which they are encoded?

That conundrum was resolved in April 1993 when a chilling proposal surfaced, ostensibly from NIST (the National Institute for Standards and Technology), to promulgate a "voluntary" government-approved cryptography system for civilian computer and phone communication. Documents obtained by CPSR (Computer Professionals for Social Responsibility) under the Freedom of Information Act reveal that, in violation of the Computer Security Act of 1987, the real initiator of this proposal is the NSA (National Security Agency)—the agency charged with intercepting all transmissions relevant to national security. The budget of the NSA exceeds that of all other intelligence agencies combined (e.g., the FBI, CIA,

DIA), and its computing power is measured not in MIPS (million instructions per second) or gigabytes but in acres of physical ground covered by the most modern computing equipment.[48]

This proposal would establish a cryptographic algorithm, called Skipjack, as a de facto civilian standard, despite the fact that the Skipjack algorithm itself remains classified as a military secret. It is customary to publish crypto algorithms so that they may be tested by all challengers to prove their mettle against attacks by cryptanalysis. But the NSA refuses to allow public testing. The Skipjack algorithm would be implemented in hardware, in a chip called Clipper or Capstone, which could be installed in computers and phones.

Central to this NSA-NIST proposal is that every user's private crypto "keys" would be registered with government authorities. In this manner, if an intelligence agency needed to decipher the encrypted communications from a wiretap or intercepted e-mail, the agency could obtain the corresponding decryption keys from the government key "escrow" authority.

In an unprecedented public appearance in July 1993 before the Computer System Security and Privacy Advisory Board in Washington, Clint Brooks, assistant director of the NSA, readily admitted that the Skipjack-Clipper system is not intended to catch any criminals. Obviously, he said, those who have something to hide will avoid inviting government wiretaps by using the system. Those sentiments were echoed by NIST's acting director, Ray Kammer: "It's obvious that anyone who uses Clipper [Skipjack] for the conduct of organized crime is dumb."[49]

Why, then, would the NSA propose a "voluntary" cryptographic standard to which the government would hold the keys? The most obvious explanation is that it is merely the first step in a process gradually to degrade people's expectations of privacy until ultimately the NSA can outlaw any nonapproved crypto algorithms or devices. Establishment of Clipper as a de facto crypto standard in the marketplace would make nonstandard crypto traffic stand out like a sore thumb. Every law-abiding citizen who used Clipper would have his or her crypto chip's serial number transmitted at the start of each communication, thus rendering the citizen's location known to authorities and the person's activities susceptible to traffic analysis, for which the U.S. government doesn't even need a search warrant.

Suppose—contrary to all historical evidence—the public trusts that no intelligence agency will mount an organized campaign of general surveillance. If government-accessible cryptography is widely used, is there a potential for rogue elements in government intelligence agencies to abuse the public trust? The same week that Dr. Brooks testified, the U.S. House Judiciary Committee held hearings on abuse by police of the FBI's National Crime Information Center (NCIC, a computerized database of criminals and suspects). In one instance, a former police officer accessed the NCIC without authorization to track down and murder one of his former girlfriends. In another case, a woman finagled access to the NCIC to check the records of prospective clients for her drug-dealing boyfriend so they could avoid undercover operatives. It is widely assumed that the broad collaboration between police agencies and private security forces means that much of the NCIC data has already been compromised and is now duplicated in numerous private databases.

Clearly the move toward outlawing any crypto system that is unbreakable by the NSA has extremely ominous overtones. But the ramifications of widespread use of unbreakably encrypted communication are not comforting either. Recall that not only data but also trillions of dollars of capital flow through cyberspace every day: "It is imaginable that, with the widespread use of digital cash and encrypted monetary exchange on the Global Net, economies the size of America's could appear as nothing but oceans of alphabet soup. Money laundering would no longer be necessary. The payment of taxes might become more or less voluntary. A lot of weird things would happen after that."[50]

Widespread use of unbreakable encrypted communications would further exacerbate the existing class-based discrimination by law enforcement agencies: "If law enforcement is left to investigate only crimes in which neither communications nor data are essential proof, it is unlikely that prosecution of crimes such as murder, assault, rape, and robbery would be significantly affected. What would be affected, however, is prosecution of business crime. The end result would be a contour to law enforcement that is decidedly class-focused."[51] Thus, it seems that neither technological alternative for communications access by government would result in an acceptable balance of power between business and government. In both cases, it seems that civil society would be on the losing side of the power struggle.

It is instructive to look beyond America's borders for insight. The French government is known to use electronic surveillance to eavesdrop on U.S. manufacturers in France. Pierre Marion, retired head of the DGSE (the French CIA), was dismayed that the Pentagon boycotted the 1993 Paris Air Show in reaction to French industrial espionage against forty-nine U.S.-based multinational corporations: "A national intelligence agency that would not consider doing that kind of intelligence work would not be fulfilling its mission. . . . Economic intelligence is a fact of life."[52]

In light of the French policy of conducting industrial espionage against multinational corporations originating in other countries, widespread international use of Clipper would certainly enhance the ability of U.S. intelligence agencies to play that same game. This explanation fits well with the struggle of U.S. intelligence agencies to justify their budgets and existence in the post–Cold War era. U.S. agencies have floated numerous trial balloons regarding their entry into industrial espionage, for both "offensive" and "defensive" purposes.[53] Perhaps this putsch to concentrate power in the hands of a central crypto authority will be sold to the American public (like so many other raw deals) with the rhetoric of "economic competitiveness."

To date, there appears in this situation to be scant middle ground between competing technological dystopias. One technological pole would doom privacy—personal and corporate—and thereby allow intelligence agencies to reign supreme. The other technological pole would elevate privacy over all other "rights" and thus could end most remaining government (and citizen) power to regulate business.

∾   ∾   ∾

Events have moved rapidly since this section was written in October 1993. Legislation (HR 4922, S. 2375) implementing much of the FBI's March 1992 "digital telephony" proposal was passed by Congress, with no floor debate, in an unrecorded voice vote in October 1994. To reimburse telecom companies for the cost of making their equipment "surveillance-friendly," this Communications Assistance for Law Enforcement Act authorized $500 million for the first four years.

The bill nominally precludes law enforcement from having remote automated surveillance capability. Yet in October 1995, the FBI published a "wiretap capacity notice" stating it intends to mandate a redesign of telephone networks to allow it to intercept simultaneously up to 1 percent of all calls.[54] Such an unprecedented level of domestic wiretapping is at least a thousand times greater than is currently reported by intelligence agencies in the United States.

As for the Clipper chip, in testimony before the Senate Judiciary Committee on February 14, 1995, FBI Director Louis Freeh sounded a newly ominous note regarding the voluntary nature of government-approved encryption: "Powerful encryption threatens to make worthless the access assured by the new digital [telephony] law." Indeed, U.S. government documents released in August 1995 in response to a Freedom of Information request by the Electronic Privacy Information Center reveal that—contrary to the administration's public statements—the FBI and the NSA had concluded as early as February 1993 that the Clipper chip encryption initiative would succeed only if alternative encryption techniques are outlawed.

The Information Superhighway—to Where?

New technologies of communication are waiting in the wings, poised to take center stage. The digital convergence of TV with computers and telecommunications networks is to culminate in a national information infrastructure (NII) or information superhighway. Once again, techno-optimistic visions of best-case scenarios are proclaimed with great and uncritical enthusiasm. "Electronic democracy" is just one magic elixir. "The information revolution is bringing with it a key that may open the door to a new era of involvement and participation. The key is the self-motivating exhilaration that accompanies truly effective interaction with information through a good console through a good network to a good computer."[55]

Some grandiose predictions regarding electronic democracy can be excused as instinctive extrapolations from current trends. Admittedly, trends in participation on the Internet are encouraging. But Internet culture is a renaissance that represents the flowering of a print culture, one composed almost exclusively of First World educated elites. An equally significant factor is that current Internet culture is primarily noncommercial. In America, much of it is subsidized by the federal government, ostensibly to promote research and education. Obviously, given that half of Americans are functionally illiterate, this print culture cannot easily be "scaled up" to engage other segments of society, despite commendable outreach efforts (e.g., to provide on-line access to the homeless in Santa Monica, California). Moreover, the only design goal for the NII that is shared by both government and the private sector alike is the perceived need for massive bandwidth—the capacity to carry gigabits of information per second. That increased channel capacity will make viable the transmission of video signals over the NII, and it is reasonable to assume that much of the Internet's current print culture will be displaced, washed away by another triumphant stream of images.

Technological frontiers are key sites in the struggle over the production and distribution of meaning. For critics to reject a technology, for opponents to abdicate the struggle, does little more than cede the field to those who remain. Contesting the meaning of "electronic democracy" by struggling to establish prototype applications on community and regional scales seems a more viable strategy than does ceding the field to electronic demagogues like Pat Robertson and Rush Limbaugh.

Moreover, to reject a given family of technological applications may be counterproductive, unless related applications similarly can be rejected. For example, suppose opponents rally sufficient forces to prevent the telcos and cable TV companies from constructing an NII of their own design. But that would ignore the electric utility companies. Through real-time residential power line surveillance, electric utilities "can sharply reduce the future costs of making power at the same time they are capitalizing the cost of building the great information superhighway."[56] Despite efforts to promote a public interest vision for the NII, the lure of profits may drive de facto mergers among telcos, cable TV providers, and electric utilities. It is ironic that allegedly decentralized, democratic technologies in fact engender such concentrations of power.

Much dispute over the NII appears to be about money: Who will pay for it, and who will profit? It is by no means clear that an NII will facilitate gains in productivity.[57] If home gambling is typical of the "killer applications" needed to induce consumer demand for an NII "product," then the NII may be the ultimate example of firms internalizing benefits as they externalize the net costs onto society at large. Economic considerations regarding an NII should not distract our attention from more fundamental issues of normative values, politics, and the distribution of power. Throughout history, media technologies have coevolved with the art of politics. The present crisis of democracy is inseparable from the ascendancy of television as the dominant source of news. In the words of computer pioneer Alan Kay, "Television should be the last mass communications medium to be naively designed and put into the world without a Surgeon General's warning!"[58]

Just as each new generation must learn for itself the lessons of war, so must each generation renew its contracts with democracy, and it must renegotiate those contracts in light of the prevailing media technologies of the times. As Hazel Henderson correctly pointed out, "Fears about the misuse of instantaneous forms of democracy—technological hardware like call-in radio, television, electronic town meetings, polling—have stifled the debate over how to design these potential tools of democratic participation so as to avoid abuse and new forms of totalitarianism."[59]

It is said that, no matter what form of government we have in the United States, it will always be called "democracy." Modern communications technologies—and the businesses that control them—already constitute a de facto information infrastructure that profoundly influences politics. Whether the meaning of "democracy" is further degraded and perverted will be determined by the struggle of contending forces. The NII is neither a hardware mechanism nor a software application. Rather, it is a new name for an old locus of struggle between those who control today's communications resources and those who have suffered the externalities imposed by previous generations of social architectures. What is needed is more open debate over various forms of electronic democracy and dictatorship so that a wider spectrum of people can be intelligent participants in shaping the decisions that determine their future.

The metaphor of the NII as an information superhighway evokes images of physical nuts and bolts—which seem inherently value-neutral until they are used for some specific purpose. But values may be embedded in the very design of telecommunications hardware, not merely in the software applications that run on particular computer platforms. Cable TV hardware provides an instructive example. Not surprisingly, the cable TV infrastructure was designed by profit seekers whose thoughts were constrained by the dominant (and dominating) paradigm—that the purpose of a network is entertainment, and that there are two separate and distinct types of entities connected to a network: information producers and information consumers.

This schema is heavily value-laden, and the asymmetric power relation it engenders already is immanent in many technologies. With cable TV infrastructure, activists who want to use existing cable TV wiring to implement a local community network typically find that the bandwidth from information producers to consumers is thousands of times greater than the capacity of the return leg. The vast majority of cable TV networking technology (repeaters on fiber optic cable) has been optimized to suit a particular set of values.

Cable TV and telecom companies try to frame NII issues in terms of hardware—which segments of the communications network should be upgraded first to fiber optic capacities, or whether satellite channels, cellular technologies, and packet-switched radio should be employed instead. The implicit assumption (embedded in the ideology of the information age) is that to upgrade a channel, it suffices to boost its bandwidth, or capacity to support information flow. The content of that information and the nature of its sources are secondary considerations. We are told that a nationwide high-bandwidth NII will usher in the next Golden Age: "Information is power, and the key to empowering Americans is to give them access to it. Information is the public's No. 1 need."[60]

To help deconstruct the dreams of computer romantics, Langdon Winner identified a complex of mistaken assumptions: "(1) people are bereft of information; (2) information is knowledge; (3) knowledge is power; and (4) increasing access to information enhances democracy and equalizes social power. Taken as separate assertions and in combination, these beliefs provide a woefully distorted picture of the role of electronic systems in social life."[61]

The gap between the info-rich and the info-poor within an industrial society is maintained partly because the info-poor are confused and divided regarding their own best interests and partly because of disparities in communications competence.[62] Mere access to data will not alleviate that state. Rather, it will exacerbate the knowledge gap because "those best situated to take advantage of the power of a new technology are often those previously well situated by dint of wealth, social standing, and institutional position."[63]

For example, much of the economic value of data lies in the timeliness of the information. Even if an info-pauper could gain access to and interpret high-priced financial data, the opportunity to exploit that data would probably pass within microseconds, as automated trading programs in global financial powerhouses rose to gobble the bait. It takes money to make money, even in cyberspace. Because of the social biases and the differential benefits of new information technology, today's underclass risks winding up as roadkill on the shoulder of tomorrow's information superhighway.

Mere information does not imply knowledge, nor does the latter necessarily entail power. To transform raw information into useful knowledge requires the application of values and the production of meaning. Thus, a sampling of principles that should be promoted for the common good includes equal access, communicative freedom, privacy, noncommercialism, collaborative education, community building, active engagement in citizenship, ongoing evolution of the NII through participatory (re)design, and more symmetric power relations between individuals and institutions.

To illustrate the complexity of these principles, it is instructive to attempt to "unbundle" the principle of equal access. The public interest battle cry of "equal access to information" neglects three important factors: (1) disparities in communications competence by receivers; (2) the problem of information overload; and (3) disproportionate abilities to communicate with targeted receivers. The first factor might be addressed by active outreach and training efforts—affirmative programs for adult literacy rather than passive availability of self-tutoring software that may be psychologically or culturally inappropriate.

The second factor—information overload—has not yet been solved satisfactorily, even for the info-rich. Nevertheless, as it becomes more widely recognized by
the info-rich as their limiting factor, methods to manage the information glut,
such as indexing and filtering tools, will become the next stumbling block for the
info-poor. We will then need equal access to metainformation. Imagine if access
to today's Yellow Pages (by readers or writers) were by invitation only or required
payment of a hefty fee. Differential access to sources of metainformation, even
among the info-rich, will engender new power disparities. Whereas the limiting
factor in many current media environments is the control over distribution, the
locus of struggle will shift to control over indexing authorities and information
filtering standards. For example, what indexing authority will decide whether
fundamentalist Christian abortion counseling centers will meet the selection criterion of a computerized search for "abortion service providers"?

To address the third factor of equal access—disproportionate abilities to communicate with targeted receivers—also treads in the realm of metainformation,
since that is very much the business of today's direct mailing list vendors. The situation is further complicated by issues of privacy and intellectual property: To reveal names and addresses on a mailing list might provoke (additional) unwanted
invasions of privacy, and it would give an advantage to competing vendors of
mailing lists.

Many fundamental concepts of industrial civilization will not make the transition to cyberspace unscathed. Besides the struggle against extensions of corporate
intellectual property rights ("wrongs"), a radical reassessment of the Cartesian
model of communication—as a conduit for data between fully autonomous individuals—will be required. When human beings are viewed from a cognitive in-
formation-processing standpoint, it is apparent that we read (and then more or
less critically interpret) printed material as data, but we execute compiled visual
images as code. In the language of computer security, this inherent vulnerability
to images will result in serious breaches of system integrity. Personal integrity and
autonomy are therefore more foundational issues than are mere notions of privacy. Human beings must be treated as subjects of communication, not as objects
of manipulation. Somehow the technologies of control must themselves be
brought under social control.

Across the grand stage of history, several acts in the saga of corporate development have passed in succession. The advent of mass production entailed a crisis
of distribution. Construction of physical infrastructure for transportation alleviated the distribution crisis. Then followed the vertical integration of production
with distribution, causing a significant shift in power from the chaotic regime of
the "invisible hand" to the controlled regime of the "managerial hand"—the institutional rationality of the corporation.[64] As manufacturing and distribution
became ever more productive under efficient, integrated managerial control, the
bottleneck in the economic system shifted to the realm of consumption. The tech-

nology of marketing and advertising then evolved to boost consumption through the cultivation of "needs."

Now, as the media monopoly gathers steam, the economic system is poised for the next stage of vertical integration. With the development of a national information infrastructure, the emerging information-age conglomerate may bring under one (distributed, virtual) roof the manufacture, distribution, and (intensively cultivated) consumption of its information products. Should the media-industrial complex ever reach that stage, the balance of power between institutions and individuals could be irrevocably tilted. Institutions engaged in the manipulation of social reality would then control the very means of production of meaning itself.

The increasing corporate influence over leisure or free time prefigures the transition from the pay-per-view society to a fragmented populace trained to pay per experience, who ultimately pay to be viewed. Undemocratic, market-driven "advances" in information technology are accelerating the commodification of existence, as citizens sacrifice autonomy and privacy for consumer convenience and surveillance subsidies.

The road to freedom via a two-way information highway may turn into a one-way surveillance street used to condition people's thoughts and control their behavior—a form of progress that benefits only the powerful. In their quest for profit and power, the wardens of the panoptic prison—both corporate and military—share a common mission: Assisted by the best computing power money can buy, they work to extend their ongoing colonization of consciousness.

The initial stages of a virtual panoptic prison planet have already been constructed, even without a conscious, unified design. Millions of people are essentially prisoners of television, even before its metamorphosis via digital convergence. Although these individuals are allowed to leave their living rooms on work furloughs, they have effectively ceded control of their free time to the rhythms and dictates of institutional marketing strategies.

The most secure prison is one in which the inmates think they are free—because then they can harbor no thoughts of rebellion or escape. As the outer walls of the new VR Panopticon solidify into completion, few Americans realize they risk a life sentence as prisoners of panoptic disinformation. To the degree that interactive feedback is linked to the engines of computerized surveillance and classification, it will become economical to distribute individually tailored panoptic disinformation.

The warning signs of this invisible Panopticon were apparent to Jacques Ellul as far back as 1954: "It will not be a universal concentration camp, for it will be guilty of no such atrocity. It will not seem insane, for everything will be ordered. . . . We shall have nothing more to lose, and nothing to win. Our deepest instincts and our most secret passions will be analyzed, published, and exploited."[65]

In 1982, Oscar Gandy predicted "the regular, patterned, and skillful manipulation of the information environment to ensure that . . . perceptions of past, present, and future lead ultimately to the selection of a preferred option or plan."[66] He subsequently noted, "Within the panoptic future, addressability and verifiability mean that it is much more likely that each of us will be exposed to a different, customized, administratively tailored image of our immediate environment, our risks, our options, and the opportunities for the realization of our dreams."[67] The panoptic information enclosure already has subverted the information flow around millions of people. Perhaps before everyone can be imprisoned snugly in virtual panoptic cocoons, the external environment will intrude on our media-induced sweet dreams. Ecosystem collapse, coupled with social collapse, may prove difficult to ignore. These disturbances may intrude even into the sanctity of the (virtual) home shopping mall, with such force that the hegemony of consumption cannot absorb them. Yet perhaps we can still get organized as autonomous publics and take back our cultural environment by introducing a new, even democratic, mode of traffic on the superhighway. To paraphrase Ronald Reagan, it's morning in America—time to wake up and cast off the chains of market-structured consciousness.

NOTES

1. Jerry Mander, *In the Absence of the Sacred: The Failure of Technology and the Survival of the Indian Nations* (Sierra Club Books, 1991).

2. Ad in *New Statesman,* May 25, 1979.

3. K. Robins and F. Webster, "Cybernetic Capitalism: Information, Technology, Everyday Life," in Vincent Mosco and Janet Wasko, eds., *The Political Economy of Information* (University of Wisconsin Press, 1988), p. 49.

4. Jerry L. Salvaggio, "Projecting a Positive Image of the Information Society," in Jennifer Daryl Slack and Fred Fejes, eds., *Ideology of the Information Age* (Ablex, 1987), p. 154: "The information industry is investing billions of dollars into manufacturing an image as a guarantee that the information age is not a futuristic illusion."

5. Stephen Sloan, "Technology and Terrorism: Privatizing Public Violence," *IEEE Technology and Society Magazine* 10, no. 2 (Summer 1991):8–14.

6. Robert A.G. Monks and Nell Minow (former Reagan economist), *Power and Accountability* (HarperCollins, 1991), p. 24: "Despite attempts to provide balance and accountability, the corporation as an entity became so powerful that it quickly outstripped the limitations of accountability and became something of an externalizing machine, in the same way that a shark is a killing machine—no malevolence, no intentional harm, just something designed with sublime efficiency for self-preservation, which it accomplishes without any capacity to factor in the consequences to others."

7. Jeremy Bentham, *Panopticon; or, the Inspection House* (1791).

8. Michel Foucault, *Discipline and Punish: The Birth of the Prison* (Pantheon, 1977).

9. Robins and Webster, "Cybernetic Capitalism," p. 55.

10. Ivan Illich, *Energy and Equity* (Harper & Row, 1974). Illich calculated that the typical American spends more than four hours each day in car-related activities, including not

only driving and idling but also earning money to pay for the car, its maintenance and insurance, and so on. "The model American puts in 1600 hours to get 7500 miles: less than five miles per hour" (p. 31).

11. The potential of home VCR technology for "temporal emancipation" through "time shifting" is utilized by only a minute fraction of VCR owners. The vast majority automatically internalize the discipline implicitly imposed by the wardens' central transmitting tower and "choose" to watch—synchronously—whatever is currently being broadcast. The new consumer choice of real-time interactive television promises to reinforce this constraint of synchronicity.

12. "Privacy Concern Raised over Lotus Marketplace," *CPSR Newsletter* 8, no. 4 (Fall 1990): 24–25.

13. K. Lenk, "Information Technology and Society," in A. Schaff and G. Griedrichs, eds., *Microelectronics and Society, for Better or for Worse: A Report to the Club of Rome* (Pergamon, 1982).

14. Business Roundtable, "International Information Flow: A Plan for Action" (New York, January 1985), pp. 6–11.

15. M. Buyer, "Telecommunications and International Banking," in *Telecommunications* (1982).

16. Andrew Clement, "Office Automation and the Technical Control of Information Workers," in Mosco and Wasko, *The Political Economy of Information*, p. 222.

17. J. Schumpeter, *Business Cycles: A Theoretical, Historical, and Statistical Analysis of the Capitalist Process* (McGraw-Hill, 1939).

18. Joseph Weizenbaum, *Computer Power and Human Reason: From Judgment to Calculation* (W. H. Freeman, 1976).

19. Carl Sagan, "In Praise of Robots," *Natural History* 84, no. 1 (January 1975):8–20, quotation at p. 10.

20. Michel Crozier, Samuel P. Huntington, and Joji Watanuki, *The Crisis of Democracy: Report on the Governability of Democracies to the Trilaterial Commission* (New York: New York University Press, 1975). The Trilaterial Commission is a club of economic elites that promotes a uniform globalized economy, with national laws standardized to benefit transnational corporations.

21. James Stanford, "Continental Economic Integration: Modeling the Impact on Labor," *Annals of the American Academy of Political and Social Science* 526 (March 1993):92–110.

22. The electric utilities' term for RRPLS is more innocuous—"nonintrusive appliance load monitoring system" (NIALMS).

23. United States v. Miller, 425 U.S. 435 (1976), U.S. Supreme Court decision.

24. Roger Clarke, "Information Technology and Dataveillance," *Communications of the ACM* 31, no. 5 (May 1988):498–512.

25. George W. Hart, "Residential Energy Monitoring and Computerized Surveillance via Utility Power Flows," *IEEE Technology and Society Magazine,* June 1989, pp. 12–16.

26. J. Douglas, "Reaching Out with 2-way Communications," *EPRI Journal* 15, no. 6 (September 1990):4–13.

27. Edward S. Herman and Noam Chomsky, *Manufacturing Consent: The Political Economy of the Mass Media* (Pantheon, 1988).

28. Mitchell Pacelle, "Makers of Automated-Home Systems See a Future of TVs Talking to Thermostats," *Wall Street Journal,* September 28, 1992.

29. S. Rivkin, "While the Cable and Phone Companies Fight . . . Look Who's Wiring the Home Now," *New York Times Magazine,* September 26, 1993.

30. K. Nussbaum, panel discussion "Computer-based Surveillance of Individuals," First Conference on Computers, Freedom, and Privacy, March 27, 1991, Burlingame, Calif., sponsored by Computer Professionals for Social Responsibility. Nussbaum is former executive director of Nine to Five, the National Association of Working Women.

31. Charles Piller, "Bosses with X-ray Eyes," *Macworld* 10, no. 7 (July 1993):118–124.

32. Cited by Nussbaum, "Computer-based Surveillance."

33. Piller, "Bosses with X-ray Eyes."

34. Cited in ibid.

35. Ibid.

36. Ibid.

37. Interview with Mike Davis, *CovertAction Info Bulletin,* Summer 1992.

38. Laura Evenson, "The Video Game Culture: How It's Changing Kids' Perception of the World, *San Francisco Chronicle,* May 25, 1993.

39. *San Jose Mercury News,* May 25, 1993.

40. "Too Violent for Kids?" *Time,* September 27, 1993, p. 70.

41. C. A. Bowers, *The Cultural Dimensions of Educational Computing: Understanding the Non-neutrality of Technology* (Teachers College Press, 1988).

42. Y. Magrass and R. Upchurch, "Computer Literacy: People Adapted for Technology," *Computers and Society* 18, no. 2 (April 1988):8–15.

43. Michael Schrage, "High-Tech Programs Are no Substitute for Quality Education," *Los Angeles Times,* May 6, 1993, p. D1.

44. "New Nielsen System Is Turning Heads: Peoplemeter That Reads Faces, and Where They're Looking, Raises Specter of Big Brother," *Broadcasting* 122, no. 21 (May 18, 1992):8.

45. Jamie Beckett, "Computer Game Enters the Ad Age," *San Francisco Chronicle,* December 16, 1992.

46. Howard Rheingol, *Virtual Reality* (Summit Books, 1991), p. 352.

47. M. Schwartz and D. Wood, "Discovering Shared Interests Using Graph Analysis," *Communications of the ACM* 36, no. 8 (August 1993):78–79.

48. J. Bamford, *The Puzzle Palace* (Houghton Mifflin, 1982).

49. John Perry Barlow, "A Plain Text on Crypto Policy," *Communications of the ACM* 36, no. 11 (November 1993):21–26.

50. Ibid.

51. F. Tuerkheimer, "The Underpinnings of Privacy Protection," *Communications of the ACM* 36, no. 8 (August 1993):69–73.

52. C. Hanley, "International Spy Business Concentrates Mostly on Business," Associated Press, June 4, 1993.

53. R. Smith, "Administration to Consider Giving Spy Data to Business," *Washington Post,* February 3, 1993.

54. *Federal Register* 60, no. 199 (October 16, 1995):53643–53646.

55. J. Licklider, "Computers and Government," in M. Dertouzos and J. Moses, eds., *The Computer Age* (MIT Press, 1979).

56. Rivkin, "While the Cable and Phone Companies Fight."

57. J. Aronson, "Telecommunications Infrastructure and U.S. International Competitiveness," in *A National Information Network: Changing Our Lives in the 21st Century* (Institute for Information Studies, 1992).

58. Alan Kay, "Four Images for the Information Superhighway Summit," paper presented to the "Superhighway Summit" sponsored by the Academy of Television Arts and Sciences, January 11, 1994, University of California at Los Angeles.

59. H. Henderson, "Perfecting Democracy's Tools," in "After the Nation-State: Reinventing Democracy," *New Perspectives Quarterly,* Fall 1992, p. 22.

60. B. Farrah and D. Maxwell, "Building America's Infostructure: Public Policy in the Information Age," *Telephony,* April 20, 1992, p. 52.

61. Langdon Winner, *The Whale and the Reactor: A Search for Limits in an Age of High Technology* (University of Chicago Press, 1986), p. 108.

62. Oscar H. Gandy Jr., "The Political Economy of Communications Competence," in Mosco and Wasko, *The Political Economy of Information.*

63. Winner, *The Whale and the Reactor,* p. 107.

64. Alfred D. Chandler Jr., *The Visible Hand: The Managerial Revolution in American Business* (Belknap Press, 1977).

65. Jacques Ellul, *The Technological Society* (1954; English translation, Alfred A. Knopf, 1964), p. 427.

66. Oscar H. Gandy Jr., *Beyond Agenda Setting: Information Subsidies and Public Policy* (Ablex, 1982), p. 197.

67. Oscar H. Gandy Jr., *The Panoptic Sort: A Political Economy of Personal Information* (Westview, 1993), p. 231.

6

Freedom, Fun, and Fundamentals: Defining Digital Progress in a Democratic Society

NICHOLAS JOHNSON

Innovation in technology seems to follow a pattern. It starts with a spark of creative imagination, develops into science fiction, and then some inventor tinkers around to see if it is possible to do what the science fiction writer said, and then a scientist actually designs it, and the engineer tests and builds it.

And then the first use is military—which has driven technology since the beginning of humans on this planet. The new creation then comes into industrial use for the Fortune 500, and then it becomes consumer electronics for the lifestyles of the rich and famous.

I remember the first satellite dishes were in the Neiman Marcus catalog one Christmas: his and her satellite dishes, $30,000 apiece. Well, the price has dropped since. At the end of this parade, lagging a few blocks behind the band, are the academics and the think-tank policy wonks who are trying to analyze the implications of all of this. Following them are the legislators and regulators who are attempting to create the laws and regulations under which we live. And when the parade is over, we may find ourselves trapped in a crisis made even deeper when virtually invisible.

Leapfrogging the Policy Process

My purpose in this chapter is to see if we can leapfrog that process a little bit so we do not wait until the end of the parade. We have the responsibility of raising

The original version of this chapter was a similarly titled speech delivered at the third conference on Computers, Freedom and Privacy, San Francisco, California, March 10, 1993.

these policy questions and helping to formulate some of the answers to the often unprecedented and certainly very complex public policy and legal issues that fly like sparks off of the new technology, systems, and services coming down the assembly line.

All too often the cynics in Washington have started by asking what is possible. "How much of a cigarette tax increase can we get the American Tobacco Institute to support?" "How strict of a children's television standard will the National Association of Broadcasters stand still for?" That is an understandable orientation after years of being beaten down by corporate interests, but it is unlikely to create policies in the best national interest.

President Lyndon Johnson, who gave me two presidential appointments along the way, was a complex fellow, no question about that, but I never had anything but very positive personal experiences with him. And one of the most impressive things he did early on in his presidency was to send out a memo to all the presidential appointees. He said:

> I want to hear from you what you think is in the best national interest in the area over which you have responsibility. I don't want you to worry about what is politically possible. A lot of things you think we wouldn't have a prayer of getting through Congress I'll show you how we can get them enacted. And a lot of things you think would be easy to do I'll explain to you why it's impossible. I'll make those decisions, and I want you to give me a lot of those decisions to make.

And we appointees responded by filling up scores of three-hole-punched notebooks on Bill Moyers's shelves and had one of the most exciting and successful legislative periods in our nation's history.

It is a different way of going about things from what has been seen recently. It is not that you never have to compromise; of course you are going to have to compromise. However, you start not with a compromise but with an ideal: that you are trying to accomplish what is really in the best interest of people. And then, if it is necessary, you back off from that to try to make it happen. But throughout the process, you know what you are losing and know what it was you were trying to gain.

My first interest in computers began when I was teaching at the University of California at Berkeley Law School. I had no more enthusiasm then for grading law students' blue book exams than any professor I have met before or since. At a Lake Arrowhead conference, I ran into an IBM executive. This was the early 1960s. I said to him, "What can you do with these computers anyway?"—hoping that perhaps I could grade essay exams with them. He said, "You remind me of a friend of mine who goes into a restaurant, looks at the menu, and says, 'Hmmm, what goes good with French fries?'" He said, "You tell me what it is you want these computers to do, and I've either got one on the shelf that can do it or I'll invent the hardware and software for you in less than eighteen months." There is software that can do some relatively unsophisticated analyses of writing. But unfortunately, I am still grading law students' essay exam booklets, as John Houseman used to say, "the old-fashioned way."

Computers Create Privacy

Some observers would note that the more computers you have in your life, the more you tend to be working for them rather than the other way around. And since—at least so far—they are not organized, they are capable of working faster and smarter than you are and seem to have no need for sleep or other breaks, the net result is that you have very little freedom left to do anything other than relate to computers. So that is one observation that can be made about freedom and computers. There are some, indeed, who view this as computer slavery rather than computer freedom. But those of us old enough to remember 1984 recall that it was George Orwell who explained to us how slavery really is freedom, and we are patient with those who have not yet sensed this truth and realize what freedom we offer them with our computer systems.

Privacy and computers, I think, constitute a much simpler concept to grasp than computers and freedom. It is truly amazing how much privacy you can get for yourself if you spend all your time with computers and then, when it is necessary to have a brief conversation with a humanoid, if you limit the subject to computers. You will find that friends no longer call or come by. Significant others and children will gradually drift away. In fact, the current state of the empirical data suggests an almost linear correlation between the quantity of computers and the quantity of privacy. Having settled that issue, I now consider the more difficult one.

Computer *Freedom*

We must, of course, begin with a definition of *freedom,* and I have done a lot of research on this. Members of my generation will remember Janis Joplin's definition—that "freedom's just another word for nothing left to lose." If Joplin was right, the employment layoffs by America's largest corporations and the national unemployment figures certainly bode well for increasing levels of freedom in this country. And when you consider the extent to which the unemployment of humanoids has been brought about by the transfer of their work to robots and computers, the relationship of computers to freedom also becomes obvious. Unfortunately, Joplin is no longer available for interviews, so my wife and I attended a Peter, Paul, and Mary concert and afterward visited with my old friend Peter Yarrow. I asked him for suggestions of any ideas I could pass along on this subject of freedom and computers. Peter said, "Don't ever take away my freedom." When I asked him what he meant by that, he said, "Don't ever take it away." In my view, Joplin and Yarrow pretty much summed up freedom.

There are many kinds of freedom. Two categories are *freedom from* and *freedom to*. Computers play a role in both. Computer networks give us the freedom to access from home or office the information in thousands of computers worldwide. But that ability also reduces our freedom from the intrusions that result when government agencies and other large institutions have comparable access to information about us. Computers give us the freedom, for example, to choose the option of working from home rather than commuting on congested interstate highways. The person for whom we work, the institution for which we work, may very well not provide us that option, but that is a human limitation and not a technological one.

My case is an example of computers expanding freedom. From Iowa City, Iowa, I write nationally syndicated columns distributed out of New York, record and uplink nationally distributed radio commentaries, write scripts for a network television show that I did on PBS for a couple of seasons—it was produced out of Madison, Wisconsin, but scripts were shipped back and forth electronically from Iowa City to Madison—and participate as a national board member in Common Cause, which has a system called CauseNet. But for others, computers may have reduced freedom from the overbearing supervisor who is now able to track their work keystroke by keystroke.

Where You Stand Is Where You Sit

It is important to recognize that how we come out on a policy question is determined by how we came in. "Where you stand is a function of where you sit." Technology creates social issues; it almost has a dynamic all its own and entails problems no one ever contemplated at the outset. Henry Ford certainly did not set out to change teenage courtship patterns. Television has not only had an impact on our lives—it has become our lives. The epitaph for many people will read "She watched TV."

In short, next to sleep and work, that is what we as a human species now do—and will do until the coming of computers transfers our attention to yet another screen. The average child has watched more hours of instruction from television by age five than he or she will later spend in life sitting in a college classroom earning a B.A. degree.

We did not have this in mind when television first came along. In the same way, computers and telecommunications are having an impact not only on how we do business and on matters of freedom and privacy but also on how human beings relate to each other—indeed, what it means to be human.

I want to give a sense of the broader public policy orientations we bring to these issues, because how you feel about freedom with regard to computers is probably heavily affected by how you feel about freedom with regard to anything else.

How do you feel about the role of the government? Are subsidies only for the rich, a system of "socialism for the rich and free private enterprise for the poor"? Many people believe that is in fact the proper role of government. The virtue of the marketplace has gone beyond an ideology to become a branch of theology in our country. I recall a cartoon that made an impression on me thirty years ago. It was Barry Goldwater walking down the street and looking at these three street urchins sitting on the curb. He looks down at them and says, "Why didn't you have the incentive to go out and inherit a chain of department stores like I did?" For such people, social good is defined as whatever comes out of the corporate struggle. It is the basis for *trickle-down economics,* which the economist John Kenneth Galbraith explained as a proposition that as long as the horses are generously fed, ultimately some food will be made available to the sparrows.

It turns out, however, that many who are prepared to explode in standing ovations of applause at the Rotary Club for free private enterprise instead panic at the prospect of its moving in next door. So we see newspapers fighting radio stations as a distributor of news, television fighting cable television, cable television in turn fighting home satellite dishes, and I would not be surprised if the home satellite dish industry is fighting direct broadcast satellites with their smaller dishes, and so forth—until, of course, they all get together on the great information superhighway to work the toll booth and abolish free enterprise altogether.

The Information-Poor

There is, in contrast, a sort of religious, ethical, and philosophically based sense of responsibility for the less fortunate. This raises an issue about the *information-poor,* the *information-rich,* and the information infrastructure.

I do not think we should ignore the needs of the military, the government, the Fortune 500, and the superrich. We need to care about the availability of telecommunications equipment and networks and services for them. I do not mean that as a joke. Our national defense, our international competitiveness, and our domestic economy are dependent on good communications systems for our major institutions. But it is also true that, in general, their members are relatively well cared for in our society—for example, with the health care services available to them and the private schools for their kids.

But if we believe in democracy and think everybody has a stake, then we need to look at some broader questions. It is not just a matter of access to national data networks. It is how everybody can get access to the hardware and software in the first place. How can they get the training they need, whether in schools or elsewhere? How can they be encouraged to have the incentive to want to participate and to see the advantages to themselves of doing so? How can we improve the quality of our public educational system generally so as to aid in this undertaking? As it turns out, anyone interested in those things also needs to be interested in how we can provide more widespread and better prenatal care (because crack-cocaine babies are notoriously poor students), head-start programs, educational day care centers, educational programs, housing programs, training and employment opportunity, and health enhancement and disease prevention programs—in general, how we can provide the kind of society in which individuals are able to achieve the most of which they are capable, including participation in the information age. But affordable and user-friendly access to national data networks is only a part of this equation.

Jefferson on the Internet

We have a number of traditions that support the notion of free or heavily subsidized access to information. Thomas Jefferson did not choose to be remembered as someone who was once president of the United States, as anyone who has visited Monticello and seen his tombstone knows. His version of democracy included several elements involving access to education. First, education was key—the notion of public education in schools—and he did much to encourage that.

His second element of access to information took the form of public libraries. Indeed, his personal library became the first library for the Library of Congress. The notion that the very poorest among us could have the same access to information as kings and nobility and the wealthiest members of society was central to Jefferson's idea of what was necessary to make self-government function. He also supported the notion of free or deeply discounted postal charges for circulation of books and magazines and newspapers, again as a part of this second element of self-governing by making information accessible to the very poorest in society.

Third was lack of censorship and the benefits that flow from the protection of the First Amendment. What are the purposes of the First Amendment? First is the notion of self-governing: If we are in fact going to engage in this incredibly radical experiment—quite frankly, it has not yet proved out that people are capable of governing themselves—we absolutely have to have access to information. Second is the notion that in a search for truth, whether scientific research or political ideas or whatever, we are more likely to be able to find it if we have a free and open marketplace of ideas. Third is the checking value that the media as well as anyone who exercises First Amendment rights can be a check on abuses of power not only by government but also by corporations and other large institutions in our society. The fourth purpose results in a self-serving benefit for the establishment: It is much cheaper and easier and less hazardous to your health, if you want to stay in control of a society, to let the disfranchised and upset folks speak of their dissatisfaction than to require them to remain silent and have them come into your neighborhood with rifles and rocks. It discourages violence and revolution to permit people to talk. And finally is the notion of what it means to be human. The very process of self-actualization, of self-fulfillment, is really the essence of liberty, of freedom, of what it is we are trying to do with our society.

We still believe in public education. It has many critics, but we are still working at it with reform. Libraries are constantly under attack from a number of directions, and they have not yet solved how to provide their patrons free access to $200-an-hour databases, but they are still there and we are still funding them. We still subsidize the movement of books and magazines and newspapers through the postal service, and the law provides a number of special privileges for the media. The Federal Communications Commission (FCC) still seems more intent on satisfying its corporate clientele than carrying out its mandate, but the applicable Communications Act still recognizes a public ownership of the airwaves and speaks of *public interest* in terms of the standard to be applied to broadcast programming. Some would probably find our interstate highway system another analogy, although paying for it with a gasoline tax does mean a charge of a fraction of a cent per mile for its use.

Such are the American traditions and laws we bring to the issues surrounding the Internet and ISDN (Integrated Services Digital Network, sometimes called "Innovations Subscribers Don't Need") and NREN (National Research and Education Network). These national data networks invoke each of the institutions that Jefferson thought central to democracy. They have a great contribution to make to public education from grade school through college. They provide access to libraries, certainly bibliographic databases, and full text increasingly is available. They are also a forum for free speech. And they present the reality of citizen communication to public officials.

Therefore, it is not at all radical to suggest that access to these networks and the information they provide is something that should be free to every U.S. citizen. Such free access would be as American as free public schools, free libraries, and free speech in the free public park. This is not to say that one could not propose charges for access; it is just that it would be un-American to do it.

Content and Conduit

An issue even more fundamental than charges is whether we will get access at all, at any price. The question might be put this way: Should telephone companies be permitted, encouraged, or forbidden (1) to offer conduits for information services, such as and including cable television, owned and provided by others and (2) to offer such information and services that they own?

I am untroubled by the possibility that such services may force cable monopolists to cut their rates and improve their services. I am also untroubled at the prospect of cable companies getting into what we have traditionally thought of as the telephone business. I am untroubled at the prospect of others offering a continuously updated, flexibly searchable database combining what we today think of as *yellow pages* and what the newspapers think of as *classified ads*—notwithstanding whatever adverse economic impact that might have on the newspaper industry. But I think telephone companies should be forbidden the second option in the two-part question.

I think it is a bogus issue to argue, as the phone companies have in full-page ads all across the country, that unless they own the information we will be deprived of access to it. These services not only can be but are being offered by others. Putting the RBOCs (Regional Bell Operating Companies) and other telecommunications companies squarely into the content business not only is contrary to the national interest and the interests of consumers but also is not even in the best interests of the telephone companies' shareholders. The problems of cross-subsidization and anticompetitive practices are virtually impossible to monitor without involved regulatory machinery—an enormous number of employees of government or some external force—with its concomitant adverse impact on the telephone companies. Leaving the companies unregulated would be unthinkable from the standpoint of consumers and small business information providers.

My baptism of fire on this issue was the ABC-ITT merger proposed back in 1965 and 1966. Question: Would ITT ever try to control ABC's coverage of the news to favor ITT's other business interests? "Oh, no," executives would testify at hearings, even while at that very moment their vice president for public relations was calling up the heads of the Associated Press, the *New York Times*, and the *Washington Post* trying to change the content of the stories being filed by their reporters. This is the most natural thing in the world. It is done all the time.

I used to do this routine—and it is nothing as good as Lily Tomlin's—in which you walk into the telephone store and you say, "Do you have any phones? I'm new in town, want a phone line, want a phone." "Well, yeah, we've got some phones." "Well, can I have one?" "Well, just a minute now. Suppose, I got you a phone, got you set up with a line, what kind of things would you be saying over the phone?"

Now you either laugh or cry at that because it is illegal, it is contrary to our custom, it is contrary to our experience. But other industries have asked for and been granted censorship power. Florida had a statute providing, in effect, that newspapers could attack politicians all they want, but when they did they had to give the politician attacked an opportunity to respond. The Supreme Court found the statute unconstitutional. The gist of its opinion was that a newspaper, with its right of free speech, has a right to censor out of its pages anybody it wants to censor. It can be as biased and one-sided a newspaper monopoly as it wants to be.

While I was an FCC commissioner, the Business Executives for Vietnam Peace had prepared a spot ad pointing out how the war was bad for business—at which point it had attracted their attention. They wanted to put the ad on WTOP in Washington and were stunned to discover they had at long last found something money could not buy. I wrote a strong dissenting opinion. The U.S. Court of Appeals overturned the FCC and upheld my dissent. Unfortunately, the case went on to the Supreme Court, which decided that my friends on the Court of Appeals and I were all wrong, and so that earlier decision was reversed.

Cable television systems are making the same argument. "We have free speech rights. We are programming these channels. We have a right to censor material that we do not like off the cable system—all 500 channels."

Freedom's Last Frontier: Free Speech by Phone

So in case anyone has not noticed, over the last few years, the only remaining free speech medium in this country today is the telephone system. Everything else is gone. Now the telephone companies argue: "Look, we are putting information out over this telephone network. We are as much a free speech provider as the newspaper publisher or broadcaster or cable operator, and therefore we have the right to censor off the system anything we want to censor." And for those who think we should trust the phone company on this, a little history is in order.

The Associated Press was formed about 1848. There was not yet an under-ocean cable across the Atlantic, so anyone wanting news from Europe had to go up to Halifax to get it. So AP said, "We will run a telegraph from Halifax down to New York City, and we can get the news quicker than it would come down normally." In order to do that, the line had to pass through a telegraph system from Maine to New York. The telegraph company that owned the line thought it would be real nifty if it became a news-gathering and -distribution source. It refused to make access available to the Associated Press. It's the most natural thing to do.

It happens every time. Many years ago AT&T was fighting vigorously to prevent a little microwave company from running a line from St. Louis to Chicago because, AT&T said, "We own it all." And that is what gave rise to Lily Tomlin's great line: "We don't care. We don't have to. We're the telephone company."

Since I made a career out of writing dissenting opinions at the FCC, I was surprised when I got a majority of the commissioners to join me in saying that this little fly-by-night outfit ought to be able to put in this private microwave system. Today that company has grown into something we call MCI. But before it got to where it is today, it endured many abuses thrust upon it by AT&T, which was both its conduit and its competitor. They led to the largest antitrust judgment in history: $1.8 billion worth of abuses by AT&T, anticompetitive practices of various kinds. And that is why we need to separate content and conduit.

PART THREE

GAPS THAT DIVIDE US

7

Writing About Poverty in the Age of Plenty

STANLEY MEISLER

Editors like to feel that their newspapers are ahead of the curve, that they spot trends before these trends burst upon the rest of us. But newspapers are also founts of respectability, the pillars of their community, the bedrock of the establishment. Journalists, for the most part, are white, middle class, well educated, and (to a lesser extent) male. For the most part, conventional wisdom rules their thinking. They would rather spot a trend than create one.

The White House sets much of the news agenda for newspapers. When the president of the United States focuses on an issue, newspapers tend to turn their spotlights on it as well. Sometimes newspapers may be sucked into an issue by the White House. In 1989, President George Bush, in a dramatic television address, waved a little packet of drugs that agents had pressured a pusher into selling in Lafayette Square across the street from the White House. The nation, the president made clear, had no greater domestic problem. He declared a war on drugs yet again and appointed a federal drug czar. The *Los Angeles Times* quickly appointed a correspondent in Washington to cover the drug scene full-time. The *Times* did not have a Washington correspondent on full-time coverage of race relations, a far more significant problem in America. But race was not on the White House agenda.

Of course, the White House agenda is influenced by television and newspapers. President Bush would probably not have dispatched the Marines to Somalia if television had not come up with the poignant footage of the starving. Despite a government of checks and balances, an American president dominates politics as do few other democratic leaders on earth, and the American media follow his every whim and turn like a hawk.

Culture Shock

After twenty-one years as a foreign correspondent, I returned home in late 1988 to a country bristling with astonishing problems, most left untended. Yet many Americans persisted in believing then that their country had a divine mission on earth—to be a model for all others. Ignorance about the rest of the world sometimes seemed total. Our son set off for high school one day in a T-shirt emblazoned with a bust of Lenin. I jokingly warned him to be careful. "Don't worry," he said, cynically, not jovially, "no one at school knows who he is."

My own newspaper, the *Los Angeles Times,* puzzled over the disgruntlement of a former foreign correspondent upon his return to Paradise. In the first weeks of my return, passed in Maine, New York City, and Washington, D.C., I set down my impressions of America for the *Times:* the cornucopia on supermarket shelves numbing the sense of choice; the enormities of shopping malls surrounding cities like ugly pillboxes; the copious, tasteless dishes in cavernous restaurants; the loud and raucous mediocrity of television; the greed and baseness of businessmen and politicians; the awesome and fearsome statistics on crime and drugs and homeless and poor; the astounding, ludicrous boast and belief of many Americans and their president that this land is God's special place on earth.

Not many newspapers have foreign correspondents returning after twenty-one years abroad. I was sure the *Times* would be eager to print my impressions, no matter what they were, but an editor refused to run the story. According to accounts relayed to me, he found it too negative and unbalanced, needlessly exposing me and the paper to angry cries from readers who would denounce me as hasty, biased, foolish, a snobbish lover of anything foreign. If I couldn't stand it here, they would surely clamor, why didn't I go back there. Perhaps the editor felt the same way. Perhaps he was justified in spiking the story. It did not really belong on the news pages.

I had not realized that almost all my impressions in my first weeks in America were negative until I set them down. Why had so many uncomfortable images piled up? I felt like those rookie, cherubic correspondents who show up in Africa for the first time and cram their dispatches full of anecdotes about planes that never depart on time, witch doctors who cast spells on university professors, servants who mangle the English language, soup that cannot be strained of tidbit ants. In the old days, I would shake my head at the ethnocentric innocence and ignorance of these correspondents. Yet was I—like them—in culture shock?

About six months later, Anthony Day, then the editor of our editorial pages, who did not know about the spiking of my story, came up with the idea of a piece on my first impressions for "Opinion," his Sunday section of columns and essays. My material had probably belonged in a home like that all the time. To meet Tony's request, I dusted off the old story, reordered my impressions, mulled over them, tried to draw some meaning out of the material, and put out an angry essay lamenting the blindness of Americans in a time of woe.

"You can hear the moments of boredom tick away," the article began, "whenever you tell Americans that no other industrialized democracy has the same dispiriting problems as the United States—not the crime, not the guns, not the homeless, not the unschooled, not the poor, not the racism, not the ugliness. Listeners may mimic interest for a short while, then their glances roll up and away."

"Opinion" published it, and the reaction was as sobering as surprising. Newspapers throughout the world reprinted the article. Radio stations interviewed me. Politicians and professors congratulated me. Governor Mario Cuomo called me in for a ninety-minute session in his office in New York City to discuss the column. One retiring professor used it as the text for his commencement address at the University of California at Santa Barbara. A frenzy of letters fell upon me. Some readers foamed in fury; one even offered to pay my air fare to Paris on condition that I pledge never to return. But the vast majority of letters came from readers who agreed with me, Americans frustrated over the refusal of their smug neighbors and leaders to look or care about the deterioration around them.

The response made me realize that a body of Americans could feel an anguish over so many cruel blights in their land at a time of general comfort. This led me to feel that it would make sense to explore one of the most intractable problems—the growth of poverty in an age of plenty. I could do so from two special perspectives. I had left the United States during the era of the Great Society and returned in the era, as President Bush put it, of "more will than wallet." On top of this, for more than two decades, I had experienced how other countries dealt with their social problems, usually more deftly than seemed the case in the United States.

Several themes guided my thinking. I felt that our social programs, compared with those of almost any other industrialized democratic nation, were a cruel shame. My father, an immigrant worker, struggled for decades to accumulate a paltry few thousand dollars for his self-respect in old age, but the void of our social security sucked it from him. Only pauperdom would allow him to qualify for the medical care that eased his way toward death. The French, the Canadians, almost anyone else in the industrialized world, feel a security that is lost to us. People elsewhere do not need to worry about the costs of education, of day care for their children, of medical catastrophe, of the fragility of age. Their doctors are rich but not rapacious. Their universities are fewer but open to all at little or no cost. Our welfare for the poorest may be extensive (though probably misguided), but our social programs for everyone else defy belief and deserve contempt.

I was also astounded by the obscene difference between growing up poor and growing up rich in America. There are enormous and shameless gaps between the rich and poor in Europe, but the gap between our most rich and most poor cannot be matched. The salaries of our corporate executives and rock stars and baseball players climb beyond reason. French television workers went on strike in jealousy and anger during the fall of 1988 over what they regarded as the excessively high salary paid to television anchor Christine Okrent. Yet she was paid less than 10 percent of what Dan Rather earns.

More important than anything else, I soon realized on my return that the gnarled shame of racism, the greatest blight of all, pressed heavily on most American social problems and nourished them. Without understanding racism, one cannot understand the desolation of our cities, the scourge of crime and drugs, the paucity of social services, the indifference of our welfare system, the mediocrity of our schools, the despairing numbers of poor and homeless, the great differences between our society and those of industrialized Europe. Yet many Americans were obviously contemptuous of blacks and tired of hearing about their problems.

The Poverty Story

The White House agenda is so important that, on rare occasions, a journalist can sometimes play against it—pushing a story on the grounds that it has been excluded from the agenda unfairly. My memo to the editors in 1990 began, "Just because the problem of poverty in America is absent from President Bush's agenda is no reason why it should be absent from our agenda." This appeal to conscience worked. The editors were persuaded that a major series on poverty in America made sense. The key decision came from Norman Miller, the national editor, who steadfastly supported the project for months and persuaded others to allot him an enormous amount of space for it. There was an irony to this. Miller was the same editor who had spiked my earlier story of first impressions upon coming home to America. But the first story had been fuzzy and gushy and whiny. The poverty series would be tough, tight, and packed with evidence. Miller obviously prided himself on caring about good journalism, not ideology.

The *Times* assigned a new Washington correspondent, Sam Fullwood III, to join me in the project. Fullwood was black, which added another perspective to the team. He had grown up in North Carolina as the middle-class son of a minister and a teacher, and his experience in no way paralleled that of poor blacks in the devastated inner cities of America. In fact, since I had grown up in the Bronx, I probably knew a bit more about that life than he did. But his sensitivity as a black—combined with his skills as a thoughtful, gentle journalist—made the project work. More than half the individuals interviewed were black, and I sensed they felt more comfortable with Fullwood in the room.

We spent six months interviewing, researching, writing, and rewriting. In talks with social workers, local officials, university analysts, and poor families, we focused on four problems of poverty: a health-care system so inadequate that infants died at a faster rate than anywhere else in the industrialized world; an educational system so deficient that it produced 20 to 30 million functionally illiterate adults; drug-fueled crime and murder rates so high that the United States put more of its population in jail than any other country except South

Africa and the former Soviet Union; and a shortage of housing so acute that half the working poor spent almost all of what little they earned on rent. We concentrated on four cities, making joint trips to Atlanta, Boston, Chicago, and Oakland, California. In addition, we made separate forays, I to the Bronx and Columbus, Georgia, and Sam to St. Louis and Baltimore. All this was supplemented by interviews of federal officials, think-tank analysts, and the poor on our doorstep in Washington.

There was one glaring omission: Los Angeles. This was mostly bureaucratic. Large newspapers have become complex systems with each editor controlling his or her own fiefdom. I was not sure how members of the Metropolitan department would react to our invasion of their territory, and it seemed like too much trouble to ask for permission to operate in Los Angeles. I told myself that it would be wiser to skip Los Angeles and send a memo sometime later suggesting that the Metro staff work up a sidebar on Los Angeles to accompany our main stories. In the end, I forgot to send the memo. That was an unfortunate mistake. But the series made clear that we were talking about problems that pervaded urban life throughout every corner of the United States. No reader could have imagined Los Angeles exempt.

We occasionally came across a new, even spectacular phenomenon. We interviewed several *crack grandmothers,* for example, older women raising their grandchildren because their own daughters were addicted to crack cocaine. One sixty-year-old woman was raising her great-grandchildren because both their mother and grandmother were addicted. There were enough crack grandmothers in East Oakland that the Schuman-Liles Clinic, a nonprofit mental health center, organized a club so that a dozen could meet and talk about their similar problems.

But, in the main, we did not break new ground. University researchers, think-tank analysts, social workers, mayors, and black leaders had been crying alarms about the crisis of poverty for years. The statistics were clear. The gap between rich and poor was the widest since the end of World War II. The richest 20 percent of American households earned an average, after adjusting for inflation, of $9,109 more in 1988 than they had earned ten years earlier. The poorest 20 percent of American families earned an average of $576 a year less. The poorest of the poor were at their worst state in fifteen years. More than 11 million Americans, almost 5 percent of the population, lived in families earning less than half the poverty-level income in 1988.

Moreover, there was a remarkable similarity of views in university and foundation circles about what needed to be done. The works of the University of Chicago's William Julius Wilson and Harvard University's David T. Ellwood were widely praised and quoted. The badly flawed welfare system cried out for overhaul, Washington had to stimulate the creation of jobs, and federal programs must help whites and the lower middle class as well as blacks and the poor.

This material, however, although familiar to specialists, was evidently out of the reach and mind of most other Americans. Our achievement, I think, was to lay down all these statistics and analyses in a coherent and colorful package for a mass audience. The *Los Angeles Times* sells more than a million copies a day and distributes a news service over the wires that reaches several hundred other newspapers.

The series, titled "Building Crisis: Poverty in America," started appearing on the front page Sunday, July 15, 1990 (the Sunday circulation of the *Times* approaches 1.5 million), and ran for five consecutive days, always on the front page, until Thursday, July 19. The front-page stories led to at least a full page inside every day. In all, the *Times* published 740 column inches of text, photos, and graphs.

The series received a good number of compliments from colleagues at the *Times* and, of course, even more enthusiastic compliments from the specialists and social workers interviewed for the articles. The editors who worked on the series felt, I think, as much pride in seeing the huge finished product as Fullwood and I did. But the series did not win any prizes and did not provoke the kind of flurry of mail that had followed my earlier article fretting over my return to America.

For the most part, readers like to read (and newspapers like to print) analysis and background only about subjects at the top of the day's news. All the stories about famine and warlord chaos in Somalia went unheeded until television footage and the White House put Somalia into the day's news—and then it misled us all.

8

Race Relations in the Suburbs

ROSALYN BAXANDALL AND ELIZABETH EWEN

The crisis in housing cuts across the great divides of American life and speaks profoundly to fundamental concerns of race, class, and democracy. Henry Cisneros, secretary of Housing and Urban Development, said that the racial crisis of American life could not be solved until the suburbs themselves were integrated. Supreme Court Justice Thurgood Marshall explained the logic behind Cisneros's claim: "Housing in our society today is more than a shelter. It includes the whole environment in which the home is maintained. A well-built house in a poorly planned, impoverished, slum area, without adequate schools, community facilities, etc., does not provide good housing. Nor does a well-built house in a ghetto provide good housing in a democratic society."[1]

Housing became a contested issue twice in the post–World War II period. After the war the issue was whether the government was obliged to ensure shelter for all Americans. In 1947 there was a large movement backing middle- and low-income public housing. Housing shortages caused by the depression and World War II made the need for public housing a pressing popular concern. Supported by President Truman and a bipartisan Congress, the Taft-Ellinger-Wagner public housing bill was a reflection of this public sentiment. However, real estate developers, along with conservative members of Congress, portrayed this bill as socialist. They played on anticommunist fears and managed to defeat this public housing bill, replacing it with government-sponsored mortgages to white veterans only. The construction of suburban single-family dwellings instead of public housing was the result. Another outcome of this conservative compromise was that public housing was built and subsidized only for the poor.

This campaign was buttressed by a public relations blitz that claimed the private sector could build housing for the many if only the construction unions would drop old practices and work harder. The bricklayer and the painter were depicted in mainstream media—such as the *Saturday Evening Post, Look, Life,* the

Wall Street Journal, and the newsreel "The March of Time"—as laggards who refused to break union rules and work at a faster pace. At the same time, all of the major media outlets created compelling images in ads, news, and feature stories of the wonders of suburban living. All residents of this world, of course, were white.

The second crisis occurred after the civil rights movement had demanded a society based on integration, not segregation. This time the issue focused on whether the public had the right to reside in integrated communities. Gains had been won in integrating public accommodations, education, and transportation. The riots of the 1960s reemphasized that inadequate housing was still a major component of poverty. In 1971, George Romney, then head of Housing and Urban Development, saw as one solution to urban poverty the building of public low-income housing in the suburbs. Again, as in 1947, the federal government opted for private solutions, subsidizing the real estate industry and guaranteeing banks low-income mortgages for individual home owners, this time minority home owners in the suburbs. This would be equivalent to ignoring public school integration in favor of subsidizing private educational firms to run the school systems.

President Nixon further clarified the direction of this policy. On the housing issue, he said, "We will not seek to impose economic integration upon an existing local jurisdiction; at the same time, we will not countenance any use of economic measures as a subterfuge for racial discrimination."[2] As a result of this decision, almost no subsidized low-income public housing was built in affluent suburbs or white middle-class suburbs. The little that was built was in preexisting ghettos or integrated middle-class suburbs that would become solidly African American.

In spite of the fact that no governmental policy mandated integrated housing until 1980, African Americans moved to the suburbs in significant numbers. In this chapter we explore the barriers these migrants encountered, from racial covenants to racial steering, block busting, suspicion, white flight, prejudice, and media stereotyping. We report the stories of three different Long Island suburbs: Levittown, a stereotypical white middle-class suburb; Roosevelt, inhabited mainly by African Americans; and Freeport, a suburb where the ideal of racial integration is still pursued, often with difficulty. Our report is based largely on interviews with black and white community activists, politicians, social service workers, lawyers, real estate brokers, leaders of political, religious, and civic associations, and members of many community organizations from sewing circles and reading groups to arts councils and neighborhood watch groups.

Suburban Dreams

Long Island, like most other suburbs, was initially developed as a bucolic haven for white upper-class families. By the 1950s, suburban development included white middle- and working-class families as well. Historically, African Americans and other ethnics were employed as servants and craftspeople who served the needs of the large estates and lived in small segregated enclaves, often near the railroad tracks.

Servant communities were built through family, church, and kinship ties. For example, a large proportion of African Americans who worked as servants on Long Island's South Shore came from towns in South Carolina and Georgia and were either recruited or brought to Long Island by relatives or agencies. This migration pattern was typical in the cities as well. In Harlem, for example, there are blocks where all the families originally came from one small town in Georgia or South Carolina, just as in an earlier period, certain buildings on the Lower East Side in New York were inhabited by families from villages in Russia or Italy.

Louise Simpson moved to Freeport in 1960 where she worked on voter registration for the NAACP (National Association for the Advancement of Colored People) for a number of years in the black community. As she filled out the voter registration forms that included information on where people were born, she began to notice a distinct pattern:

> I realized that they were all from the same area in South Carolina, a lot from Charleston. So many of them were from the same area. Freeport was a hub; it had good transportation for people migrating to do domestic work. For domestics, it was okay, you had one day off and every other Sunday. So you come to where you can find transportation and Freeport got to be a meeting place for people who did domestic work, and they were able to find work in the large homes. There were rooming houses, so when they quit a job they could find a room. This is how friendships developed—if you're from my hometown, I'm going to seek you out. You felt comfortable, you knew each other. If you didn't go that route of family and friends, there was this particular woman who was sort of like a personnel person for employment. She would go to where she came from in Carolina and bring people up [north] or tell them to get in touch and their transportation would be paid. Freeport blossomed like that.[3]

Harve Sinklar-Herring, who came from South Carolina, ran an agency like this. Her first contact with Freeport was in 1927 when she came north with her cousin to work as a domestic servant for the summer. She also found work as a chauffeur and a caterer. Using these skills, she opened a domestic service agency, first in her own home and then in a large house that encompassed an office, a dormitory, and a staff of twenty. She not only recruited women from South Carolina but trained them in domestic work as well. She claims to have "had the only agency like this. I advertised in *Newsday*. I charged employers who hired the women. I charged the domestics room and board while I trained them. By 1957, I had two agencies. I was so busy I had to send my children home to South Carolina."[4]

By the 1940s, many of these servants and artisans had accumulated enough money to own their own houses or plots of land. In addition, World War II had brought employment opportunities through the burgeoning aerospace industry, Mitchell Field (a huge army base), and other related defense industries. Even though the opportunities were not equal and most blacks were employed in the service and maintenance area, some managed to work in the industrial sector despite ongoing discrimination.

Charles and Meta Meredy, for instance, came from South Carolina to Long Island in 1927. He worked as an artisan: blacksmith, mechanic, and all-around handyman. She worked briefly as a domestic servant. For years they lived with various relatives in Hempstead looking on and off for property they could afford. In 1940, they finally discovered a piece of land in an undeveloped area of Roosevelt and slowly built a house. Although he was a skilled mechanic, Charles got a job at Grumman as a porter and supplemented his income by driving a truck. When war broke out he was finally given a temporary job as Grumman's first black mechanic. "I worked at Grumman for three and a half years and never got a raise or was promoted. I took every course which was supposed to qualify me for a raise, but I never got one. I even invented a special pliers and several other tools, but Grumman took all the credit. All they ever gave me was a $25 prize."[5]

With the end of the war in 1945 came a major housing shortage and persistent demands from veterans and others for affordable housing. The response to the housing shortage, however, did not include open housing even to black veterans. Preexisting segregated suburban communities relied on "interlocking friendships, mutual loyalties and existing social pressure . . . as an adequate barrier against Negroes."[6] In new suburban boom communities such as Levitton, financed in large part through Federal Housing Authority (FHA) mortgages, racial covenants were common.

In 1938, the FHA, in its underwriter manual, stated that housing under its auspices was limited by the "prohibition of the occupancies of properties except for the race for which they are intended." In plain English, this meant whites only. A 1947 FHA guidebook for suburban development, "Planning Profitable Neighborhoods," described covenants: "Protective covenants are essential to the sound development of proposed residential areas, since they regulate the use of land and provide a basis for the development of harmonious, attractive neighborhoods." Although the NAACP charged that the FHA was supporting racist housing practices and the Supreme Court outlawed racial covenants in 1948, the FHA waited two years after the decision to announce that it would no longer officially issue mortgages in restricted neighborhoods. Unofficially, the FHA accepted unwritten agreements and "existing traditions of segregation" as late as 1968, long after the suburban boom was over.[7]

Levitt and Sons, the nation's largest home-builder, argued that it would be committing economic suicide if it opened Levittown to blacks while other developers sold only to whites. William Levitt repeatedly made this argument: "Most whites prefer not to live in mixed communities. . . . The responsibility (for this) is society's. . . . It is not reasonable to expect that any one builder could or should undertake to absorb the entire risk and burden of conducting such a vast social experiment."[8]

By the 1960s, the cities were the site of riots, agitation, fights over urban renewal, and struggles over employment. As a response to the civil rights movement, there were new governmental initiatives in education, health, social welfare, housing, and law enforcement. Partially as a result of these government programs, a new black middle class emerged. At the same time, there was an expanding civil service with jobs in the post office, transportation and sanitation, and the armed forces. From 1960 to 1976, the black middle class tripled in size.[9]

Middle-class black families seeking better housing, schools, and integrated neighborhoods were drawn to the suburbs as a means of achieving these goals. Long Island had a special lure. Roosevelt resident Clara Gillens claimed, "When you move out to Long Island everyone thinks you're living in the gold coast; after all, you live in suburbia and you own a house."[10] Jean Wyatt, for example, who worked for the motor vehicle bureau, and her husband, who worked for the post office, lived in a deteriorating housing project in Brooklyn. They thought of moving to the suburbs when their son reached the first grade. Jean explained:

> We thought our son would have a better life in suburbia. We began looking in the newspapers and found a place in Freeport. I transferred my job to Long Island. We were both city kids, but we thought we'd give the suburbs a try. We'd live the suburban dream. We tried it and it was a bit of a dream and a bit of a nightmare. I loved my house, not having to come into an elevator. But I was lonelier here than in the city. The projects were an automatic community. Here it was more difficult to make friends, and generally people didn't need to be as supportive here.[11]

Like Jean Wyatt, Helena White, a schoolteacher, and her husband, an accountant, lived in the city but felt their children needed open space. They moved into a modern house in an integrated neighborhood in Freeport. Her husband wanted to move there because "he wanted a house with push buttons and a garage you drive into."[12]

Unlike the Wyatts and the Whites, Barbara Patton, who became the first minority representative from a suburban district to the State Assembly, moved to Freeport from Brooklyn when she got divorced. Her children were in a city Catholic school where she was paying more than she could afford for tuition. According to her:

> I decided that if I was going to raise my children by myself, I wanted to do it in suburbia. Like everyone else, I wanted to make the leap to Long Island. I was fortunate in that I was an only child and my parents bought me a house. When I was deciding where to move, I had white friends in Baldwin and I told them, 'Now, look, I don't want to move in and then have a cross burned on my lawn.' They said to me that I could probably move to Baldwin, but as a Jewish family, they didn't feel comfortable on their block, so as a black family I wouldn't feel okay here. They said there is a com-

munity next door, Freeport, and it's integrated with neighborhoods with beautiful houses. So I bought a four-bedroom Tudor house where an integrated public school was right around the corner.[13]

These dreams, however, in large part, could only be realized in older suburban communities that already had a sizable black presence. At the same time, real estate brokers, agents, and speculators, recognizing that there was quick money to be made from these new migrants, began to engage in two policies that deeply affected black suburban migration: blockbusting and racial steering.

Blockbusting and Racial Steering

Although Levittown was racially closed, the already established communities of Roosevelt and Freeport drew African-American families and single people through word of mouth, family ties, and job opportunities. According to the *New York Times,* for example, in the 1960s, in addition to white families, Roosevelt was becoming an ethnically mixed community where "houses sell anywhere from $15,000 to $50,000. Many of the Negroes who have moved in are college graduates who are teachers, personnel managers and other professionals. Another group is made up of such workers as truck drivers and gardeners."[14]

Blockbusters were also moving in on the community. Blockbusting is a tactic used by real estate agents and developers to create an unstable housing market through an atmosphere of fear and intimidation. Linking the idea of falling property values to the influx of racial or ethnic minorities, blockbusters rely on a campaign of racial innuendo whispered into the ears of white homeowners. Through the use of the telephone, leaflets, and word of mouth, families would succumb to scare tactics—"The value of your house is dropping $1,000 a month" or "You have a twelve-year-old daughter. What if she were raped? You'd have a mulatto grandchild"—and make deals with agents to sell their houses. One blockbuster, twenty years after, described what he was told to do:

> We were told you get the listings any way you can. It's pretty easy to do; I just scare the hell out of them. And that's what we did. We were not only making money, we were having fun doing what we were doing. We all liked selling real estate—if you want to call what we were doing selling real estate. And it got to a point that in order to have fun while we were working, we would try to outdo each other with the most outlandish threats that people would believe and chuckle at the end of the day. . . . I had fun at it. I'd go down the street with a (black) buyer and ask, Which house do you want? He'd pick one, and I'd ring the door bell and say, these people want to buy your house. If the lady said no, I'd say the reason they're so interested is that their cousins, aunts, mother, whatever, it's a family of twelve, are moving in across the street, and they want to be near them. Most of the time, that worked. If that didn't work, you'd say their kid just got out of jail for housebreaking, or rape or something that would work.

In some cases, blockbusters resorted to more extreme measures. "There were instances of housebreaks that were arranged only to scare people out. That was the worst. . . . I don't think anybody to this day is aware that anybody arranged this. Nobody was ever arrested for it, convicted of it, or anything else."[15]

Blockbusting is akin to the domino theory on a block-by-block basis. Neighbors start to hear that families down the street moved in the middle of the night, and soon large numbers of whites become susceptible to the offers of real estate brokers. Before 1968 brokers and speculators benefited through a game called multiple mortgages. As New York Secretary of State John Lomenzo testified before the Senate Judiciary Committee, "Let's say the market value of the house was $15,000. The speculator would offer to buy it for $10,000, all cash, with the homeowners readily accepting as they became panicked." The next step was to offer it at double the price or more to a minority family with the incentive of an automatic mortgage qualification with no money down. This was a complex scheme of buying triple money mortgages on the purchased house and selling them to banks and finance and insurance agencies at discounts. This scheme usually allowed the broker to make a profit of nearly 90 percent. The major flaw was that the high mortgage carried by the minority family was usually far in excess of the worth of the property. After 1968 and the FHA decision to bring the American dream of homeownership to poor and middle-class minorities, loans guaranteed by the FHA made blockbusting much easier.[16]

Another aspect of the blockbusting campaign was the fear that the government would move welfare families next door who would have no stake in the preservation and upkeep of their homes or communities. This was another profitable tactic used by real estate agents. In Roosevelt, for example, most of the houses were one-family dwellings, but landlords and real estate speculators subdivided single-family houses and then offered each subdivision to the Welfare Department at triple the rent. Willie Pyatt, father of eight, told a *New York Times* reporter that he had encountered difficulty finding an apartment for his family in communities other than Roosevelt. Pyatt said that the Welfare Department had put him in a subdivided house, paying $200 for five rooms. In all, the Welfare Department was paying $360 a month to an absentee landlord in behalf of the house's eighteen occupants. Pyatt said, "The Welfare Department is spreading the cancer by putting four or five families in a one-family house and paying exorbitant rents for them."[17]

Yvonne Simmons, one of the few African-American real estate agents in Roosevelt, confirmed Pyatt's observation and blamed the Nassau County's Welfare Department for placing large numbers of welfare families in Roosevelt.

> It's the fault of people in power. The county is in charge of the welfare system. If you have welfare families it would seem that you could divide them equitably, so that there wouldn't be a whole influx of them in one area. So many landed in Roosevelt. Of course when people don't own their own homes they tend not to take care of

them as well as someone who can afford to take care of them. If you get your welfare check and you have a certain amount of money for A, B, C and D, when it comes to getting some grass seed for the lawn, they're not going to think about that; they just think about survival.[18]

Another essential component of blockbusting was racial steering. Racial steering was a conscious policy of segregation. Real estate brokers and agents designated certain communities as either white or black and deliberately showed houses to families based on race. No matter what specific community a family desired to live in, the family would be taken to communities defined by race. In order to attract particular constituencies, agents advertised in papers like the *Amsterdam News* in New York and in southern papers read by blacks. Billboards on major roads leading out of southern cities showed black families living in attractive suburban houses in Roosevelt.[19] Similarly, whites were shown houses in white communities, even if they asked about other places, and ads in newspapers and magazines read mainly by whites emphasized images of white suburban homeowners.

For example, Alvin Dorfman, a lawyer with a long history of civil rights work in Freeport, and his wife Shelly, a community activist, moved to Freeport in 1963 from Brooklyn. They wanted to buy a house in an integrated neighborhood, but real estate agents wouldn't show them houses in black areas. "When we pressed them, they showed us poor houses in Roosevelt and a few that were much too expensive. Then they showed us good houses in Freeport, near the Baldwin school district, an all-white neighborhood."[20]

Louise Simpson, an African American who worked at the Federal Reserve Board, and her husband, who worked for the post office, had to move from their Brooklyn project because they were earning too much for the housing authority guidelines. Louise described their experience:

> We had to move. I really wanted to live near the city, but since there were no fair housing ordinances in 1960, we didn't find any houses close to the city. We were steered to northeastern Freeport, really a part of Roosevelt. We were going to move to Lakeview which was also being developed but I felt the realtor pulled a deal and we ended up here. I'm sure I could not have purchased a house except in northeast Freeport.[21]

Ramona Crooks, who headed a town-run antiblockbusting real estate agency, comfirmed the existence of steering:

> There were brokers in Massapequa, brokers in Seaford, brokers in Merrick [nearby nonintegrated towns], and when a black person went to them, they weren't going to show them a house in Seaford or Merrick. Most black people I interviewed wanted to live in an integrated neighborhood, but if you and your wife were black, if you went to a broker in Massapequa, you'd end up buying a house in Roosevelt or Freeport.[22]

Roosevelt: A Community Transformed

The effectiveness of blockbusting and racial-steering campaigns can be seen across the nation. Roosevelt is an excellent example of a successfully blockbusted South Shore Long Island community. Roosevelt is a small unincorporated village in Nassau County without a local government, train station, or sizable commercial center. From 1920 to 1960, it was a predominantly white middle- and working-class village with a small black community. Suddenly it became prey to blockbusting and racial steering. Yvonne Simmons explained how this happened:

> The houses were less out here. Real estate agents would steer black people to certain areas, and the white people got nervous as they do sometimes. The real estate agents wanted to make money, and this was the way to do it—to steer people to certain areas and create fear in white homeowners. It's all about money. For people that were prejudiced, this was like pushing their buttons. This was great for the people doing the steering. There are myths that when blacks move into an area, the property values go downhill.

These prejudices were precisely what blockbusters counted on, as Simmons noted:

> Frightened people would sell cheap. They would try to get the most they could, but their overriding desire is to leave. On the other hand, blacks wanted better living conditions than they had in the city. They wanted their kids to go to better schools. So the brokers would sell to blacks at inflated prices, really upping the price. After a while some families who couldn't really afford it would get into financial trouble and lose their houses. But the brokers were long gone.[23]

In analyzing the blockbusting phenomenon, local residents who were interviewed almost uniformly described the transformation of their town as like a prairie fire happening almost overnight. Actually, blockbusting takes considerable time. In Roosevelt it took at least fifteen years. In 1957 the population of Roosevelt was 80 percent white and 20 percent African American. In 1967 it was 60-40. By 1980 it was 80 percent black.[24]

For the new black middle class, Roosevelt, first seen as a model for integration, became an all too familiar and disappointing situation. Take the story of John Rice Jr., a black Harvard graduate in 1950 and an Air Force major in the Strategic Air Command in the 1960s, who moved into a split-level house in Roosevelt in 1968 with his wife and three children. At the time, all his neighbors were white. He felt he had arrived. Within ten years all his white neighbors had moved and his block was inhabited totally by African-American families; the community, once well-off, was now impoverished. One would not know this by looking at his house, his two Jaguars, or his extensive gardens. All his life he sought a place among the American elite, yet this prospect, in many ways, still eludes him.[25]

In the early 1960s, when black families began moving to Roosevelt in significant numbers, there ensued a protracted struggle over school integration, the beginning of a policy of placing welfare families in subdivided housing, and the media-fed perception that Roosevelt was becoming a ghetto. As African-American families moved to Roosevelt, they were steered to the southeastern section of town, where a small number of blacks already lived. These new families enrolled their children in the Theodore Roosevelt elementary school in the area. As black children began attending this school, white parents withdrew their children and enrolled them in the Centennial school on the other side of town, the largely white northeastern section. By 1965 this led to de facto school segregation.

As a result, the New York State Education Department ordered the integration of the Roosevelt school system by March 1966. The local school board responded by proposing the Princeton Plan, which would require all students of the same age to attend one school. Part of the plan's implementation included busing children out of their neighborhoods and levying taxes to support the building of new schools. The NAACP criticized the plan because it did not integrate with "all deliberate speed" and demanded new taxes that most certainly would be rejected.[26]

The effect of this proposal was that white parents, rather than put their children in desegregated classes, enrolled them in private or parochial schools, as had occured in the South. "For sale" signs began to appear in larger numbers, and the school integration plan, though formally successful, backfired. In 1967, Daniel Terry, superintendent of the Roosevelt school system for eighteen years, told a *New York Times* reporter that integration had gone smoothly in school: "We have no feuds in school, no gangs against the Negroes." But he conceded that "it hasn't reached the parents. Many parents have said to me that their child is getting along just fine, but 'we' are going to move anyway.'" He noted that "Negro and white children play together on the sidewalks and the community had had no racial disturbances. Still, there will be quite an exodus again at the end of this year."[27]

At the same time, the news media were writing sensationalistic stories about Roosevelt that focused on the threat of school busing, the "dumping" of welfare families, and the fear of lowered property values. The media added fuel to white flight. Ironically, the media used the voices of concerned black residents, particularly welfare families, in Roosevelt to sharpen their points. Stories such as "The Making of a Black Ghetto," "Harlem Comes to Long Island," and "Negroes Invade Roosevelt" played on racial stereotypes and created a constant fear on the part of white homeowners. To this day, local Roosevelt residents blame the media for what happened to their town and particularly denounce what they call "the yellow journalism" of *Newsday.*[28]

Blockbusting did not occur without a struggle. Catholic, Jewish, and Protestant religious leaders and community leaders formed a united front called the Roosevelt Community Relations Council to counter the fear and intimidation. By 1967 there was a United Civic Organization composed of twenty civic, fraternal, and church groups to discourage blockbusting and maintain the existing 60-40 racial ratio. Morton Decker, president of the organization, sang the praises of his small bucolic town but was cautious about the ability of the organization to stop white flight: "How do you get through to white people who have stereotyped images and have never known a Negro socially or as a neighbor?" The organization's program called for federal intervention in the form of money to maintain racial balance and for an end to blockbusting in all its forms, including the collusion between the Nassau County Department of Welfare and absentee landlords who were placing welfare families in houses recently abandoned by white flight.

Unfortunately, these attempts were unsuccessful. By 1980 Roosevelt was 80 percent black and 20 percent white, economically depressed, educationally deprived, and seen by many as a ghetto. However, Ruth Grefe, one of the few white residents still living in Roosevelt, described it as a hospitable community. Grefe, whose family was among the founders of Roosevelt, married a jack-of-all-trades, and they built their own house in Roosevelt in the 1940s. They raised a family and were pillars of their church and community. In the 1960s, the Grefes decided to stay in Roosevelt and not succumb to the blockbusting scare. She felt she had permanent roots in the community despite the change in racial balance. Even after her husband died, Roosevelt remained her town. Her black neighbors looked in on her and helped her out, and she had many black friends. She remained active in her church (as one of three white members) and in the community. She described Roosevelt not as a ghetto but as "a big family where everyone cares for everyone else."[29]

Freeport: The Battle for Integration

The lessons residents learned from the Roosevelt experience benefited their neighbors in Freeport. Freeport was a very different community. In the 1920s, it had been the economic and recreational hub of southern Nassau. A seaport community composed of elegant mansions, solid and active middle-class neighborhoods, and a black servant quarter, Freeport had its own railroad station and utility company. The town also had a strong commercial center with many locally owned department stores as well as light industry, fishing, and leisure-based businesses. This gave the town a strong tax base and a cosmopolitan atmosphere.[30]

Unlike Roosevelt and many other towns on Long Island, Freeport, with a population of 38,000 in 1960, was an incorporated village with its own government, police, and fire department. Because it had its own government, residents had more stake and could have more direct involvement with town hall. Therefore, local civic associations dating to the 1920s were developed. This governmental structure encouraged independent political parties, usually male led, loosely affiliated, and somewhat independent of the dominant Nassau County Republican Party.

Before 1960, most of the neighborhoods of Freeport (south, southwest, northwest) were predominantly white and defined by class. Most blacks lived in the center of town in low-income projects and were slowly moving to the northeast.

Blockbusting began in Freeport around 1959 with the usual tactics: unscrupulous brokers bringing in families on welfare, panic selling, and threatened neighborhood decline. In response, the northeast Civic Association in 1964 collected petitions by homeowners who refused to be solicited by real estate agents. Over 240 homeowners signed the petitions. These were sent to the New York secretary of state, who said, "We will instruct realtors in the Freeport area not to solicit homeowners who listed their names."[31] Then the secretary of state issued cease-and-desist orders to real estate brokers based on these petitions, and four licenses were revoked.

In the early 1960s, black middle-class families began to move to Freeport, although still in a segregated pattern—blacks on one side, whites on the other. The elementary schools were successfully integrated in 1964 without incident. But residential segregation had an impact on school life as well: "In the early days, blacks would walk in one door to get the buses to the northeast; the whites would use the other to go south."[32]

By 1968 about 4,000 black families lived in Freeport, half of whom were above the poverty level; some began to integrate the traditionally white neighborhoods. *Newsday* described Freeport then as a community that was "neither a ghetto nor snow white."[33] Yet under this peaceful facade were long-standing practices reminiscent of the segregated South.

The population was changing by 1968, but these older practices and convictions were not. The high school, for example, had segregated buses with "blacks loading and unloading at the rear of the school and whites in the front. Blacks were forced to sit in the back of buses on the way to school."[34]

Black parents and their children responded to televised images of the southern civil rights confrontations and were eager to address similar grievances in Freeport. The high school, which was 22 percent African American, was the site where built-up racial tensions and frustrations in the community were expressed. Black and white students hearing the attitudes of their parents at home acted them out in school. In this heightened racial situation, small incidents became major confrontations. Laura Jean Campbell, a white student, told a *Newsday* reporter, "The parents have been hearing rumors out of proportion."[35]

Sides were being drawn. From December 1968 to April 1969, there was increased political activity in Freeport High School, including sit-ins, walkouts, confrontations with the faculty and principal, demands, a growing polarization, and attempts to hear grievances and bring black and white students together. In December 1968 black high school students demanded that the segregated bus system end; that the school teach African-American history to all students; that the school hire black teachers, guidance counselors, and administrators; and that January 15 be celebrated as Martin Luther King Day and made a legal holiday.[36] These demands were accepted. Marquita James, one of the few black teachers, taught social studies and race relations; she later recalled:

By April the black students put real pressure on the principal to desegregate the school buses and other things. The principal said that he wasn't strong enough to make a change and that the Klan members on the school board didn't even want to make it an issue. Students were having meetings in their houses and a plan was hatched to confront the principal. . . . I came into the cafeteria and the principal, who was six feet, was standing on a table, his head bowed and students surrounding him firing questions. After this incident the principal threatened to resign unless the school policy changed. The vote on the school board was very narrow; the buses were desegregated by one vote. After the results of the vote were announced, the black students stood in front of the building with clenched fists for victory. A backlash followed. Fights broke out, the mass media had a field day, and all hell broke loose.[37]

The next day white students met with the principal to protest the way the authorities had handled the sit-in in the cafeteria. What is commonly referred to as the Freeport "riots" by the press and local residents began on the evening of April 24, 1969. However, what is considered a riot in the suburbs is not the equivalent of an urban riot. In a sense, what happened could be considered small incidents, but in a suburban context, these became major confrontations revealing unsolved issues and problems.

On April 24 the student council called a meeting at the village recreation center to try to defuse the growing polarization between white and black students. Ironically, this meeting only exacerbated the tensions. The meeting revealed three clear constituencies: a group of militant black students, a group of white racist students, and a group of white and black students who supported the black demands but who were eager to heal wounds and make peace. The rhetoric of the meeting escalated; groups of black and white students began to walk out. Outside the meeting, "the action was confused and fast." The result was that two black youths were stabbed and another was wounded by white students, and the white racist student leader was attacked by a group of black students and hospitalized.[38]

The next day, after much deliberation and added police power, school was in session. Again, whites and blacks clashed, tables and chairs were tossed, windows were broken, village police were wounded, and the American flag was torn down. Outside the school, cars were damaged and passersby attacked. Interestingly, the only arrests that occurred were of two black students on charges of disorderly conduct.

The riot spread to Roosevelt as about 200 black students gathered to discuss what had happened in Freeport. The group took to the streets and ran through the small business district breaking windows. Four white adults were injured. The press reported these events in melodramatic fashion. Headlines like "200 Youth in Racial Rampage" and "4 Hurt as Negro Youths Roam" further inflamed the situation.[39]

Both black and white parents were afraid to send their children to school the next day. School and village officials responded to this fear by lining the corridors and the outside of the school with more than sixty Nassau County and village police. Still, some 50 percent of the student body stayed away entirely. For black parents, the police were there to protect their children, but they worried about whether the students needed protection from the police as well. As one black parent put it, "This is like Selma and Detroit and Montgomery. Isn't this a mess? I know they're not here to protect my brother."[40]

It was 1969 and students all over the country were demanding, demonstrating, rioting, and confronting power from the hills around San Francisco State University to the shores of Columbia University and all through the heartland as well. Violence, police intervention, and arrests were often the result of these encounters. In Freeport, high school students were involved, but as Dan Mandel, a local lawyer and activist, put it:

> The core of this black upheaval isn't in the schools. It is more vocal there because youth often react with less restraint in many instances than adults. The problem is the economic inequality which forces a poor black child to go to school knowing he can't achieve the same material things as his white classmate. This community has not anticipated the needs of minority groups or tried to better the situation.[41]

In addition, black middle-class parents who had moved to Freeport had the expectation that suburban schools would offer their children more educational opportunities in a safe environment. They did not expect segregation, tracking, and unequal disciplinary practices.

Disturbed by the violence and the fear that their children would be suspended, black parents began to organize. Louise Simpson, for example, had a daughter attending Freeport High School who was active in the protests:

> My daughter told me that there were serious things happening in school because of the black demands and that she might be suspended. Over the weekend I met with some black parents who said they would be at the school on Monday. That Monday I took off work and went down to the school to be there in case anything happened. I saw a lot of parents I did not know. They were new homeowners who had moved to Freeport and were concerned about their children. What impressed me the most was that there was a car full of black men sitting there to protect the children. It was the first time I had seen black men take off work to do something like this. And we really needed them.
>
> We were there for several days. The white boys would come out with their chains and belts and so forth. I remember going to a school board meeting during the week and the black parents sat down in front to make their demands about what was going to happen to their children. . . . These white youngsters, about 200 of them, marched around to show their power. Talk about intimidation. I had my daughter with me and I was intimidated. Even with the police department, would we be protected?[42]

One of these new homeowners was Chris Sprowal, a longtime labor organizer and community activist. Before moving to Freeport, he had been involved in CORE (Congress of Racial Equality) in both the North and the South and been an organizer for the Drug and Hospital Workers Union. He and his family moved to Freeport because he was burned out from intense activity and wanted a break—something he thought the suburbs offered. Instead, Chris quickly became a leader in the community and helped form an independent organization, the Black Coalition. He was one of the men Louise Simpson met that Monday morning. Sprowal said he became involved in the school struggle

> because the black kids said that no one was supporting them in their demands and that they were being suspended at higher rates than white students. They had to riot to get basic demands. They said their parents didn't support them and the Black Coalition was doing nothing. That's why when a group of twenty black men showed up at the school the kids cheered and were proud of us for taking off work and staying all day.[43]

Julius Pearse, the first black policeman hired by the Freeport Police Department, recalled how tense the atmosphere was on all sides. He, like Chris Sprowal, felt that the "black kids had real gripes but no one was listening. They acted to make people listen." However, this was a difficult time for him because he had to wear two hats and was often called an Uncle Tom. As *Newsday* noted, "Julius Pearse was expected to go to Freeport High School in a dual capacity as one of the policemen on guard against disruption and as a Community Relations officer quietly trying to bring black and white students together."[44] He had access to community organizations as well as the white establishment and the police:

> I met with community groups to tell them I would protect them, but I couldn't tolerate broken windows. But windows were broken. I then told the local leaders to talk to the kids. I told them this because I knew my side would call in the National Guard and the state police. I had to pacify the militants under the law. There was organization and agitation on both sides. There were white agitators as well.[45]

One parent whose daughter had complained about unsafe school conditions in the past was electrified by the riot. Jomer Rand became a leader overnight and the most notorious white conservative in town. He lived on the south side of Freeport in a white working-class neighborhood that was not yet integrated and had had no contact with black people. He had been a professional wrestler, a teamster, and an active union member with aggressive instincts and a lot of pent-up anger. Rand said that before the riots he was a "couch potato" who spent his considerable leisure time watching "the boob tube" and tuning out. "From 1952 to 1969, I was the average tax-paying, truck-driver, functioning alcoholic." This routine abruptly ended the night of the riot.

> This friend of mine, Gus, who was an electrician—his daughter was beat up. I happened to run into him and he said, "We're going to a meeting tonight." I said, "What kind of meeting?" And he said, "There's trouble." And I said, "yeah, I heard it over the radio." And he was livid. . . . He said, "I'm gonna get a shotgun and I'm gonna shoot some niggers." I said, "Gus, let me calm you down." So I went to the meeting and I became a community leader by default.[46]

At this meeting of about fifty white parents, Rand, using his union experience, proposed action to this inchoate group. Although many had never heard of a picket line, he organized them to picket the high school and junior high on that same Monday. Bright and early Rand and his group came prepared with placards that read "No School Until It's Safe," "How About Our Civil Rights?" and "Safe Johns for our Janes."[47] The press immediately approached the group and Rand became the spokesperson.

Calling themselves the Concerned Parents of Freeport (CPF), they decided to hold a mass meeting that night at the Sons of Italy hall. Crowds packed into the small hall; accounts ranged from 400 to 600. Black parents tried to attend the meeting but were barred entry. According to Rand, this was "because we don't know any blacks and they're the ones who are beating up our kids. Let's get to know ourselves before we invite any blacks." The crowd refused to listen to then Mayor Robert Sweeney or the president and vice president of the school board but did listen to Rand, who exclaimed, "We feel our children are like a bunch of white sheep that have been attacked by black wolves while the shepherd stands around."[48]

Speaker after speaker, some with voices shaking with emotion, criticized the mayor and school board officials for "handcuffing the cops and going easy on the Negroes." Rand drew wild applause when he said, "If you want to take the hand-cuffs off our police—tell them." He also brought the crowd to its feet with this statement: "If some of the black people have decided to declare war on white peo-ple, they should know that war works two ways. . . . I'd rather have my kids out of school with heads empty of knowledge instead of in school with heads full of welts."

The CPF demanded the suspension of any student who left school without per-mission or carried a weapon or participated in an unauthorized meeting during school hours; arrest of any student found in the halls without permission who re-fused to return to class; patrol of the halls during school hours; and "public re-view" of demands made by black students. School officials must grant these con-ditions or resign.[49]

Sixty black students were expelled or suspended for participation in demon-strations. One black parent, on behalf of her daughter, got a court injunction to block the suspensions. In court papers, she charged the school board with "com-plete capitulation to white racist parents," claimed that the hearings were being held in "an atmosphere of hysteria," and alleged that top-ranking school board members attended a "white extremist meeting where blacks were systematically excluded."[50] She also charged that no white students were suspended even though they had been involved in activities. One board member admitted that none of the suspended or expelled students was white but added that "there is absolutely no racial motive behind our actions." Ultimately, after much pressure and legal maneuvering, the suspensions and expulsions were dropped, although some stu-dents were taken out of the day session and sent to night school.[51]

The Blockbusters Outwitted

The riots and polarization, combined with intensive media coverage, created an image of a community that appeared to be coming apart at the seams. During this period, blockbusters moved in on Freeport, flush with victory from Roosevelt and ready to begin their campaign of scare and sell. Some white families moved out to less turbulent white Long Island enclaves, and black middle-class and poor families started to move into areas where there had been few blacks before. Local residents feared that their town would be forever marked by the riots and might go the way of Roosevelt. This fear was fueled by the media depiction of Freeport as a town about to become a ghetto. Even the Republican mayor objected to this kind of biased coverage and argued in a letter to the editor of *Newsday* that the paper "seems determined to present the most negative, most distorted view possible of what is really a fine community."[52]

Residents wrote letters as well. Kathleen Glass, for example, "vehemently protests the slanted conclusions and racist implications reported. Suburban problems (soaring crime rates, taxes, etc.) germane to most Long Island communities are depicted as cause and effect results of black migration to heretofore unblemished white neighborhoods." She concluded, "No I am not the Mayor of Freeport, but rather a wholly satisfied resident, living on a lovely and longtime integrated block, only asking that Freeport be given the positive media attention it deserves.[53]

A black resident comparing Roosevelt with Freeport explained one reason why whites would not abandon this community. "Freeport will never turn all black because Freeport has resources that Roosevelt does not have—a waterfront and mansions. No one is going to give up something you can make an economic entity. . . . Freeport has too much to offer to give it to blacks, to afford it to be a total black community"[54]

Another aspect was the unusual amount of political organization in the town itself. Since Freeport was an unincorporated village and had decades-old civic associations and independent parties, coalitions of people with divergent politics could work together for the good of the town. For example, during the 1960s, Freeport was governed by the Village Party, which although nominally Republican included a range of perspectives, from left-wing Democrats to the mayor, who described himself as a neoconservative. Former Mayor Robert Sweeny said, "The Village Party was a strong coalition. We had many arguments because it was a diverse group, but we were all interested in what was good for Freeport. So it worked out."[55]

Dan Mandel, a lawyer and the Democrat on the mayor's council, confirmed the cooperative atmosphere: "The thing that always used to amaze me about Freeport is that we would go to meetings and yell and shout. But after the meeting was over, we would shake hands and talk. This made it possible to function and accomplish things without becoming embittered and drawing lines that no one would step across."[56] Alvin Dorfman noted about Freeport, "There are liberal, active, cultural families here that are dedicated to their community. People here are committed to Freeport and feel that they have more control because, unlike in Hempstead, you can really badger the mayor."[57]

Residents felt that the antiblockbusting campaigns were beginning to show signs of stopping the speculators. One resident told *Newsday* that the reason for this success was that "we want Freeport integrated. We stress that. It should be a self-sustaining community. We don't need panic."[58] In a further effort to stop blockbusting, the village banned For Sale signs, which had been an intimidating symbol of the blockbusting mania. This was the only ban of its kind on Long Island.[59]

Out of this activity came Homefinders, a village-subsidized real estate bureau, which listed houses in an attempt to balance the community racially. This bureau eliminated the real estate broker's fee and allowed direct contact between buyer and seller. Volunteers introduce homeowners, show houses, and sometimes conduct tours of the neighborhood. The buyers and sellers privately arrive at the price. Homefinders advertises in the *New York Times,* the *Long Island Catholic* and the *Jewish Weekly,* the *Village Voice,* and *Metropolitan Home* magazine and sends pamphlets to newlywed apartment dwellers on Long Island and to colleges and corporations throughout the country.[60]

The problem facing Homefinders was that during the 1960s black families had been moving into new neighborhoods that had begun to be blockbusted. By 1970 the older white middle-class neighborhoods were becoming more integrated, and another big blockbusting effort would have tipped the balance. The challenge was to find new white homeowners who would want to live in integrated neighborhoods. Ramona Crooks, head of Homefinders, explained:

> If you want to keep this village so that people won't have to say, well, we want to leave Freeport because there are too many blacks or too many anythings, the only way you can do that is to keep everybody coming in. If there are too many blacks, then there have to be whites coming in too. It's as simple as that. The more racist whites leave, but they are replaced with white people who want to live in an integrated cosmopolitan community.[61]

Real estate brokers felt that Homefinders restricted their power and prevented a free market. Harry Berman of Berman Real Estate said, "We as brokers are like merchants in the village. Why should we have competition from the village itself? This is unfair competition, especially since we have to show to blacks and whites. If a person knows he can get a house without a broker's commission, he'll tend to go to them.[62]

Some black activists saw Homefinders as a mechanism for subsidizing white families by allowing them to buy houses below market value to balance a neighborhood. Despite these criticisms, a powerful alliance of Homefinders, civic associations, local political parties, and city hall consciously portrayed Freeport as one of the few communities on Long Island where integration was a success. Those who didn't want to live in a multicultural environment left. Those who did stayed. As one white resident said, "Freeport has become a little U.N."[63]

Dorothy Storm, the mayor, stated in 1985, "We in Freeport work hard to maintain a stable, healthy integrated Village." But she acknowledged the challenge:

> We have always recognized that there are outside forces working against us by steering away those who may have wished to buy a home here and steering others to us who were made to feel they had no other option. However, the people of Freeport, all of us together, fight back. We believe everyone has the right to choose whether or not they wish to live in Freeport. They must have the same right in every community in this County, on Long Island and in the nation. It is indeed the law of the land.[64]

Not only were students and teachers and new and old residents trying to find common ground, but the parent organizations that originally clashed with each other, the Concerned Parents of Freeport and the Black Coalition, were beginning a process of reconciliation. Jomer Rand, head of the CPF, explained what was changing his attitudes: "There is a renaissance in Freeport. At first, every black face was an enemy, but the scars are being healed. We found that the problem we had in Freeport was not a black problem but a community problem."[65] Black leader Chris Sprowal was less enthusiastic but also saw progress: "There has been a lot of hassle and there still is, but for the most part there has been a conscientious effort on the part of the school administration to sit down with the community and make the system work better. The lines of communication are open."[66]

Private enterprise, the construction industry, and the banks, which control housing, still rely on segregated markets. Media constructions of the "good life" and governmental policies that have long determined who would be excluded from that life contributed greatly to the history of postwar suburbanization and are still critically important in the segregation of the suburbs.

Contrary to the prevailing media myth about suburban life, some blacks and whites fought together to forge integrated, cosmopolitan, and multicultural communities. But there is still a national housing crisis, one that reverberates in the suburbs as well as the cities. Two issues that remain unsettled is whether housing is a right or a privilege and what responsibility the government, private industry, and the media should assume in the creation of integrated equitable communities.

NOTES

1. Letter, Thurgood Marshall to Harry Truman, February 1, 1949, NAACP file, Box 751, as quoted in Andrew Wiese, "Driving a Thin Wedge of Suburban Opportunity: Black Suburbanization in the Northern Metropolis, 1940–60" (master's thesis, Columbia University), p. 80.

2. *Federal Policies Relative to Equal Housing Opportunity Statement by the President,* 7
Weekly Compilation of Presidential Documents, 892 (January 14, 1971).

3. Interview with Louise Simpson.

4. Interview with Harve Sinklar-Herring.

5. Interview with Charles and Meta Meredy.

6. John Dean, "None Other than Caucasians," *Journal of Land and Public Utility
Economics* (University of Wisconsin), November 1947.

7. Gwendolyn Brooks, *Building the Dream* (New York: Pantheon, 1981), pp. 247–248.

8. William Levitt, quoted in Michael Danielson, *The Politics of Exclusion* (New York:
Columbia University Press, 1976), p. 132.

9. See Michael Brown and Steven Erie, "Blacks and the Legacy of the Great Society: The
Economic and Political Impact of Federal Social Policy," *Public Policy* 29, no. 3 (Summer
1981); and Nicholas Lehman, *The Great Black Migration and How it Changed America*
(New York: Alfred Knopf, 1991), pp. 201–202. Also Thomas Edsall and Mary Edsall, *Chain
Reaction: The Impact of Race, Rights, and Taxes on American Politics* (New York: W. W.
Norton, 1991), p. 18: "Fully half of all blacks holding professional and managerial jobs are
employed by local, state or federal government agencies as compared to just over a quarter of whites."

10. Interview with Clara Gillens.

11. Interview with Jean Wyatt.

12. Interview with Helena White.

13. Interview with Barbara Patton.

14. *New York Times,* June 27, 1967, p. 75.

15. "Confessions of a Blockbuster," in *Metropolitan Real Estate Journal,* 1967, quoted in
Hillel Levine and Lawrence Harmon, *The Death of an American Jewish Community: A
Tragedy of Good Intentions* (New York: Free Press, 1992), pp. 195–196.

16. Ibid., p. 196.

17. *New York Times,* July 6, 1967.

18. Ibid.

19. Marquita James, "Blacks in Roosevelt, Long Island," in Salvatore La Gumina, ed.,
Ethnicity in Suburbia: The Long Island Experience (1980), p. 95.

20. Interview with Alvin and Shelly Dorfman.

21. Interview with Louise Simpson.

22. Interview with Ramona Crooks.

23. Interview with Yvonne Simmons.

24. Ibid., *New York Times,* June 27, 1967.

25. Interview with John Rice.

26. *Newsday,* November 24 and 25, 1965; James, "Blacks in Roosevelt," p. 96.

27. *New York Times,* June 27, 1967.

28. James, "Blacks in Roosevelt," p. 27. Interview with John Rice. Interview with Ruth
Grefe, Reginald Rembert Brown, and Ilda Northern.

29. Interview with Ruth Grefe.

30. Freeport is one of the more attractive towns on Long Island's South Shore. It has a
long history of being a summer resort town for Broadway actors and actresses, and a number of its streets are named for celebrities, the most famous of which is Guy Lombardo. In
the 1920s, as this artists' colony developed, Freeport was also important in the then illegal

trade in alcohol, an activity that made money for many of the town's older fishermen and clam diggers.

31. *New York Herald Tribune,* December 20, 1964; *Freeport Leader,* February 4, 1965; *Newsday,* November 17, 1964: *Long Island Press,* October 3, 1964.

32. Interview with Ramona Crooks and Michael Kirwin.

33. *Newsday,* April 13, 1968.

34. Interview with Marquita James; *Newsday,* December 20, 1968.

35. *Newsday,* January 23, 1969.

36. *Newsday,* December 20 and 23, 1968.

37. Interview with Marquita James.

38. *Newsday,* April 25, 1969.

39. *Long Island Press,* April 26, 1969; *Newsday,* April 26, 1969.

40. *Newsday,* April 29, 1969.

41. Dan Mandel quoted in *Newsday,* April 30, 1969.

42. Interview with Louise Simpson.

43. Interview with Chris Sprowal.

44. *Newsday,* November 16, 1970.

45. Interview with Julius Pearse.

46. Interview with Jomer Rand.

47. *New York Daily News,* April 29, 1969.

48. *Newsday,* April 29, 1969.

49. Ibid.; *Long Island Press,* April 29, 1969.

50. *Long Island Press,* May 16, 1969.

51. Ibid.

52. *Newsday,* July 21, 1970; *Kernel,* July 23, 1970.

53. From Freeport Library Ethnic Groups files, May 1981.

54. Interview with Louisa Monteiro.

55. Interview with Robert Sweeny.

56. Interview with Dan Mandel.

57. Interview with Alvin Dorfman.

58. *Newsday,* June 4, 1971.

59. *Newsday,* June 24, 1974; *The Leader,* June 24, 1974; *Long Island Graphic,* June 24, 1974.

60. *Newsday,* January 11, 1985.

61. Interview with Ramona Crooks and Michael Kirwin.

62. *Newsday,* May 6, 1974.

63. Interview with Popkin.

64. *Newsday,* December 19, 1985.

65. Interview with Jomer Rand.

66. Interview with Chris Sprowal.

9

National Amnesia, Cultural Darwinism, and the Pursuit of Power, or What Americans Don't Know About Indians

JERRY MANDER

In 1981, when my sons Yari and Kai were attending San Francisco's Lowell High School, they complained to me that their American history class began with the arrival of whites on this continent and omitted any mention of the people who were already here. The class was taught that Columbus *discovered* America and that American *history* was what came afterward.

That same year, Ronald Reagan gave his first inaugural speech, in which he praised the "brave pioneers who tamed the empty wilderness." Still, I was surprised to hear that the wilderness was also empty for the faculty at Lowell High, a school usually considered among the top public high schools in this country.

The American history teacher asked my kids why they were so keen on the subject of Indians, which led them to mention the book I was planning to write. This, in turn, led to an invitation for me to speak to the class. As a result, I received some insight about the level of Indian awareness among a group of high school kids.

The youngsters I met had never been offered one course, or even an extended segment of a course, about the Indian nations of this continent, about Indian-Anglo interactions (except for references to the Pilgrims and the Indian wars), or about contemporary Indian problems in the United States or elsewhere. These teenagers knew as little as I did at their age and as little as their teacher knew at their age—or now, as he regretfully acknowledged to me. The American educational curriculum is almost bereft of information about Indians, a deficiency that makes it

Based on Chapter 11, "What Americans Don't Know About Indians," in Jerry Mander, *In the Absence of the Sacred: The Failure of Technology and the Survival of the Indian Nations* (San Francisco: Sierra Club Books, 1991). Reprinted by permission.

difficult for young non-Indian Americans to understand or care about present-day Indian issues. European schools actually teach more about American Indians. In Germany, for example, every child reads a set of books that sensitizes them to Indian values and causes. It is not surprising, therefore, that the European press carries many more stories about American Indians than does the American press.

In the sixty minutes I was allotted to speak to the Lowell class, I tried to communicate five points: (1) There were many Indians living here before whites arrived; (2) they were not savages but lived in very well-organized, stable societies spanning thousands of years; (3) the white European settlers killed most of the Indians on the continent and massively stole from the rest; (4) nonetheless, there are still many Indians within the United States facing problems similar to those faced by their ancestors; and (5) there are millions of Indians (and other native people) all over the world.

I posted one of the excellent maps prepared by the Bureau of Indian Affairs (BIA) showing Indian land areas prior to the arrival of white colonists. The students were shocked to learn that nearly every acre of what is now the United States was once part of some Indian nation. I pointed out that by the time this map was drawn, some of the Indian nations had been in place for thousands of years. So much for *empty wilderness.*

Some of the Iroquois tribes have been living in the northern United States for at least 5,000 years. In the Southwest, the Hopi Indians are estimated to have been living in what is now called the Four Corners area (the junction of Colorado, New Mexico, Arizona, and Utah) for at least 10,000 years. (Some archaeologists have lately put the Hopi arrival as long as 40,000 years ago. The Hopi themselves say, as do many Indian nations, that they did not *arrive* at all—that their genesis was in the Grand Canyon.)

Whatever the millennium, Indian people were living on this continent thousands of years before the Hebrews came down from the steppes into what is now the Middle East, long before Christ, long before the establishment of European nations, and very long before Columbus.

By 1776, when the United States was established, about 100 Indian nations had survived the slaughter of the fifteenth, sixteenth, and seventeenth centuries, and some 2 million to 5 million Indian people (depending upon whose estimate you accept) were living in the lower forty-eight states, speaking more than 750 distinct languages. In California alone—where climate and conditions were hospitable— more than 200,000 Indians lived in several hundred *subtribes,* each with its own language. And in Hawaii in 1776, there were still, by the most conservative estimates, at least 300,000 natives. By 1830, the number was reduced to 80,000 as a result of massacres and disease brought by the white followers of Captain Cook.

When I got to this point in my lecture, one of the students asked, "What do you mean by the word *nation,* as applied to Indian tribes?"

As defined by such international organizations as the U.N. and the World Court, nation includes the following components: common culture and heritage, common language, stable geographic locale over time, internal laws of behavior that are accepted by members of the community, boundaries recognized by other nations, and formal agreements (treaties) with other nations. By those standards, Indian nations were and are just that. Moreover, the colonial powers on this continent—the British, French, and Spanish—openly recognized the Indian nations as such and made treaties with them, affirming boundaries, mutual alliances, peace, and friendship as well as land exchanges and concession. The Indian nations also made thousands of treaties with each other.

From the late eighteenth to the late nineteenth centuries, the United States made 370 formal treaties with Indian nations, following the same procedure of congressional and presidential approval that was followed with France or Great Britain. There were no distinctions between Indian treaties and any others; all became the *law of the land* as the Constitution requires. The fact that we violated virtually all of these Indian treaties resulted from our feeling that we could get away with such violations, that the violations were acceptable in the eyes of the European community of nations, and that the United States would not be as heavily criticized as it would if it violated treaties with Spain or England. Clearly, there was a sense that Indians somehow are not people in the same category as the English, and so deals with them can be made in a less earnest fashion.

European doubts about the peoplehood of Indians extend back to the murderous explorations of Hernando Cortés in the mid-1500s among the Indians of Central America and Mexico. The fate of the Indians became the subject of fierce disagreements within the Catholic Church. The argument became focused in the historic sixteenth-century debates between Spanish scholar Juan Gines de Sepulveda and Dominican friar Bartolomé de las Casas as to whether Indians had souls and ought to be saved for the church or whether they should be slaughtered or made into slaves. Sepulveda argued the Aristotelian viewpoint that some people are born to slavery. De las Casas, who had traveled in Mexico with Cortés and had been impressed with the Indians, was horrified at the invaders' brutality. He argued that murder and slavery contradicted the Gospels. Pope Pius V finally sided with de las Casas in 1566, ruling that Indians should be converted rather than killed. Apparently no consideration was given to permitting Indians to live as they had before the Spanish invasion.

By the eighteenth century, the case for Indian inferiority was no longer predicated on the issue of souls but on the fact that Indians had no concept of private property: Their religions were based on nature, they lived by subsistence economics, and they believed that rocks, trees, and the earth were alive. Such beliefs were held to be prima facie evidence that Indians were less evolved than Europeans and that they stood against the tide of history. That viewpoint has not fundamentally changed for the past 300 years.

Next on my agenda at Lowell High was a discussion of Indian governmental structures. Like most Americans, the young high school students assumed that Indian or aboriginal people had no forms of government other than despotic chiefs, such as the Shaka Zulu characterization we have seen on television. This lack of information about Indian governments represents another tragic omission from American education, since many Indian governmental forms were highly evolved and democratic. Some of them, notably the Iroquois, apparently had considerable effect upon concepts later incorporated into the U.S. Articles of Confederation and the Constitution. The systems of checks and balances, popular participation in decisionmaking, direct representation, states' rights, and bicameral legislatures were all part of the Great Binding Law of the Iroquois Confederacy dating to the 1400s. But there may not be one American in ten thousand who knows this.

Another shocking fact was that very few of the students were aware of the degree to which or how recently Indian lands had been expropriated. Between 1776 and the late 1800s, Indian landholdings were reduced by about 95 percent, from about 3 million to 200,000 square miles. This was accomplished in a variety of ways, from massacres to duplicitous treaty-making. Some treaties exacted land cessions in exchange for guarantees of safety and permanent reserves, but these treaties were soon violated. Usually the Indians were driven off because the settlers wanted gold or farmland or mineral rights or railroad rights. Wherever there was resistance, the cavalry ensured compliance. All of this was in the cause of Manifest Destiny: God willed it.

My hour was nearly gone. I had only enough time left to say that to ignore the past reality of the Indians is bad enough, but to ignore the current situation is worse. In this country there are still 1.5 million Indian people, more than half of whom live on the lands where their ancestors lived thousands of years ago. Some of these Indians maintain traditions that have survived for millennia. But when the U.S. government or private corporations seek to get oil, coal, or copper from Indian land, they behave exactly as they always have. Since the Custer period, the methods have switched from violent assault to legal manipulations that separate Indians from their lands as surely as the guns once did. I gave the students three brief examples:

- *The Dawes Act (1887).* This law provided that individual Indians could own their own plots of land. It was hailed as a liberal reform when introduced, but the real purpose and effect of the law were to break the communal-tribal ownership of land. Tribes were rarely, if ever, willing to sell land. But individuals could be persuaded to sell for cash, guns, or liquor. Millions of acres moved from Indian to white ownership.
- *The Indian Reorganization Act (1934).* Another liberal reform, it offered U.S. assistance in converting Indian governments to modern democratic systems. Like the Dawes Act half a century earlier, this law was designed to break the hold of traditional Indian governance—based on slow-moving consensus processes—because it invariably led to refusal to negotiate leases for oil, coal, gas, and other minerals that the U.S. government was

seeking. *Democracy* had nothing to do with it. In fact, as the new American-style governments were put into place, the great majority of Indians refused to participate in the voting. This enabled the Bureau of Indian Affairs to train and run its own complaint candidates—ready to make deals—who were elected by the tiny handful of Indians willing to participate in the alien process. As a result, corporations gained inexpensive access to Indian resources, and the new Indian tribal councils effectively became part of the U.S. bureaucracy, as most still are, though a sizable resistance on many reservations now threatens this cozy arrangement.

- *The Indian Claims Act (1946).* Theoretically established to settle Indian grievances about stolen lands, in practice the Indian Claims Commission is a fraud. The commission refuses all requests to grant land title to Indians, offering only compensation for lands that it determines were lost by Indians (at per acre rates that are often a century old). So Indians entering claims to land find that accepting payment amounts to a permanent extinguishing of their aboriginal title, which is the opposite result of the one they sought.

I ended my talk by mentioning that there are hundreds of millions of indigenous people all over the world who continue to live on their ancestral lands and who experience varying degrees of domination by invading colonial interests. Most of these people are suffering even more violent assaults than were visited upon American Indians a century ago. As in the past, these acts are justified by an assumption of cultural and spiritual superiority and by the fact that the indigenous people stand in the way of the orderly progress of technological and industrial development.

The bell rang. The kids leaped up. Out the door to lunch.

The Media: Indians Are Non-news

That the Lowell High students should know nothing about Indians is not their fault. It is one of many indicators that this country's institutions do not inform people about Indians of either present or past. Indians are nonhistory, which also makes them non-news. Not taught in schools, not part of American consciousness, their present-day activities and struggles are rarely reported in newspapers or on television. On the rare occasions when the media do relate to Indians, the reports tend to follow very narrow guidelines based on preexisting stereotypes of Indians; they become what is known in the trade as *formula stories.*

My friend Dagmar Thorpe, a Sac-and-Fox Indian who until 1990 was executive director of the Seventh Generation Fund, once asked a network producer known to be friendly to the Indian cause about the reasons for the lack of in-depth, accurate reporting on Indian stories. According to Dagmar, the producer gave three reasons. The first reason was guilt. It is not considered good programming to make your audience feel bad. Americans do not want to see shows that remind them of historical events that American institutions have systematically avoided discussing.

Second, there is the *what's-in-it-for-me?* factor. Americans in general do not see how anything to do with Indians has anything to do with them. As a culture, we are now so trained *to look out for number one* that there has been a nearly total loss of altruism. (Of course, American life itself—so speedy and so removed from nature—makes identifying with the Indians terribly difficult, and we don't see that we might have something to learn from them.)

The third factor is that Indian demands seem preposterous to Americans. What most Indians want is simply that their land should be returned and that treaties should be honored. Americans tend to view the treaties as ancient, though many were made less than a century ago—more recently, for example, than many well-established laws and land deals among whites. Americans, like their government and the media, view treaties with Indian nations differently from treaties with anyone else.

Just like the rest of us, reporters and producers have been raised without knowledge of Indian history or Indian struggles. Perhaps most important, media people have had little personal contact with Indians, since Indians live primarily in parts of the country and the world that lack much media presence. Indians live in nonurban regions, in the deserts and mountains and tundras that have been impacted least by Western society, at least until recently. They live in the places that we did not want. They are not part of the mainstream and have not tried to become part of it.

As a result, some of the most terrible assaults upon native people never get reported. If reports do emerge, the sources are the corporate or military public relations arms of the Western intruders, which present biased perspectives.

When reporters are flown in to some region where Indians are making news, they are usually ill prepared and unknowledgeable about the local situation. They do not speak the language and are hard pressed to grasp the Indian perception, even if they can find Indians to speak with. In addition, these reporters often grew up in that same bubble of no contact, no education, and no news about Indians. A reporter would have to spend a great deal of time with the Indians to understand why digging up the earth for minerals is a sacrilege, or why diverting a stream can destroy a culture, or why cutting a forest deprives people of their religious and human rights, or why moving Indians off desert land to a wonderful new community of private homes will effectively kill them. Even if the reporter does understand, to translate that understanding through the medium successfully and through the editors and the commercial sponsors—all of whom are looking for action—is nearly impossible.

Prevalent Stereotypes and Formulas

The dominant image of Indians in the media used to be of savages, of John Wayne leading the U.S. Cavalry against the Indians. Today the stereotype has shifted to noble savage, which portrays Indians as part of a once great but now dying culture—a culture that could talk to the trees and the animals and that protected nature but that sadly is a losing culture, which has not kept up with our dynamic times.

We see this stereotype now in many commercials. The Indian is on a horse, gazing nobly over the land he protects. Then there is a quick cut to today: Two oil company workers are there to protect against leaks and to preserve the environment for the animals. We see quick cuts of caribou and wolves; these images imply that the oil company accepts the responsibility the Indians once had.

The problem here is that the corporate sponsor is lying. It does not feel much responsibility toward nature; if it did, it would not need expensive commercials to say so, because the truth would be apparent from its behavior. More important, however, is that treating Indians this way in commercials does terrible harm to their cause. It makes Indians into conceptual relics, artifacts. Worse, they are confirmed as existing only in the past, which hurts their present efforts.

Another stereotype we see in commercials these days is the Indian-as-guru. A recent TV spot depicted a shaman making rain for his people. He is then hired by some corporate farmers to make rain for them. He is shown with his power objects, saying prayers, holding his hands toward the heavens. The rains come. Handshakes from the businessmen. Finally the wise old Indian is shown with a satisfied smile on his flight home via United Airlines.

Another very popular formula story is the one with the headline "Indians stand in the way of development," as, for example, in New Guinea or Borneo or the Amazon Basin. These stories concern resistance by Indians to roads or dams or the cutting of forests and their desire for their lands to be left inviolate.

The problem with these formula stories is not that they are inaccurate—Indian people around the world most certainly are resisting on hundreds of fronts and do indeed stand in the way of development—but that the style of reporting carries a sense of foregone conclusion. The reporters tend to emphasize the poignancy of the situation: stone-age people fighting in vain to forestall the inevitable march of progress. In their view, it is only a matter of time before the Indians lose, the forests are cut down, and the land is settled by outsiders. However tragic the invasion, however righteous the cause of the Indians, however illegal the acts being perpetrated against them, however admirable the Indian ways, reporters will invariably adopt the stance that the cause is lost and that no reversal is possible. This attitude surely harms the Indians more than if the story had not been reported at all.

Finally, and perhaps most outrageous, is the rich Indian formula story. Despite the fact that the average per capita income of Indians is lower than that of any other racial or ethnic group in the United States, and that they suffer the highest disease rates in many categories and have the least access to health care, the press loves to focus on the rare instance of some Indian hitting it big. Sometimes the story is about an oil well found on some Indian's land or about someone getting rich on bingo, but often the stories emphasize someone's corruption. This formula story has a twofold purpose: It manages to confirm the greatness of America—where anyone can get rich, even an Indian—and at the same time manages to confirm Indian leaders as corrupt and despotic.

A corollary to this story is how certain Indian tribes have become wealthy through land claims cases, as, for example, the Alaska natives via the Alaska Native Claims Settlement Act. A little digging into the story—if reporters only would— exposes that settlement as a fraud that actually deprived the Alaska natives of land and money.

The press's failure to pursue and report the full picture of American Indian poverty while splashing occasional stories about how some Indians are hitting it big creates a public impression that is the opposite of the truth. The situation is exacerbated when national leaders repeat the misconceptions. Ronald Reagan told the Moscow press in 1987 that there was no discrimination against Indians in this country and the proof of that was that so many Indians, such as those outside Palm Springs (oil wells), have become wealthy.

Cultural Darwinism

There is yet a deeper widespread rationalization for our avoidance of Indians and the news they bring us. On some level we think that however beautiful their culture once was, however inspiring their religious ideas, however artistic their creations and costumes, however wise their choices of life within nature, our own society has advanced beyond that stage of evolution. They are the *primitive* stage, and we have grown beyond them. They have not adapted as we have. This makes us superior. We are the survivors. We are the *cutting edge.*

A good friend of mine (who now works in television) put it this way: "There is no getting around the fact that the Indian way is a losing way. They are no longer appropriate for the times. They are anomalies."

In saying this, my friend was essentially blaming the Indians themselves for the situation that befell them. They failed to adapt their lifestyle and belief systems to keep up with changing times. Most important, they failed to keep up with technological change. They were not competitive.

This statement reflects a Darwinist, capitalist outlook of survival of the fittest, with fitness now defined in terms of technological capability. If you can use the machine better than the next fellow or the next culture, you survive and the other dies. This may be sad, the reasoning goes, but that is the way it is in today's world.

This view sees Western technological society as the ultimate expression of the evolutionary pathway, the culmination of all that has come before, the final flowering. We represent the breakthrough in the evolution of living creatures; we are the conscious expression of the planet. Indians helped the process for a while, but they gave way to more evolved, higher life forms.

Our assumption of superiority does not come to us by accident. We have been trained in it. It is soaked into the fabric of every Western religion, economic system, and technology. They reek of their greater virtues and capabilities.

Judeo-Christian religions are a model of hierarchical structure: one God above all, certain humans above other humans, and humans over nature. Political and economic systems are similarly arranged: Organized along rigid hierarchical lines, all of nature's resources are regarded only in terms of how they serve the one god—the god of growth and expansion. In this way, all of these systems are missionary; they are into dominance. And through their mutual collusion, they form a seamless web around our lives. They are the creators and enforcers of our beliefs. We live inside these forms, are imbued with them, and they justify our behaviors. In turn, we believe in their viability and superiority largely because they prove effective: They bring us power.

But is power the ultimate evolutionary value? We shall see. The results are not yet in. *Survival of the fittest* as a standard of measure may require a much longer time scale than the scant 200 years' existence of the United States or the century since the industrial revolution or the two decades since the advent of high technology. Even in Darwinian terms, most species become unfit over tens of thousands of years. Our culture is using its machinery to drive species into extinction in one generation, not because the species are maladaptive but because pure force wins out. However, there is reason to doubt the ultimate success of our behavior. In the end, a model closer to that of the Indians, living lightly on the planet, observing its natural rules and modes of organization, may prove more fit and may survive us after all. Until that day, however, we will continue to use Darwinian theories to support the assertion that our mechanistic victory over the primitives is not only God's plan but nature's.

PART FOUR

GLOBAL FAULT LINES

10

Beaches Without Bases: The Gender Order

SUE CURRY JANSEN

A growing body of feminist research suggests that news, especially international news, is a form of communication that can be fully and critically understood only when seen through the prism of gender.[1] This research indicates that the cultural forms of objective journalism are currently alienating a significant segment of the audience: women, especially young women. From a pragmatic perspective, journalism's apparent indifference to the female audience makes no sense. In the United States, where commercialization of news production is most pronounced, women control or influence 80 percent of consumer decisionmaking. When news organizations ignore women, they are ignoring market imperatives.[2]

How can this apparent resistance to the logic of capitalism be explained? I explore this question by arguing that journalism's indifference to female audiences is a socially significant extension of current structures of global power, not simply a provincial souvenir of traditionalism. I treat gender as an important, perhaps even decisive, category in articulations of *all power* relations, including relationships among heterosexual men. By continuing to ignore the role gender plays in communications and international relations, critical communication scholarship contributes to the invisibility of "critical conditions and developments whose imagery would pose an unacceptable challenge to the structure of culture-power."[3]

The argument is developed in the following steps. First, I examine recent data that support my claim that news, especially international news, is gendered and that this gendering both reflects and contributes to current global crises. Second, I unpack some of the gendered constituents of the mythology of the Cold War. Third, I analyze some of the opportunities and obstacles that the end of the Cold War poses for the global feminist movement, for the practice and study of international relations, and for media organizations themselves. Fourth, I briefly identify some crises that become fully visible only when gender is treated as a significant category for analyzing and reporting global politics.

News as a Gendered Form

In the United States men write most of the front-page newspaper stories. They are the subjects of most of those stories—85 percent of the references and 66 percent of the photos in 1993. They also dominate electronic media, accounting for 86 percent of the correspondents and 75 percent of the sources for U.S. network television evening news programs.[4] According to Margaret Gallagher,[5] "Prevalent news values define most women and most women's problems as unnewsworthy, admitting women to coverage primarily as wives, mothers or daughters of men in the news: in their own right, they make the headlines usually only as fashionable or entertaining figures."[6]

Newspaper readership research indicates that women are turned off by conflict-based news narratives.[7] Yet stories framed in terms of conflict, confrontation, extremism, and sensationalism are the staples of journalism.

Men are typically assigned to *hard* news, news that has significant public implications. Women, in contrast, cover *soft* news stories and stories related to topics traditionally associated with female responsibilities. Figures for U.S. newspapers show that men dominate coverage of war and the military (81.8 percent), sports (81.2 percent), government and politics (78.1 percent), human interest (75.4 percent), economics (75.3 percent), and foreign relations (72.6 percent). Women are most prominent in coverage of education (66.7 percent), health and medicine (43.9 percent), accidents and disasters (45.5 percent), and social issues (42.4 percent).[8] Gender also makes a difference in reading the news. Although women in the United States read more than men generally, men read more newspapers than women: Approximately 65 percent of men and 60 percent of women are daily consumers of newspapers.[9]

Kay Mills maintained that Western journalism still views women as "outsiders, suspect, 'the other' . . . the anomaly, exceptions to the male norm."[10] As a result, "coverage of issues affecting women is not institutionalized, not part of the 'normal' media mind-set."[11]

In international news coverage, women not only are marginal but also are normally absent. As Cynthia Enloe pointed out, only on those rare occasions when women such as Margaret Thatcher or Indira Gandhi are present in news photographs of world leaders do we become consciously aware that nearly all leaders are men.

Women's experiences—of war, marriage, trade, travel, factory work—are relegated to the "human interest" column. Women's roles in creating and sustaining international politics have been treated as if they were "natural" and thus not worthy of investigation. Consequently, how the conduct of international politics has depended on men's control of women has been left unexamined.[12]

The socially structured silences or erasures produced by the routine practices of international news production contribute to the maintenance and reproduction of an international gender order that is secured by what Bob Connell called "hegemonic masculinity."[13] According to Connell, at the level of mass social relations, highly stylized and impoverished definitions of masculinity form the basis for dominant males' relationships to subordinate males and for the relationships of all males to females.[14] This hegemonic principle is replicated, in an abstract form, in the global ordering of relationships of dominant and subordinate nations.

Research stimulated by the feminist, gay, and lesbian liberation movements has, however, made it increasingly difficult to ignore the salience of gender as an explanatory category in social research. According to Stuart Hall, nothing less than a "revolution in thinking" follows "in the wake of the acknowledgment that all social practices and forms of domination—including the politics of the Left—are always inscribed in and to some extent secured by sexual identity and positioning."[15]

This revolution requires radical reconstructions of the theories, research protocols, and journalistic practices used to conceptualize international relations and international news. Connell critized the outmoded approach: "The habit of mind that treats class, or race, or North-South global relationships as if gender did not matter is obsolete—and dangerous."[16] To ignore gender is to ignore a major generative principle of international conflicts. Such ignorance contributes to practices that allow incipient conflicts to remain invisible until they escalate into major international crises. As Connell pointed out, even when gender is ignored,

> the facts of gender do not go away. Aid programs to Third World countries, by ignoring gender in principle, in fact give resources to men rather than to women. Industrial and nationalist militancy that ignores questions of gender reinforces men's violence and the patterns of masculinity that lie behind it. The question of human survival, in the face of a global arms race and widespread environmental destruction, requires us to understand a play of social forces in which gender has a major part.[17]

Under the present global gender order, policymakers and journalists find it more *manly* to deal with guns, missiles, and violent conflicts than with matters like female infanticide in China, the increased trade in children in the sex markets of Manila and Bangkok in the wake of the AIDS epidemic, the impact of the intifada on Palestinian women, or the political activism of groups such as the Women in Black, Israeli women who support the intifada.

The Gender Order and Cold War Mythology

E. P. Thompson maintained that the power knowledge of the Cold War hung "the hinge of history" on an extremely narrow frame.[18] It restricted the exercise of political imagination and rhetoric to the reductive terms of a binary code. The ideologies this code supported "nourished and reproduced reciprocal paranoias" and "deadened imagination with a language of worst-case analysis and a definition of half of the human race as an Enemy Other."[19]

This code also nourished and fed cultural imagery of a heterosexist gender order where good women stayed in the kitchen and the bedroom and supported manly men in their valiant attempts to contain an "evil empire" (to use former President Ronald Reagan's description of the Soviet Union). Within this binary semantic code, homosexuals were conceived as security risks: *enemies within,* to be coerced, brutalized, and confined to closets.

The gendered constituents of the *dangerous-world* syndrome that fueled the mythology of the Cold War have been excavated by Brian Easlea,[20] Helen Caldicott,[21] Carol Cohn,[22] and others. In a world pervaded by threats and violence—in which two superpowers were locked into a deadly game of brinksmanship—risk taking was justified in the name of avoiding a bigger risk.[23] Thus, for example, U.S. defense policy justified wars in Korea and Vietnam as necessary to stop Chinese and Soviet expansionism and thereby avoid a nuclear holocaust. The rationale for these bloodlettings, the *domino theory,* put forth by John Foster Dulles, secretary of state in the Eisenhower administration, is an exemplary case of a Cold War policy that "nourished and reproduced reciprocal paranoias."[24]

The Cold War may be over, but the dangerous worldviews of men in power show few signs of pacification or imaginative reconstructions. The Persian Gulf War was, among many other things, *a boy thing,* in which George Bush demonstrated—live and in color—that his missiles were bigger, better, and much more potent than Saddam Hussein's.[25] Bill Clinton dramatically invoked the dangerous-world syndrome to justify new bombings in Baghdad and to initiate nuclear saber-rattling with the last fully intractable Cold War enemy, North Korea.[26] Like George Bush, who demonstrated that he was no wimp to the U.S. media and to the world, Clinton's moves also have closely followed the Cold War's prescriptions for *manly men* at the brink.

When elite males define the world as a dangerous place, "masculine men and feminine women are expected to react in opposite but complementary ways."[27] In such a world, manly men are supposed to suppress their own fears and assume the role of protector of women and children. Women, in turn, are expected to look to their fathers, husbands, and brothers or their symbolic surrogates for protection against the dangerous men on the other side. In exchange for this protection, women are expected to be self-sacrificing: to put the interests of their husbands, children, and nation before their own. According to Easlea,[28] Cohn,[29] and by extension, Keller,[30] the erotics of the power knowledge of this masculinist order are, paradoxically, homoerotic, misogynist, and necrophilic—involving male bonding secured by exclusion of women and sealed by the daring defiance of death.[31]

Under the form of hegemonic masculinity that has defined global politics since the end of World War II,

Ideas of masculinity have to be perpetuated to justify foreign-policy risk-taking. To accept the Cold War interpretation of living in a dangerous world also confirms the segregation of politics into national and international. The national political arena is dominated by men but allows women some select access; the international political arena is only for those rare women who can successfully play at being men, or at least not shake masculine presumptions.[32]

A dangerous world is an unambiguous world. For this reason, it is, paradoxically, a comfortable world for some (males) in the defense establishment and the press. As Larry Eichel noted in a September 11, 1989, article in the *Philadelphia Inquirer* entitled, "Wall Kept Things Simple," some experts on international politics already *miss* the Cold War: "They say the day may come when the world looks back on the 40 years after World War II as the good old days—when life was simple, people knew which side they were on and a standoff between superpowers kept the peace." In a 1990 interview, Jeremy Azrael, a Rand Corporation Soviet analyst, acknowledged that "the Cold War world has been very good" to the military, the defense industry, and its apologists. With the prescience of a seasoned warrior, he worried: "There is a terrible danger that defense intellectuals will have to go whoring. Folks in the services will go looking for threats out there."[33]

The rest, of course, is already *instant history.*[34]

Opportunities and Obstacles
to Expanding the Political Imagination

In 1990, Thompson announced that history is now turning on a "new hinge."[35] At the time, Thompson was optimistic about the possibilities for expanding the breadth, depth, and quality of the political imagination.

Nevertheless, the semantic void left by the spies and speechwriters who came in from the cold remains unfilled. Moreover, neither subsequent historical events nor most mass-mediated discourses they have generated support Thompson's optimism.

While he was president of the new, now former Czechoslovakia, Vaclav Havel offered a much different and far more pessimistic take on recent events. Havel maintained that the collapse of communism has not only profoundly challenged the assumptions of Eurocentric political and social theories but has also undermined the very foundations of rational inquiry itself:

> The end of Communism has brought a major era in human history to an end. It has brought an end not just to the 19th and 20th centuries but to the modern age as a whole. . . . The large paradox at the moment is that man—a great collector of information—is well aware of all this, yet is absolutely incapable of dealing with the danger.[36]

According to Havel's postmodern dangerous-world scenario, the modern West's uncritical faith in scientific and technological progress—its instrumentalism—has delivered us to the eleventh hour: "We are looking for new scientific recipes, new ideologies, new control systems, new institutions, new instruments to eliminate the dreadful consequences of our previous recipes, ideologies, control systems, institutions and instruments."[37]

If Havel's analysis and the cultural practices he described are reexamined through the lens of gender, very different readings not only are possible but in fact are already well advanced in the work of many feminist and some postmodern theorists. James Hillman unpacked this legacy eloquently and succinctly:

> The specific consciousness we call scientific, Western and modern is the long sharpened tool of the masculine mind that has discarded parts of its own substance, calling it *Eve, female and inferior.* What is required to recover and heal *political man* is not simply to add woman and stir. Rather masculinity and femininity must be reinvented, new political and social theories must be written, and new forms of politics and eroticism must be created.[38]

Enloe suggested a new feminist (and, I believe, planet- and species-friendly) recipe that may contribute to this political and personal renaissance.[39] She reflected on the rhetorical power that the slogan "the personal is political" had in mobilizing the second wave of U.S. and global feminism, a phrase C. Wright Mills maintained is like a palindrome.[40] Enloe explained how it can be read backward as well as forward:

> Read as "the political is personal," it suggests that politics is not shaped merely by what happens in legislative debates, voting booths or war rooms. While men, who dominate public life, have told women to stay in the kitchen, they have used their public power to construct private relationships in ways that bolstered their masculinized political control.[41]

According to Enloe's recipe, to understand a nation's political order, its gender order must be analyzed. The "political is personal" concept not only renders visible the roles women play in the global assembly line—as laborers, servants, guest workers, diplomatic wives, immigrants, refugees, tourists, sex workers, bank clerks, and peace activists—but also exposes men *as men.* As Enloe pointed out, governments qua elite males devote considerable resources to controlling women, and women, it should be noted, devote considerable resources to developing multiple overt and subterranean strategies for resisting these efforts.[42]

Elite males' efforts to control women usually have much more to do with optimizing control over other men than women: men as migrant workers, soldiers, diplomats, intelligence operatives, overseas plantation and factory managers, even bankers. This control includes control over what Herbert Marcuse called political linguistics: "the right to establish enforceable definitions of words."[43] Legitimacy arises under the terms of the current international gender order: "Ideas about *adventure, civilization, progress, risk, trust,* and *security* are all legitimized by certain kinds of masculinist values and behavior, which makes them so potent in relations between governments."[44]

Within the economy of signs produced by prevailing patterns of political linguistics, icons of popular culture such as Rambo, the Terminator, and their Japanese-manufactured technocounterpart, Super Mario, are not simply entertainments. The extreme exaggerations and sexualization of differences present in the imagery currently produced by the U.S. culture industry for global consumption would suggest that the gender order of the Cold War is playing its trump card: the threat of brute force. In this deadly contest, air-brushed images of violent, steroid-pumped, manly men with suprahuman bulging muscles are presented as counterpoint to starving, anorexic, pencil-thin, fashion-modeled forms of femininity. Within this reconstruction of the gender order, however, corporations—advertising, fashion, sports, film, video, and related consumer industries—and not governments define and police the new internalized landscapes of the dangerous-world syndrome.

The gender-based news blackout does not involve malevolent plots or conspiracies by retro-male editors. Women editors and journalists also create and enforce policies and practices that perpetuate it. This blackout is a structural artifact of both Cold War and commercial news values that privilege dangerous-world scenarios: sensational stories about violent conflicts and disruptions of order. There are, to be sure, real dangers in the post–Cold War world that are news. Within the terms of current formulas for international news production, however, the stories about women that do make the news typically represent them as sexualized objects or victims of male violence, whether in Bosnia, in Kuwait, or in the mean streets of urban centers throughout the world. Such stories are news: hard political news, not just human interest or crime stories. Nevertheless, this kind of news represents a very narrow range of women's experiences: the actual and narrative terrain where hegemonic masculinity overtly and often brutally surveys and disciplines them into *political* subordination.

There are many significant stories about women that seldom make the news: stories about women's collective efforts to become agents rather than victims of history. Some dramatic and dramatically underreported efforts, which fit within the agonistic frames of conventional news, are, for example, women's organized efforts on behalf of "the disappeared" in Argentina, Chile, and Guatemala; the political mobilization of women's rights organizations in the wake of the slaughter of female engineering students in Montreal; mass demonstrations of Moroccan women to protest police violence against women after a police commissioner was convicted of raping more than 500 girls; and the takeover of highways in northern Buenos Aires by 300 women on foot and bicycles to protest privatization of Argentine highways.[45]

The news blackout is nearly total when women organize to address issues that involve structural exercises of elite male power. Examples can be found world-wide: women meeting in Japan to examine and redress the status of migrant workers and proxy brides; women in New York tracking the global prostitution industry; women in the Netherlands and Finland monitoring gender-related impacts of global trade and arms agreements; women in Mexico City organizing to address labor issues; women meeting in Brussels to examine the implications of the unification of the European Community.[46]

How many readers of this book know that women have established a feminist radio station, Radio Tierra, in Chile? How many know that they are producing and distributing feminist videos throughout the Americas?[47] How many know that women in Sri Lanka have formed underground media collectives to produce videos documenting human rights violations?[48] How many are aware that women in Uruguay have used the division in that country between commercial and non-commercial speech to win concessions from advertisers that have resulted in less sexist images of women in the media of that country?[49] How many know that the Manushi collective in India has published a successful magazine that confronts the oppression of women in that society?[50] Conversely, how many media scholars are aware that similar efforts in Kenya by the editorial staff of *Viva* magazine were halted by transnational advertising agencies? These agencies threatened to withdraw advertisements if the advertising-dependent magazine continued to address issues like prostitution, birth control, female circumcision, polygamy, and sex education.[51] How many know that the Asian-Pacific Institute for Broadcasting Development in Kuala Lumpur is distributing internationally a resource kit on changing media images of Asian women?

Such stories have low or no news value within the framing conventions of mainstream objective media. To locate such stories, readers must seek them out at the margins of journalism in feminist and leftist magazines and periodicals and in low- or no-budget newsletters. History will not be hung on a new hinge until the gender-related constituents of commercial news practices and the forms of power knowledge they represent are critically analyzed and reconstructed.

What Gender Analysis Makes Visible

In this section, I briefly identify and discuss three crises that either become visible or look quite different when they are examined through the lens of the global politics of the gender order.

Global Overpopulation

In a book that received extensive praise in U.S. media, *Preparing for the Twenty-first Century* (1993), Paul Kennedy examined demographic projections indicating that the world's population has more than doubled in the past forty years to 5.5 billion. Current projections indicate that it will reach between 7.6 and 9.4 billion by 2025, with most of that growth occurring among people currently living in developing nations. In Kennedy's dangerous world, imbalances between "richer and poorer societies form the backdrop to all other important forces for change that are taking place."[52] The developing nations will face famine, ecological devastation, and massive emigration, but Kennedy pointed out that the effects of the population explosion are also going to be very "painful for the richest one-sixth of the earth's population that now enjoys a disproportionate five-sixths of its wealth."[53]

Until the appearance of reviews of the Kennedy book, population issues had received very little coverage in the U.S. press since the early 1980s. Coverage had been so meager that some media treated Kennedy's thesis as if it were *news*, even though it drew on data that are readily available in undergraduate sociology textbooks. Why?

The absence of the population question on news agendas can be explained as extensions of both the domestic gender politics of the Reagan-Bush era (antichoice, antifeminist) and of U.S. global media dominance. Neither the Reagan and Bush administrations—which banned U.S. aid to international population planning agencies that condoned abortion in any way—nor U.S. advertising-driven commercial media had anything to gain by covering the population crisis, an issue that is tied to the right of women to control their reproductive capacities. To the contrary, in the highly politicized climate created by antichoice groups, it became a lose-lose issue. Putting it on the agenda could invite boycotts, loss of advertising revenues, and loss of votes.

To view the population issue as a national issue is, of course, absurd. Overpopulation in the developing world produces migration to the developed world. To view it as a gender-neutral problem is even more absurd. Women have babies.

Kennedy said nothing about global feminism in any of his well-informed 428 pages but devoted four pages to "The Role of Education and the Position of Women." He noted that for the developing world, "the evidence linking the depressed status of women to population explosion, acute poverty, and economic retardation seems clear."[54] In his view, education of women in the developing world is the essential key to solving the population explosion.

Who is depressing women? Who is denying them access to education? Kennedy did not take the next obvious analytic step. He did not see or analyze the gender-related constituents of the structures of power that are producing the ecological nightmare. As a result, Kennedy did not see an obvious ray of hope on the horizon: the global feminist movement, a movement committed to expanding women's literacy rates and reproductive choices. Research that focuses on human reproduction without analyzing the gender order does not have the power to analyze effectively the related constituents of international trade policies, employment practices of paranational corporations, the global communications and financial revolutions, the growing homogenization and commodification of culture, or international law.

Child Sex Trade in Poor Nations

The AIDS pandemic has received enormous global media coverage since the mid-1980s. Much of the coverage has, of course, been shown to reflect strong heterosexual and heterosexist biases.[55] Coverage of the AIDS crisis in Africa has also been widely criticized by both Africans and international media critics.[56]

The AIDS crisis is highly visible. Factors that remain relatively invisible are its impact on child slavery and prostitution in poor nations and the role men from prosperous nations are playing in dramatically increasing the sexual traffic in children.

Stories about prostitution are not usually framed as political news, let alone as international news. The single exception appears to be sex scandals involving princes and presidents. Routine practices in the sex trades are generally unreported or underreported. The roles global structural inequalities play in trafficking in children typically make the papers only when special commissions of the U.N. or human rights watch groups produce press releases. Such reports indicate that "child catchers" in poor countries like Thailand, Haiti, Bangladesh, the Philippines, Indonesia, and war-torn parts of Africa frequently purchase or kidnap children for employment in mines, plantations, and sex trades.[57]

An unintended side-effect of AIDS education, according to a 1993 UNESCO-sponsored conference, has been an increased demand for very young girls or boys, who are marketed by pimps as being clean or virgins. In Manila, Bangkok, Rio de Janiero, and Frankfurt, such children draw premium prices on the international sex market. In Vietnam, the influx of businessmen from Japan, Hong Kong, and Taiwan is generating a boom market in children. Statistics are both rare and of questionable reliability, but one UNESCO study estimated that 2 million Thai women work in the sex trades and that as many as 800,000 of them may be adolescents or children. The report indicated that the demand for young girls comes mainly from Asians, and the demand for young boys comes primarily from Westerners.[58] Another UNESCO study estimated that more than 10,000 boys between ages six and fourteen work as prostitutes in Sri Lanka, where most of their clientele are foreign men.[59]

The silence around this issue represents the routine workings of the news organizations under a gender order secured by hegemonic masculinity. The repellent practices of the international sex trades do not pose any *immediate* threats to manly men, their wives, or their children. (However, one version of this story finally made the papers because it contained an important advisory for elite male travellers: The preadolescent prostitutes of the developing world, no matter how young, are not clean and not free of the HIV virus or other sexually transmitted diseases.) The wall of silence shielding the sexual abuse of poor children and the long-term global health crisis their abuse precipitates become visible through the lens of gender-order theory.

Female Genocide in Bosnia

In response to activism by international women's organizations protesting "gynocide" in Bosnia, rape has finally been defined as a war crime.[60] Although sexual forms of torture, including rape, were documented at the Nuremberg trials, perpetrators were not prosecuted.[61]

Female gynocide in Bosnia represents an extreme case, one that is thoroughly repugnant to most men and women throughout the world. Naming it as a gender behavior marks a turning point in the history of war. Women have become historical agents by organizing, publicizing, and seeking international political condemnation of these acts as *war crimes*. In doing so, they are making visible a form of military aggression that has historically violated men as well as women. Because women were regarded as the property of men under patriarchy, rape not only brutalized and dehumanized enemy women but also robbed, emasculated, and demoralized enemy men. In short, it was a strategy that powerful males used to motivate their own troops and to dominate enemy males and all females.

Conclusion

War may be hell, as Ernest Hemingway claimed, but it is a form of hell that has some beneficiaries: the commanders, commissars, and capitalists on the winning side. The efforts of human rights, peace, and feminist organizations to make the gender order of war visible may make it more difficult for anyone to benefit and to stoke the fires of future hells. It may also make it more difficult to maintain the media blackout that marginalizes or erases women's politics qua politics.

A new journalism dedicated to breaking this code of silence is emerging in the wake of global feminism. As a result, the old Western journalistic establishment may be approaching the eleventh hour in its crisis of credibility if not of survival.

NOTES

1. The title of this chapter is a play on Cynthia Enloe's *Bananas, Beaches, and Bases: Making Feminist Sense of International Studies* (Berkeley: University of California Press, 1989). Without Enloe's groundbreaking work, this chapter could not have been written.

2. Susan Miller, "Opportunity Squandered: Newspapers and Women's News," *Media Studies Journal* (Winter/Spring 1993):167–182.

3. Certainly Gaye Tuchman did pioneering work in the study of gender and media. See Tuchman, "The Symbolic Annihilation of Women by the Mass Media," in Gaye Tuchman, Arlene Kaplan Daniels, and James Benet, eds., *Hearth and Home: Images of Women in Mass Media* (New York: Oxford University Press, 1978); Tuchman, *Making News: A Study in the Construction of Reality* (New York, 1978), and Tuchman, "Objectivity as a Strategic Ritual: An Examination of Newsmen's Notions of Objectivity," *American Journal of Sociology* 77, no. 4 (1978):660–679. This work laid the foundations for current social constructivist fem-

inist critiques of journalistic objectivity. Yet it left intact a self-privileging form of scientific objectivity that most contemporary feminist epistemologies no longer support.

4. Freedom Forum, "Who's Covering What in the Year of the Woman?" *Media Studies Journal* (Winter/Spring 1993):135.

5. Margaret Gallagher, *Unequal Opportunities: The Case of Women and the Media* (Paris: UNESCO, 1981), p. 71.

6. See also H. Leslie Steeves, "Gender and Mass Communication in a Global Context," in Pamela J. Creedon, ed., *Women in Mass Communication: Challenging Gender Values* (Newbury Park: Sage Publications, 1989), p. 91.

7. Miller, "Opportunity Squandered," p. 172.

8. Freedom Forum, "Who's Covering What," p. 138.

9. Miller, "Opportunity Squandered," p. 169.

10. Kay Mills, "The Media and the Year of the Woman," *Media Studies Journal* (Winter/Spring 1993):20.

11. Ibid. p. 29.

12. Enloe, *Bananas, Beaches, and Bases,* pp. 3–4.

13. Robert W. Connell, *Gender and Power* (Stanford: Stanford University Press, 1987).

14. Although Gayle Rubin in a classic article, "The Traffic in Women: Notes on the Political Economy of Sex," in *Toward an Anthropology of Women* (New York: Monthly Review Press, 1975), identified and theorized this dynamic long before Connell, Connell's formulation is nevertheless more extensively developed. It is particularly useful since it recognizes that the global pattern of subordination of women in industrial societies is nevertheless negotiated and accommodated in culturally specific ways. Women are not passive objects in this *sex trade.* In *Gender and Power,* pp. 183–184, Connell noted: "One form is defined around compliance with this subordination and is oriented to accommodating the interests and desires of men. I will call this *emphasized feminity.* Others are defined centrally by strategies of resistance or forms of non-compliance. Others again are defined by complex strategic combinations of compliance, resistance and co-operation. The interplay among them is a major part of the dynamics of the gender order as a whole."

15. Stuart Hall, "Brave New World," *Marxism Today* (October 1988):29.

16. Connell, *Gender and Power,* pp. 17–18.

17. Ibid., p. 18.

18. E. P. Thompson, "End and the Beginning: History Turns on a New Hinge," *The Nation,* January 28, 1990, p. 120.

19. Ibid., p. 120.

20. Brian Easlea, *Fathering the Unthinkable: Masculinity, Scientists, and the Nuclear Arms Race* (London: Pluto Press, 1983).

21. Helen Caldicott, *Missile Envy: The Arms Race and Nuclear War* (New York: Morrow, 1984).

22. Carol Cohn, "Sex and Death in the Rational World of Defense Intellectuals," *Signs* 12, no. 4, (1987):687–718.

23. Enloe, *Bananas, Beaches, and Bases.*

24. Thompson, "End and the Beginning," p. 120.

25. Abouali Farmanfarmaian, "Sexuality in the Gulf War: Did You Measure Up?" *Genders* 13 (Spring 1992):1–29.

26. Even Fidel Castro has sent some mixed signals in speeches and interviews.

27. Enloe, *Bananas, Beaches, and Bases,* p. 12.

28. Easlea, *Fathering the Unthinkable.*

29. Cohn, "Sex and Death."

30. Evelyn Fox Keller, *Reflections on Gender and Science* (New Haven: Yale University Press, 1985).

31. Conversely, the presence of this homoerotic element in the mythos of the Cold War gender order may, in turn, explain the centrality of its taboo on practicing homosexuality. Perhaps the idea could be entertained without threatening the dominance of manly men, only if homosexual acts were strictly proscribed.

32. Enloe, *Bananas, Beaches, and Bases,* pp. 12–13.

33. E. J. Dionne Jr., "'Defense Intellectuals' in a New World Order: Rand Analysts Rethink the Study of Conflict," *Washington Post,* May 29, 1990.

34. George Gerbner, "Instant History: The Case of the Moscow Coup," *Political Communication* 10 (Spring 1993):185–194.

35. Thompson, "End and the Beginning," p. 117.

36. Vaclav Havel, "The End of the Modern Era," *New York Times,* March 1, 1992, p. E15.

37. Ibid., p. E15.

38. James Hillman, *The Myth of Analysis* (New York: Harper and Row, 1972), p. 250.

39. Enloe, *Bananas, Beaches, and Bases,* p. 195.

40. C. Wright Mills, *The Sociological Imagination* (New York: Oxford University Press, 1959).

41. Enloe, *Bananas, Beaches, and Bases,* p. 195.

42. Ibid.

43. Herber Marcuse, *An Essay on Liberation* (Boston: Beacon Press, 1969), p. 73.

44. Enloe, *Bananas, Beaches, and Bases,* p. 200.

45. Catherine MacKinnon, "Turning Rape into Pornography: Postmodern Genocide," *Ms* (July/August 1993):24–30.

46. Enloe, *Bananas, Beaches, and Bases,* p. 1089; Angharad Valdivia, "International Communications and Feminist Studies," *Feminist Scholarship Interest Group Newsletter, International Communication Association* (Spring 1993).

47. Valdivia, "International Communications."

48. "Women Breaking the Silence," *Index on Censorship* 19, no. 9 (October 1990):2, 7–36.

49. Valdivia, "International Communications."

50. Steeves, "Gender and Mass Communication."

51. Gallagher, *Unequal Opportunities;* Steeves, "Gender and Mass Communication."

52. Paul Kennedy, *Preparing for the Twenty-first Century* (New York: Random House, 1993), p. 46.

53. Ibid., p. 46.

54. Ibid., p. 341.

55. Randy Shilts, *And the Band Played On: Politics, People, and the AIDS Epidemic* (New York: St. Martin's Press, 1987).

56. *Assignment Africa,* written by Belinda Cowdy and David Royle, an *Inside Story* special edition produced by David Royle, New York, New Atlantic Productions, 1986, VHS videotape, 58 minutes.

57. Marlise Simons, "The Sex Market: Scourge on the World's Children," *New York Times,* April 9, 1993, p. A3.

58. Ibid.

59. Ibid.

60. Anna Quindlen, "Gynocide," *New York Times,* April 9, 1993, p. A15.

61. MacKinnon, "Turning Rape into Pornography."

11

The New World Intellectual Order

JOHAN GALTUNG

The world is shrinking, they say. So is the space between the components of gun-powder when hit by a hammer. If there is only one component present, maybe it is not so dangerous, only tight. But a very different matter emerges if the mix is potentially explosive and the components start interacting.

Human capacity to take differences well is limited. There is comfort in inter-acting with a mirror image of Self; behind differences dangers may be lurking. No doubt the capacity to accept the different Other may be expanded—through pos-itive experiences, by cultivating the spirit of "you are different from me, how fas-cinating, what can we learn from each other?" (and not "you are different from me, how dangerous, how can I change, teach, convert, control, eliminate you!")—through education. But these are long-term projects. And we are dealing with soon 6 billion humans divided into about 2,000 nations in 200 states (including 20 nation-states).

Simple reasoning applies to well-known fault lines in the human construction, such as gender and generation, race and class, religion and language; the latter is the raw material for nation constructs. In this chapter, another cultural category will be explored: epistemology, intellectual style. What do major groups see as valid knowledge? How does that shape behavior, including internation behavior? And how can that constitute fault lines for future upheavals?

On the New World Order: A World of Civilizations

By the "new world order," I shall mean the post–Cold War organization of the world in hegemons, with their hegemonic systems, not all of them equally crystallized at present (late 1994) but sufficiently so for reasonable hypotheses to be formed.[1] More particularly, the basic hypothesis is that the successor system to the Cold

War—which was bipolar, although the Third World at times was strong enough to act as a third pole—is a seven-polar world, or more correctly, seven unipolar regions in conflict and cooperation, to some extent lorded over by the hegemons' hegemon—the United States of America. Among the seven (or eight) are some that are potentially in ascendancy as superpowers (indicated here by the symbol +):

United States: Protestant, the Western Hemisphere, Middle East
European Union (EU): Catholic, the rest of Europe, the Africa-Caribbean-Pacific system
Russia+: the Slavic-Orthodox parts of the former Soviet Union
Turkey+: Muslim parts of the former Soviet Union, Iran, Pakistan, Afghanistan
India+: Hindu, over South Asia parts of the former British Empire
China: Buddhist-Confucian, over itself, possibly minus Tibet
Japan: Buddhist-Confucian, a *dai-to-a* (Great East Asian Coprosperity Sphere) with China, Korea, Vietnam

In addition, there is a very important regional power:

Israel: Judaic, over itself, possibly minus Palestine, Golan Heights

With the exception of Japan, all of them, as far as we know, are nuclear powers. But that is not the aspect to be discussed. They are also civilizational powers, with the power to program vast parts of humanity and to organize intellect, not only to disorganize matter. In saying this, we are following the line of Ali Bhutto, then Pakistan's minister of energy, when in 1973 he referred to a possible Pakistani nuclear capability as an "Islamic bomb."[2]

If, instead of geography and countries, we use civilizations as the point of departure, we get five instead of eight:

1. **Christian:** U.S., EU, Russian versions
2. **Muslim**
3. **Jewish**
4. **Hindu**
5. **Buddhist-Confucian:** Chinese, Japanese versions

"West" is here taken to mean U.S. and European Christian; "East" means Russian Christian; "Occident" means Christian, Muslim, and Jewish; and "Orient" means Buddhist-Confucian.

Two of the civilizations are divided: Christianity among three major powers to some extent corresponding to the three branches of Christianity (Protestantism in its WASP fashion, the basically Catholic European Union, and Orthodoxy) and Buddhism-Confucianism between two (the Daoist and the Shintoist countries).

In truly global, as opposed to merely regional, struggles along civilizational lines, the divided civilizations—Christian and Buddhist-Confucian—will probably come together economically, militarily, politically, with the cultural substratum as crystallization nucleus.

The world system has in its midst something approximating a state in a national system, the United Nations, which means that who owns the U.N. at least owns some of the world. A corollary, rather obvious, is that we are probably in for a major struggle over U.N. ownership—in other words, some kind of world revolution. Several contenders may announce their claims, sometimes backed up with more than voting power: the non-U.S. West (meaning the European); the non-West (meaning Russia+, Turkey+, India+, China, Japan); the non-Occident (meaning India+, China, Japan); the Orient (meaning China, Japan); the non-hegemons (meaning the United Peripheries, of all seven hegemons);[3] the peoples (meaning a future United Nations Peoples' Assembly). The last two possibilities are perhaps more remote. But struggle among the hegemons is a very clear and present reality. The only problem is how it will shape up and how the struggle will shape the world.

On Cosmology, Epistemology, and Intellectual Style

By "cosmology," I mean deep culture,[4] the very basic assumptions of a civilization, not artifacts, not the countless schools and individual variations, but something more solid. By "epistemology," I mean a basic part of the cosmology, basic assumptions about what constitutes valid knowledge, maybe with some ontology, assumptions about reality. By "intellectual style," I mean the way epistemology expresses itself in the verbal behavior of intellectuals, academics as well as laypeople.[5] Cosmology is the broadest of the three concepts, epistemology focuses on *episteme,* and intellectual style underlies what is ultimately expressed. All three are constructs to be refined and redefined by developing theories ultimately to be tested along their edges.

I shall use the following scheme to arrive at a typology for the *episteme:*

Episteme I	Monism: The real and the ideal are inseparable;
	Dualism: The real and the ideal exist separately
Episteme II	Contradictory versus noncontradictory reality
	Contradictory versus noncontradictory discourse, speech
Episteme III	Deductivism: a priori reasoning, from *ratio*
	Inductivism: a posteriori reasoning, empirically based

This discourse, or something similar to it, is indispensable for discussing intellectual style. However, what I attempt in this chapter is to show that a discourse of that kind is also indispensable for discussing how knowledge is validated around the world, which in turn is indispensable for understanding how power is organized around the world. In other words, even a short excursion into philosophy may carry us far into geopolitics.

Episteme I.   The basic point about philosophical dualism, from this point of view, is not abstraction, for instance based on generalization to arrive at universals. It is hard to see how life would be possible if humans (and also other forms of life) saw all situations, including from one second to the next, one degree of viewing angle to the next, in terms of *particularia,* with no carryover of some *universalia,* some essence, some generalization, by necessity abstract, meaning detached from the concrete and the particular, from one situation to the next. Of course we impute invariances. Of course we do not see everything new "in a new light." Of course there are halo effects.

But the point is whether we attribute to this idealized, abstract essence a separate existence somewhere. Is the essence separable, in one way or the other, from the concrete, particular reality around us? If yes, where is it (apart from in our mind, which, as mentioned, is trivial)? To postulate hypotheses about the concrete, or to proclaim norms prescribing ideal behavior, is not tantamount to saying that there is somewhere a world that follows these hypotheses and fulfills these norms.

The answers handed over from this medieval, scholastic debate—*in rebus,* within the thing, the treeishness in the tree, and *ante rem,* before or independent of the thing—leaves out neither-nor and both-and: Inside it is an ideal waiting to be liberated, the pure type that has been caught in the impurities of this world, the noise, random or not. A strong faith in the reality of this *ante rem in rebus* may make one see it, hear it, smell it as the real reality, but only temporarily, and only for those who are unable to see, hear, and so on, overshadowed by concrete noise. For example, for some 2,500 years, we have been seeing Euclidean shapes everywhere, lines and planes and right angles and triangles and circles, although it is plainly evident to the naked eye (but then, which eye is really naked, meaning unguided?) that this is not nature's geometry at all.[6] Instead, we construct houses and cities with planes and right angles and all that, including circular plazas and roundabouts, shaping the real in the image of the ideal.[7]

Philosophical monism would deny the separability of the two, defining as real the sense-able (capable of being sensed, Sorokin: *sensate*) or the idea-able (capable of being expressed as an ideal, Sorokin: *ideational*) but not both separately (for Sorokin, that would be the *idealistic*).[8]

Episteme II.   The issue of the contradictory versus the noncontradictory, unfortunately, uses the term (*contra dicere*) that has built into it a bias in favor of language analysis rather than empirical (intersubjectively observed, communicated, and reproduced) reality.

For the discourse, it means a proposition and its negation. For empirical reality, it means the presence of incompatible goal-states in the same goal-seeking system—in other words, conflict. We shall use both meanings and arrive at four combinations (Table 11.1).

Table 11.1.   Empirical Contradiction, Contradiction in Speech

	Empirical World	
	Contradictory	Noncontradictory
Speech contradictory	Daoism	Talmud?
Speech noncontradictory	Mathematics?	Cartesianism

Daoism departs from the assumption that there are yin-yang contradictions everywhere, including in yin and yang, leading to an infinite regress of a Chinese-boxes view of reality. Daoism also uses contradictory language, a reason why reading *Dao de ching* is such a delight. Thus, a principle of *adequatio* may be at work: Only contradictory (discourse) can mirror contradictory (reality).

The Talmud could serve as the archetypical example of *pro et contra dicere*, even typographically, with texts within texts within texts and so on. But from that it does not follow that readers view reality as contradictory. Reality could be non-contradictory, consistent, only that there are different views as to what this non-contradictory reality is, as expressed in dialogues *sans fin*. There is no final answer, as that would be tantamount to assuming that ultimate reality is within the reach of the human mind. A final answer is tantamount to dogmatism: The issue is settled.

Mathematical modeling would be based on the opposite pattern. Mathematics as a discourse carries with it a ban on contradictions, not to be confused with undecidability (Godel) or polyvalent logic (the theorems are formulated in bivalent logic). But assuming that reality has a yin-yang character, how can the noncontradictory be used as a model of something contradictory, except in the small, and in the very specific, where contradictions may be minor?

Finally, there is the second epistemologically consistent category of having the noncontradictory reflect the noncontradictory. "Your speech should be yes,yes or no,no,"[9] presumably because reality is (yes,yes) or it is not (no,no). If reality is and is not at the same time, then the speech may be yes,no. Roughly speaking, that is the Daoist position and definitely not a hard-line Aristotelian-Cartesian position of *contradiction = error*, in speech, in observing reality, or both.

Episteme III.   An examination of deduction versus induction demonstrates that deduction departs from axioms and rules of inference, such as *tertium non datur*, the axioms are either true or false. As the inference is either valid or invalid, then, by *modus ponens*, the conclusions are also either true or false, meaning that the whole system (also known as a theory) is consistent, harboring no contradictions. Induction, as a process, presupposes data (sense-impressions) *particularia* and then proceeds to establish *universalia*, possibly linking them together in hypotheses to be tested. If confirmed hypotheses can be correctly inferred, and correctly inferred hypotheses can be confirmed, then we have an inductive-deductive system.[10]

Intellectual Styles Around the World I:
Occident-Hindu-Orient

From a combination of the preceding sections, the task ahead is easily defined: a description of the intellectual styles of the eight hegemons (including Israel more for reasons of intellectual than political hegemony). The task is made easier by the circumstance that in today's post–Cold War world, the hegemonic systems, so the hypothesis, are essentially civilizational systems. That they also turn out to be carriers of relatively distinct intellectual styles is a tautology but a tautology with deep geopolitical implications.

I start by painting with a very broad brush indeed, dividing the world into *Occident, Hindu,* and *Orient,* with *Occident* and *Orient* as megacivilizations; the former comprises (here, by definition) the Christian, the Muslim, and the Jewish, the latter the Chinese and the Japanese and not everything "east of Europe" or some other geographism. Thus, Indonesia and the Philippines are obviously not in the Orient by the definition used here, being Muslim and Catholic. Table 11.2 serves only as a preliminary overview, to be refined and modified immediately. The positions taken here are as follows:

The Occident Is Basically Dualist.   Human reality is divided in two, body and soul; the soul, eternal, being the carrier of the real person, waiting to be liberated (by death). The world is divided in two, this side and the other side; the other side (itself coming in two versions, up and down) being the more real, being the carrier of eternity, waiting to be liberated (by apocalypse). Each side, the temporal and the eternal, has its own noncontradictory logic to be expressed in noncontradictory discourses. When the essence has been properly grasped by the ratio, then deductive reasoning is appropriate. If not, some inductive reasoning may be in order, as a first guide to reality.

The Orient Is Basically Monist.   There is no soul, eternal and individual; no heaven or hell; there is life and the effort to make the best of it, including improving oneself for the sake of the family, clan, system (Confucianism), or all life (Buddhism).

Reality is filled with contradictions, cut through with fault lines (Daoism). Adequate speech should also be contradictory, whether in the semantics through

Table 11.2.   World Intellectual Styles I

	Occident	Hindu	Orient
Separability	Yes	Both-and	No
Contradiction, speech	No	Both-and	Yes
Contradiction, empirical	No	Both-and	Yes
Deductive-inductive	Both-and	Both-and	Inductive

enigmatic expressions such as the *koan,* riddle (Chinese), or already built into the syntax (Japanese).[11] As deduction presupposes contradiction-free discourses, deduction *strictu sensu* is only meaningful in discourses like mathematics, which only in a very limited way can reflect a contradictory reality. Reasoning, hence, will basically have to be inductive.

Hinduism Is Basically Eclectic. It combines all of the above and provides possibly the richest set of metaphors-archetypes in the world.

Intellectual Styles Around the World II: Judaism-Christianity-Islam

The next step is to differentiate the preceding Big Three in the direction of the eight we are supposed to characterize, five of them in the Occident (Protestant, Catholic, Orthodox, Muslim, Jewish) and two of them in the Orient (Chinese, Japanese).

Differentiating the Occident according to the three religions of the *kitab*— roughly Old Testament Christianity, Islam, and Judaism—reveals some basic differences, not similarities (Table 11.3). All three cases involve belief systems that command allegiance as the only truth. Then, in addition to being singularist, Christianity and Islam are also universalist, valid for the whole world, forever. Judaism is for Jews, however. Conversion into Judaism is problematic and proselytism rare, to say the least. Moreover, Judaism is hardly dualist, or at least much less so than the other two, soul-heaven-hell being more metaphorical, less a reality, even the salient reality, as for the other two. What is real is *Zion, Eretz Israel,* the Promised Land for the Chosen People. With recognition of Palestine, not only the Palestine Liberation Organization, that Other Reality may become more liberated than it ever was for the 3,000 years ensuing after Israel I (1000–920 B.C.).

But the particularity of Judaism within the Occident goes further. The polyprophetism is as pronounced as the monotheism, meaning that even if there is only a single Yahweh, what can be said about him is pluralistic; there is this view, there is that view.[12] And even if the Talmud is concluded as a book, the Talmudic tradition of *pro et contra dicere* continues, forever, there being no final word. Just as the Torah tradition constitutes the archetype for the chosen-people-promised-land concept, the Talmud tradition constitutes the archetype for intellectual pursuits. No minor contributions to humankind, or at least to the Occident, are these two, the latter perhaps more applaudable than the former.

Table 11.3. World Intellectual Styles II

	Judaism	*Christianity*	*Islam*
God	Monotheistic	Polytheistic	Monotheistic
Prophets	Polyprophetic	Monoprophetic	Monoprophetic

Even if reality may be noncontradictory, speech can be contradictory. The total tradition of contradictory speech is what matters, not one noncontradictory prophet alone. The Christian profile, as described here, is the opposite. The theoscape is pluralistic, with a contradiction between the masculine (God the Father, Jesus Christ the Son, and the Holy Spirit?) and the more compassionate feminine (Maria the Mother). Protestantism is less contradictory deemphasizing the feminine. In monoprophetism one might expect efforts to arrive at the ultimate understanding of what that single prophet, the Christ, said. That search has, in principle, an *Endzustand*—an end state—through asymptotic convergence.[13]

Islam is the purest type, monotheistic and monoprophetic.[14] The theoscape is noncontradictory and not easily understood. But there is an equally noncontradictory and infallible guide, the Prophet, *al rasul*. In this respect, Islam is not that different from Protestantism.

What happens when the three secularize? The faith in a personal God, accessible through prayer, in an eternal soul, and in eternal salvation and damnation disappears (in Judaism the last elements are less important anyhow). But what is left is considerable:

Judaism: a possibly noncontradictory, monist, nonseparable reality, best understood through an ongoing, contradictory discourse combining deductive and inductive reasoning.

Christianity: noncontradictory, dualist, separable realities, possibly one within the other waiting for purification or pure circumstances, best understood through noncontradictory speech, deduction being the adequate style for potential reality, induction for empirical reality. As there are *Zwei Regimenten,* two regimes, God's and Caesar's, there are also two intellectual regimes, with inductive reasoning being more prominent in the Saxonic intellectual style and deductive reasoning more prominent in the Teutonic-Gallic intellectual style.[15] As the Saxonic (essentially the United Kingdom and the United States, with Cambridge I, England, and Cambridge II, Massachusetts, among the intellectual capitals) is more Protestant, or at least less Catholic, one might speculate that individualism gives people more freedom to follow the leads of their sense impressions rather than the dogma derived from hierarchy *ratio*. Because they admit some contradiction, Orthodox and Catholic theoscapes may also serve as more realistic guides to empirical reality, meaning that deductive reasoning from more complex first principles (e.g., about human frailty) may render deeper insights. A good guide based on deduction presupposes wisdom; induction presupposes only knowledge.

Islam: noncontradictory and nonseparable dualist realities in which the temporal can be brought to approximate the eternal by imposing the *shari'ah*, best understood through noncontradictory speech. Subdivision would bring out more differentiated views.[16]

So do I side with those who say that Islam tends to be dogmatic and fundamentalist? In a sense yes, but with four comments:

1. Thinkers in the Islamic world can of course be intellectuals as much as any others if by that is meant the never-ending ability to question assumptions, including one's own, as in the Talmudic exercise. But I doubt that they are intellectuals qua Muslims. To say "Allah the Compassionate and the Merciful" may prove that the writer or speaker has some allegiance to Islam, but any intellectualism may be in spite of rather than because of it.[17]

2. That Islam is "dogmatic" in the sense of being nonempirical does not necessarily make it bad: The doctrine could be superb in terms of its consequences, when enacted, in the natural, human, social, and world spaces. Whether it is, is another story.

3. That Islam is "fundamentalist" in the sense of believing in its own dogma and in the face of Western cultural, economic, and military power does not necessarily make it bad either, but may prove that some people are real believers, not hypocrites.

4. If "dogmatic fundamentalism" means an apodictic faith in the superiority of an ideal world, to be imposed upon the empirical world come what may, then this is also a Western characteristic that has survived secularization. Two exemplars: the legal system, municipal and international, and *mainstream economics*.

Intellectual Styles Around the World:
An Overview

We are now ready to reap the harvest of these more preliminary explorations: a mapping of intellectual styles on the seven (eight) hegemons with a focus on male elites.

1. **The U.S. hegemonic system.** The U.S. elite has been characterized as WASP, (white, Anglo-Saxon, Protestant). This is probably still valid to a large extent, although the importance of Jewish intellectualism—the Jews after the first aliyah being an important component of the intelligentsia of the country—is considerable, more important than their alleged economic power.

Dualism and separability are expressed in a high level of idealism, both in the sense of sacrifice for ideals and in the sense of belief in the nonempirical. Behaviorist reward-punishment models will direct the use of the carrot and the stick, assuming a universal human rationality along individual cost-benefit lines, for social behavior of individuals, economic behavior of economic actors, and world behavior of states.[18] That in the real world values could differ, that the evaluation of the values could differ, even to the point of changing sign or having infinite utility (absolute values), will cause hardly a dent in the models.[19] Rather, the world will be interpreted so as to fit the models. More work will be put into making the models noncontradictory (consistent) than making them reflect reality.

But dualism also expresses itself as "barefoot empiricism," a never-ending search for more data, not necessarily to confirm or disconfirm any theory but just to know. Data banks will abound.

The level of accurate, concrete knowledge will be high. Careful induction will be engaged in, not even theories of "the middle range" but low-level generalizations. Biography, sociography, and geography become inexhaustible empirical bases.[20]

How can these styles coexist, the styles that elsewhere have been referred to as Teutonic and Saxonic?[21] One way would be as the "inductive-deductive style," perhaps more pronounced in the Nordic intellectual style. Another way would be as "eclecticism," as two ways of being intellectual within the same mind. And a third, and for our purposes the most important way, would be as two intellectual styles in the same society; in that case deductive would be for the elites and inductive for the people, the latter presumably having their deductive inclinations satisfied religiously. And, possibly, deductive-inductive would be in the middle, as in the Nordic countries, also in the middle. General conclusion: There will probably be little or low elite learning, if learning is defined as letting experience from the empirical world have an impact on deductive, rationalist schemes.

2. **The European hegemonic system.** As long as this system is run by a Germany-France axis, with the Teutonic-Gallic intellectual style high up in the system, ideal models will have considerable staying power over and above data ("facts"). Of course, there is an undercurrent of the Saxonic, particularly in England, meaning that England and other countries in northern Europe constitute an epistemologically subversive fifth column, some kind of empiricist resistance movement against the schemes deduced from first principles by the German-French (and particularly the latter, less Americanized?) elites. A political split will usually be explained in terms of political and economic controversies over the distribution of new power and profit; for these, an explanation in terms of epistemology may be more appropriate and at any rate deeper.

3. **Russia+.** Christian dualism will be accentuated by the Teutonic deductive intellectual style we can stipulate as an outcome of Russia because of its long tenure as an intellectual periphery of Germany. Utopias and abstract scientific models will attract true believers. The strongly dichotomous Bogomil tradition will favor strict dichotomous thinking, at the expense of dialectic thought,[22] and jumps in thought, ideology, and praxis. The distinction between the Western-oriented *zapadniki* and the people-oriented *narodniki* concerns only the source of inspiration: The former fetch their utopias from Marxism with local apostles (Lenin and Stalin) or from mainstream economics with Harvard professors and apostles,[23] and the latter derive theirs from the Russian tradition, the village community,[24] the Orthodox church, the lake, the birch tree forest, again with local apostles (Aleksandr Solzhenitsyn, Vladimir Zhirinovsky).

Thus, we get the three major factions of the more pluralistic Russia of today: the socialists, the capitalists, and the nationalists, all with the fascist overtones that derive from being carriers of a singular, universal truth. For democracy a higher level of inductive thinking is needed in order to see more clearly the flaws in the ideal, using empiricism as an antidote to dogma.

4. **Turkey+.** This is essentially a coming Islamic superpower, more likely to come out of the non-Arab than the Arab world given the divisions of the latter and the dynamism of the former. The Islamic aspect will become more pronounced in a process involving all the contradictions in pan-European space, divided into Catholic-Protestant, Orthodox, and Muslim with Yugoslavia and Bosnia as its meso- and microcosm model. The intellectual style will be dualist with a strong tendency to superimpose models and utopias, noncontradictory and deductive—in other words, like the Teutonic style but less tempered by Saxonic subversive empiricism.

5. **Israel.** Although the major impact of Jewish intellectualism, or primordial intellectualism, is felt in the United States and may be a major reason for the intellectual vitality of that country, we might expect interesting initiatives from an Israel liberated from its major trauma: of being not only colonialist but of treating the colonials, the Palestinians, as objects of displaced hatred of the Nazis. Being more monist and capable of harboring very contradictory speech (and thought, presumably), being both inductive and deductive in the sense of being theory builders but not in the sense of attributing to a world run by the axioms a separate existence, the Jews are ideally suited as intellectual guides in a very confusing and complex world. But the condition, as mentioned, is the liberation from the chosen-people-promised-land complex, in the sense of seeing Israel as one land among many, neither above nor below the rest. Maybe that perspective would help others see Israel the same way.

6. **India+.** The intellectual style is profoundly eclectic but with the hypothesis[25] (or suspicion!) that the Indian caste system is also epistemologically divided, between *brahmin* and *shudra,* between twice-born separatists, noncontradictory deductionists and nonseparatists, nonconsistents, inductionists of the lower orders. The eclecticism of the total system is nonintegrated, the strands being separated by enormous social differences. The net result may be confusion rather than something interesting for the world.

7. **China.** The message of the columns in Table 11.2 is that Buddhist-Confucian space is an epistemological counterpoint, not only a geographical antipode, to the West. In general, there is less separability between real and ideal. The professor of ethics who is a rascal in social life is not only doing wrong; he invalidates his theories.[26] The idea of separating theory and praxis or, say, macrolevel conflict from microlevel conflict is in principle alien to Chinese (and Japanese) thought. What follows from this is not necessarily high ideals meticulously followed but more realism in formulating ideas and ideals and more pragmatism in praxis in order not to become victims of separation. But that means facing a reality filled with contradiction, not only because of the conflict between real and ideal but because escape into a noncontradictory model of reality, as if it were empirical reality, is inadmissible. Speech has to reflect this, being less assertive and absolute than in the West, more "maybe-ish." More pragmatic, more inductive.

8. **Japan.** The same points made about China are applicable, possibly even more so. The system is also based on three teachings, *san fa,* with Shintoism instead of Chinese Daoism.[27]

Geopolitics as Encounters of Intellectual Styles

We now have eight intellectual styles, some of them very similar, some of them highly discrepant. How do they relate to each other? What happens when the carriers of these intellectual styles not only meet each other but also engage in serious dialogue, bearing in mind that the carriers are the elites from the major actors in the new world order? In other words, how does the intellectual order impact on the new world order?

Encounters among these intellectual styles could lead to twenty-eight possible combinations (Table 11.4). At this point we keep Israel out of it; being a giant in intellectual style is not the same as being in the world league of major world powers. We also brush aside the idea that all these elites have a common language, not only English in the trivial sense but the Saxonic intellectual style as mode of presentation and the more problematic aspects of the Occidental style at a deeper level of the consciousness. The appearance may be in this direction. However, this means only that the dialogue takes place somewhere else. I offer two concrete hypotheses about where: (1) inside the minds of bicultural persons, between the shallow Western style and the original style located deeper down; (2) between that bicultural person and others, inside the vernacular.

What passes for internationalization, talking one tongue, hence being of one mind, may mean only that the real dialogue is out of sight, like seeds under asphalt. Springing forth, sooner or later, leading to paralyzing dilemmas and bitter disputes. Fundamentalism.

Let us first clarify the basic assumptions, remembering all the time that the focus here is on intellectual style, not on all the other matters (myths, traumas, interests, etc.) that these powers may have at the back of their mind or at the tip of their silver tongues.

Table 11.4.   Encounters of Intellectual Styles: An Overview

	United States	EU	Russia+	Turkey+	India+	China	Japan
United States	1	2	3	4	5	6	7
EU		8	9	10	11	12	13
Russia+			14	15	16	17	18
Turkey+				19	20	21	22
India+					23	24	25
China						26	27
Japan							28

One assumption would be that the combination of separable, noncontradictory reality with noncontradictory deduction (SNND) as the dominant intellectual style is potentially dangerous. An idealist world will be imprinted on adherents' minds, sometimes even referred to as "realist," from there to be imprinted on the empirical world. There is blindness to the fault lines in the real world; the speech opens for no fruitful ambiguity where doubts may be rooted; the line of reasoning is flawless. The construction is perfect—and that is the problem. However, a caveat: We do not know whether the human mind is inherently incapable of conceiving of a utopia whose perfection would presuppose the imperfect, more contradictory, less deductive. But that is hardly the Occident!

It is the devotion to the Islamic idealist scheme that evokes so many fears in the United States, the EU, and Russia+. The blindness of these regions to their own tendency to do exactly the same is interesting; consider the fundamentalist devotion to "free market principles" in the United States, to "rule of law, national and international," in the EU, and to "socialism-communism" in Russia until recently (Russia is now switching to the other two fundamentalisms). The *maya* (veil) for the eyes of the non-Islamic Occident has the word "secularization" engraved on it; the faith or hope that dualism and separability will prevail and that fundamentalist faith and devotion will disappear with secularization. Secularists fail to see that this also applies to their own fundamentalisms.

That argument is usually backed up with the idea that these are not apodictic truths but are theories on trial, to be tested in practice. The argument disregards the way in which devotion to the axioms of a secular system may attain religious character, causing both imaginative blindness to the many disconfirmations and a general rejection of any need to test anything. The truths have become apodictic. And yet there may be more willingness to test and pay serious attention to disconfirmations in the West than in the rest of the Occident, Russian (Slav-Orthodox) as well as Islamic. There is a recessive undercurrent of separable, noncontradictory reality combined with noncontradictory induction (SNNI), mainly in the Saxonic regions.

At the other extreme is the MCCI syndrome, monism combining contradictory speech for a contradictory world with a generally inductive mode of reasoning. By and large this is seen as typical of the Orient, both in its Chinese and Japanese articulations. And then there is the Hindu eclectic style, which combines all the other styles.

The scheme can now be simplified to four intellectual styles only—SNND, SNNI, Hindu, and MCCI—as show in Table 11.5 (the numbers from Table 11.4 fit into the appropriate cells). Instead of twenty-eight relationships, there are now only ten to consider, but for some of them we have to resort to Table 11.4 for more refined explorations.

Table 11.5 spells nothing good for a major geopolitical triangle possibly taking shape on the European continent in the wake of the Cold War: the EU-Russia+-Turkey+ triangle. Because the regions are polarized economically as center versus

Table 11.5.   Encounters of Intellectual Types: An Overview

	SNND	SNNI	Hindu	MCCI
Separable, noncontradictory, noncontradictory, deductive (EU, Russia+, Turkey+)	EU-Russia+-Turkey+ Triangle	Triangle to the United States	Triangle to Hindu	Triangle to Orient
Separable, noncontradictory, noncontradictory, inductive (United States)		Intra–United States	U.S.-Hindu	U.S.-Orient
Hindu			Intra-Hindu	Hindu-Orient
Monist contradictory, contradictory, inductive (China, Japan)				Intra-Orient

periphery, and politically as EU and NATO members versus the marginalized, and are militarily given to mutual suspicion, keeping arms "just in case," spiraling trilateral arms races will bring into the open the deep cultural schisms.

Of course, the schisms have been there all the time but have to some extent been hidden under a veneer of secular economic (free market) and political (democracy) discourses. And since the acronym "SNND" stands for "true believer," we would expect the discourse to be about these beliefs, in the old form of religious beliefs, in the modern form of secular beliefs in different economic and political systems, and in the form of mixed interaction with one party being religious and the other secular.

The basic point about the intellectual styles that are mobilized to carry these faiths into the open is the lack of space for compromises. There are too many first principles involved, such as departing from the Bible or the Koran, from Adam Smith or Karl Marx. Augustine had the useful formula: *Credo quia absurdum,* I believe because it is absurd. There will be much *absurdum* and much *credo* in these debates.

Is the United States different? Perhaps not when it comes to "market principles" and "free trade" or to the U.S. secular religion with the United States itself as God.[28] But there is a pragmatic current both underneath and on the surface, possibly derived from the more plebeian origins of the U.S. emigrants from

Europe.[29] On the other hand, what will be openly at stake in the EU-Russia+-Turkey+ interface will probably be precisely the aspects about which the United States is at its most apodictic: the economic and political orders.

This U.S. deductive-inductive mix, which features both true believers and true pragmatists, should go well with the Hindu mix, even if its members are more separated by class than in the United States. They will understand and value positively, having both a faith and a distance to that faith. Because this reflects the Saxonic style, one might add that it was good luck India was colonized by the British. Had it been from the continent, the clashes would have been more pronounced, and a Gandhi treating law as if it were a scientific hypothesis—he conducted "Experiments with Truth,"[30] including with the law—would hardly have been possible.

But these clashes should be even more pronounced in the MCCI Orient, which is both very pragmatic and very contradictory. For the Occident that pattern is hard to understand. There must be some faith in an ideal existence somewhere, some paradise, some utopia. Words are then picked up. A Chinese (meaning Oriental) "communist" party must necessarily stand for the same as a Russian (meaning Occidental) communist party, with a relatively clear image of the *Endzustand:* the communist society. It does not.

The notion that "communist society" could be an experimental hypothesis whose proponents take for granted that it will be revised in the light of experience would be difficult to believe and strains credulity. Additional strain will be provided by the many contradictions in speech and references to reality as contradictory,[31] all of this neatly summarized under the heading of "Orientals are devious." The flip side of this, the Oriental view of the Occident, will be in terms of extreme rigidity, hypocrisy (people preaching an ideal without even trying to practice it, claiming that "time is not yet ripe"), a clarity of speech out of touch with the fuzziness of reality, hence naïveté and reckless, shortsighted behavior. With both-and Hindus, however, there can be more understanding.

What about the relation intra-Orient? Of course, that China and Japan share intellectual style does not mean agreement, as little as it does for intra-Occident. Interests and values are still there, structures and actors. There may be less of the true believer and the image of the other as true believer, however. There may be more meeting ground in the sense of sitting down and talking it over, and also a longer time perspective and less of an urge to bridge the gap between the real and the ideal in one jump, a "shock therapy" as the free market believers in the World Bank tend to say (which of course results in more shock than therapy).

This is important, because it may be indicative of more cohesiveness in the pragmatic Orient than in the apodictic Occident. And, interestingly, there may be an argument for both the United States and India+ ending up closer to the pragmatic Orient than to the European Occident with its endless wars over—well, exactly over what? Basically just over one thing: not over different ways of seeing empirical reality but over different ways of seeing ideal reality. Wars of true believers, in other words, as seen by comparing the kind of wars envisaged by a Clausewitz and a Sun Tzu.

So far we have explored the styles of the seven hegemons but not their hinterland. How much misunderstanding, not to mention basic conflict over understanding of reality, is actually built into these hegemonic systems? The United States, for instance, believing itself to be mainly pragmatic, may think the Marxist idealism of the Latin American continent to be dead so U.S. believers can all meet in piecemeal realization of market principles.

They may be right that market idealism fits Catholic, Continental-style idealism, but they are not right that this is pragmatic, steered by broad and deep attention to empirical phenomena. Nor are they right in discounting the possibility that another idealism may soon appear in Latin America—for instance, religious fundamentalism instead of secular market fundamentalism. There may be more religious fundamentalism in the U.S. hinterland than Muslim fundamentalism in the Middle East, and some of it is right inside the United States, among people who used to say during the Reagan administration that they "had a friend in the White House."

The same applies to the European Union. To the extent EU members think of the rest of Europe as their hinterland, the Yugoslav experience should already have taught them what that means. Thus, if ideal reality is more real than empirical reality, and the EU lives in democracy and *Rechtsstaat*, nationally and internationally at the same time as Serbs, Croats, and Muslims are in ideal reality theoscapes—as chosen people enacting their myths with "pan" in front of their names for their countries—then the gap is considerable. The former Yugoslavs, less concerned with the details of empirical reality, will be perceived as liars by the EU. The EU members, in turn, will be seen as idealists, detached both from the empirical and the ideal reality of the combatants. Their epistemes are not different; they are very similar. And that is precisely the problem.

In the Africa-Caribbean-Pacific hinterland, however, the EU faces the problem of highly discrepant epistemes ready to surface, highly incompatible. A "backyard" asserting itself?

In a sense, eclectic Hinduism would be the ideal center of hegemonic systems, bridging them all. And China and Japan would be spared much of the problem by being so similar and also similar to the entire Buddhist-Confucian region. Again, the conclusion is one of cohesiveness in the Orient and not in the Occident.

What about the United Nations? If that is the homologue of the state in the international system, does it not stand to reason that it has to have a fairly cohesive intellectual style to operate? As I have been argued elsewhere, the solution to that problem has been found: the inductive Saxonic intellectual style as the style of the civil servants making "studies" and "reports," combined with the deductive Teutonic-Gallic intellectual style for people higher up, such as the higher echelons of the secretariat and the elites from the member states.[32] The reason is not that

English is so important as a world language, nor that British colonialism became one of the nuclei around which global governance could be built, nor that Americans and British together played a major role in the founding of the U.N. There is also a question of finding an intellectual style, the SNNI style, which permits collection of data without committing the data to the realization of a policy. That is the monopoly of the decision makers—hence the reflection of the general class nature of inductivism versus deductivism in such a large bureaucracy as the U.N.

And at that point, I prefer to stop. The assumption is that intellectual styles change very slowly if at all. Geopolitics is also geointellectualism, each causing the other. Hence, no serious geopolitical change will take place unless these geocultural roots are challenged, particularly in the Occident.

NOTES

1. See Johan Galtung, "The Emerging Conflict Formations," in K. Tehranian and M. Tehranian, eds., *Restructuring for World Peace on the Threshold of the Twenty-first Century* (Cresskill, NJ: Hampton Press, 1992). The essay was originally presented as a paper in June 1991. Also see Johan Galtung, "Geopolitical Transformations and the 21st Century World Economy," in K. Nordenstreng and H. Schiller, eds., *Beyond National Sovereignty: International Communication in the 1990s* (Norwood, NJ: Ablex, 1993), ch. 3, where the same argument is pursued for some of its economic implications.

2. In other words, the bomb may have more important geopolitical implications than in an Indo-Pakistani context only.

3. It might well be in their interest to found their own organization, particularly if the veto powers (United States, France, and Britain in the EC-EU and Russia and China) do not give up their veto and the other three (Turkey+, India+, and Japan) do not try to get one.

4. For some explorations, see Johan Galtung et al., "On the Last 2,500 Years in Western History and Some Remarks on the Coming 500," in Peter Burke, ed., *The New Cambridge Modern History,* vol. 13 (companion volume) (Cambridge: Cambridge University Press, 1979).

5. See Johan Galtung, "Intellectual Styles: Saxonic, Teutonic, Gallic, Nipponic," in Galtung, *Methodology and Development,* (Copenhagen: Ejlers, 1988), ch. 1.2, with further explorations in 1.3.

6. Benoit Mandelbrot's insistence on totally different geometries where the number of dimensions are *fractals* of integers—transcending Euclidean insistence on zero (point), one (line), two (plane), and so on, geometries—may well prove to be as significant for our views of reality as Einstein's breakthroughs earlier this century. Suddenly a geometrical language reflecting nature became available.

7. Does this mean that we shall soon come "back to nature" by building houses embodying some of the shapes of fractal geometries? More like adobe houses? Probably yes.

8. See Pitirim Sorokin, *Social and Cultural Dynamics* (Boston: Porter and Sargent, 1957), table 1, pp. 37–39.

9. Matthew 5:37: "Say just a simple 'Yes, I will' or 'No, I won't.'"

10. For one presentation, see Johan Galtung, "Theories," pt. 2, ch. 6, of Galtung, *Theory and Methods of Social Research* (New York: Columbia University Press, 1967).

11. See Johan Galtung and Fumiko Nishimura, "Structure, Culture, and Languages: An Essay Comparing the Indo-European, Chinese, and Japanese Languages," *Social Science Information* (1983):885–925.

12. Raphael Patai, in his *The Jewish Mind* (New York: Scribner's, 1977), identified this as one factor in explaining Jewish "Giftedness and Genius" (chapter 12 of the book): "Inquisitiveness and argumentativeness—both related to 'a skeptical frame of mind'— have been Jewish mental characteristics for many centuries, nurtured by a concentration in halakhik study with its method of *pilpul,* questioning and arguing over apparently contradictory statements contained in the Talmud" (p. 333). But Patai added that for this talent to be brought to bear on the more general human intellectual enterprise, not only the *Halakha,* the Jews had to join the world or to be let into the world, which for Patai was the sixth of the great encounters the Jews had with the Gentile world, from the Enlightenment (chapter 9).

13. This is probably still the basic model for intellectual pursuits: We come closer and closer—just one more foundation grant and we shall close the gap between pursuit and final truth. The convergence toward such constants as the equivalence between mechanical and heat energy (Joule) or as absolute zero (Kelvin) are used as inspiring models. But such models may be irrelevant given paradigm changes in the search for "truth," "knowledge," "insight."

14. For interesting explorations of the Islamic assumptions, see Raphael Patai, "The Islamic Component of Arab Personality," in Patai, *The Arab Mind* (New York: Scribner's, 1973), ch. 9, pp. 143–155; and Basil Bernstein, "Thoughts on the Trivium and the Quadrivium," in Donald Broady, ed., *Education in the Late Twentieth Century* (Stockholm: Stockholm Institute of Education Press, 1992), pp. 9–16.

15. Galtung, "Intellectual Styles," p. 32.

16. Thus, the bias I have because I am a product of the West shows up clearly in naming subdivisions for the West and not for the other parts of the Occident. Where is sufism, for instance? In short, let this serve only as a very simplistic and distorted first guide.

17. The comparison would probably be to ritualistic Marx-Lenin quotes in the former Soviet Union and to the early presidents and de Tocqueville in the United States.

18. Some of the more obvious problems with Skinnerism (e.g., in the form of rewarding with sugar and punishing with electric shocks) would be diabetes and masochism. Take Saddam Hussein and the Gulf War: If his values are what Patai (*The Arab Mind,* ch. 6, pp. 89–96) postulated as "Bedouin values"—courage, honor, and self-respect—then the more he is beaten in the technical arena, the more he demonstrates these values. But such points will do little to sway Western a priori reasoning.

19. The "benefit" of cost-benefit analysis as a basic paradigm in mainstream economics is probably more important than the enormous "cost" incurred when absolute values are denied, because they wreak havoc with product sums (infinities are bad for that level of mathematics).

20. It might have been useful if the more descriptive sciences or parts of sciences all ended with *-graphy* and all explanatory sciences with *-logy.* But geography and geology dif-

fer in other ways, as do biography and biology (and sociography and sociology but to a lesser extent).

21. "Teutonic" and "Saxonic" have been chosen in order not to tie the concepts to such geographisms as "German" or "English."

22. It may be objected that the Bogomils were Marxists and that there is dialectics in Marxism. However, Marxist dialectics is only a shadow of Daoist dialectics: The former is primarily along economic lines, equipped with an *Endzustand* as opposed to a highly multiple and never-ending dialectic. Moreover, in Soviet communism even that trickle of dialectic disappeared soon after the revolution, the essentially and officially contradiction-free society already having been attained. From that point on real-life contradictions were not only errors in thought or speech but also indicative of "deviations" to be uprooted or at least overcome.

23. Like Professor Jeffrey Sachs, used as a substitute for own thinking.

24. In Russian *za miru mir* may mean Peace to the world! to the cosmopolitans and Peace to the village! to the localists.

25. I am indebted to R. K. Srivastava of the Centre for the Study of Developing Societies in New Delhi for this point.

26. Charles A. Moore, in his *The Chinese Mind* (Honolulu: University of Hawaii Press, 1967), p. 5, listed twenty-one "basic principles of Chinese philosophy." The second is "the profound and all-pervading inseparability of philosophy and life and even of theory and practice—a major attitude of the Chinese philosophical mind, old and new."

27. In a sense the Orient is the ultimate indicator of ability to accommodate contradiction: To be daoist (or Shinto)-Confucian-Buddhist is perfectly acceptable in the Orient; try the combination Jewish-Christian-Muslim in the Occident and see what happens.

28. Johan Galtung, *United States Foreign Policy as Manifest Theology* (San Diego: University of California Press, 1987).

29. Again the same hypothesis: There is something lower-class about empiricism; rationalism is rooted higher up in society. One reason is simple: Down at the margin of social, even biological existence, one cannot take the risk of indulging in a priori thinking; barefoot empiricism is a condition for survival.

30. From the title of his autobiography.

31. As John Gittings pointed out in his insightful reflection on Maoism, "Communists Have Parents Too," *London Review of Books*, August 5, 1993, pp. 3–4: "Mao was as full of contradictions as his theory of the same name."

32. See my forthcoming work on the United Nations.

12

Whose Whispers Are in the Gallery?

ERSKINE B. CHILDERS

Information that was once the exclusive possession of a favoured few is now the common property of all. News of events that transpire at the other side of the globe and in our most distant dependencies is flashed here in a few hours. The world has become a vast whispering gallery.

—Joseph Cowen, M.P., 1882[1]

Not quite forty years after Morse sent the world's first telegraph message only from Baltimore to Washington, Joseph Cowen gave the House of Commons a dramatic view of an entire world that was shrinking. His cautions about the meaning of all this are very pertinent over a century later.

The House had before it a motion by Mr. Gladstone that a majority should have the right of cloture (to close a debate). The prime minister urged that the House was becoming too long-winded, unable to conduct the business of state efficiently, and that the elected majority would adequately reflect public opinion. One of the most spirited protests came from Cowen, in terms that sound eerily familiar today.

He acknowledged the role of a telegraphized press in directly informing citizens. It was certainly true, he said, that "this rapidity of communication and this multiplication of the means of publicity have quickened public life and intensified discussion. Opinion, as a consequence, ripens more rapidly." But whose opinion, derived from what information?

It was being argued, Cowen said, that public questions were now "sifted and settled in the columns of the Press [and] all that this assembly is required to do, or indeed can do, is to give force and form to the decisions thus arrived at." To this the eloquent libertarian took particular exception:

164

The press . . . is vested with no representative function. . . . Newspapers express, often in a discursive and cursory way, the opinion of their conductors . . . but it is ignorance on the part of politicians, and vanity on the part of journalists, to pretend that the opinion of the newspapers and the opinion of the public are always synonymous.[2]

The ensuing sixty years provided hideous demonstration of the vulnerability of democratic processes to what information—and consequently what images—citizens actually possessed about other peoples and events. Bertrand Russell's sad expression of hope on the eve of a second world war reflected how little the expanding media and education had as yet achieved.

Amid the myths and hysteria of opposing hatreds it is difficult to cause truth to reach the bulk of the people, or to spread the habit of forming opinions on evidence rather than on passion. Yet it is ultimately upon these things, not upon any political panacea, that the hopes of the world must rest.[3]

Russell continued to rest prime faith in the intelligence of citizens, if this could be nurtured and applied in international relations: "This, after all," he said in 1950, "is an optimistic conclusion, because intelligence is a thing that can be fostered by known methods of education."[4]

This precept emerged strongly from the ruins of World War II. It was reflected in the very constitution of UNESCO, the education arm of the new United Nations: "Since wars begin in the minds of men it is in the minds of men that the defenses of peace must be constructed." The idea of positive education for international understanding and of peace education took root in Europe and in the United States. It suffered deeply from but was not entirely crushed by McCarthyism. The corrosive equation of *international* with *red communist* was to linger in many minds throughout the Cold War.

The 1960s brought a considerable burst of optimism. The informational prison of colonialism had crumbled far more rapidly than even the founders of the U.N. had anticipated.[5] All humankind was now going to become accessible and be heard at the U.N. It was also in the 1960s generation of students and youth, in Europe as well as North America, that a sense of planetary solidarity began to rise through a new kind of music.

In the same years, not only communications specialists but many liberal and internationally minded people took heart in Marshall McLuhan's announcement of the advent of a *global village*. Real-time television information flows would enable citizens to learn directly of problems and views in other, distant cultures. Education in schools and colleges would be immeasurably enhanced. With a far better informed democracy, the United States would surely conduct its international relations, as its founders had pledged, with "a decent respect to the opinions of mankind."[6]

The element of this optimism that has indeed been fulfilled is the hardware. More than one billion TV sets are alive on Planet Earth, with an increase projected at 5 percent annually. There are now over 300 satellite-delivered TV services (CNN alone reaches some 140 countries), and several dozen more communications satellites will be launched before the end of the century. At one time a newspaper for an American in Paris, the *International Herald Tribune* is now printed in eleven countries and read in 164. Telefax technology is expanding so exponentially that the number of pages transmitted within the United States alone quadrupled from 1986 to 1987 and is probably now over 60 billion a year. Nongovernmental networking by fax and electronic mail, using lowest-rate telephone times, is one of the more socially hopeful hardware benefits.

However, it is all too clear that something was seriously wrong with the rest of the optimism of the global village. We are confronted by extraordinary paradoxes. In examining these it is important to keep in mind that the *white* Judeo-Christian portion of humankind in the industrial North is a 23 percent minority in the global village.

Paradox 1

Anyone who has worked in developing countries knows that with the poorest educational opportunities their secondary students learn far more about the rest of the world and the U.N. than do their peers in the most richly endowed countries.[7] Visiting Third World professionals, well-read in the history, culture, and politics of the North, are invariably astonished at the ignorance of citizens and the shallowness of perspective of politicians and journalists about the vast majority of humankind.

This huge disparity has gravely affected every facet of North-South relations—of world relations. This can be demonstrated through a number of prisms on international relations, each with its own further paradox.

In the 1980s, not the 1880s, a democratically elected U.S. president accepting his welcome in Brasilia thanked the people of Bolivia. For blatantly commercial purposes, American TV networks ran daily live broadcasts about U.S. hostages in Iran. Thus constantly inflamed, most U.S. citizens still learned little about Iran, only that Iranians were Moslems (as discussed later, a deeply provocative image) and certainly not that the United States with other Western governments had overthrown Iran's one popular government and had reinstalled and protected a hated Shah.[8] Not realizing the depth of this ignorance and bias, the Iranians daily used television to try to present their case—and, of course, only exacerbated the hostage crisis.

Further and potentially explosive damage was done to Western-Islamic relations in this period. It was part of a wider phenomenon in which, on virtually every issue involving major popular movements in the South, orthodox Western commentators managed to transform cause into effect, which was then made the cause conveyed to Western citizens. Two examples illustrate the approach:

The United States and South Africa covertly supported an Angolan gang to destabilize the *Marxist* (meaning popular) government. The Angolan government sought and received Cuban military aid. This *Cuban presence* promptly became the *cause* of whatever the West did further to ravage Angola thereafter.

Palestinians resisted the seizure of their homeland and their mass forcible expulsion. The cause was virtually concealed by media from the Western citizen's view for decades; the effect was called *terrorism,* which was converted into the cause of Israeli attacks and more expansion and of U.S. support for the Zionist state.

Language plays crucial roles in such disinformation in the supposedly benign global village. It is, for example, highly symptomatic that *radical,* which means of the *root*—going to cause—has been made a menacing word in the North.

Paradox 2

The global village can actually be dangerous if it does not actively foster greater knowledge and understanding of peoples and their aspirations beyond the frontiers of the West. If modern transnational public communication only perpetuates ignorance, strengthens disinformation, and exacerbates tensions, it may prove more dangerous to peace and the rule of international law than the world was without it. Two examples again are illustrative:

In 1990, in violation of numerous international laws, Panama was abruptly invaded by an American military force that killed thousands of civilians and destroyed the very shelter of more thousands; the entire action was successfully presented to the American public as a neat *surgical* move to arrest Manuel Noriega, whose employment by the CIA was hushed as much as possible.

Later in 1990, a U.S. president and others with a special agenda in the Persian Gulf abruptly stopped financing and arming Iraq as an ally against Iran when the Saddam Hussein government invaded Kuwait. The full story of the origins of that invasion has yet to be verified. But every promising effort to negotiate Iraq's withdrawal was either sabotaged or ignored, and a U.S. president and his coterie used an array of mendacious means—even stories of Kuwaiti babies ripped from incubators—to whip up a desert storm of anger in favor of war.[9]

As the largest military force assembled since World War II was attacking Iraq, most citizens in the universally educated and media-wealthy countries of the coalition had no idea where Kuwait was. After the guns fell silent, these citizenries, ostensibly the best informed in human history, accepted reports from their superbly equipped media that the destruction of the basic civil and development infrastructure of a country of some 18 million people was a little *collateral damage.*

Paradox 3

Expanded access to information for citizens of democracies through supposedly independent media does not necessarily strengthen their democratic influence on their governments' foreign policies.

As the Cold War ended, much of the South lay ravaged and ruined in the most crucial underpinnings of normal life; but after thirty years of global village, there was little sign that the causes were understood, not even the economic ones. In the 1970s, the Third World had tried to advance a *new international economic order* at the U.N. in terms identical with those the young United States had advanced when Europe discriminated against it in trade and finance.[10] (A parallel advocacy of a *new international information order* was grossly misinterpreted by Northern media leaders, including the fiction that UNESCO was promoting it as an official program.[11] The United States and Britain withdrew their membership in UNESCO.)

The major Northern powers refused even to discuss adjusting the international economic system to the fact that there were now not 80 but 165 nation-states each seeking its rightful share of world product and trade in a climate of reasonably stable monetary conditions and equitable international finance. The debt of the South has since increased fourteen times since 1970, to $1.4 trillion. The U.N. Development Program calculates that the developing countries are losing $500 billion a year in potential income because of Northern barriers to their exports, Northern manipulation of interest rates, and other North-South inequities.[12]

This annual income loss is ten times all official Northern aid to the same countries. None of this makes sense, tragically so for the developing countries but no less for the North, which sooner than later will need the South as a market, only to find its billions of people without purchasing power. Every appeal to negotiate an all-win global economic and financial strategy has fallen on deaf ears in key Northern capitals.

The amount of misleading information about world money and trade purveyed through Northern media to the North's own citizens is staggering. For example, the International Monetary Fund (IMF) is routinely depicted as the world's money manager. The G-7 powers invoke it as a key reason for refusing to discuss monetary issues at the U.N. proper. The IMF long ago abandoned any serious pretense of intervening in Northern monetary questions; it has been converted by the powers that control it into an instrument of intervention in Third World economies that uses criteria for its *structural adjustment* diktats for which the United States, among other Northern countries, should be a prime candidate. The IMF influences less than 10 percent of global liquidity.[13]

The GATT (General Agreement on Tariffs and Trade) is routinely depicted as the commanding global trade machinery. The G-7 powers invoke it to legitimate their refusal also to negotiate genuinely global trade strategies at the U.N. The *agreement* ending the Uruguay Round in December 1993 was hailed by orthodox media as a decisive benefit to the *global economy.* The vast majority of countries on the globe were kept on the sidelines of the negotiations for seven years. The agreement will further impoverish most of the countries where most of humankind tries to eke out a marginal existence.

So grossly misrepresented are these issues in Northern media and so ill-educated are their editors that they automatically reproduce references in G-7 summit communiqués to the "global economy" without any comment on the fact that the fine print of the communiqués refers solely to the economy of the North.[14]

Paradoxes 4 and 5

The North's enormously superior access to economic information about the entire world has resulted in no better knowledge about the real economic conditions of the whole of humankind. Furthermore, the existence of communications capacities truly spanning the real world has had no effect on the proclivity of Northern elites to depict to their citizens a world and its economy that in fact apply to less than a quarter of humankind. If not urgently addressed, these conditions will produce catastrophic convulsions between the North and the South.

The apparent end of the Cold War seems only to have compounded these perceptual weaknesses. The Reagan-Bush-Thatcher era enabled an enormous increase in the communication power of right-wing ideologues, who subtly conveyed that all brands of social democracy must have neural connections with Moscow because there could be no other, no indigenous, explanation for them. The collapse of Soviet command statism has thus made it even more difficult for the North to comprehend the political forces that can be fueled by impoverishment.

This was instantly evident when popular rebellion erupted in the Mexican province of Chiapas in early 1994. The editors of the august *New York Times* could actually print a news report that quoted a young Zapatista as saying, "Our thinking is that we have to build socialism," and then went on to advise readers: "That the cold war had ended seemed to mean nothing to the hundreds of insurgents who stunned their countrymen [by] declaring war on the government."[15]

Paradox 6

The Cold War was a monumental distraction and source of perceptual confusion of what really moves human beings anywhere if they are exploited, impoverished, and discriminated against. Notwithstanding that the distraction has disappeared, there is little sign that the North has straightened out its thinking and is better able to comprehend the gigantic political forces being generated by poverty.

It is worth pursuing the paradoxes revealed by the end of the Cold War: A wave of euphoria swept across the North. Washington and London proclaimed *a new world order;* Western media supinely echoed this with little serious examination. Democracy, now to be married with the new fundamentalist religion of *the magic of the market,* would sweep across the former Soviet empire. An essay announcing the *end of history* became the rage of diplomatic and think-tank circles. Peace in our time would now need little more than continued vigilance over essential Northern interests, as in the Gulf, and economic assistance for market democracy in the former Soviet regions.

Paradox 7

This new world order simply never happened. The USSR has dissolved. In precisely the region of the world on which the West had focused a massive intelligence apparatus and a preponderance of its ultramodern public information capacities, within months there were secessionist insurrections in places most Western citizens had neither heard of nor been informed as to their aspirations. Whereas media and political commentators had given Western citizens to understand that brutal internal strife and mass human-rights violations were Third World phenomena, suddenly these things were also happening in Europe, especially in the former Yugoslavia.

As for the new world order in the South, it was to mean an end to dictators and corruption. Few Northern citizens were aware that almost every dictator had been installed outright by their own intelligence agencies, and the handful who had gained power on their own had been quickly co-opted. The support extended to weapons, loans, training of secret police and torturers, and bribes for Western investments—then denounced as *Third World corruption.*

Few knew of decades of deliberate, systematic destabilization by Western governments to weaken any Third World government adopting nonalignment. Among leaders with access to every kind of historical, cultural, and current political information and with the most powerful intelligence agencies in the world, there had been abject ignorance of the most fundamental precepts of national liberation struggles.

Throughout the Cold War, to be nonaligned was to be portrayed in the North as communist or dangerously so inclined, notwithstanding that maneuvering between rival powers is a time-honored practice in Northern diplomacy (and was also, indeed, in the diplomacy of the young nonaligned United States). Yet throughout the Cold War, officials in the key Western governments refused to accept that a nonaligned government would resist any Soviet attempt to control it as much as it would any Western effort. Virtually all media parroted this basic misperception.

The cumulative impact of these decades of support of dictators, of destabilization, and of disinformation was that as the Cold War ended almost every country in the South had also been ravaged politically. Northern media showed as little cognizance of this history as did Northern leaders.

With remarkable rapidity the continuing conflicts in already devastated Angola and Mozambique were being reported as civil wars. In the early 1990s, media ventilated increasing indignation about the Swiss bank accounts of President Mobutu of Zaire, conveying to their audiences that this was but another instance of an inherent corruption in the Third World. The much-vaunted communications of the global village had not informed Northern citizens that Mobutu had been continuously funded, armed, protected, and used (i.e., to destabilize neighboring Angola) by Western intelligence agencies ever since they arranged the assassination of the Congo's first and only independent leader in 1961.

And all across the South, the ghastly detritus of the North-North contest lay like volatile minefields. In Somalia alone the USSR had provided $270 million of arms in the 1970s until sides were switched and the United States took over, delivering to its protected dictator Siad Barre another $154 million of weapons between 1981 and 1991, with Italy providing another $520 million worth—in a country of only 8 million people.[16]

The perspective of reporting on this ravaged South in the wake of the Cold War was, however, overwhelmingly that its own peoples were responsible. Soon, *aid fatigue* was on the rise; the Third World had turned out to be a big disappointment.

Paradox 8

Whether in crucial policies or in daily media commentary, there was no improvement in Northern knowledge and sensitive perception of the huge human majority remotely commensurate with the North's expanding access to it.

This massive flaw in the thesis of the global village has crucially affected the U.N. After the arrival of its Third World *new majority,* the U.N. was either treated with scorn or deliberately weakened by major Western powers. Western media dutifully followed their lead, reducing their correspondents at the U.N. until, instead of its once prized status as an assignment, it became a journalistic Siberia.

In the 1980s, the Reagan administration deliberately provoked a furor about the cost of the U.N. and lack of control by its major contributors over its budget. Sweden's prime minister, the late Olof Palme, urged that no member should pay more than 10 percent of the budget; the U.S. administration hastened to make it clear that it had no objections to its 25 percent share provided it had concomitant influence, and the redistribution proposal was shelved. With a glaring inconsistency that went entirely unnoticed by the mainstream media, U.S. officials continued to claim that the cost of the U.N. to the treasury was outrageous. Congress responded by refusing to pay the legally obligated U.S. share of dues.

By the early 1990s, the U.N. was bankrupt, with unpaid assessments totaling $2.23 billion. The United States owed $834 million, and the Russian Federation, plunged in economic chaos by its pressured rush to the market, owed $598 million.[17] However, the U.N. was badly needed to cope with the unexpected eruption of conflicts all over the world, but it was ill-prepared. By 1993 there were some sixty active conflicts. The powers had refused to authorize more than forty professionals at U.N. headquarters for all peacekeeping work.

Paradox 9

In the period of the most powerful array of information-gathering and -disseminating capacities the world has ever seen, the leaders and orthodox media of the very countries possessing such capacities have been massively wrong in all their most critical analyses and projections of world affairs. Meanwhile, the powers with the greatest access to information about global dangers have nearly crippled the capabilities of the international community as a whole to cope with them.

In a brilliant special issue on "Media, Societies, and Democracy" in the aftermath of the Gulf crisis in 1991, France's *Le Monde Diplomatique* reflected the deep disjunctures that had surfaced between the optimism of the global village and the realities. The very titles of the essays spoke volumes: "The Era of Suspicion," "On the Orders of the North, the Information Order," "Manipulating and Controlling Hearts and Minds," "The Military-Media Complex," "The Spectacle of Propaganda," "Fax It or Perish: A Culture of Urgency," and "Too Fascinating Virtual-Reality Worlds."

The journal's special issue included an essay on the history of an international information order by Jacques Decornoy, who perhaps summed up the fate of the heady optimism since Cowen proclaimed that the world had become "a vast whispering gallery."

> The lack of presentation of the cultures, histories, and great social phenomena of the Third World, as well as the polarization of information around the pressures of violence, engender the most primitive judgments (in the North) if not also irrational or dangerous political decisions. It is also true that the emptiness of information produced by the North about itself has perverse effects on democracy.[18]

What went wrong? What can be learned from some of the salient characteristics of the *emptiness* of information in the North?

The Inheritance of Perceptions

> What ideas, notions, and images do we have in our heads about these hitherto distant lands and peoples? Insofar as we have had to [react to them] what did we have from our past to react with?
>
> —Harold R. Isaacs, 1958[19]

Modern global communication did not grow on perceptually neutral soil. This, indeed, is the most underlying paradox. The deep chasms in Northern perception of the South cannot be explained as the problem of a culture only recently coming into contact with the great majority of humankind.

Much of western Europe has been in contact with most of the cultures of the South for up to 500 years, ever since the rise of the various contesting imperial slave and other trading powers of Venice, Portugal, Spain, France, Britain, Holland, and Belgium. Within those five centuries, all of the indigenous cultures of the Western Hemisphere were conquered and devastated by genocide and exploitation. European empires were established over all of southern Asia except Siam (Thailand), with effective dominion over parts of China at various times. In the early sixteenth century, the Portuguese set up colonies in Angola and Mozambique, and after growth of the slave trade around the coast and inland penetrations over the next 300 years, Africa was effectively carved up among Britain, France, and Germany by 1886.

European contact with Arab and Islamic culture began 1,200 years ago in the Iberian Peninsula, and religious and temporal elites of Europe became deeply engaged in the Arab east between 900 and 700 years ago during their Crusades. The modern-day conquest of the Arab world began with Napoleon in Egypt nearly 200 years ago.

In the mysteries of today's Northern void of information about the South, then, we are not dealing with an ignorance born of no contact—far from it. The Western-Northern mind was already subconsciously filled with images of Southern cultures as being either exotic and primitive or threatening, even before Joseph Cowen noted how news could be flashed "from our most distant dependencies" in a few hours.

Undoubtedly the most deeply embedded and most powerful of these perceptual inheritances is about Islam and Arabs. The sudden rise and rapid geographic expansion of a religion having the effrontery to claim Jesus and others as prophets were regarded with shock and fear by medieval Christian leaders. Moreover, Islam was more tolerant of other religions and even helpful to Jews whom the Christians were persecuting.[20] The defeat of the Moslem Arabs at the battle of Tours in A.D. 732 was perpetuated as a dreaded memory in Europe; a thousand years later the great historian Gibbon was still recalling with an implied shiver how the Koran might otherwise have been taught in Oxford "to a circumcised people."[21]

The Crusades ended in frustration for Europe; the largely Moslem Arabs could not be conquered. Worse, they had manifest superiority in virtually every discipline. The intellectual and scientific foundations of Europe's brilliant advance in all the social and the physical sciences came from the *Third* World—which in fact was *First*—through texts in which Arab authors had assembled and enriched Chinese, Indian, Persian, Greek, African, and Meso-American knowledge. So heavily dependent was Europe on this store of knowledge that entire centers of translation scholars had to be opened.[22] As Europe's universities began using Arab works for their first textbooks, a kind of collective subconscious decision was apparently made that this debt must never be acknowledged. To this day, very few Western students at any level even learn that the West's Greek inheritance arrived in Europe in Arabic via the Arabs who had enriched it.[23]

Parallel with this—and probably the largest fit of cultural amnesia ever induced—Europe's literature and language acquired consistent negatives about treacherous "Moors," dishonest "Mahomedans," and the "malignant and turban'd Turk."[24] For centuries the prophet Mohammed was always described in European literature as "the impostor."[25] For as many centuries one of the standard poems every Western schoolchild learned was the "Song of Roland," in which the Basque brigands that chivalrous warrior fought at Roncesvalles were converted into evil "Saracens." In the second half of the twentieth century, one of the cited definitions of *Arab* in English dictionaries is "street urchin," and in French, "miser, screw, usurer." To all these negatives were of course added the romantic-exoticisms of Western travelers.[26]

The development of images of other Southern cultures was not as religiously infused because their religions were less challenging, more easily dismissed as quaint or simply pagan. Nonetheless, ignorance combined with negative and distorted images about these other cultures abounded and remains widespread.

Generations of press-ganged and conscripted working-class soldiers of the major empires—in the aggregate, millions of Europeans, over centuries—spent long years in colonial wars and garrisons, filtering back into their home societies inevitably only the worst impressions of the peoples they had been sent to suppress. Their officers provided the same in the upper classes. An acronym was evolved in India as a sardonic code for Indian employees who tried to behave like Europeans—WOG, for *Westernized Oriental Gentleman.* Significantly, this was transmuted geographically and linguistically into a new word in English for any Arab, a *wog.*[27]

The United States was not to get into external imperialism for its first hundred years, but most of Europe's accumulated images of the non-Christian world crossed to North America with European settlers. Color prejudice was massively expressed not only in the existence of slavery but also in the virtual extinction of even the slaves' knowledge of their homelands, even their very names, for they had to acquire Anglo-Saxon ones. Cultural and ethnic prejudice was rampant toward the Chinese, who were inducted for cheap labor on the West Coast and then inland on the railroads. People of one degree or another of Hispanic origin were equally degraded as *dagos,* a word imported from Europe.[28]

Mark Twain, an energetic activist against imperialism, was evidently well aware of many deep, antagonistic biases. He himself traveled in the Middle East. Of seeing the sword of the Crusader Godfrey of Bulloigne in Jerusalem, he reported that "I tried it on a Moslem and clove him in twain like a doughnut," but his intent was probably missed by most of his readers.[29]

Nor was the United States without its version of the French imperial *mission civilisatrice* (civilizing mission). A heady strain of this, strongly mixed with financial motivations, entered the mind of the nineteenth-century American elite after the 1840s when leaders like Senator Thomas Hart Benton extolled the unfolding benefits of opening up the West to the Pacific and beyond:

> The Mongolian, or Yellow race is there, four hundred millions in number, spreading almost to Europe; a race once the foremost of the human family . . . far above the Ethiopian, or Black—above the Malay, or Brown (if we must admit five races)—and above the American Indian, or Red . . . but still far below the White. . . . The apparition of the van of the Caucasian race (after) having completed the circumnavigation of the globe, must wake up and reanimate the torpid body of old Asia (and) political considerations will aid the action of social and commercial influences.[30]

In the 1840s the notion that America had a *Manifest Destiny* was born. A continuous tension entered American foreign policy between the morality of the founders and a pragmatism and expediency as to means that could be adopted by liberal and conservative alike.

Fundamental white-settler justifications could be drawn into foreign policy—that the "natives" have not properly used their abundant resources and are "not of a self-governing race."[31] Whether "a nation shows that it knows how to act with reasonable efficiency and decency in social and political matters" or whether "chronic wrongdoing may . . . ultimately require [U.S.] intervention" was enunciated by President Theodore Roosevelt eighty years before Reagan-Bush imperialism.[32]

Original foreign-policy moralities are also weakened by the extremely ahistorical, always future-oriented American outlook. As an occasional lecturer during the Cold War years of official hostility to nonalignment, I always prompted audible astonishment in audiences on reading "a very good statement of Non-Alignment by the president of a newly independent developing country"—and then announcing that it was, of course, by President George Washington.[33] In the past decade, when economic *sticks and carrots* have been brutally used to secure votes or silence from weak Third World countries at the U.N., Washington's voice on that very practice has long been forgotten: "I believe it is among nations as with individuals, that the party taking advantage of the distresses of another will lose infinitely more in the opinion of mankind and in subsequent events than he will gain by the stroke of the moment."[34]

A ritually renewed national egotism also arose with the *spread-eagling* fervor of the westward movement.[35] Ever since Manifest Destiny, it has been obligatory for every American candidate for national office to state that it is the will of God or the wish of all other (never consulted) peoples that the United States be "the moral leader of mankind . . . the last best hope of humanity . . . Number One now and always."

The Arrogance of Being Number One

This fundamentally arrogant nostrum is, of course, as dangerous in a democracy as in a dictatorship, possibly even more so. In the classic pattern of demagoguery, it excites in a (macho) proportion of American citizens an assumption that their elected leaders will demonstrate being Number One against all declaredly dangerous foreigners. In turn, knowledge of what they have excited becomes a conscious element on the leaders' political checklist.

Ronald Reagan had not played military officer, and countless cowboys, never then to play commander in chief sending the forces into battle; no other possible explanation accounts for the invasion of Grenada. A wimp image helped propel George Bush into his massively destructive aggression into Panama and the carefully orchestrated Gulf massacre. At an awkward early moment in approval ratings, even President Clinton exploited Kuwait-inspired and unproven charges of an Iraqi assassination attempt against Bush to launch cruise missiles against Baghdad.[36] Being Number One is ever a prophecy that may require fulfillment before the next elections.

By itself, the Number One mentality creates a subconscious mind-set of antagonism toward any *upstart* nation or foreign leader who is *intransigent* (usually meaning one who resists or seems to thwart the prophecy). If that nation happens to come from one or another culture about which the American external mind is already loaded with negative images, then the fulfillment of the prophecy is made easier.

The character choices and depictions of mystery and thriller novels and films in the Western world during the twentieth century have been excellent barometers of the state of stereotypy and baleful images. There was an early concentration on menacing central Europeans, inscrutably evil Orientals, oily and imposturing Arabs and Turks, silly Negro servants, mafiosi wops, devious dagos, and of course, in and from the United States, savage Red Indians. After World War II came an inevitable literature of resurrectionist Nazis, a growing volume of Cold War Armageddon-threatening Communist spies and insane Russian leaders, and a steady injection of Zionist-inspired thrillers about terrorist Arabs (often brought down by heroic Israelis on behalf of Western civilization).

As the Cold War wound down, new or regrouped enemies of all good Northern values had to be found. These reflect and of course very powerfully reinforce contemporary negative images: The Red Menace is now being replaced by the Islamic Menace (still containing the Arab Menace), with or without evil recidivist Russian generals who can sell nuclear missiles. A growing tributary to the current fiction mainstream concerns ultraefficient Japanese nuclear and other hi-tech killers and commercial predators.

There is by now a huge volume of stereotyped images of the people of virtually every non-Judeo-Christian culture being fostered in American and other Western novels read by hundreds of thousands and in film and television seen by tens of millions, including Third World audiences. Especially since the Persian Gulf massacre, no people anywhere in the South can feel safe. Among over one billion people of Moslem faith, it is now widely believed that the United States and the North in general are continuously and permanently at war with Islam.

The contrast between the presumption of world leadership and the realities of world attitudes toward the presumer offers two more essential paradoxes.

Paradoxes 10 and 11

Even in a democracy, even with all the late-twentieth-century panoply and paraphernalia of real-time worldwide communication (into every home), it is entirely possible to create a virtual screen of reverse reality between the great majority of all human beings alive on the planet and a small but powerful minority.

Although the United States never formally acquired an empire, otherwise decent American citizens can be misinformed into supporting—or acquiescing in—any and every brutal and unlawful foreign action by their government in the name of *world leadership* or *national security,* or *making country X safe for democracy* against

Red or other dangerous hordes. There is profound contrast between the decent behavioral standards most American citizens try to uphold and the viciousness abroad that U.S. foreign-policy postures can so quickly prompt.

Only an *emptiness* of real information that decent Americans could use to inform their judgments on international issues can explain these paradoxes. The same deep lacunae in perception exists in one or another degree across most of the Northern world. If long and negatively tinted contact provides part of the explanation, it does not provide enough. We have to search further, and in so doing we encounter another amnesia, one I call "amnesia after midnight."[37]

Amnesia After Midnight

> *Were all humanity a single nation-state, the present North-South divide would make*
> *it an unviable, semi-feudal entity, split by internal conflicts. Its small part is ad-*
> *vanced, prosperous, powerful; its much bigger part is underdeveloped, poor, powerless.*
> *A nation so divided within itself would be recognized as unstable. A world so divided*
> *should likewise be recognized as inherently unstable.*
>
> —The South Commission, 1990[38]

As earlier noted, the citizens, leadership elites, and media directors of the North were not in any way prepared for the grassfire of national liberation that raced across the South from the late 1940s on and that made the U.N. universal by the early 1970s. If we are to understand our perceptual problems and the dangerous socioeconomic disparities now dividing humankind, it is essential to understand this extraordinary moment in a confrontation of cultures.

Suddenly, if we see it against the long canvas of history, the orderly arrangement of the world had come undone. Numerically huge populations had been kept relatively docile by admixtures of the machine gun, indirect rule, and harsh imprisonment or execution for subversive intellectuals. Suddenly, in ceremony after ceremony at midnight in ancient forts and sports stadiums, the imperial flags were being quietly lowered in darkness so that none would see them fall. And in their place as the lights went back on were strange independence flags, and there were unfamiliar new figures on the world stage.

A phrase used about these historic events by the dean of British radio commentators instantly conveyed perhaps the most fundamental misperception of all. The late Richard Dimbleby would say over the BBC, "Now yet another people is free to begin making their own mistakes."

The perspective was widely expressed in the North that whatever the past, these peoples were now responsible for themselves. One could discern in some who used it a rather hasty and nervous wish to have the colonial chapter of world history quickly closed.[39] In others one could sense sour grapes. Many, however, did seem at once to assume it was true, and the basic concept has passed into general perspectives on the South.

For elites who had become obsessed with the East-West confrontation, this perceptual greeting of decolonization made it quite easy to forget that there were two billion human beings in the South whom it might be important at last to get to know and understand. Only the Nordic countries and Canada exhibited an early concern for what was called *development education* and made a decision to support it by public grants; elsewhere nongovernmental organizations and teachers groups had to try to introduce some information about the Third World on their own. There is no significant evidence that media directors organized crash training courses for their staffs but much evidence that if any did it was disastrously unsuccessful.

In addition, the U.N. charter already contained the principle of *one nation, one vote*—ironically, for the benefit of the original smaller members. There was, therefore, no political contest over the South's admission to the U.N.; the *new majority* simply arrived. This was as much a profound, history-changing event as the popular revolutions in Europe that led to the democratization of its parliaments—and that generated a permanent constituency of defense of that achievement. Yet the equivalent implications for the U.N. were never publicly debated by citizens in the North. No constituency of support for a universal U.N., and of acceptance that the great majority of humankind is entitled to influence the U.N. agenda and priorities, has ever been generated.

It has, of course, been argued that few of the U.N.'s new-majority members have democratically elected governments; therefore, there is no reason the Northern minority should respect the majority. Unfortunately for this argument, Northern governments have shown no more respect for the views and proposals of Third World governments that indeed have been democratically elected. No government more continuously irritated key Western powers and had its views spurned more continuously than that of the largest pluralist parliamentary democracy on earth, India. In this, again, is revealed evasion of the necessity of a minority of humankind coming face to face with a non-Christian, *non-white* majority with far older cultures.

It is interesting to note the implications of the term *non-white,* still in usage in the North. It continuously conveys by the negative that human beings who are not white are a minority; indeed, in terms of cognition, they do not exist in any number. A part of the problem is precisely this inability to *see* people of color.[40] If Northerners' perceptions of their cultural and demographic place in humankind were even nominally correct, they would be calling themselves noncolored.

The free-to-make-their-own-mistakes idea was, of course, so far from the truth as to build by itself a chasm of misperception that affects Northern attitudes to the present day. A report in 1993 in the *New York Times* describing the political impasse in Nigeria averred that "there are deeper causes: decades of mediocre government, pervasive corruption, a military leadership stubbornly clinging to power, and ethnic and religious rivalries that have kept this country from establishing a social consensus more than 30 years after independence from Britain in 1960."[41]

The key words are "more than 30 years after independence from Britain." In this and in countless daily reports and commentaries on every country in the South, a second huge perceptual amnesia is revealed. It is actually a double amnesia. It involves, in the first place, total forgetfulness in the North of the condition in which the colonialized South was left upon regaining independence only—*not more than*—thirty years ago. It also involves forgetfulness of how long in some respects, and how very short in others, has been the comparable experience of Northern countries themselves.

The Colonial Legacy

The nature of information filtered back from the South into Northern countries before decolonization was sporadic and, as has been noted, consisted largely of negative *image-bites* from the experiences of the occupiers. Only a handful of progressive writers and scholars (and some parliamentarians) made it their business to know the real conditions of the colonies, including those of the United States, as in the Philippines or in disguise in Central America. These reports were shunned by orthodox media and foreign-policy elitists as the fulminations of cranks or left-wing radicals.

Thus, there has been no understanding that colonialism placed entire peoples in intellectual and institutional stasis. For one or more centuries the entire South, except Iberian-settled South America (and there including the indigenous survivors of genocide), was not allowed to continue to evolve its own endogenous intellectual, technological, political thought or its political and social institutions. In a very real sense, the majority of all humankind was put to sleep, while a minority in the North proceeded with evolution of these crucial elements in any society's progress.

Education is fundamental both to the evolution of endogenous, democratic institutions appropriate to cope with the modern world and for effective governance and economic management. It is again symptomatic how unknown are the facts about the educational stasis that was imposed under colonial rule. For example, Ghana was left in 1960 with a ratio of university graduates to total population that, had it applied in the United States, would have left that country in 1960 with fewer than 3,000 graduates for all purposes (instead of more than 400,000); Britain would have had only 600. It may at least be imagined in what condition either Northern country would be "more than thirty years" later. A comparable dearth of educated, trained people applied all over Africa—only tens (even fewer in some cases) of university graduates among populations of ten or more million people.

Even those countries, like India, that regained independence with a somewhat higher education ratio shared the full range of other legacies of colonialism. Economies had been kept stunted (India's, in fact, ruined by compulsory British textile imports) and grossly distorted for extractive purposes. Crucial elements of physical transport infrastructure, of the kinds it took a century or more to build in the North, were either nonexistent or had also been built for extractive or suppressive purposes.

Onto all societies of the South, without exception, there was also dropped the wholly alien political and administrative structure of the centralist post-Westphalian nation-state. These societies were not political tabulae rasae, for the South had vibrant institutions of governance before the white conquerors came. After the long colonial sleep during which no political discussion was allowed and even the ancient governance structures were unused or distorted, the Western nation-state was simply imposed (often as the price of self-determination). Yet it has been a basic unspoken Northern assumption that people whose political and institutional evolution had been stopped during the several centuries when the North's democracy was being evolved should imitate it neatly and dutifully in less than thirty years.

Frozen Frontiers

One other unperceived legacy, whose all too certainly conflictual effect has yet to be fully experienced, concerns frontiers. With the exception of parts of the Chinese, Thai, Egyptian, and Ethiopian frontiers, the national boundaries of the whole of the South are totally exogenous and artificial. They were imposed by imperial demarcation without any local consultation. National liberation movements had to accept them because the empires did not dissolve synchronously, not even within themselves; a movement gaining independence in a territory at a certain moment in the 1950s or 1960s had continuing colonial authority all around it. In other instances last-minute partitions were imposed, with invariably bloody consequences.

Ironically, U.N. membership then immediately made each of these artificial frontiers sacrosanct. Local elites, usually nurtured by outside powers for their own Cold War purposes, then acquired vested interests in these *sovereignties* along with the transnational investments pressed upon them. Although repeatedly asserted before Saddam Hussein was even born, Iraq's claim that Kuwait was detached from Basra Province by force of British arms was significantly muffled in Western information. So was Kuwait's accession to U.N. membership only under direct British military protection. The South is studded with equivalents.

Again, the history of these frontiers of most of humankind is in no way esoteric information, difficult to come by. It is part of a body of what can only be called primary information essential to the very beginning of understanding events and attitudes among the vast majority of humankind. It remains virtually unknown in the North.

The other facet of this amnesia is, of course, an astonishing inability—even in a history-conscious Europe—to recall for how little time the North's political and socioeconomic structure has itself been functioning.

The essential attitude underlying the North's increasing *aid fatigue* and conditionalities upon such aid, is that it offers to developing countries ready-made and well-proven models of democracy, governance, and economy, and they had better follow these. Yet universal adult franchise is scarcely seventy years old (except in New Zealand), and the West's (and Japan's recently adopted) multiparty democracies are even now being exposed one after the other as riddled with corruption. The socioeconomic model of compacting populations in dense urban-industrial centers and leaving the land to be farmed by chemical-intensive mechanized agriculture is only a hundred years old.[42] It is, at the least, in deep social, psychological, and ecological difficulties. And models of economy that have sharply increased poverty, homelessness, and the collapse of financial institutions would equally call, at the least, for a little modesty.

The point is not to denigrate these models, in which there are numerous fine features. It is to say that they are in reality very brief and local experiments in the long human experience. But for some forty years the basic construct of Northern official and media attitudes toward the South is that these models, imperfectly operating in only one cultural arena among only a minority of humankind, are so assuredly sound that they should be adopted by the great majority of all humankind.

The Northern minority in an increasingly riven world is in need of leaders, intellectuals, and media directors who might recall the words of a Scottish poet:

> *O grant me, Heaven, a middle state,*
> *Neither too humble nor too great;*
> *More than enough, for nature's ends,*
> *With something left to treat my friends.*[43]

Otherwise, by the year 2000, those who will number only one in every five on a planet of 6.25 billion human beings will have very few friends among the vast majority. This will be the ultimate failure of all in media, education, and political leadership who have the most powerful communication tools the world has ever known.

For the whispers will become an angry, despairing roar.

NOTES

1. Joseph Cowen, "Speaking in the House of Commons, November 10, 1882," in Edgar R. Jones, ed., *Selected English Speeches* (New York: Oxford University Press, 1929), pp. 340–341.

2. Ibid. I have taken some liberty in rearranging the sequence of Cowen's famous speech for the sake of brevity.

3. Quoted in Noam Chomsky, "On Changing the World," in *Problems of Freedom and Knowledge* (London: Fontana, 1972), p. 49.

4. In his remarks on accepting the Nobel Peace Prize, quoted in Ibid.

5. In 1945, for all but a handful of people considered to be *cranks* and *radicals*, decolonization was not envisaged even within this century. The architects of the U.N.'s head-

quarters were advised to anticipate only another twenty or so member states for a total membership of some seventy (and these to be largely from Europe). See U.N. Document A/311, 1947.

6. In the preamble to the Declaration of Independence, adopted at Philadelphia on July 4, 1776.

7. Surveys by the National Geographic Society and the National Education Association indicate that less than 5 percent of American secondary school students are taught either geography or anything about international relations.

8. See James A. Bill's authoritative history, *The Eagle and the Lion* (New Haven: Yale University Press, 1988).

9. A teenage Kuwaiti girl told the incubator babies story at a congressional hearing. This was nationally promoted by Bush, congressional hawks, and media as well as by "Citizens for a Free Kuwait," depicted as a nongovernmental organization financed by the contributions of individual U.S. citizens. The teenage witness turned out to be the daughter of the Kuwaiti ambassador to the United States. The *citizens* organization turned out to have a handful of citizens' donations and nearly $12 million in a check from the Kuwait government. Doctors and nurses at Kuwaiti hospitals possessing incubators denied the story. Neither human rights organizations nor, in the end, an official investigation could find a single case of a baby being ripped from an incubator during the Iraqi occupation.

10. See Secretary of Treasury Alexander Hamilton's Report on Manufactures, December 5, 1791.

11. Advisory from the U.S. National Commission for UNESCO, 1984.

12. United Nations Development Program (UNDP) Human Development Report 1991, United Nations, New York.

13. Mahbub ul-Haq, senior advisor, UNDP, in a paper presented at the North-South Roundtable, Bretton Woods, N.H., September 1–3, 1993.

14. Of special irony, the chairman of the giant Sony Corporation recently published an open letter to President Clinton and his G-7 colleagues about a *new world economic order,* urging that the transnational corporate community did not favor the present lack of system and regulation in international money and essentials of a trading environment. Morita also referred frequently to the *global economy,* when his entire article was only about the triad of Japan, North America, and Europe. See Akio Morita, "Toward a New World Economic Order," *Atlantic Monthly,* June 1993.

15. Tim Golden, "News," *New York Times,* January 4, 1994.

16. Report of the U.S. Congressional Research Service, U.S. Congress, November 1, 1993.

17. Report of the Secretary-General on the Financial Situation, U.N. Document A/C.5/47/13/Add.1, June 24, 1993.

18. Jacques Decornoy, "Aux ordres du Nord, l'ordre de l'information" (On Northern orders, the information order) *Le Monde Diplomatique* (May 1991):13. My translation.

19. Harold R. Isaacs, *Scratches on Our Minds* (New York: John Day, 1958).

20. After A.D. 600, Jews in Spain were forced to accept Christian baptism under the Visigoths. In 711, they were one of the key groups that successfully appealed to the Arab leader Tariq to cross into Iberia from Morocco (hence "Gibraltar," from Jebel al-Tariq, the hill of Tariq).

21. Edward Gibbon, *Decline and Fall of the Roman Empire* (Oxford: Bury, 1777), ch. 52.

22. There were seventeen libraries in Arab Cordova alone, one containing over 400,000 volumes. In the twelfth century, the Primate of Spain, Archbishop Raymond, established an entire college at Toledo to translate Arabic works on Aristotle, Ptolemy, Archimedes, Hippocrates, Galen, and Euclid. Albertus Magnus, Thomas Aquinas, Roger Bacon, and William of Auvergne were all preoccupied with translating Arab texts. The Europeanization of the names of the great Arab scholars also helped suppress knowledge of them. For example, "Averroes" was ibn-Rushd, "Avicenna" was ibn-Sina, "Maimonides" was al-Maimoun, "Rhazes" was ar-Razi, "Alhazen" was al-Haytham. Few Westerners in the late twentieth century know that the word *algebra* is from the centuries-used treatise "Restoration and Equation" by the eleventh-century Arab mathematician al-Jabr w-al-Muqbala al-Khwarizmi.

23. On this intellectual debt, see Sir Richard Southern, *Western Views of Islam in the Middle Ages* (Cambridge: Cambridge University Press, 1980); Nabih Amin Faris, ed., *The Arab Heritage* (Princeton: Princeton University Press, 1944); P. K. Hitti, *History of The Arabs* (London: Macmillan, 1944); Jacob Bronowski, *The Ascent of Man* (Boston: Little Brown ,1973).

24. Shakespeare, *Othello,* v.ii.; also Hamlet's metaphor of his fortunes "turning Turk."

25. For example, Martin Luther ("shameful abominations and deceptions"); Robert Burton ("the lying perjuryose Machomete"); the Dean of Norwich in 1697 ("The True Nature of Imposture fully display'd in the Life of Mahomet"); Barthelemy d'Herbelot in 1718 ("le fameux imposteur Mahomet").

26. Edward Said, *Orientalism* (New York: Vintage, 1979), is the classic study of all these processes.

27. The military maps used by the British forces landing in Port Said in the 1956 Anglo-French-Israeli aggression actually named the indigenous part of the city *Wog Town.*

28. A corruption of the Spanish name Diego.

29. Mark Twain, *Innocents Abroad* (London: Chatto & Windus, 1881).

30. Speech by Senator Thomas Hart Benton, U.S. Senate, May 28, 1846, from Warfel, Gabriel, and Williams, eds., *The American Mind* (New York: American Book Co., 1947), pp. 478–479.

31. As Senator Beveridge asserted when calling for annexation of the Philippines, U.S. Senate, January 9, 1900.

32. Quotations from his Fourth Annual Message to Congress, December 6, 1904.

33. In President George Washington's Farewell Address on September 17, 1796, in Henry Steele Commager, ed., *Documents of American History* (New York: Crofts, 1945), pp. 169–175.

34. Observations on July 28, 1791, from the collection by Edward S. Morgan reprinted in the *New York Times,* February 22, 1981.

35. The verb *spread-eagle* evidently came into use in the 1840s with a totally different meaning from its recent usage: the wings of the American eagle extending outward over the planet.

36. On the dubious Kuwait charges, which not even a Kuwait court trial based on testimony extracted by torture has yet adjudicated, see especially, Seymour M. Hersh, *New Yorker,* November 1, 1993, pp. 80–92.

37. This phrase is copyrighted by the author (the title of a book in preparation).

38. *The Challenge to the South: The Report of the South Commission* (New York: Oxford University Press, 1990), p. 4.

39. An analyst living in London in the 1960s soon learned that it had already become "impolite" to mention "colonialism."

40. During his first job as a hygiene inspector in Nairobi, Kenyan leader Tom Mboya was working in a white-settler dairy when a settler woman came in, looked all around the room, and asked, "Is anybody here?" Tom Mboya, *Freedom and After* (London: Deutsch, 1963), p. 29.

41. Kenneth B. Noble, *New York Times*, October 31, 1993.

42. Throughout western Europe and North America in the early 1890s populations were 95 percent rural and 5 percent urban; by the early 1990s these percentiles had been almost exactly reversed.

43. David Malloch, early eighteenth century, in *Imitation of Horace*.

13

The Crisis of Political Legitimacy and the Muslim World

HAMID MOWLANA

Why does the world seem to be fragmenting, a process too often characterized by disintegration, violence, and such phrases as *nationalism, ethnicity, tribalism,* or *fundamentalism?* One school of thought holds that the nation-state system, which for years gave people a sense of binding and belonging, is no longer the guarantor of social peace and protector of the national economy. More specifically and according to this school of thought, national sovereignty has eroded because the modern world system of consumer capitalism under the sponsorship of transnational companies has moved beyond the confines of the nation-state in search of an ever-expanding market. Increasingly, national governments are unable to serve as a domestic champion against globalism or globalization. As the nation-state fails to deliver the required sense of security to citizens, a feeling of anchorlessness develops in the individuals, and thus people turn to local identity, shifting their loyalty to their own immediate groups for protection.

When the process of secularism was completed in Europe and capitalism had engendered a measure of personal freedom, the nation-state replaced communitarian and feudal systems in the West. In the Islamic world the process was quite different, since the concepts of the state and the community were in sharp contrast to those developed in the West. The nation-state system was never accepted by large segments of the Muslim world in the first place, and this continues to be the major source of crisis in Islamic countries. Unlike in the West, it is not the changing or shifting role of the nation-state but the very existence of it that is responsible for fragmentation and disunity as well as the ongoing crisis in the Islamic world. The crises of the modern nation-state system in the Islamic world must be analyzed in their cultural context, since the process of *nation building* has been incompatible with the cultural settings of these societies.

The discourse on the nation-state in the Western industrialized world deals almost exclusively with evolution of a particular kind of state that had its origin and development in western Europe over the past 200 years in predominantly Christian and capitalist or socialist countries. In the Islamic countries, the conception of the state, however, historically offered a radically different version of the relationship of governing bodies to society. Over the past fourteen centuries, the notion of the state in an Islamic context has undergone the process of articulating its unique identity in the contemporary world. The division of different geographical, linguistic, and national groupings in this part of the world into the modern nation-state system since the turn of the twentieth century has created an ongoing crisis of political legitimacy and identity that requires close scrutiny.

The crisis of political legitimacy in the Muslim world was and continues to be ignored by many writers and analysts because of the emphasis they put on the study of formal political institutions such as the state, political parties, bureaucratic institutions, and modern parliamentary and governmental infrastructures. Yet the traditional Islamic political and social institutions, the informal political channels through which interest articulation and political demands are expressed, and the deep Muslim feelings and reservations about the nation-state system that persist beneath a modernizing culture in the last two decades all have altered the balance of political forces nationally and regionally.

For years it was assumed that certain Islamic countries had fairly strong institutions that contributed to the continued legitimacy of government: monarchy in Iran and the modern state in Turkey. However, Islamic movements in both countries have stood apart from the mainstream of political thought. The most formidable challenge to modern nation-states in Iran, Turkey, Egypt, and other countries has come from the mobilized forces of political Islam, a reminder that modern politics has failed to solve the spiritual and material needs of these societies. In Algeria, a deep desire for change among the country's restless population has locked the government and the underground Islamic movement into a cycle of violence that many believe will ultimately end the long rule of the secular elite that admired the West and its culture. In 1992, after the cancellation of multiparty elections that would have given the Islamic Salvation Front vast representation in and control of the government, Algerians fought against one another for the first time since their country gained independence from French colonial rule in the early 1960s.

The U.S.-led intervention in Somalia in 1993 was met by formidable resistance not from the modern nation-state system of postcolonial Somalia that collapsed after the end of the Cold War (and the rivalry of the two superpowers in the Horn of Africa) but from the combination of traditional Islamic authorities and the centuries-old clan politics that had characterized the societies of East Africa.[1] The Islamic Union Party (Ittihad), Somalia's armed Muslim group, which seeks to establish an Islamic state based on *shari'ah* (Islamic law), was credited by the Western media for moving into areas where there was a power vacuum and for bringing "an end to the kind of violence and banditry that have wracked this country for nearly two years."[2] In neighboring Sudan, where European-inspired political elites and Islamic authorities were at odds with each other, the Islamic movement group, considered a few years before as a minor irritant by the media and the West, has managed to outlast the old Sudanese dictatorship and to establish in its place the first Islamic republic in Africa. "Islam is a wave of history. It will come through evolution or by revolution," declared Hassan al-Turabi, a scholar and leader of the Islamic movement in the Sudan and the African continent.[3]

Ever since their independence immediately after World War II, modern nation-states of Muslim South and East Asian countries, such as Pakistan, Bangladesh, Indonesia, and Malaysia, have faced fundamental problems arising from the contradictions created between a modern secular polity and an Islamic notion of the state and community. For example, in 1993, Islamic movements won two victories over their secular opponents in Indonesia and Malaysia, an outcome that underlined the growing importance of Islam in the region's politics. In Jakarta, the Indonesian government bowed to pressure from student and religious leaders and abolished a national lottery after weeks of demonstrations, as gambling is prohibited under Islam. In Malaysia's Kelantan state, the state assembly unanimously passed a bill to introduce an Islamic criminal code. Jakarta has ruthlessly suppressed an Islamic rebellion in Aceh, northern Sumatra, but both Indonesian and Malaysian governments have sought to co-opt militant Muslims by encouraging interest-free banking and establishing a number of Muslim organizations. Indonesia, with 90 percent of its 190 million inhabitants nominally Muslim, has the world's largest Muslim population. Nearly one-fourth of the world's population (more than 1 billion people) is Muslim.

The Muslim Central Asian republics of the former Soviet Union, from Azerbaijan to Tajikistan, not only were subject to the geopolitical struggle of the nineteenth century between the Russian and British empires for the dominance of the region but also were later forced to accept the nation-state system with political and ideological boundaries where none existed before. If the erosion of state legitimacy in Central Asian republics began with the people's disillusionment in the Soviet system, the current U.S. attempt to keep the nation-state systems of the region tuned to capitalism and the Turkish-style secular state is no better. Today's crisis focuses on Islamic movements throughout the region, but it is replete in the media with echoes of the domino theory once invoked for communism. Many Central Asian people consider themselves as part of the Islamic world with historical, political, and economic ties to such countries as Iran, Turkey, and Afghanistan, but the Russians still view the area as their Central America with a frightening vision of an Islamic ideological insurgency.

Today, the Islamic nations face one of the most severe dilemmas of their contemporary existence, yet how they will deal with this issue remains largely problematic because the very political structure of the nation-state (upon which they have been erected) is in part the cause of their underlying instability. Many

Muslim nation-states proudly include the words *democratic* or *socialist* (or any number of other descriptive political adjectives) in their official names, which have little or no relevance to their society. In fact, regardless of what type of government the names appear to represent, most of those states are dominated by a small number of political elites who are highly uncharacteristic of the general population and are indifferent to Islamic political and cultural values. These elites are generally supported by monarchical, tribal, ethnic, or military regimes and rely almost entirely upon Western ideologies (beliefs, ideas, values, and emotions) to legitimize their existence. To understand the crisis of political legitimacy, one must understand (1) the Islamic concepts of state and community; (2) the syndrome of nationalism as a symbol of the modern nation-state system; and (3) the process of domination and hegemony imposed by the great powers.

The State and Community

The major crisis facing the Islamic countries is that, with a very few exceptions, their political systems and their governments are inconsistent and incompatible with the core of their cultural systems and values, that of Islam. The political tone of the Islamic countries from the beginning of the twentieth century was distinctly dominated by two streams of political forces: the politics of modern ideology and material interest. The prominence of modern ideological politics can be last seen in the constitutional movements and the ideas of European liberalism in Iran, Egypt, and the Ottoman Empire at the turn of the century; in the rise of Arab nationalism during World War I; and in the movements of national socialism and the development of military governments in a number of Islamic countries after World War II.

This ideological flood, which had its course in modern political parties, secular intellectual elites, and the officers corps, was paralleled by the system of material politics, which was rooted in traditional monarchy, in intertribal coalitions and competition, and most recently in the growing sector of industrial and transnational infrastructure. This resulted in an attempt to alter the political and economic segments of society in order to meet the requirements of a global market system. The elites and the so-called modern institutions and groups pursued their material interests with disregard to society as a whole and often without any accountability, thereby increasing the disparity in strength between the state and society. However, both the politics of modern ideology and the politics of material interests were counterproductive in Islamic societies because they were inconsistent with the principles and precepts of the politics of *ummah* (Islamic community) that were perceived as the core of political legitimacy and the doctrine of both spiritual and temporal powers and authorities.

For example, the issue today causing the greatest instability in the Middle East is the fact that the very basis upon which the modern political structure of the region is built (i.e., the nation-state) is a concept that is alien to and in many ways diametrically opposed to the fundamental principles of Islam. Historically, the great Islamic empires that began their expansion in the seventh century were in no way related to those concepts that are integral parts of the modern nation-state. Rather, they were based primarily on the precepts of the Islamic faith, which helps to explain the great diversity and viability characterizing Islamic societies in the past. However, as almost inevitably occurs throughout history, the Islamic empires eventually eroded and were encroached upon by newly expanding powers. Thus, beginning with Napoleon's invasion of Egypt near the turn of the eighteenth century, a political system was imposed upon the Middle East that was not a system resulting from indigenous evolution but rather was a system that had grown to meet the needs of feudal Europe. The imposition of this concept of government (and with it an entirely new way of thinking) has been one of the primary causes of instability in the Middle East for the past 200 years.

In many current analyses, great confusion arises from the failure to make a distinction between a nation-state and an Islamic state. It should be emphasized that whereas the nation-state is a political state, the Islamic state is a *muttagi,* or religio-political, *God-fearing* state.

The foundation of the Islamic state is based on the Koran, the *sunnah* (tradition), and the *shari'ah* (Islamic canonical law). Whereas in a secular nation-state system sovereignty rests in the people, in an Islamic order the sovereignty of the state rests in God and not in thrones, individuals, or groups of people. Where the state does not acknowledge the sovereignty of God, religion becomes a private affair for the citizens. In Islam, religion is not a private affair; it is a public affair. The spiritual and temporal powers are not separated but are united.[4] When Islam appeared as a world power in the seventh century, the concepts of the nation and the state as we know them today did not exist. Instead, Islam developed the concept of the *ummah,* the community of the faithful who professed to believe in both the spiritual and temporal dimensions of Islam. The concept of the *caliphate* as head of the community was formulated after the death of the Prophet to represent the political and spiritual powers of Islam. The political theories of the classical period of Islam identify the *caliph* or *Imam* as the head of the *ummah.*[5] In the Islamic context the power of the *caliph* is limited and can be removed by the community if the *caliph* fails to exercise the Islamic tenets and exceeds the power conferred upon him.

From an Islamic perspective, the study and conduct of state affairs cannot be separated from the methods of ethics; the need is to determine what ought to be and not to analyze what merely is. The concept of *ummah* transcends national borders and political boundaries. Islamic community transcends the notion of the modern nation-state system: An Islamic community is a religio-political concept and is present only when it is nourished and governed by Islam. The notion of community in Islam makes no sharp distinction between public and private; therefore, what is required of the community at large is likewise required of the state and every individual member of society. Race, ethnicity, tribalism, and nationalism have no place in distinguishing one member of the community from the rest. Nationalities, cultural differences, and geographical factors are recognized, but domination based on nationalism is rejected. Both the concept of the state and *ummah* emphasize communality and collectivity based on Islamic tenets and not interindividualism. Communication in society and by the state must have ethical and moral dimensions. The social contract that becomes the basis of *ummah* is not based on free will of undefined choice but is subject to higher norms through the will of Allah. The classical period of the Islamic state that began with the Prophet (A.D. 572–632) and continued through the first four *caliphs* (632–661) exemplifies the ideal period in which communication between the state and society was most harmonious. The general political principles in Islam directed the affairs of the state. These principles called for just leadership, provision for the weak, and a critical yet constructive dialogue between the government and the members of society.

The emergence of the modern nation-state system in the Islamic countries partly arose out of the shift from traditional Islamic politics toward secular government that manifested itself in Turkey's abolition of the *caliphate* in 1924. Turkey's decisive move toward secularism, in turn, had serious repercussions on the rest of the Muslim world. Although Islamic political thought had been undergoing scrutiny by both religious reformists and traditionalists since the end of the eighteenth century, Turkey's action compelled the Islamic countries to realize alternatives to the *caliphate* that had divorced itself from the original ideas of the Islamic state. Hence, different religious viewpoints surfaced with Turkey's move toward secularization. On the one hand, the reformists or Muslim revisionists perceived the abolition of the *caliphate* as an auspicious event marking the overthrow of an old and corrupt hierarchy. For the more orthodox Muslims, on the other hand, the Turkish and modernist trend toward Western thought and secular practice reinforced the traditional view that Islam must be preserved as an all-encompassing way of life guiding moral, political, and communication actions of society. Indeed, as history showed, the cultural agenda of Kemal Ataturk in Turkey and his contemporary ruler in Iran, Reza Shah, exemplified an effort to diminish the Islamic aspects of the Turkish and Iranian peoples.[6]

To see the effects of grafting the Western political mind-set onto a region for which it is not suited, one need look no further than the chaotic turmoil of the modern Middle East. The region is littered with the remnants of regimes that relied directly upon imported Western values and ideals as the primary justification of their existence. Both the Shah of Iran and the former monarchs of Egypt had very little if anything to do with the historical processes of Middle Eastern political development and everything to do with the ambitious leaders who saw modernization along Western lines as the only viable option in a secular world. Even today the majority of the governments in the region follow the same pattern.

In Egypt, for example, the so-called modern government of President Mubarak (which for all practical purposes is secular) is scarcely representative of the

Egyptian population at large. After taking office in 1981 following the assassination of President Anwar el-Sadat by Islamic militants, Mubarak's government, which governs under emergency law, set up a special military court that has sentenced many of his opponents to death—"the largest number of executions for political crimes in Egypt this century," according to the *New York Times*.[7] Among other things, he is being criticized for supporting the interests of the West and especially the United States in Egypt and the Arab world and for surrounding himself "with sycophants and old military cronies, [who issue] edicts and decrees in the splendid isolation of seaside palaces in the manner that doomed British colonial rulers and monarchy."[8]

For two decades Egypt has been the beneficiary of one of the world's most ambitious assistance programs, a multibillion-dollar aid program involving the United States, as well as a number of conservative Arab states and European countries—all provided to secure the current political regime in Cairo and, as Mubarak himself has declared, "to push Egypt toward a market economy."[9] The Islamic militants are calling for the establishment of an Islamic state in Egypt at a time when more than 20 percent of the country's 18 million workforce is unemployed and another 20 percent is underemployed. In addition, the nation's tourism industry, which once brought in $2.2 billion a year, has been crippled as a result of insecurity and violence. In 1993, in response to the criticism of the referendum in which for the third straight election he was the only presidential candidate, Mubarak said, "Until we have stability and economic reforms this is the best way to run the country,"[10] and he later rejected calls to appoint a vice president, saying that there was no one who was qualified.

Saddam Hussein of Iraq and President Hafiz al-Assad of Syria are no more Islamic leaders interested in the physical and spiritual well-being of their people than they are ambitious men who see the opportunity to expand their personal authority and prestige according to purely Western principles. Even the countries of the Arabian peninsula, though perhaps more Islamic than other countries of the region, operate primarily according to Western rules and have been able to avoid the severe internal turmoil that plagues other Middle Eastern states only because they are able to placate their citizens through the distribution of their extraordinary wealth. But the Saudi Arabian and other Arab kingdoms' well of petrodollars is running dry, and a potential for a major financial and political crisis is building.

Saudi Arabia, the major U.S. ally in the Arab world and one of the world's wealthiest countries, has undermined its financial stability with decades of unrestricted spending on military and Western-oriented developmental projects to a point that the kingdom's debt has risen to almost $10 billion. Large deficits are expected, and the financial reserves that in the early 1980s totaled $121 billion have melted away.[11] It was the *special relationship* between the United States and the kingdom that evolved in the 1970s that led the U.S. government to recycle petrodollars by issuing special, nonmarketable Treasury debt to the Saudis. Now this strategic relationship has become an obstacle and is preventing fiscal regulators from limiting lending by new banks to Saudi Arabia. Referring to the U.S. relationship with the Shah of Iran in the 1970s, a 1993 editorial in the *New York Times* summed up Washington's worry and Wall Street's concern about Saudi Arabia: "In the short run, this recycling of American dollars spent on oil for U.S.-made weapons is good for the American economy. But in the long term, it could bring trouble. The rough economic equilibrium that is achieved comes at considerable risk to the Middle East's stability."[12]

Yet it was exactly this *special strategic relationship* that was in the making again in the early 1990s, this time between another troubled kingdom, Morocco, and the United States and Europe. The thirty-two-year authoritarian reign of King Hassan II of Morocco as both a monarch and an *Imam* has created one of the most contradictory crises of the postcolonial era in North Africa. He has pleased the West by introducing free-market reforms in Morocco's economy and "wants to be repaid with the kind of economic and political cooperation with Europe that Mexico enjoys with the United States."[13] As King Hassan established new economic and strategic ties with Europe by opposing the Islamic movement, his legitimacy and Morocco's drive for a modern nation-state sank to an all-time low. To overcome the challenge to his regime by a nation where two-thirds of the 25 million people are under age twenty-five and unemployment remains very high, Hassan in 1993 inaugurated a billion-dollar mosque that bears his name and was built by the French architect, Michel Purseau. But the only visitors among the Middle Eastern leaders included prime ministers of Israel and Lebanon, which made a clear political statement that the inauguration "was widely seen as a flop."[14]

The Syndrome of Nationalism

The aspect of the nation-state system that has been the most destabilizing of the imported ideologies in the Islamic world has been nationalism. In Muslim countries attempts to create a sense of loyalty to an entity that is for all practical purposes foreign has led to seriously destructive consequences. Largely as a result of instigation from those in authority, the peoples of the Islamic world are divided more than ever before along the lines of ethnicity, language, and the possession of geographic territory. Islam has thus not been used to capitalize on its assimilative capability, which had made it the unifying force behind one of the greatest political powers the world has ever known. Islam has been subordinated to the powerful ideology of nationalism and has created a dependency upon the West for the understanding of the basic rules of both domestic and international policymaking.

Until the nineteenth century, the Turks, the Arabs, and the Persians thought of themselves primarily as Muslims yet with a distinct nationality, known as *melliet.* Their primary loyalty belonged to Islam and not to the state, the empire, or the dynasty. Under the Islamic system of *ummah,* they identified themselves as separate cultural and linguistic groups within Islam. For example, when the power of the Ottoman Empire was supreme, different *millat* (national) groups, including Arabs, enjoyed cultural autonomy, and various religious minorities, including Christians and Jews, were given autonomy and protection. The concept of an *Ottoman nation* or the *Arab nation* as a primary focus of unity and loyalty under the nation-state system were new innovations under European influence. When the creed of Islam was replaced by nationalism as a result of internal decay and external influences, the interethnic and internation rivalry increased, with nationalism and imperialism often finding themselves in an unholy alliance.

The most conspicuous example among numerous others is the exchange of letters between Sherif (and after 1916, King) Hussein of the Arabian Hejaz and Sir Henry McMahon, then the British high commissioner in Cairo, in 1915. The latter promised the former a united Arab state from the Euphrates to the Nile if the Arabs would fight with the British against the Turks. Under the banner of Arab nationalism and aided by an annual British subsidy of 2.4 million pounds, Sherif Hussein ordered the Arabs under Faisal and Lawrence during World War I to side with British imperialism against their Muslim brothers and against the only state that had maintained Islam as a major world power for centuries and that was the only possible challenger to European powers.

British promises to Sherif Hussein and the Arab nationalists were not kept. Through the Sykes-Picot Agreement at the end of World War I, the French and the British divided the spoils of the Arab Ottoman Empire.[15] However, for serving the cause of British imperialism, Sherif Hussein, instead of being the *king of the Arab World,* had to settle for the province of Hejaz. His first son, Amir Faisal, was set on the throne of Iraq, and his second son became the king of Jordan. In place of independence and unification, the Arab world had been divided into either protectorates or the so-called small nation-states often quarreling with each other as the Balfour Declaration opened a new era in the Middle East.

So-called *decolonialization* under the nation-state system drew political frontiers in the Islamic world where none existed before. It created competing national leaderships among a people with a long common history and, in the case of Arabs, even a common language and culture. Decolonialization from imperialism and imperial powers became the beginning of the recolonialization process under the banner of nationalism. As one Western scholar observed about polity and society:

> If the subject of government in Muslim society has been left almost until the end, that is because it was never, or almost never, anything other than superimposed; never, or almost never, the emanation or repression of that society. It is in its solidarities at the individual level that the true social coherences and structures of Islam are to be found, not in the princes, their soldiers, and their tax collectors.[16]

Since individual Muslims consider themselves part of the *ummah,* government authority and legitimacy are further eroded when armies of various Islamic countries are used against each other. For example, European colonial powers in Africa always employed Muslims as their local and regional troops and used them against other Muslims. Somali and Galla Muslims served Italians against Arabs and Turks in North Africa, Hausa Muslims were forced to fight against the Congo Arabs, and Sudanese served Germans against Abushiri as Senegalese Muslims served the French in the Algerian war of liberation.[17] More recently, in the Iran-Iraq war and the Persian Gulf War, Muslims were forced to fight each other, and in the U.S.-U.N. intervention in Somalia, Pakistani soldiers were confronted by Muslim Somalis. In the Muslim community, the holy war is a religious duty pertaining to the entire Muslim community, but this principle conflicts with the concept of the modern secular army that is supposed to be loyal to the nation-state. This tension has created further instability within Islamic countries.

The crisis of political legitimacy in the Islamic world was further reinforced by a series of humiliating events during the four decades after World War II. They included the failure of secular democracy in Turkey, Pakistan, and Indonesia; the defeat of the Arabs in the Six Day War with Israel in 1967 and later in 1973; the Pakistani war with India in 1971; the Israeli occupation of Lebanon in the early 1980s; the Soviet occupation of Afghanistan; and in the 1990s the devastating Persian Gulf War and the massacre and genocide of Muslims in Serbia-Herzegovina. The Islamic revolution in Iran for many Muslims was a landmark and a watershed in their campaign against illegitimate governments in their own countries.

Arab nationalist discourse has tried to replace the term *Islamic* with *Arab* in an attempt to influence the population and eventually to change the backdrop of the analysis of political and social facts. However, the fact that Islam is not recognized as an important element of Arab nationalism characterizes two contradictions in its ideology. In the first place, the Arab nationalist movement emphasizes the unity of all Arabs based on history, language, interests, and blood ties. But the Arab nationalist movement is contradicted in geographic terms when it appeals to Arabs of the *homeland,* from the Persian Gulf to the Atlantic. Not only does this disregard other Arabic lands, but it also overlooks the fact that the notion of the homeland comes from Islam. In the second place, Arab nationalists are contradicted again in their view of Islam as a social growth, since it was also the motivating factor for the spread of the Arab homeland. Nationalist thinking recognizes certain uniting factors such as language, common history, and heritage but ignores Islam because of nationalism's secular foundation. Ironically, it was Islam that united the warring tribes of Arab prehistory and created a true Arab identity. Arabic language and culture are a result of Islam, not vice versa. In reality, Arab nationalism reflects ideas of Western origin, even though the movement's name implies that it is anchored by Arab culture and thought. Secularism, the defining idea of the nationalist movement, is Western.

The nationalist movements in Muslim countries, which have rallied around the idea of independence, defined the word as freedom from external domination and influences. Yet this interpretation did not give a positive defining character to the word; rather they rejected Islam as this defining character. For example, Arab nationalists have clung to the idea that nationalism has priority over religion as the supreme identity for the people. However, the Israeli example of religion as the basis of its nationalist movement contradicts the Arab idea.

In their search for a solution to the conflict with Israel, Arab nationalists rejected the resources of the Muslim world, as these would have jeopardized their secular beliefs, yet chose to jeopardize their so-called independence by seeking help from international sources. Yasser Arafat and his PLO (Palestine Liberation Organization) leaders suffer from this nationalism syndrome. Hence, the accord between Israel and Arafat's faction faces a crisis of legitimacy because of Arafat and his colleagues, problems with identity, secularism, and their ties with the most conservative and delegitimized leaders in the Arab world and their Western supporters. Arab nationalism is flawed by its tendency to unite Islamic and Arab history, as a majority of contributors to Islamic civilization were not Arabs. Muslims created a civilization that tolerated populations of Jews and Christians, which further complicates the problem.

The Young Turk Movement leader Ziya Gokalp, a Turkish nationalist thinker, helped to restore nationalistic thought in the country and contributed to Ataturk's subsequent success in exploiting Turkish national pride. Nationalism has also led to an almost inevitable conflict between the Turkish and the Islamic identities. Gokalp associates his feelings for Turkey with pre-Islamic tribal identity rather than with the Islamic *ummah* identity. However, he contradicts himself on this point because he invokes the image of defending the homeland, which is derived from Islam.

Historically, Gokalp considered the Turks a part of the Islamic *ummah*, but he condemned Turkish history, which he associated with the Byzantine and Iranian civilizations, and sought to implement the teachings of Western civilization. He advocated European secularism in his declaration that nations or modern states could not be part of an *ummet,* thus abolishing the political status of the *ummah* identity of the Turk. Gokalp did, however, strive to maintain the *caliphate* as a spiritual guide but not as a way to unify Muslims politically. Gokalp's ideal was to protect his homeland and to adopt a *new life* for that homeland. Though this idea had no predefined goal, it did have a disciplined method, through which Gokalp attained his ideal. He wanted to adopt a *moral and secular* value system for Turkey but did not explain the supposed *immorality* of religion that had dominated traditional Ottoman society.

Eventually, the Republic of Turkey became a one-party state. Secularism dominated, as European dress, romanized script, prayer in the Turkish language, and even a proposed change in the method of worship replaced the early declaration of Islam as the state religion. Mustafa Kemal, however, did not consult the common people during this formation of a new national identity for the Turks, which weakened the process of secularization. Westernization became synonymous with modernization. Government-controlled education was the key to Westernizing the population, with the goal of shifting loyalty from the Islamic *ummah* to the Turkish national identity. Ethnicity became the new central idea as religion and the Arabic and Persian languages were banned in schools. Turks educated in this new system became much more European-oriented, although the overall success of the educational reforms was difficult to measure. A new constitution was declared in 1961 under the auspices that the principles of Kemalism and secularism were at risk. Article 2 of the constitution declares secularism as the foundation of the state, and Article 19 makes it unlawful to use religion to invoke social, economic, political, or legal change in order to promote that religion or personal or political interests. In the 1960s, however, the exploitation of Islam for political reasons grew. Today, Turkey continues to suffer from an identity crisis.

During the next seventy years, Iran paid dearly for the contradiction between a secular state being tailored on European models and an Islamic state based on *ummah*. From 1925, when the Iranian monarchy was handed from the Qajars to the Pahlavis, mainly as a result of British instigation and support, until the Islamic Revolution of 1978–1979, an authoritarian system of the secular nation-state was imposed on Iran. The reign of Reza Shah, the founder of the Pahlavi dynasty, was a period of wholesale Westernization. Religion, which had always dominated national life, was subordinated to the interests of the state. Reza Shah undercut religious power in the country in many ways. For example, he took away the judicial authority of the *ulama* (religious leaders) and gave it to civil courts. He sent many religious leaders and well-known *ayatollahs* of the time into exile, and as a result, the state gained considerable influence over its new bureaucracy and much of urban society.

Reza Shah's official ideology did not survive the fiasco of 1941 when British and Russian troops marched into Iran during World War II resulting in his abdication. However, the concept of public communication he had laid out continued under his son, Mohammad Reza Shah, with the exception of several short periods of relaxation in which the religious authorities as well as the secular liberals succeeded in challenging the state's dominance of political discourse and its monopoly of communication. Two decades of Reza Shah's rule had not succeeded in separating religion from politics to the degree that it was carried out under Kemal Ataturk in Turkey. From 1951 to 1953, a combination of religious and secular movements, under the leadership of Ayatollah Sayied Abul-ghasem Kashani and the nationalist liberal Mohammad Mossadegh, who had succeeded in becoming the prime minister, not only waged an antiimperialist war against the British by nationalizing the Iranian oil companies but also nearly toppled the regime of Mohammad Reza Shah, who had fled the country after an unsuccessful attempt against this religio-political coalition. However, a coup instigated by the U.S. Central Intelligence Agency (CIA) in August 1953 ended this short period of religio-political expansion and convergence and reinstated Mohammad Reza to power. The second challenge to the state's power came a decade later in 1963, when Imam Ayatollah Ruhollah Khomeini, mobilizing the population behind religious authorities and using traditional channels of public communication such as the mosques, bazaars, and *hozah* (religious colleges), waged a campaign against the Shah's authoritarian regime as well as his Western model of development, only to be exiled first to Turkey and then to Iraq.

It is important politically (and in terms of leadership) that Shia religious leaders could maintain their independence from the semisecular or monarchical states that had come into power in the past.[18] In the Sunni-tradition countries, such as Egypt and Saudi Arabia, religious leaders' power was consolidated within the existing political structure, which left the *ulama* little autonomy. It was precisely this power of checks and balances between the *ulama* and the state or monarchs in Iran that allowed Imam Khomeini, and others before him, to be in the center of power when disputes arose. Mohammad Reza's wholesale Westernization through his so-called *White Revolution* failed in making Iran a modern nation-state system modeled after Europe. In addition, his propensity toward reliance on the United States and certain European powers as well as the systematic intrusion of foreign powers in the internal affairs of Iran further eroded the legitimacy of the state on which his power was based. Indeed, it was the publication of an article against religious authority placed by the Shah's regime in the leading Teheran daily newspaper, *Ettella'at,* on January 7, 1978, that quickened the revolutionary uprising and accelerated the outburst of popular anger, which finally led to the overthrow of the Pahlavi dynasty in February 1979.

In sum, three major elements underlined the process of communication and the state before the Islamic Revolution of 1978–1979. First, the concept of a secular nation-state was never fully realized in Iran because of the contradiction it generated with Islamic notions of the state and community. Second, two lines of contradictory and competing communication channels were created, one directed by the state and the other rooted in the Iranian religio-political tradition. Whereas the state, by its *modernization* attempts, generated specific lines of communication along with the development of bureaucracy, university systems, military and telecommunication systems, mass media, and managerial systems, the community leaders and the *ulama* maintained control over vast, highly complex and sophisticated cultural and communication systems never yielding to the authority of the state.

As long as the state bureaucracy and infrastructure remained fairly small, it was possible to control and socialize members of the bureaucracy along the state party line; however, with the growth of population and the expansion of education and bureaucratic and information communication systems, the process of secularization was indeed difficult to sustain. In other words, control of political power in Iran requires control over the traditional channels of communication rather than over the mass media alone. It is the power of traditional authorities that determines the legitimacy of the modern media rather than the other way around.

The third element has been a historically systematic interference of foreign powers in both communication and state affairs of Iran. This interference has further eroded the legitimacy of governments in power and deliberately blocked any attempt to establish a religio-political state that might have served as a model for the Islamic community in general.[19]

Parallel developments occurred in other Muslim countries. Postwar development in South and East Asian countries is a case in point. Pakistan was created as a refuge for Muslims who wanted to escape British India in an effort to preserve their identity. Muhammad 'Ali Janah, leader of the Pakistan movement, articulated the need of a new nation because of differences in culture, heritage, and law. Yet after Pakistan was created, his argument seemed to change, which led to disagreements over the secular or Islamic basis of the country's constitution.[20] The goal of the British educational system in India was to create a group of people to serve as liaisons between the British government and the people of India, whom the British felt should be "English in task, in opinions, in morals and in intellect" (Lord Macaulay). Ironically, Indian nationalism grew out of this system, as nationalism was inherent in a British education and was therefore passed on to Indians. This eventually led to the formation of the Indian National Congress and to Indian independence. Muslims, however, felt threatened by Hindu India and pressed for a separate homeland, which led to the formation of Pakistan in 1947. The educational system in Islamic society precipitated the identity crisis among Muslims. Colonialism had instilled European ideas for so many years that students who chose to identify with Islam did not even understand its history because it was not taught to them. Students who accepted the European ideology suffered because they had not learned about scientific and technological developments in Europe and were not European in color or background.

The Paradigm of Domination

The penetration and the intrusion of the major European powers in the affairs of the Islamic lands had profound impact on the relationship between the state and communication institutions. It must be recalled that this direct incursion of the European powers in the affairs of the Muslim world signaled the beginning of both colonialism and the spread of modern communication technologies, including navigation, telephone and telegraph systems, transportation, and railroads.

The introduction of the European powers in the Middle East, beginning with the Portuguese attempt of hegemony over the Persian Gulf in the sixteenth century and continuing later with the Dutch, the British, and the French penetration into Islamic lands from Egypt to India, had two important consequences. First, it reduced the authority of the state in the Islamic Middle East, subjecting it to the political and economic will of colonial interests. Second, this colonial influence established communication dominance over the affairs of governments in the region and controlled channels of modern communication whenever possible.

Introduction and adoption of the nation-state system in Islamic countries created an atmosphere of crisis in which foreign intervention was succeeded by concealed control. Internally, political power was shifted from community and religio-political leaders to army and bureaucratic elites. In short, the nation-state system introduced other aspects of modern Western ideologies and institutions. In general, the public considered modern leaders and elites either agents of foreign powers or elements through which new systems of colonialism and ideological politics were imposed on society. Thus, each victory of the modern nation-state system in such countries as Turkey, Iran, Pakistan, Egypt, and Indonesia toward modernization was overtaken by a new crisis of economic and social fragmentation. In short, a crisis of political legitimacy grew beneath a modernizing culture.

Internally, a divisive force in Islam sprang out of the ascendancy of Muslim rulers who valued the political authority of the state more than their religious duties. From the seventh century of the Christian era, beginning with the Umayyad and the Abbasid dynasties until the demise of the Ottoman Empire at the end of World War I, the Islamic state gradually became separate from its original concept. Power became divided between the rulers who issued laws under their jurisdictions and the religious scholars and leaders who announced verdicts under the *shari'ah*. Thus, the two lines of communication established in the Islamic countries were often in an adversarial position that gradually evolved into conflict.[21] The situation was well captured by an Islamic observer of the eleventh century, Abul Malli, who said that "we obey the King in matters of State, but in matters of religion the King must consult us,"[22] and in time, contradictions between the state and religion ensued. The system of *caliphate* as a governing body gradually lost its authority yet attempted to retain its communication dominance resulting in repressive measures.

The changing nature of the Islamic state during this period resulted in the alienation and separation of the community from the state. In many cases there existed only the community and its leaders, but the state as such had no place in their scheme of things. The rulers were more preoccupied with repressing disorders and reestablishing themselves against rebellion. In short, the state authority was not evenly effective throughout the territory or the communities claimed by it but tended to assert itself forcefully only in the immediate surroundings of the ruler. The separation of the *ummah* and the state characterizes the current dilemma of the state in almost all the Islamic countries.

For example, whereas the state attempted to centralize the institutions of communication by controlling the traditional channels such as the mosques and traditional schools of education, the community under the leadership of the *ulama* maintained competing channels of communication that challenged the conduct of the state. The seventeenth- and eighteenth-century political systems in a number of Middle Eastern countries, including Iran and Egypt, were characterized by the proverb "If you see the *ulama* at the gates of kings, say there are bad *ulama* and bad kings. If you see the kings at the gates of the *ulama*, say there are good *ulama* and good kings." Thus, the contradiction between Islamic domination and secular power spurred further antagonisms within the Islamic world throughout this period. With the public denouncement of the state, the *ulama* were pressured to act independently of the state. This type of conflict is best illustrated by the Constitutional Revolution (1906) and the Islamic Revolution (1979) in Iran. The resistance of the *ulama* to becoming mere instruments of the state and the correlating division between Islamic and secular leadership triggered these eventual revolutions.

The power of the state and the *ulama* was further distinguished by their relationship to foreign actors. The government tended to yield to the influence of outside courtiers and ministers, whereas the *ulama* held a clear concept and practice of authority, despite restrictions, that resisted outside pressures. The steadfast quality of the *ulama* nurtured a close relationship with the community through the mobilization of traditional communication channels; the state typically ignored its subjects and used modern communication channels and the emerging mass media systems to maintain its legitimacy, collect taxes, or recruit soldiers. Hence, the *ulama* became an intermediary channel of communication between the people and the state, acting on behalf of the *ummah* as well as the nation; however, the foremost loyalty of the community remained toward Islam rather than the state. Muslim disfavor of both the state and imperialism was proclaimed in an Islamic rather than a nationalistic framework.

The contacts between the Islamic world and the West in the nineteenth and twentieth centuries increased the absorption of many Islamic countries into quasi-secular political entities ranging from hereditary monarchies to modern Western- or military-style republics. This also resulted in pronounced conflicts between modern secularism and the Islamic tradition of *shari'ah,* which until the nineteenth century provided the main if not the complete legal underpinnings of social and economic conduct in Muslim societies.[23] The intimate contact between Islam and modern Western industrial countries, coupled with the process of colonization of substantial parts of Asia and Africa, introduced a number of Western standards and values to these societies. Thus, at the beginning of the twentieth century and with the introduction of modern means of communication, transportation, and technologies, the fields of civil and commercial transactions proved particularly prominent for change and new methods of conduct. The first foothold of European law, criminal and commercial, in the Islamic countries (particularly in the Ottoman Empire) was advanced as a result of the systems of capitulations, which ensured that the European citizens residing in the Middle East and a large part of Africa would not be governed by the Islamic laws and conduct of ethics but by their own laws and traditions. Furthermore, the reform movements such as the Tanzimat (1839–1876) in the Ottoman period and the Constitutional reform in Iran (1906–1911) were indeed direct translations of French and other European codes, which tended to establish secularism and European rules of conduct. In Egypt from 1875 onward, that process went even further in the adaptation of European laws in such fields as commerce and maritime and included the enactment of civil codes that basically were modeled on French laws and contained only a few provisions drawn from *shari'ah*.

The development of Islamic law and the state can be explained by reviewing briefly the classical period of Islam during which the general political principles directed the affairs of the state and the manner in which communication took its course. These principles during the first four decades of Islamic history called for just leadership; provisions for the weak; a critical yet conservative dialogue between government and the members of the community; government and individual responsibility in the fight against evil; collective mobilization to defend faith; government compliance with regard to conduct that is permitted and prohibited; and rules of inheritance, penalties, and retaliation. During this early period that extended to the fourth *caliphate* under the leadership of Ali, the Prophet's son-in-law, the state exemplified the enactment of many of these principles. The success of their application can be attributed to strong leadership and piety, cultural homogeneity, and spiritual and moral familiarity with the meaning of the Koran, especially as it is related to the solidarity between the government and the governed.

The Turkish state, as the governing force over Islam during the Ottoman Empire, provides a model of Muslim reaction to Europe in the late nineteenth century. During the Tanzimat, the reform movement of 1839–1876, the young Ottomans criticized the initial trend toward Europeanization. In turn, three reactions to Europe prevailed throughout the Islamic world. Critics in Iran and a number of Arab countries perceived the influence of Europe as a threat to the *shari'ah*. Others, primarily in the Indian subcontinent, advocated a balance between European modernity and Islamic tradition. A third group, led by Mustafa Kemal Ataturk of Turkey, called for a total embrace of Europe and secularization of the Turkish state divorced from Islamic rule.

Those who claimed the middle ground integrated elements of pan-Arabism derived partially from the elements of radical social policies to form an Arab nationalist movement that could resist Western imperialism. In particular, the Arab nationalists, as prior subjects of the Ottoman Empire, rejoiced at the abolition of the *caliphate* that had monopolized religious power for so long. Muhammad Iqbal, an influential Islamic modernist in India, supported Turkish secularism and made an attempt to reconstruct the Islamic religious thought in light of development in Europe. Hence, different religious viewpoints surfaced with Turkey's move toward secularization. On the one hand, the modernists or Muslim *revisionists* perceived the abolition of the *caliphate* as an auspicious event marking the overthrow of an old and corrupt hierarchy. For the more orthodox Muslims, on the other hand, the Turkish and modernist trend toward Western thought and secular practice reinforced the traditional view that Islam must be preserved as an all-encompassing way of life guiding moral, political, and social actions. The traditionalists thus regarded Turkey and its supporters as compromising Islamic integrity.

During the twentieth century, the ideological and cultural differences between those who embraced modern Western ways and those who retained traditional Islamic thought became increasingly pronounced. The birth of new Islamic movements during the closing decades of the twentieth century to a large degree can be attributed to the fact that the rise of the nation-state system and the promotion of the brands of nationalism of the Arab, Iranian, Turkish, and Pakistani nature did not lead to any unity of Islamic countries.

Today, those who oppose nationalism and question the basic notion of the nation-state system in Islamic lands propose that foreign encroachment can be resisted through spiritual, moral, and ethical principles of Islam that serve to mobilize Muslims for their cultural autonomy. In the universalistic realm of Islam, patriotic and national views can be transcended through the new principle of *al-watan al-Islam* (the Islamic homeland), or *ummah,* once perceived as the abode of Islam.

It must be recalled that in the past millennium Islam has at least twice become a major military, economic, cultural, and scientific power in Europe, a status that often resulted in hostility and antagonism between the two cultural styles. The first occasion was the rise of the Islamic state in Spain and Sicily and the spread of its influence to France and the Mediterranean region from about the seventh to thirteenth centuries. The second, from the fourteenth century to the beginning of the twentieth, was when the Ottoman Turks dominated the entire part of eastern and central Europe and especially the Balkan region. The gradual loss of political and economic sovereignty in the Islamic world, which began with the rise of the European powers—especially Holland and Portugal, then Germany, France, England, and Russia—and their intrusion into the Islamic community created a wave of internal crises in Islamic countries continuing up to the present time.

The increasing military and economic clout of the United States immediately after the end of World War II coincided with its influence and interventions in the Middle East and a number of other Islamic regions. The Soviet dominance over the Islamic republics of Central Asia and the Cold War system of the postwar period further fragmented the Islamic world and widened the gap between the ruling political elites and the community at large. Increasingly, the great powers' involvement in the internal affairs of the Middle East took on concrete forms. Throughout the twentieth century not only direct but also indirect control through missionaries, educational institutions, mass media, and transnational corporations led to the rise of technocratic elites in many Islamic countries that widened the economic and cultural gap. Indeed, because they owed their allegiances to Europe and America, their ascendancy delegitimized the very foundations of polity.

The nationalistic reformers of the post–World War II era—such as Mohammad Mossadegh of Iran, Jamal Abdul Nasser of Egypt, Sukarno of Indonesia, and counterparts in Ba'athist Syria and Iraq—in part challenged the traditional conservative system inherited or dominated by European and American powers and demanded a new polity. However, as the experience showed, the modern nationalist programs and ideology were derived from the ideology of Western systems and thus were unable to maintain either a sustained level of mass mobilization on behalf of their programs or the legitimacy to assert an alternative independent and culturally compatible system of governance with the Islamic community. The resurgence of the Islamic movement throughout the world, which was touched off by the Islamic Revolution in Iran, led subsequently to instability in Turkey, in the hands of the military officers; to the assassination of Anwar Sadat of Egypt, a close friend of America; and to the downfall of the secular francophone nationalists who had governed Algeria for three decades. The fact that the Islamic Revolution in Iran was willing and able to chart an independent, alternative path to community development not only challenged the hegemony of the superpowers in the Islamic world but also struck a very sensitive chord in the region, altering the unresolved claims to self-determination within many Muslim countries, especially among the Palestinians, the Lebanese, and the Kurds.

The Persian Gulf War and the intervention of U.S. and European powers in support of conservative regimes and nonrepresentative regimes further eroded the state legitimacy in such countries as Kuwait, Saudi Arabia, and Iraq without any basic reform and thus helped destabilize these countries for years to come. The Persian Gulf War also provided for new forces that were unleashed against the conservative as well as the modern secular elites in the Islamic countries. Petitions submitted to the ruling elites in Saudi Arabia and Kuwait to uphold democratic and Islamic principles of constitutional governance and similar demands in Algeria, Egypt, Morocco, Tunisia, and Pakistan were only the beginning of widespread protests that have been made and that, if unanswered, will continue to destabilize the political systems in the Middle East, North Africa, and South and East Asia.

The Question of Identity

The crisis of political legitimacy was further enhanced by a number of conceptual as well as policy developments during the post–World War II period. With the triumph of romanticism and secularism after the French Revolution, naturalism came to occupy and dominate the worldviews of the West. In the Islamic view of the natural and transcendent orders, the latter governs the flow of the former. A large part of the law of Islam deals with the social order, and Muslims today are concerned not with the state of modernization but the state of transformation. The most important difference between transformation and modernization is that the former is out of time (since time is a category of understanding), and the latter is in time.[24] Under the slogans of modernization, economic development, and technological progress, the Islamic countries were deprived of the right to recognize a unique and distinct civilization and culture of their own. For the sake of convenience in terminology and world political hierarchy, they were merely lumped together with less industrialized countries under the vague category *Third World.*

Political stability as a prerequisite for *economic development* was a justification for keeping repressive regimes in power, but the dominant world economic and political systems by then also had claimed the right of access to valuable natural resources in Islamic lands. It was the economic and not the political infrastructure of such countries as Iran, Indonesia, and Saudi Arabia that had become vital for the well-being of the industrialized countries.

In the 1970s, when the oil-producing Islamic countries demanded their rightful share, President Gerald Ford threatened to seize the oil fields by force. If production and distribution of oil and access to world markets dominated the politics of the Persian Gulf and Central Asia in the early part of this century, it was the price tag of oil exported from the fields of the Islamic lands and the surplus capital that determined international political and military maneuvering that led to the Persian Gulf War in 1991.

Indeed, the Persian Gulf War sharpened the cultural and historical division between the state and community in a number of Islamic countries. It provided for new forces, which were unleashed in Algeria, Tunisia, Jordan, Saudi Arabia, Kuwait, Palestine, and a number of other countries in the Islamic world.

Today, in the so-called post–Cold War period, when the fear of communism has disappeared, the governments and the media of the West portray the growth of Islamic movements as a threat and as a major source of national, regional, and international crises. The term *Islamic fundamentalism* is used everywhere and on about every occasion to refer to those states, leaders, and organizations that have challenged many of the presuppositions of the Western ideologies regarding secularism and development theories. The fact remains that the major crisis facing these countries is the contradiction created by a secularist fundamentalism, which insists that its worldview and polity be a self-evident truth, and the Islamic culture and precepts, which have resisted the ontological and epistemological foundations of such theories and proxies. In short, the imposed system of the modern nation-state, with its internal and external hegemonic elements, including the supportive political and economic institutions, has been and will continue to be the major source of crisis in the Islamic world.

The perpetual crisis outlined here and its future course can be better understood if it is realized that Islam historically has been the major force in the world that has resisted the Western modernization. It seems that all other societies, including communistic ones, have surrendered without a great struggle. One consequence of this downfall is that the modernizing political systems of the Islamic world, such as Egypt, Algeria, Syria, and Indonesia, which at times could lead toward socialism in their search for new legitimacy and identity, are now at the mercy of Western financial and political institutions. Freed from the inhibition of the communist threat, the West has now a total, monolithic view of international development, where its globalizing mission under the *free market* (a phrase replacing capitalism after the collapse of the Soviet Union) and an international monetary regime attempt to impose those systems on all countries, including the new republics of Muslim Central Asia. The current ruling elites of modern nation-states of the Muslim world suffer from an acute lack of legitimacy and strategic thinking, simply because they have divorced themselves from the larger community of *ummah* and do not represent the aspirations and worldviews of Islam and their peoples.

NOTES

1. A. H. Nimtz Jr., *Islam and Politics in East Africa* (Minneapolis: University of Minnesota Press, 1980).

2. K. Richburg, "Somali Muslims Warily Eye GIs," *Washington Post,* December 21, 1992, p. A1.

3. H. al-Turabi, "A Gathering Force," *Newsweek,* June 15, 1992, p. 48.

4. Ayatollah Imam Ruhollah Khomeini, *Islam and Revolution: Writings and Declarations of Imam Khomeini,* trans. by Hamid Algar (Berkeley, Calif.: Mizan Press, 1981); Ayatollah Imam Ruhollah Khomeini, *Islamic Government,* trans. and annot. by Hamid Algar (Kerala, India: Islamic Foundation Press, Malappuram District 1988).

5. Q. Khan, *The Political Thoughts of Ibn Taymiyah* (Islamabad, Pakistan: Islamic Research Institute, 1973); M. Umar-ud-din, *The Ethical Philosophy of Al-Ghazzali* (Lahore: Muhammad Ashraf Publishers, 1962); I. Khaldun, *The Muqaddimah: An Introduction to History* (London: Routledge & Kegan Paul, 1967).

6. Hamid Enayat, *Modern Islamic Political Thought* (Austin: University of Texas Press, 1982).

7. Chris Hedges, "As Egypt Votes on Mubarak, He Faces Rising Peril," *New York Times,* October 4, 1993, p. A8.

8. Ibid.

9. Chris Hedges, "Mubarak Promising Democracy, and Law and Order," *New York Times,* October 12, 1993, p. A3.

10. Ibid.

11. Stephen Engelberg, Jeff Gerth, and Tim Wiener, "Saudis' Stability Is Hit Hard by Heavy Spending over the Last Decade," *New York Times,* August 22, 1993, pp. A1, A12.

12. "Saudis Without Dollars," *New York Times,* August 25, 1993, p. A14; Jeff Gerth, "Saudi Stability Hit by Heavy Spending over Last Decade," *New York Times,* August 22, 1993, p. A1; and Christopher Whalen, "The Saudi Well Runs Dry," *Washington Post,* August 29, 1993, p. C2.

13. William Drozdiak, "Morocco Building Ties with Europe by Opposing Islamic Militancy," *Washington Post,* February 6, 1993, p. A17.

14. Roger Cohen, "World's Tallest Minaret, but Short on Popularity," *New York Times,* October 5, 1993.

15. George Lenczowski, *The Middle East in World Affairs,* 4th ed. (Ithaca: Cornell University Press, 1990), pp. 76, 80–82, and 574–575.

16. Claude Cohen, "Economy, Society, and Institutions," in P. M. Holt, H. Fisher, A. Lambton, and B. Lewis, eds., *The Cambridge History of Islam,* vol. 2 (Cambridge: Cambridge University Press, 1970), p. 530.

17. Humphrey Fisher, "The Western and Central Sudan," in Holt et al., *Cambridge History of Islam,* p. 397.

18. Hamid Algar, *Religion and State in Iran: 1785–1906* (Berkeley: University of California Press, 1969).

19. Hamid Mowlana, "Technology Versus Tradition: Communication in the Iranian Revolution," *Journal of Communication* 29, no. 3 (Summer 1979):107–112.

20. Ziauddin Sardar, *Islamic Futures: The Shape of Ideas to Come* (London and New York: Mansell Publishing, 1985), pp. 126–156; and Ziauddin Sardar, *The Future of Muslim Civilization* (London and New York: Mansell Publishing, 1987), pp. 53–76.

21. Hamid Mowlana, "The New Global Order and Cultural Ecology," *Media, Culture, and Society,* special issue of *Islam and Communication* 15, no. 4 (1993): 9–27.

22. Quoted in Altaf Guahar, "Islam and Secularism," in Altaf Guahar, ed., *The Challenge of Islam* (London: Islamic Council of Europe, 1978), p. 306.

23. For a review of this phenomenon, see Mohammad Rafi-ud-din, *Ideology of the Future* (Lahore, Pakistan: SH. Muhammad Ashraf Publishers, 1946); Ahmad Hasan, *The Doctrine of Ijma in Islam* (Islamabad, Pakistan: Islamic Research Institute, 1978); Mumtaz Ahmad, ed., *State Politics and Islam* Washington, D.C.: (American Trust Publications, 1986); Isma'il Raji al Faruqi, *Tawhid: Its Relevance for Thought and Life* (Kuwait: International Islamic Federation, 1983).

24. Hamid Mowlana and Laurie J. Wilson, *The Passing of Modernity: Communication and Transformation in Society* (White Plains, N.Y.: Longman, 1990).

14

The Crisis in Mobility

NANCY E. SNOW

Give me your tired, your poor, your huddled masses yearning to breathe free, the
wretched refuse of your teeming shore, send these, the homeless, tempest-tossed, to me:
I lift my lamp beside the golden door.

— Emma Lazarus, "The New Colossus," etched on the Statue of Liberty pedestal, 1886

There are only the pursued, the pursuing, the busy and the tired.

— F. Scott Fitzgerald, *The Great Gatsby*, 1925

There must be a halt to the relentless flow of immigrants to this country, especially
from the Indian sub-continent in order to preserve the British way of life.

— Winston Churchill, grandson of the Prime Minister of Great Britain, 1993

The free market triumphs of NAFTA (North American Free Trade Agreement) in 1993 and of GATT (General Agreement on Tariffs and Trade) in 1994 with its creation of the World Trade Organization (WTO) were portrayed promisingly in the mass media as global economic growth indicators with a trickle-down prosperity quotient for everyone. Not until the Zapatista revolt in Chiapas, Mexico, on January 1, 1994, the day NAFTA became effective in Mexico, did the world awaken to the fact that big payoffs for transnational corporations and their corporate statist friends in government do not mean equal gains for the poor and marginalized. The fact that capital knows no borders should put us all on notice that population movements are increasingly mobile and answer the pull of a better life somewhere else and a push from unlivable conditions.

Two of the globe's most pressing crises—mass migration across borders and displacement of people and national minorities within borders—are "invisible" to the eyes of most public officials and receive far too little attention in our mass media. The result of an ever-widening disparity between the economic and political "haves," a global minority, and the global majority of "have-nots," this *crisis in mobility* is occurring at a time when populations of the industrialized nations of the North are stable or in a decline while the populations of the South[1] are increasing rapidly. It is estimated that the world's population may double by the middle of the next century from the current 5.5 billion to nearly 11 billion, and 95 percent of that increase will occur in the poorest regions of the world.[2] This growth rate comes at the same time that the world income gap is widening. Today the richest 20 percent of the world's population, basically the people in the Northern industrialized countries, accounts for 85 percent of the world's income. The share of the billion people at the bottom is 1.4 percent.

Some governments of the North sound occasional alarms that the economic pull to migrate will result in a "mass exodus" from the South, but few have taken the initiative to devise policies, outside of draconian measures, that address the underlying root causes of this crisis in mobility. Instead, the wealthy industrialized countries of the North, which include the OECD (Organization for Economic Cooperation and Development) countries of Europe, the United States, Japan, Canada, and Australia, have chosen to react to the crisis by increasingly closing off their borders to any newcomers and thereby limiting accessibility to some, including the world's refugees, who have nowhere else to go.

In the United States alone, 1994 will be remembered as the year that it was politically expedient to slam shut America's golden doors. Proposition 187, known as the "Save Our State" initiative on the California ballot, handily passed muster by fear-ridden voters convinced that illegals were bleeding the state of already scarce revenues. Such legislation promised not only to outlaw all services to illegal immigrants but also to require that public officials, teachers, and health care workers report anyone "suspected" of being illegal, in effect to make them de facto INS agents. Such a startling state initiative was preceded by an even greater surprise at the federal level—detainment of Cuban rafters in internment camps on the U.S. naval base at Guantanamo Bay. It would not have caught the eye of the average television viewer except that most Americans were aware that Cubans for the past thirty years had been considered the most privileged immigration-seeking refugees, offered automatic asylum as an example of American moral superiority for those yearning to be free. Now some Cubans were being shipped off to detainee camps in Panama and no one seemed to notice.

Immigration, both illegal and legal, will become the hot-button issue for countries of the North in the next five years preceding the new millennium. Whereas in the past fear was centered around economic insecurities that jobs would be lost to late arrivals, today's anxieties are increasingly xenophobic given that most current immigrants are poor and of non-European origins. The picture of Cubans and Haitians on unseaworthy vessels symbolized for most Americans that the world is steadily losing its order and ability to control people's movements. These fears come at the same time that Northern nations continue knowingly to admit illegals who can perform two primary functions: (1) fulfill as yet unfilled labor demands that service the high rates of economic growth the Northern countries demand and (2) accept jobs that are beneath the sense of dignity for most of the settled population.

In this age of instant history[3] in which modern communications can link deprived people in the South to images of consumerist lifestyles and economic opportunities in the North, the pull to migrate is strong, and modern, more affordable travel opportunities provide transit. Features of the global market economic structure with its regional economic trading blocs such as NAFTA and APEC (Asia-Pacific Economic Cooperation), coupled with liberalization in the movement of goods and services, have likewise increased mobility pressures to emigrate for political and economic reasons.

Persons who are the least likely to emigrate are the poorest who become refugees—the world's homeless. Unable to finance distant travel, refugees often seek refuge in adjacent countries, such as has occurred in sub-Saharan Africa, where a nearby country is not much better off than their own. Despite fears of a mass exodus of the poorest, most deprived refugees breaking through the immigration barriers of the North, the migration numbers do not reflect such a pattern. The greatest mobility pressure falls upon the most economically viable and ambitious as well as upon persons whose home countries rank higher on the national GNP scale. This latter group is most likely to respond to the opportunity for upward socioeconomic mobility portrayed by advertising campaigns and television programs as the affluent lifestyle. Increasingly, this latter group also typifies most asylum seekers and illegals living in countries of the North.

Global "Blinders"

The crisis of mobility is likely to intensify when set against a backdrop of an overall lack of vision and foresight among international relations policymakers. Unless representatives of the North address the South-North mobility flux, a new chapter of internal social disruption will result that pits newly arriving immigrants against established citizens. But tension will not exist solely between immigrants and citizens. There is likely to emerge a tension over foreign policy that pits nationalists against internationalists. Author Alan Tonelson declared that a fault line is emerging in American politics and foreign policy, one that pits nationalists who want the United States to disengage from overseas conflicts against internationalists, whom Tonelson identified as the best-educated and wealthiest Americans and the group most staunchly globalist on security and economic issues.

A new realist nationalism shows signs of becoming a full-blown alternative. . . . Such [an] approach would break decisively with internationalism by abandoning the quest for worldwide security, prosperity and democracy as the best guarantors of American well-being. Instead, it would conclude that in a world likely to remain highly unstable, America's future is best assured by restoring and consolidating its own military and economic strength, and the health of its social and political systems.[4]

Such a nationalist position, if Tonelson is right, is unlikely to be amenable to providing humanitarian assistance or international aid designed to staunch the rising tide of the world's asylum seekers, migrants, and refugees. Such a position is also likely to emerge as a cornerstone of the isolationist-friendly conservative movement in the United States and in European countries.

Displacement Within Borders

A second invisible crisis is that of ethnic, religious, and national minorities who are forging linkages with their uprooted diaspora. The end of the Cold War and the collapse of the Soviet Union have produced numerous national minorities who, barring redrawing of international borders, seek to establish their cultural sovereignty within host national borders. Upward of 26 million Russians are politically and economically "stranded" in what has become other people's countries, 12 million alone in the Ukraine, a country of 51 million. Russians in the Ukraine could through their sheer numbers pose a significant threat to the Ukrainian state if antagonized.

A 1994 U.S. intelligence analysis that was circulated in draft form among senior U.S. policymakers and reported in the *Washington Post* predicted that Ukraine's highly inflationary economy would spawn ethnic conflict and result in a partitioning of the state along ethnic and geographical lines, with the Russian minority in the eastern region pressing for secession and the Ukrainian majority in the western region seeking independence and the prevention of the eastern territory falling into the hands of Russia.[5] Such projections raised two possibilities: that Ukraine would renege on its recent historic agreement to give up its nuclear weapons in exchange for economic and political benefits from the West (which it later did not), and that Russian secessionist movements in other NIS countries would follow the Ukrainian example (which they later did in the Chechnya region).

Growing tension also exists in the Balkan states, where many Russians are arriving in Estonia, Latvia, and Lithuania to escape the declining living standards in Mother Russia. Other tensions exist throughout central Europe as well. Albanian nationalists seek to unite with their ethnic brothers and sisters in neighboring Kosovo and Macedonia with hopes for a Greater Albania.

Nearby Hungary, a country of only 10.5 million national citizens, is laying claims to ethnic Hungarians, the largest minority group in Europe. The late prime minister Jozsef Antall declared in 1990 that his country represented the interests of all 15 million Hungarians, including the 2 million Hungarians in the Transylvania region of Romania, the nearly 400,000 Hungarians in the Vojvodina province of Serbia, and the 600,000 Hungarians in southern Slovakia. In late 1991 Hungary signed an agreement with Russia that would provide rights to a national minority autonomy "on a territorial basis." In 1992 Hungary went so far as to establish a special Office for Hungarian Minorities Abroad to monitor the living conditions of ethnic Hungarians living outside its borders.

In light of Serb tactics used in Bosnia-Herzegovina, Hungarians have reasons to fear for the security of ethnic Hungarians in Vojvodina, Romania, and Slovakia, although the nationalists of those states are worried that Hungary will seek the kind of ethnic reunion that has been so brutally accomplished by the Serbs and practically unanswered by the Atlantic alliance. In early 1994 ethnic Hungarians in Slovakia met in public assembly to demand a separate self-government and to ask for special status as a majority population in southern Slovakia. The harsh denunciation by the Slovak government of the assembly as "illegal and unconstitutional" served to forebode the rise of yet another ethnically based secessionist movement in eastern Europe.[6]

Other national minority groups include the 3.5 million ethnic Germans in eastern Europe and the Gypsies, who number 3 million and have been discriminated against for years. During the Cold War, German governments concentrated their efforts on repatriation in exchange for trade and aid with the Soviet bloc. With the rising pressure from immigration and the economic strain of unification, government policy has shifted to encouraging the diaspora not to immigrate. Nevertheless, in 1992 alone, more than 191,000 ethnic Germans left the former Soviet Union and returned to Germany.[7] Most originated from Kazakhstan, which has the highest concentration of Germans, many of whom were once part of the Volga German Autonomous Republic. Ethnic Germans are understandably eager to reestablish links with their rich uncle in the west, and some German right-wing groups have taken up the slack to forge political links with the diaspora. There is even some movement toward reestablishing a new Volga German Republic that could receive significant amounts of aid from the Federal Republic of Germany.

Fear of the Other

Post–Cold War Europe is providing a picture of rising xenophobia and racism as the ready response to immigration numbers and a foreign presence. A Eurostat public opinion poll from July 1993 indicated that for the first time in the history of such polling, a majority (52 percent) of European Union (EU) members interviewed agreed with the view that there were too many foreigners in their countries. Such sentiments were matched in the extreme with a rise in violent attacks on immigrants by neofascist and racist groups from Germany and Spain to Italy and the United Kingdom.

This is not to say that the number of asylum seekers in Europe over the last several years is not an astonishing figure. In the early 1980s there were fewer than 70,000 people seeking asylum in European countries. By 1993 the figure was over 500,000. Between January 1992 and June 1993, Germany alone accepted close to 340,000 refugees from the former Yugoslavia.[8] The number of asylum seekers in Europe in general has increased ten times over the 1970s. Germany has been the main recipient of asylum seekers over the past twenty years, receiving on average 15,000 annually in the 1970s. In the 1980s that figure rose to an annual average of 77,000. With the collapse of the Soviet empire and the war in former Yugoslavia, the figures skyrocketed to 193,000 in 1990 and 266,000 in 1991. By 1992 the figure had risen by 40 percent to 438,000. Comparison numbers in 1992 show that Sweden took in 83,000, France absorbed 29,000, and the United Kingdom accepted 25,000.

Despite decline in the numbers seeking asylum in the period 1993–1994 as a result of stricter asylum procedures, and in spite of the reality that most asylum applications are eventually rejected, it is estimated that more than 80 percent of all rejected asylum seekers remain in the country of destination.[9] Many now resort to illegal networks for transit, methods that increase drug smuggling, prostitution among women migrants, and smuggling of people for high fees. The tragedy in former Yugoslavia has further exacerbated the mobility crisis in Europe. More than 600,000 people overall have left the conflict areas to seek refuge in western Europe. Within the former Yugoslav republics, nearly 4 million people remain displaced.[10]

The European Union has not had much success in grappling with the asylum or migration problems existing within its borders. Simplistic solutions, which often have racist or xenophobic overtones, appeal to the masses but do nothing to resolve the deep-seated causes of movement. The Dublin Convention, which was agreed to in June 1990, makes it harder for an asylum seeker to "shop around" for asylum by requiring that a first country of asylum adjudicate on the application, which if refused would lead to an automatic rejection by the other eleven member states. As a response to the high numbers of asylum seekers, on July 1, 1993, Germany severely restricted its generous asylum law protection (Article 16), which offered asylum to anyone who paid witness to political persecution. Article 16 stems from the uniqueness of German international law, which in turn is a reaction to the persecution and abuse suffered by national minorities under Nazism. Now Germany will not accept or will send back any person from another EU country or third country in which the application and implementation of the conventions on refugees and human rights are guaranteed. This restriction will severely limit the asylum requests from neighboring eastern countries such as Poland, Czechoslovakia, and Hungary, to which asylum seekers can now be remitted. Other EU countries are expected to follow the German example.

The European asylum issue is reflective of a rise in mass movements of people worldwide. According to UNHCR (U.N. High Commissioner for Refugees) statistics, there were 2.5 million refugees worldwide in 1970 and nearly 11 million by the early 1980s. Today there are nearly 20 million refugees and close to 25 million people who are internally displaced within national borders. Western news media have highlighted the foreign bashing in western Europe, but it must be emphasized that the vast majority of refugees and displaced people originate and find protection in the developing countries of the South such as Afghanistan, Bangladesh, and Pakistan. Refugee numbers are growing for a number of reasons—famine, war, civil unrest, economic and environmental disintegration. Increasingly, the world's response is one of "compassion fatigue," not just from the public at large but also from multilateral organizations like the United Nations. This fatigue is coupled with what Sadako Ogata, U.N. High Commissioner for Refugees, called "an alarming upsurge of hostile and xenophobic attitudes."[11]

The U.N. High Commissioner has recommended a five-point plan to address problems of asylum and refugee flows in the European states. The first element, protection, must be enforced for those asylum seekers and refugees who cannot rely on their home governments to safeguard their human rights and social security. The basis for such protection is still the 1951 convention relating to the status of refugees, but this should be updated to include concepts of temporary asylum for those who wish to be repatriated when conditions in their home countries improve.

Second, a clearer distinction must be made between refugees and migrants. Refugees look to the international community for assistance because their home governments are unable or are unwilling to help them. Migrants may also face life-threatening situations, but they are in a better position to receive international assistance through cooperation between their governments and multilateral institutions. Such assistance may improve the home situation enough to serve as a preventive measure against the need to emigrate.

The third element of a progressive refugee policy would involve increasing assistance from wealthier donor countries to poorer countries that bear the greatest burden of hosting refugees. Such an assistance program for economic and social development would establish a framework that unites development, refugee, and migration policies.

The fourth element, prevention, is most important for mobility issues. Prevention of the causes of refugee flows involves the promotion of sustainable development and the establishment of human rights that are enforced. The majority of the world's population, at least 70–80 percent, lives in conditions of socioeconomic decline that are ripe for creating displacement among ethnic groups, social classes, or regions. Economic growth alone will not prevent these groups from trying to advance their positions against one another. Respect for human rights and minority rights is the fundamental glue that will hold many countries together, especially those that are continuing their development toward democracy. Without protection of human rights in general and minority rights in particular, groups will continue to feel marginalized and vulnerable, thereby becoming susceptible to fascist or nationalist remedies. As internal displacement of population grows, a legal framework must be developed to bring together refugee law, humanitarian law, and human rights statutes that all states will honor.

Finally, a new refugee policy must include factual information on migration and refugee issues that will inform and not incite the public. The global reach of television continues to beam the fantasy of Western affluence (e.g., "Lifestyles of the Rich and Famous") into the rooms of the poor, creating unrealistic expectations of "the good life." Such commercially based images must be countered with accurate information that will allow potential migrants to make an educated decision after weighing the costs and consequences of leaving their home countries.

Western governments have a tendency to emphasize political and civil rights in developed countries over socioeconomic rights of people in developing countries. Increasingly, the issues of minority rights and migratory pressure are ones that leaders of the industrialized democracies of the North (and the compliant capitalists of the South) would like to leave to the "invisible hand" of the free market. The Clinton administration's decision to focus almost exclusively upon economics in Russia led to a backlash by nationalists who did not want to have their politics or economics dictated from the outside.[12] Zhirinovsky's sudden rise to prominence, which came as such a surprise to the West, was in part a result of the Western nations' inattention to the overwhelming psychosociological displacement that economic reforms brought upon the Russian masses. The almost religious devotion to the marvels of the free market economy can lead to disastrous consequences or at least to situations in which governments are ill-prepared to react, as President Salinas of Mexico found out on New Year's Day, 1994.

Addressing the Crisis

The world's leaders are still grossly unresponsive to issues related to global coexistence of disparate races and cultures. Part of the problem is that states are no longer the key players in the international system and do not serve as the welfare provider of last resort. States increasingly are serving other masters, as was reported at a January 1994 conference organized by Jesuits and held in San Salvador. Their report concluded that the state is serving a new master—the transnational corporation—and this arrangement is thereby creating a new transnational state that dictates economic policy through interstate institutions such as the International Monetary Fund, World Bank, International Development Bank, U.S. Agency for International Development, European Union, and U.N. Development Program.

This new world configuration favors a top-down management style and a rigid hierarchy of domination. States can no longer protect their citizens from the vagaries of the global marketplace or give citizens a voice in globally rendered decisions such as GATT and NAFTA that seal their economic fate. Citizens who no longer can look to the state as provider or job securer are looking closer to home to social, ethnic, or religious ties that bind. This is creating a cacophony of autonomous groups that harbor no safe haven for disposable populations of refugees or environmental migrants. As "Gastarbeiter" or, worse yet, "illegal aliens" and "political or economic refugees," displaced persons are not likely to be able to organize themselves as citizens and are thus more easily disposable and vulnerable.

The mass media, which expose large audiences of people to each other in all parts of the world, are likewise ill prepared to deal with worldwide problems. Most media, especially the entertainment and popular media, still stress the local over the global, deal with problems in isolation from one another, and present often stereotypical if not racist images of foreign people and their cultures.

What, then, does the invisible crisis of mass migration and displacement spell for the future? A new world order based upon human rights and social and economic justice seems remote. A new world disorder, even anarchy, seems likely. Samuel Huntington's much talked about *Foreign Affairs* article, "The Clash of Civilizations," pointed to a world that shows a rise in clashes between distinct groups or civilizations rather than between nation-states: "The Velvet Curtain of culture has replaced the Iron Curtain of ideology as the most significant dividing line in Europe. As the events in Yugoslavia show, it is not only a line of difference; it is also, at times, a line of bloody conflict."[13] Fouad Ajami, professor of Middle East studies at Johns Hopkins University, replied to Huntington in *Foreign Affairs* that states still control civilizations and that "men want Sony, not soil."[14]

Ajami and many of Huntington's critics consider events such as the nationalist vote in Russia, the Hindu separatist movement in India, and Islamic fundamentalism to be blips on the international screen and no match for liberal Western ideals of free market economies and the rule of law. But those individuals who want Sony over separatism may not be inclined to want to work for development measures that empower displaced persons. Displaced persons are need-rich and consumer-poor, not anyone's best bet for Sony profits.

Some would argue that the answers are not so simple because even developed societies tend to follow a social structure that results in a "two-thirds society."[15] This term refers to the two-thirds of a state's population that tends to gain from the ongoing process of modernization and expanding services. The other one-third of the population is at great risk of becoming marginalized and aggressive toward foreign asylum-seekers who are often resented for receiving shelter and support. Right-wing nationalists try to mobilize these resentments and incite negative and often aggressive reactions. Because those in the marginalized one-third feel disempowered, they detest their situation and find it further exacerbated by the presence of foreigners. Still others paint a much bleaker picture that includes neither Sony nor soil.

Atlantic Monthly headlined its February 1994 issue with "The Coming Anarchy" and made these observations as a prelude to an article by Robert Kaplan: "Nations break up under the tidal flow of refugees from environmental and social disaster. As borders crumble, another type of boundary is erected—a wall of disease. Wars are fought over scarce resources, especially water, and war itself becomes continuous with crime, as armed bands of stateless marauders clash with the private security forces of the elites. A preview of the first decades of the twenty-first century." Kaplan's article presented an equally dismal scenario for the future, one that has all the signs of occurring but that meets with inadequate response in international policy circles:

> It is time to understand "the environment" for what it is: *the* national-security issue of the early twenty-first century. The political and strategic impact of surging populations, spreading disease, deforestation and social erosion, water depletion, air pollution, and possibly, rising sea levels in critical, overcrowded regions like the Nile Delta and Bangladesh—developments that will prompt mass migrations and, in turn, incite group conflicts—will be the core foreign policy challenge from which most others will ultimately emanate, arousing the public and uniting assorted interests left over from the Cold War.[16]

In a later article historian Paul Kennedy and colleague Matthew Connelly portrayed migration as a much greater threat to the globe than has been recognized. They described "fast-growing, adolescent, resource-poor, undercapitalized and undereducated populations on one side and technologically inventive, demographically moribund and increasingly rich societies on the other" as a relationship that we will find "early in the next century dwarfs every other issue in global affairs."[17]

Perhaps it is up to the growing nongovernmental organizations that are involved in resolving global problems on a daily basis to inform their media and governments about what is really happening. Harold Saunders, former assistant secretary of state for Near Eastern and South Asian affairs and now director of international affairs at the Kettering Foundation, has argued that people outside of government, those involved in nongovernmental (or what he terms "public") organizations, are often better informed and more able to act upon situations that affect permeable borders.[18] In internal conflicts that create displaced persons within borders, the state is less able to provide security or preserve the body politic. Public citizens involved in nonofficial organizations can be excellent resources to inform governments and media of the problems of mobility that affect us all. In the long run, public citizens with a global consciousness may be the only answer as state resources dwindle and are increasingly overshadowed by global economic elites who seek out security and sound environments in which to invest. In the end, it may be up to communities and grassroots organizations to become the voice of the discarded and the discouraged, the weak and the weary, the pursued and the pursuing.

NOTES

1. The term "South" is meant here as a developing country where per capita income is not only lower than in the industrialized countries of the North but also more unevenly distributed. Both terms, "South" and "developing country," cover disparate and demographic situations, however; notably the newly industrializing countries (NICs) of East

and Southeast Asia now have rates of economic growth and per capita incomes similar to those of some countries in the North.

2. Robert D. Kaplan, "The Coming Anarchy," *Atlantic Monthly,* February 1994, pp. 44–76.

3. The term "instant history" is used by George Gerbner to define our global communications era in which history is packaged in quick, isolated media events that offer little context and are soon shelved for ever newer occurrences.

4. Alan Tonelson, "Beyond Left and Right," *National Interest,* Winter 1993/94, pp. 3–18.

5. *Washington Post,* January 25, 1994, p. A7.

6. For statistics and map, see David B. Ottaway, "Ethnic Hungarians in Slovakia Are Demanding Self-Government," *Washington Post,* January 10, 1994, p. A12; and Carol J. Williams, "Ethnic Tension Poses Threat to Hungarians," *Los Angeles Times,* Washington edition, January 7, 1994, p. A3.

7. "Volga Germans Seek Lost Homeland," *Christian Science Monitor,* September 8, 1993, p. 8.

8. Statistics for this chapter were collected from the United Nations High Commissioner for Refugees (UNHCR) and the U.S. Mission in Geneva's Refugee and Migration Affairs Office (RMA).

9. This statistic is according to a fifteen-country study by the European Consultation on Refugees and Exiles, an umbrella organization for refugees.

10. A displaced person is an individual who has been temporarily uprooted from his or her homeland but who is expected eventually to return home.

11. As Ogata told Washington journalists during a press conference to announce the release of the first UNHCR global study of refugees, Washington, D.C., National Press Club, October 1993.

12. Secretary Warren Christopher's statement before the Senate Foreign Relations Committee, Washington, D.C., November 4, 1993.

13. Samuel P. Huntington, "The Clash of Civilizations," *Foreign Affairs* 72, no. 3 (Summer 1993):22–49.

14. Fouad Ajami's reply is in *Foreign Affairs* 72, no. 4 (September–October 1993):1–14.

15. Jurgen Fijalkowski, "Aggressive Nationalism, Immigration Pressure, and Asylum Policy Disputes in Contemporary Germany," *International Migration Review* 27, no. 4:850–869.

16. Kaplan, "The Coming Anarchy," p. 59.

17. Paul Kennedy and Matthew Connelly, *Atlantic Monthly* 274, no. 6, December 1994, pp. 61–91.

18. Harold H. Saunders, "Enlarging U.S. Policy Toward Ethnic Conflict: Rethinking Intervention," paper prepared for symposium "Ethnic Conflicts: Threat to Domestic and International Peace," November 9, 1993, jointly sponsored by the National Defense University and the Joint Center for Political and Economic Studies of Washington, D.C.

PART FIVE

THE NEW TYRANNIES

15

Let Them Eat Pollution

JOHN BELLAMY FOSTER

On December 12, 1991, Lawrence Summers, chief economist of the World Bank, sent a memorandum to some of his colleagues presenting views on the environment that are doubtless widespread among orthodox economists, reflecting as they do the logic of capital accumulation, but that are seldom offered up for public scrutiny and then almost never by an economist of Summers's rank. This memo was later leaked to the British publication *The Economist*, which published part of it on February 8, 1992, under the title "Let Them Eat Pollution." The published part of the memo is here quoted in full:

Just between you and me, shouldn't the World Bank be encouraging more migration of the dirty industries to the LDCs (Less Developed Countries)? I can think of three reasons:

(1) The measurement of the costs of health-impairing pollution depends on the foregone earnings from increased morbidity and mortality. From this point of view a given amount of health-impairing pollution should be done in the country with the lowest cost, which will be the country of the lowest wages. I think the economic logic behind dumping a load of toxic waste in the lowest-wage country is impeccable and we should face up to that.

(2) The costs of pollution are likely to be non-linear as the initial increments of pollution will probably have very low cost. I've always thought that under-populated countries in Africa are vastly under-polluted; their air quality is probably vastly inefficiently low [*sic*] compared to Los Angeles or Mexico City. Only the lamentable facts that so much pollution is generated by non-tradeable industries (transport, electrical generation) and that the unit transport costs of solid waste are so high prevent world-welfare-enhancing trade in air pollution and waste.

(3) The demand for a clean environment for aesthetic and health reasons is likely to have very high income-elasticity. The concern over an agent that causes a one-in-a-million change in the odds of prostate cancer is obviously going to be much higher in a country in which the mortality of children under five is 200 per 1,000. Also,

221

much of the concern over industrial atmospheric discharge is about visibility-impairing particulates. These discharges may have very little direct health impact. Clearly trade in goods that embody aesthetic pollution concerns could be welfare-enhancing. While production is mobile the consumption of pretty air is a non-tradeable.

The problem with the arguments against all of these proposals for more pollution in LDCs (intrinsic rights to certain goods, moral rights, social concerns, lack of adequate markets, etc.) [is that they] could be turned around and used more or less effectively against every Bank proposal for liberalization.

The World Bank later told *The Economist* that in writing his memo Summers had intended to "provoke debate" among his bank colleagues, and Summers himself said that he had not meant to advocate "the dumping of untreated toxic wastes near the homes of poor people." Few acquainted with orthodox economics, however, can doubt that the central arguments utilized in the memo were serious. In the view of *The Economist* itself (February 15, 1992), Summers's language was objectionable but "his economics was hard to answer."

Although its general meaning could not be clearer, this entire memo deserves to be summarized and restated in a way that will bring out some of the more subtle implications. First, the lives of individuals in the Third World, judged by "foregone earnings" from illness and death, are worth less—the same logic says frequently hundreds of times less—than those of individuals in the advanced capitalist countries where wages are often hundreds of times higher. The low-wage periphery is therefore the proper place in which to dispose of globally produced toxic wastes if the overall economic value of human life is to be maximized worldwide. Second, Third World countries are "vastly *underpolluted*" in the sense that their air pollution levels are "inefficiently low" when compared with highly polluted cities like Los Angeles and Mexico City (where schoolchildren had to be kept home for an entire month in 1989 because of the abysmal air quality). Third, a clean environment can be viewed as a luxury good pursued by rich countries with high life expectancies where higher aesthetic and health standards apply; worldwide costs of production would therefore fall if polluting industries were shifted from the center to the periphery of the world system. Hence, for all of these reasons the World Bank should encourage the migration of polluting industries and toxic wastes to the Third World. Social and humanitarian arguments against such world trade in waste, Summers concluded, can be disregarded, since they are the same arguments that are used against all proposals for capitalist development.

It is important to understand that this policy perspective, with the utter contempt that it displays both for the world's poor and the world environment, is by no means an intellectual aberration. As the World Bank's chief economist, Summer has the role of helping to create conditions conducive to world capital accumulation, particularly where the core of the capitalist world system is concerned. Neither the welfare of the majority of the population of the globe nor the ecological fate of the earth—nor even the fate of individual capitalists themselves—can be allowed to stand in the way of this single-minded goal.

Perhaps the most shocking part of the Summers memo is the openly exploitative attitude that it demonstrates toward the world's poor. And yet nothing is more characteristic of bourgeois economics. *The Economist,* which went on to defend Summers's general conclusions about the desirability of the migration of polluting industries to the Third World in subsequent commentaries, nonetheless dismissed as "crass" Summers's specific references to the valuation of life, denying that such exploitative attitudes about human life are likely to play an explicit role in government policy in free societies. "Few governments," *The Economist* stated in its February 15, 1992, issue, "would care to defend a policy based on differences in valuations among groups—arguing, for instance, that society values an extra year of life for a white-collar worker more highly than for a blue-collar worker. Yet this is the counterpart, within a rich country, of what Summers appeared to be suggesting for the Third World." The truth, however, as *The Economist* itself admitted at another point in the same article, is that governments constantly do make decisions—whether in regard to health, education, working conditions, housing, environment, and so on—that are "based on differences in valuations" among classes, whether or not they "care to defend" their policies in this way. Indeed, such differences in valuation, as anyone with the slightest knowledge of history and economics must realize, are at the very core of the capitalist economy and state.

To illustrate this, we need only turn to the United States. The OMB (Office of Management and Budget) under the Reagan administration endeavored to promote calculations of the dollar value of a human life based on "the wage premiums that workers require for accepting jobs with increased risk." On this basis a number of academic studies concluded that the value of a worker's life in the United States is between $500,000 and $2 million (far less than the annual salary of many corporate CEOs). The OMB then used these results to argue that some forms of pollution abatement were cost-effective, and others were not, in accordance with President Reagan's executive order number 12291 that regulatory measures should "be chosen to maximize the net benefit to society."

Barry Commoner noted the consequences of this argument:

> Some economists have proposed that the value of a human life should be based on a person's earning power. It then turns out that a woman's life is worth much less than a man's, and that a black's life is worth much less than a white's. Translated into environmental terms, harm is regarded as small if the people at hazard are poor—an approach that could be used to justify locating heavily polluting operations in poor neighborhoods. This is, in fact, only too common a practice. A recent study shows, for example, that most toxic dumps are located near poor black and Hispanic communities.

In 1983 a study by the U.S. General Accounting Office determined that three out of four off-site commercial hazardous waste landfills in the southern states were located in primarily black communities even though blacks represented only 20 percent of the population in the region.[1]

Summers's argument for dumping toxic wastes in the Third World is therefore nothing more than a call for the globalization of policies and practices that are already evident in the United States and that have recently been unearthed in locations throughout the capitalist world. The developed countries export millions of tons of waste each year, much of it to the Third World and eastern Europe. In 1987, dioxin-laden industrial ash from Philadelphia was dumped in Guinea and Haiti. In 1988, 4,000 tons of PCB-contaminated chemical waste from Italy was found in Nigeria leaking from thousands of rusting and corroding drums, poisoning both soil and groundwater.[2] There can be few more blatant examples of the continuing dominance of imperialism over Third World affairs.

This same frame of mind, which sees toxic pollution less as a problem to be overcome than one to be managed in accordance with the logic of the free market, is evident in the approach adopted by orthodox economists toward issues as fateful as global warming. In an article in the May 30, 1992, issue of *The Economist,* Summers illustrated this perspective and the general attitude of the World Bank:

> The argument that a moral obligation to future generations demands special treatment of environmental investments is fatuous. We can help our descendants as much by improving infrastructure as by preserving rain forests . . . as much by enlarging our scientific knowledge as by reducing carbon dioxide in the air. . . . The reason why some investments favored by some environmentalists fail . . . a [rigorous cost-benefit] test is that their likely effect on living standards is not so great. . . . In the worst-case scenario of the most pessimistic estimates yet prepared (those of William Cline of the Institute for International Economics), global warming reduces growth over the next two centuries by less than 0.1 percent a year. More should be done: dealing with global warming would not halt economic growth either. But raising the specter of our impoverished grandchildren if we fail to address global environmental problems is demagoguery.

The problem with such arguments is that they are based on forms of economic calculation that consistently undervalue natural wealth and underestimate the dependence of the economy on ecological conditions. The rebuilding of infrastructure cannot be equated with preserving the world's tropical rain forests because loss of the latter would be irrevocable and would mean the extinction of both a majority of the world's species and the world's greatest genetic library. The absurdity of William Cline's attempt to quantify the potential economic damages of "very long-term global warming" up through the year 2300—to which Summers referred—should be apparent to anyone who considers the obvious impossibility of applying economic values to the scale of climatic change anticipated. Thus the Cline estimates are based on a projected rise in global mean temperatures of between 10 and 18 degrees Celsius (18 and 32 degrees Fahrenheit) by the year 2300. The cost of this to the U.S. economy, Clines expects us to believe, will be long-term damages equal to 6 to 12 percent of GNP under the best assumptions, 20 percent under the worst.[3] All of this is nonsense, however, from an ecological standpoint, since a temperature rise of 4 degrees Celsius would create an earth that was warmer than at any time in the past 40 million years. In the midst of the last ice age, the earth was only 5 degrees Celsius colder than it is today. Viewed from this standpoint, the question of whether long-term damages would equal 6, 12, or 20 percent of GNP must give way to the more rational question of whether human civilization and life itself could persist in the face of such a drastic change in global temperatures.

An even more alarming example of the same general argument was provided, again in the May 30, 1992, issue of *The Economist,* in a special report published in advance of the June 1992 Earth Summit in Rio de Janeiro. After examining estimates on the economic costs and benefits of averting global warming and the political obstacles to change under existing capitalist regimes, *The Economist* declared:

> The chance that the climate treaty will significantly change the world's output of fossil fuels over the next century is extremely slender. Does this matter? If the figures for the costs of damage likely to be done by climate change are accurate, then the honest answer is "no." It would be, of course, wise for countries to take the free lunches available to them . . . and to price their energy sensibly. It might be wise to go some way beyond that point, in the interests of buying insurance against nasty surprises. . . . Beyond that, adapting to climate change, when it happens, is undoubtedly the most rational course, for a number of reasons. Most countries will be richer then, and so better able to afford to build sea walls or develop drought resistant plants. Money that might now be spent on curbing carbon-dioxide output can be invested instead, either in preventing more damaging environmental change (like rapid population growth, the most environmentally harmful trend of all) or in productive assets that will generate future income to pay for adaptation. Once climate change occurs, it will be clearer—as it now is not—how much needs to be done, and what, and where. Most of the decisions involved in adapting will be taken and paid for by the private sector rather than (as with curbing greenhouse-gas output) by government. Above all, adapting requires no international agreements.[4]

The answer, then, is "let them build sea walls or develop drought resistant plants"—and this in response to "very probable" rises in global mean temperature of 1.5–5.0 degrees Celsius (2.7 degrees–9 degrees Fahrenheit) over the next century if "business as usual" continues, a prospect that scientists all over the world regard as potentially catastrophic for the entire planet![5] The threat of heat waves, droughts, floods, and famines suggests the likelihood of incalculable losses in lives, species, ecosystems, and cultures. Nevertheless, for *The Economist* the adaptation of the capital accumulation process and thus world civilization to irreversible global warming once it has taken place and many of its worst effects are evident is easy to contemplate, whereas any attempt to head off disaster—however defensible in social, moral, and ecological terms—besides being difficult to institute under present-day capitalist regimes, would interfere with the dominance of capital and must therefore be unthinkable.

The wait-and-see attitude promoted by *The Economist* was of course the general stance adopted by the United States (and to a lesser extent Britain) at the Earth Summit. Through its actions in watering down the climate treaty, refusing to sign the biological diversity treaty, and hindering initiatives on weapons of mass destruction and nuclear waste, the United States signaled in no uncertain terms that it was prepared to take on the task of opposing radical forces within the global environmental movement, adding this to its larger role as the leading defender of the capitalist world. According to the U.S. government's position, the concept of "sustainable development" means first and foremost that any environmental goals that can be interpreted as interfering with development must be blocked. Thus, in his defense of U.S. intransigence on global environmental issues at the Earth Summit, George Bush explained, "I think it is important that we take both those words—environment and development—equally seriously. And we do." No environmental action could therefore be taken, Bush declared, that would jeopardize U.S. economic interests. "I am determined to protect the environment. I am also determined to protect the American taxpayer. The day of the open checkbook is over . . . environmental protection and a growing economy are inseparable." In what was intended not only as a reelection ploy but also as a declaration of U.S. priorities where questions of environmental costs and controls are concerned, Bush declared, "For the past half century the United States has been the great engine of global economic growth, and it's going to stay that way."[6]

The consequences of such shortsighted attention to economic growth and profit before all else are of course enormous, since they call into question the survivability of the entire world. It is an inescapable fact that human history is at a turning point, the result of a fundamental change in the relationship between human beings and the environment. The scale at which people transform energy and materials has now reached a level that rivals elemental natural processes. Human society is adding carbon to the atmosphere at a level equal to about 7 percent of the natural carbon exchange of atmosphere and oceans. The carbon dioxide content of the atmosphere as a result has grown by a quarter in the past 200 years, with more than half of this increase since 1950. Human beings now use (take or transform) 25 percent of the plant mass fixed by photosynthesis over the entire earth, land, and sea and 40 percent of the photosynthetic product on land. Largely as a result of synthetic fertilizers, humanity fixes about as much nitrogen in the environment as does nature.

With human activities now rivaling nature in scale, actions that in the past merely produced local environmental crises now have global implications. Moreover, environmental effects that once seemed simple and trivial, such as increases in carbon dioxide emissions, have now suddenly become threats to the stability of the fundamental ecological cycles of the planet. Destruction of the ozone layer, the greenhouse effect, annihilation of ancient and tropical forests, species extinction, reductions in genetic diversity, production of toxic and radioactive wastes, contamination of water resources, soil depletion, depletion of essential raw materials, desertification, the growth of world population spurred by rising poverty—all represent ominous trends the full impact of which, singly or in combination, is scarcely to be imagined at present. "With the appearance of a continent-sized hole in the Earth's protective ozone layer and the threat of global warming," Barry Commoner noted, "even droughts, floods, and heat waves may become unwitting acts of man."[7]

The sustainability of both human civilization and global life processes depends not on the mere slowing down of these dire trends but on their *reversal*.[8] Nothing in the history of capitalism, however, suggests that the system will be up to such a task. On the contrary, there is every indication that the system, left to its own devices, will gravitate toward the "let them eat pollution" stance so clearly enunciated by the chief economist of the World Bank.

Fortunately for the world, however, capitalism has never been allowed to develop for long entirely in accordance with its own logic. Opposition forces always emerge—whether in the form of working-class struggles for social betterment or conservation movements dedicated to overcoming environmental depredations— that force the system to moderate its worst tendencies. And to some extent the ensuing reforms can result in lasting, beneficial constraints on the market. What the capitalist class cannot accept, however, are changes that will likely result in the destruction of the system itself. Long before reform movements threaten the accumulation process as a whole, therefore, counterforces are set in motion by the ruling interests, and the necessary elemental changes are headed off.

And there's the rub. Where radical change is called for, little is accomplished within the system, and the underlying crisis intensifies over time. Today this is particularly evident in the ecological realm. The nature of the global environmental crisis is such that the fate of the entire planet and social and ecological issues of enormous complexity are involved, all traceable to the forms of production now prevalent. It is impossible to prevent the world's environmental crisis from progressively worsening unless root problems of production, distribution, technology, and growth are dealt with on a global scale. And the more that such questions are raised, the more it becomes evident that capitalism is unsustainable—ecologically, economically, politically, and morally—and must be superseded.

NOTES

1. Barry Commoner, *Making Peace with the Planet* (New York: New Press, 1992), pp. 64–66; Robert Bullard, "The Politics of Race and Pollution: An Interview with Robert Bullard," *Multinational Monitor* 13, no. 6 (June 1992):21–22.

2. Bill Weinberg, *War on the Land* (London: Zed Books, 1991), pp. 37–39; Edward Goldsmith et. al., *The Imperiled Planet* (Cambridge, Mass.: MIT Press, 1990), p. 147; Center for Investigative Reporting and Bill Moyers, *Global Dumping Ground* (Cambridge: Lutterworth Press, 1991), pp. 1–2, 12.

3. William R. Cline, *The Economics of Global Warming* (Washington, D.C.: Institute for International Economics, 1992), pp. 4–6, 55–58, 130–133, 300.

4. See also Frances Cairncross, *Costing the Earth* (London: Economist Books, 1991), pp. 30–31, 130–133.

5. National Academy of Sciences, *One Earth, One Future* (Washington, D.C.: National Academy Press, 1990), pp. 67–71; Helen Caldicott, *If You Love This Planet* (New York: W. W. Norton, 1992), p. 24; Mostafa K. Tolba, *Saving Our Planet* (New York: Chapman and Hall, 1992), pp. 27–28; Intergovernmental Panel on Climate Change (IPCC), *Climate Change* (New York: Cambridge University Press, 1990), p. xxii.

6. *The Guardian* (London), June 13, 1992.

7. IPCC, *Climate Change*, p. xvi; Donella Meadows et al., *Beyond the Limits* (London: Earthscan, 1992), pp. 65–66; Jim MacNeill et al., *Beyond Interdependence* (New York: Oxford University Press, 1991), pp. 8–9; Paul R. Ehrlich and Anne H. Ehrlich, *Healing the Planet* (New York: Addison-Wesley, 1991), pp. 26–27; Peter M. Vitousik et al., "Human Appropriation of the Products of Photosynthesis," *Bioscience* 36, no. 6 (June 1986):368–373; Commoner, *Making Peace*, p. 3.

8. Paul M. Sweezy, "Capitalism and the Environment," *Monthly Review* 41, no. 2 (June 1989):6; Meadows et al., *Beyond the Limits*, p. xv.

16

The Silent War: Debt and Africa

JILL HILLS

The debt war is undeclared and silent so as not to provoke alarm or protests from the media or the public. It is another episode of silent surrender—conquest without gun battle. The debt crisis satisfies the motives, mechanisms and effects of conventional war.

—Bade Onimode, 1992[1]

This is a collective murder of Africans by the IMF and France.

—Mali civil servants commenting on devaluation of African currency, 1994[2]

Gradually and inexorably Africa is fading from the West's consciousness except as a continent that is an economic *basket case,* a black hole down which the world's largess disappears. Ethnic violence, civil wars, the overthrow of democratically elected regimes, drought, famine, and starvation are reported. In this context Africa's ongoing debt to the West is not newsworthy.

Economic *spheres of power* are replacing the previous East-West military dissection of the world. No longer the geopolitical arena where capitalism fights communism for hearts and minds, sub-Saharan Africa is simply an economic arena for the expansion of Western capitalism. Gone is the need for strategic military bases and authoritarian puppet regimes supported by Western governments, except, as in Algeria and Egypt, where the backing of existing regimes might keep at bay Islamic fundamentalism. Sub-Saharan Africa belongs to no major regional bloc and holds little strategic interest.[3]

In fact, according to Western governments and the Western media, the Third World debt crisis has ended. In September 1993 the governor of the Bank of England was reported as saying that the debt crisis was over—for the banks.[4]

Similarly, in October 1993, Reuters reported that the attendees at the annual meeting of the International Monetary Fund (IMF) and World Bank were concerned with global issues and equity markets rather than with developing-country debt. In fact, the swapping of debt for equity has allowed banks to buy developing-country assets cheaply, and a secondary market in debt has become a world market in itself.[5]

To a large extent developing-country debt interests the Western media only insofar as it affects the Western financial system. Even within the topic of debt the American mass media display indifference to Africa. A search of American databases for 1993 could find hardly one reference to debt and Africa. This lack of concern mirrors the 25 percent reduction in U.S. aid to the continent during the 1980s.

The British media give Africa more coverage—a result perhaps of its colonial heritage—yet most coverage occurs only when the aid agencies issue new reports.[6] Debt renegotiation with the commercial banks, as for instance in the case of Brazil, is newsworthy. But African debt is primarily owed to the multilateral financial institutions. It threatens no banks and is small in relation to total developing-country debt—$194 billion (12 percent) out of a total debt of $1,662 billion. Debt forgiveness is newsworthy, and calls by Britain for the bilateral debt of the poorest African countries to be forgiven by other G-7 members receive coverage. But when the response of other industrialized countries, particularly Japan, is negative, the news value vanishes.

Poverty has no news value. And unlike in the rest of the world, poverty in black Africa is increasing, not decreasing. The Western media may report the bare facts as given by the World Bank—that Africa alone will see increasing numbers in poverty until after the year 2000—yet the underlying causes go unanalyzed and unchallenged. Linkages between increasing poverty and debt to the West, or among trade, debt, and capital flows, or among environmental degradation, debt, and poverty remain unexplored.

To a large extent the Western media reflect the underlying attitude of the international financial institutions (IFIs) and Western governments—that Africa's plight is all its own fault, that African leaders have not done as they were told by the IMF and World Bank. Yet as Oxfam has pointed out, the truth is in many instances the opposite of this Western-inspired myth.[7] Appointees from the IFIs have taken up posts in the financial institutions of African countries, virtually controlling many African countries and demanding the implementation of set economic prescriptions.

Anxious to explain and legitimize its failure to alter the downward spiral of African economies, the World Bank began in 1989 to focus on politics within Africa.[8] Whereas in the 1980s the bank's Deepak Lal concluded that only authoritarian regimes would be able to impose World Bank policies on an unwilling populace, this stance became progressively untenable.[9] The problem with Africa, said the bank in 1989, was lack of good governance.

These overtly political concerns of the IFIs chimed with the altered strategic considerations of the industrialized West following the collapse of the communist bloc. In 1990, led by France, came a new emphasis on human rights and *political conditionality* as a feature of lending by Western governments. Both Western governments and multilateral financial institutions—which when geopolitical strategy so demanded supported African dictators and military regimes—began to threaten that they would cut financial aid to those who did not produce democratic credentials.[10] In particular, multiparty elections were seen as essential.

In turn, African leaders saw this new concern as reflecting the West's new agenda and the competition for financial aid from eastern Europe and the former USSR. Some saw it as a legitimation for a redirection or curtailment of aid.[11] By placing the blame for Africa's position on internal factors, the West and the IFIs could wash their hands of Africa.

From recent statements one might think that Western governments, financial institutions, and multinationals bear no responsibility for what has happened in Africa. In April 1990, the U.S. assistant secretary of state for African affairs, Herman Cohen, asked donors "to be more disciplined and selective about assistance to Africa and to ensure that their assistance is not squandered on military spending, luxury consumption and capital flight."[12]

Yet the major arms exporters to the Third World have been not only the former USSR but also the United States, Britain, and France, and the home for capital flight from Latin America in particular was U.S. commercial banks. Cynics might point out that for the U.S. government to target African regimes in this way might have something to do with British and French armament sales to previous colonies and the declining fortunes of American banks. Furthermore, despite such sentiments, the U.S. administration has not followed through on its initial post–Gulf War calls for an arms ban to the Third World. The implication, however, is that the Africans have been at fault, not that the West may bear responsibility for African demands for *luxuries.* Accordingly, it is not the U.S. government and the European Union, by subsidizing exports, that have encouraged Africans to eat wheat rather than local produce, and it is not Western multinationals who have marketed Coke or Pepsi by mass advertising, encouraged the use of powdered baby milk rather than breast feeding, or promoted Hollywood exports that produce images of Western lifestyles in African townships. Not surprisingly, media silence is pervasive on the linkages among such imports, debt, and poverty.

Misinformation and mists of silence surround African debt. That $10 billion per year is transferred to the West from the poorest countries is not reported. That the IMF has received $2 billion more out of Africa than it has paid in new loans since 1985 is not reported. On the impact of debt there is silence.

Nor has the downside of the December 1993 agreement on GATT (General Agreement on Tariffs and Trade) been widely publicized. In the new race for industrialized-country power through exports and foreign investment, GATT has been presented as of universal, worldwide benefit. According to widely quoted figures generated by the Organization for Economic Cooperation and Development (OECD) and the World Bank, each year the world will be $200 billion better off because of GATT.[13] Yet within that figure is hidden another—that black Africa will be $2 billion per annum worse off. For Africa, GATT threatens a worsening in its terms of trade, which will exacerbate its poverty. And GATT threatens to prevent Africa from feeding its own people, from upgrading its agriculture, and from ever industrializing into competition with the West.

To a large extent the media follow agendas set by the IFIs, thereby accepting that the discourse on poverty in Africa and its environment, trade, and debt should be segmented and separate. For example, to follow up on their own reports documenting the seeming inexorable rise of poverty in Africa until the year 2000 and the international criticism provoked, in 1993 World Bank officials undertook a tour of London and other European Union centers. They were to meet poverty experts to find out where they thought the World Bank was going wrong. Neither debt nor trade was mentioned in the media report.[14] It was as though poverty in Africa could be divorced from debt, from the payments required to service that debt, from the exports required to service those payments, from the trade policies of the industrialized world, from the programs imposed by the multilateral financial institutions, and from the structural conditions that created the debt.

It is the silence on those issues that I set out to remedy in this chapter. Discussion is needed about the African debt and its myths, the origins of that debt, the programs of the IFIs (including the IMF and the World Bank), the impact of those mechanisms on the everyday lives of the poor, especially women and children, and the worsening future promised as the newly agreed GATT regime comes into effect. Indeed, the very name *debt crisis* is a misnomer. For Africa, the debt crisis is a food crisis, a health crisis, an education crisis, a deindustrialization crisis, an environmental crisis, an export crisis, a crisis of sovereignty, a crisis of political influence in world affairs. It is a crisis for survival, not only at the individual level for millions of people but at the political level in a world system becoming ever more racist and undemocratic.

I argue that for the West the debt crisis has produced costs in terms of lost jobs in exports but it has also been a means of economic gain for consumers and financial institutions. It has produced cheaper tea and coffee on the tables of Western consumers, cheaper raw materials for Western business, and larger profits for Western multinationals. It is also the means for political gains—the control of African governments in the interest of multinational capital and the integration of Africa into the global capitalist economy primarily on American terms.[15]

The debt war and the parallel GATT agreement are a means of international stratification in which the international division of labor is taken to its logical conclusion: that those who work but cannot sell their labor or goods at a price sufficient to support life must starve, even if they work. It is not simply the replication within the international community of the American domestic social stratification—of rich whites living separate lives from blacks confined to ghettos. For those American blacks, there is some possibility of education to improve their lives, and there is some form of welfare to prevent starvation and death.

Nor, as some Africans suggest, are the results of the New Right political economy simply the old system of colonialism reimposed by IFIs and multinational corporations. Colonialism was not only based on a racial division of labor. It denied political and economic rights to the indigenous black population of Africa.

Instead the New Right political economy pays lip service to internal African democracy. Its assumption is that political rights can be exercised without economic rights. It assumes that one can vote even if one is dead from starvation. Hidden in the new world political economy is a reintroduction of a racist division of labor—but this time on an international basis and sanctioned by Western governments. Lack of democracy in the international economic system is legitimated by Western appeals to *market forces,* as though such markets were other than a social construct of the policy of Western companies and governments. Hidden by the silence of the Western media, the African black poor, especially women and children, suffer and die from an international dictatorship of wealth, a dictatorship that, in time-honored fashion, seeks to blame the victim for her misery.

Origins of the Debt Crisis

In Africa one can trace the debt crisis back to the economies put in place by the colonial powers, which until the 1960s used the colonies as external markets for manufactured goods and the site of resource extraction—mineral and agricultural. Internal processing of those resources was discouraged in view of the competition it would pose to labor markets in the colonialist countries. In some countries indigenous manufacturing was forbidden or dismantled, and traditional rural industries were undermined by imports. Unlike in Latin America, agriculture in Africa was based on small holdings, often with communal ownership of land. The colonialists introduced mines, plantations, and cash-cropping schemes and either physically forced indigenous labor to work for European companies (French colonies) or used a poll tax that had to be paid in cash to achieve the same effect (British colonies). Exports of commodities were exclusively to colonial masters and provided them with cheap food and minerals.[16]

The economies taken over at independence were therefore overwhelmingly agricultural in terms of the labor force and were dependent for exports on primary commodities. Despite initial advances in industrial output of 15 percent per annum following independence in the 1960s, within ten years output had fallen back, so that by the mid-1980s industry's share of GDP was only 17 percent and manufactures made up only 7 to 8 percent of nonfuel exports.[17] The most productive parts of the economies continued under the control of multinational corporations (MNCs) for the previous colonial state or were bought by them.

These MNCs continue to control about 80 percent of Africa's trade in mineral and agricultural raw materials.[18] As a result of takeovers and buyouts, they have become further concentrated. They include Unilever, Gill and Dufus, General Foods, Allied-Lyons, and Nescafe, but one of the most powerful is American Cargill Inc. (a private company), which controls 23 percent of world trade in cereals and protein crops, 15 percent of all oilseed trade, 10 percent of coffee, and 6 percent of jute and sisal and is the world's largest trader in cotton. It also deals in cocoa, rubber, soya, potatoes, hard timber, and fish flour and is the world's largest trader in fertilizer.[19]

There is no free trade in commodities. Rather, these multinationals control prices, often fixing prices before the crop is harvested. Companies such as Nescafe own no coffee or cocoa estates.[20] Renting land prevents the threat of nationalization being used against the multinational by the state in which it operates. Elsewhere, the monopoly marketing boards of the colonial regimes were taken over postindependence by the new states, which often continued to pay the peasant well below the international price for the commodity produced and used the surplus for industrialization.[21]

During the early 1980s, foreign direct investment into Africa was approximately $1 billion per annum as foreign companies moved into oil and mining. It rose to $1.7 billion per annum in the late 1980s, all of which went to oil-exporting countries and half of this to Nigeria. In general, foreign direct investment is an expensive way of gaining investment capital. The original capital investment is positive, but in a short while the flows become negative as royalties are paid and profits are remitted. Export of capital by MNCs in the form of repatriation of profits is difficult to quantify. One estimate suggests that a total of $25 billion was repatriated from Africa as profits between 1974 and 1990 at a rate of about $1.5 billion annually,[22] a sum matching or exceeding inward investment. In addition, import substitution also demanded technology royalties be paid to the West, payment estimated to have been $35 billion in 1982 alone.[23]

A further structural problem was bequeathed to African countries by their colonial masters in the form of the states that they constructed artificially. Fourteen states are landlocked, which makes both incoming and outgoing trade expensive. In addition, the colonialists determined state boundaries according to their interests, often including several hostile tribes within a single state. Following independence, after Westminster democracy had been tried and failed, one-party states could be legitimated on the basis that multiparty democracy would degenerate into tribal conflict. Even in the 1990s, the legacy of these divisions is evident in political parties based on tribal loyalties and in the degeneration of democracy into tribal slaughter in Burundi.

At the same time, education before independence was geared to a replacement of the colonial administration and limited to an elite. Almost 80 percent of the population was illiterate at independence, and there were only a few thousand graduates. Inevitably, the incoming elite was as far removed from the rural village and subsistence agriculture as the previous colonial administration, its power resting on literacy and Western education and on keeping the urban population happy.[24]

The modernization theory of development emphasizing industrialization, import substitution, and cheap food for the urban population served the interests of those urban elites. Often Western-educated, they saw the future of their countries as aspiring to the Western model. At the same time, they took over the previous colonial structure in which the only potential instigator of industrialization was the state. The state was also the primary site for personal accumulation of wealth, of which leaders and their personal families or networks availed themselves. A *winner-take-all* system of state patronage and clientele developed. However, in these displays of personal corruption, African leaders were also aided by the alacrity of Western companies in paying bribes and of Western banks in accepting the proceeds.[25]

As Cheryl Payer pointed out, the modernization theory also served the interests of Western capital and Western industrialized governments. The World Bank lent governments money primarily for capital-intensive projects until the 1980s. By lending to capital projects, Western interests could be assured of an export market for the inputs of goods and expertise into those projects and, if some of the money was used for purposes other than investment, could also benefit from export markets for consumer goods.[26] Companies winning World Bank project contracts were under no obligation to source locally, and where the privatization of state assets was concerned, as in Ghana in the 1960s, then the conditions under which multinationals bought them, often financed by indigenous capital, included the unrestricted repatriation of profits.[27]

Payer demonstrated how American economic thinking of the 1950s ignored the question of the repayment of loans, assuming instead that loan principal could be rolled over with new loans repaying interest on the old. In this way the repayment of loans through increased exports of goods and services from recipient countries to the industrialized would not have to take place.[28] Other scholars have made the same point: "There was no thought of servicing the debt by generating trade surpluses and reverse transfers."[29] In other words, industrialization was pressed on developing countries through the IFIs, but the implications in regard to the ensuing trade regime were not accepted. The two discourses were kept separate. Over the years, although the IFIs have lobbied on trade liberalization, their influence on the industrialized West in the trade area has not been noticeable.

The principle of industrialization in developing countries was accepted within GATT in 1969. Developing countries were allowed to impose tariffs to protect their infant industries. Agriculture was also exempt from GATT, which allowed developing countries to impose tariffs on the import of foodstuffs. Food imports into Africa at this time were negligible. In 1970, Africa produced enough food to feed itself. Arms sales and public procurement in general were also not subject to GATT, and because these were not subject to open competition, they could be abused with impunity.

Where loans were given by IFIs, each project in theory had to generate enough hard currency to repay both principal and interest. Since loans were short-term and infrastructural projects often only of long-term value, an imbalance was bound to arise. Yet it was in the interests of both developed and developing countries that a country should not default on payments, so the bias was toward long loan periods and long *grace periods* (periods before debt repayments began) and toward new loans to pay the interest and principal of the old, with some left over for new imports.

From the developing-country perspective, it was possible in the 1960s and 1970s to organize loans from a variety of sources, so that the overall indebtedness of a country was not visible. At the same time, commodity prices (copper, tea, sugar, coffee, cotton) in world markets were high, which gave lenders the impression that exports from producing countries could generate the hard currency required to service loans. However, the economies of the African countries were very vulnerable to external market fluctuations.

It was not simply that sub-Saharan economies were dependent on the production of commodities. Worse, the majority were and still are dependent on the export of one commodity. For example, cocoa accounts for about 60 percent of Ghana's exports; coffee for 50 percent of Tanzania's, 70 percent of Rwanda's, 90 percent of Burundi's, and 95 percent of Uganda's; and copper for 60 percent of Zaire's and almost 100 percent of Zambia's.[30] The majority (up to 80 percent) of government revenue depends on export proceeds. Hence, changes in the supply or demand for a commodity or a fall in prices could drastically affect the balance of payments of these countries, as could an increase in the prices of essential imports.[31]

The Origins of African Debt

Most analysts of the debt crisis argue that it was caused both by factors exogenous to the developing countries and by factors specific to the domestic circumstances of the debtors themselves. As for the exogenous factors, the oil shock of 1973–1974 resulted in the cost of oil increasing to oil-importing developing countries. They either had to increase exports to meet that rising cost, borrow money to cover the increased import bill, or cut down on imports. Since exports in primary commodities are inflexible—it takes three to five years for a coffee bush or cotton plant to become profitable—and levels of consumption were politically sensitive, many borrowed to meet the import bill. "The first oil shock was particularly hard, producing in the nonoil developing countries combined deficits of nearly 31 percent of exports of goods and services in 1975."[32] To some extent it also made sense to borrow, since the real rate of interest on loans was below the rate of inflation in these countries, and debt could be eaten up by that inflation.

After the election of Ronald Reagan in 1980, U.S. policy on development issues switched toward market-led theories in which outward-looking development would be partly financed by private funds from abroad. In this strategy American commercial banks were expected to play their part. However, all the industrialized countries supported the role of the private banks "in channeling financing from surplus to deficit nations."[33] By 1985 nine of the most important American banks and two British counterparts had begun to borrow from the Eurodollar market and to lend money onward, so that they actually lent more capital to developing countries than they had in reserves.[34] The Eurodollar debt crisis of the commercial banking sector was primarily a U.S. and British phenomenon.

At this juncture the experience of most Latin American countries and that of most African countries diverged. Whereas Latin American countries borrowed heavily from commercial banks, in Africa commercial banks lent mainly to oil exporters, such as Nigeria. The rest of Africa borrowed from the IMF, from the World Bank in the form of soft loans from the International Development Association, from the African Development Bank, and from Western governments in the form of bilateral loans and export guarantees for the purchase of equipment. Nevertheless, despite the lower proportion of loans owed to commercial banks, Africa was not unaffected by the ensuing Eurodollar crisis.

Overall, the proportion of debt owed to commercial banks by developing countries in 1973 was 11.6 percent, a proportion that had risen by 1983 to 43 percent. In the case of Latin America the commercial bank proportion rose from 23.8 percent to 62 percent.[35] In the case of Africa commercial banks' share of the debt rose from 32.5 percent in 1971 to 40 percent in 1980.[36]

The second oil shock of 1979 exacerbated balance-of-payments problems, not simply by increasing the import bill for oil-importing developing countries but by inducing recession in the industrialized West. The price of cocoa, coffee, tea, copper, bananas, and oil products declined during the period 1979–1981, leading to foreign exchange losses of $2.2 billion with a further $13.5 billion lost up to 1983.[37]

At the same time, interest rates increased as the United States sought to attract foreign money to pay for its federal budgetary deficit and to clamp down on inflation. U.S. interest rates were hiked by 1 percent on October 6, 1979. Within twelve months rates had climbed to 21.5 percent.

These increases were directly attributable to American domestic politics in which President Reagan, rather than accept the political costs of dealing with the internal and external deficit through tax increases, higher oil prices, and budgetary cuts, preferred instead to adopt a policy of more defense spending and no tax increases. Interest rates had to rise to finance the federal deficit through overseas borrowing, which in turn led to a high dollar value. The high dollar meant that imports to developing countries, such as oil, denominated in dollars, increased. As a result, the purchasing power represented in Africa's exports fell by 25 percent during the period 1981–1983.

Subsequently, all interest rates increased as the other Western countries raised theirs to support their currencies. Loans previously agreed on at variable interest rates as well as new borrowing became subject to the higher interest charges. The average interest on all types of loans to Africa rose from 4.2 percent in 1971 to 10.1 percent by 1982, and the real interest rate rose from 0.7 percent in 1970 to 1.7 percent in 1986. The Organization for African Unity (OAU) estimated that $20.4 billion would be required between 1986 and 1990 to pay rising interest charges alone on Africa's existing debt.[38] In addition, the average maturity for loans was reduced from twenty years in the 1970s to fifteen years in the 1980s, grace periods were reduced from six to four years, and a greater proportion of loans (20 percent) were contracted on variable interest rates.[39] As terms of lending tightened, new loans were insufficient to cover debt servicing. According to Payer, net transfer in Africa became negative in 1984, which was roughly when countries began to fall behind with their payments to the IMF.[40]

When net transfer became negative, the IMF was again called in. By 1985 fifteen sub-Saharan countries had rescheduled their debts. The largest outstanding debts were owed by Cote d'Ivoire ($10 billion), Nigeria ($19 billion), Sudan ($9 billion), Zaire ($6 billion), and Senegal ($3 billion). But for others, such as Uganda and Malawi, a much smaller total debt of $1 billion represented for each about 40 percent of export revenue.[41]

The next issue is whether indigenous factors contributed to African debt. As Harold Lever pointed out, it is virtually impossible to trace a given amount of money, but African authors and others have argued that much of the borrowing of the 1970s was squandered. Money went toward luxury imports, arms sales, and prestige development projects, and there was capital flight by elites. Although it is evidently true that these factors affected individual countries, I would argue that the current emphasis upon them is part of the mythology of debt built up by the IFIs and banks to eschew responsibility.

The term *capital flight* is itself negative terminology used by those who otherwise promote freedom of capital movement. Capital flight occurs not only where leaders and bureaucrats steal money but also where high exchange rates give incentives to convert local currency into dollars and where exchange controls fail to prevent it. Onimode quoted Adedeji's estimates of capital flight in 1989 from Africa as about $2.5 billion. On the other hand, the World Bank estimated in 1991 that the stock of flight capital from sub-Saharan Africa held abroad was equivalent to 95 percent of the region's GDP.[42] One reason cited by the IMF for the need to devalue the CFA against the French franc in January 1994 was that overvaluation had increased capital flight.[43] *Capital flight* is itself part of the terminology used to blame governments for policies (high exchange rates) of which the IFIs disapprove, although they also disapprove of exchange controls.

During the second Cold War period, military regimes and civil wars, often backed by the superpowers, brought increased arms spending by African governments. In 1980 sub-Saharan governments spent an average of 12 percent of their annual expenditure on defense, but the proportions varied from 30 percent in Ethiopia to 25 percent in Uganda and Zimbabwe, 19 percent in Somalia, 17 percent in Burkino Faso, 16.4 percent in Kenya, 16.8 percent in Senegal, and 13 percent in the Sudan.[44] In many cases, a far larger proportion was spent on arms than on health or education. However, it has to be pointed out that each year the U.S. government and others were providing millions of dollars in *arms aid* through bilateral loans to Africa, thereby creating an export market for Western defense industries.

Much of the increase in developing-country borrowing between 1974 and 1982 in fact seems to have been for higher oil costs. The additional cost to nonoil-exporting developing countries has been estimated as $260 billion between 1974 and 1982. With additional interest charges, the cost would have been $335 billion out of an increase in debt of $482 billion.[45] In other words, oil and interest rates accounted for 70 percent of developing-country debt during this period.

Nor should it be forgotten that the World Bank itself and Western governments backed massive infrastructural projects, such as the Turkwel Gorge Dam in Kenya, which were wasteful of resources, often reduced the income of the poor, and contributed to environmental damage.[46] The World Bank itself now concedes that a large number of its projects within Africa show negative or poor returns—in other words, the beneficiaries were the Western companies and consultants originally involved, not the African people.[47] Nor is this picture new. Harrison quoted a 1985 World Bank evaluation of 1,000 projects that showed the failure rate in West Africa to be 18 percent and in East Africa to be 24 percent—double that of Asian projects. In agriculture the position was worse, with one in three projects in West Africa a failure and one in two in East Africa.[48] However, because payment of the loans involved is in hard currency, the African people must continue to pay for those projects through the generation of exports.

Structural Adjustment, States, and Trade

Once African countries had gone into negative transfer of resources and called in the IMF, they had to undertake structural adjustment in order to receive loans. IMF lending is short term and based primarily on rectifying balance-of-payments imbalances rather than facilitating growth. In this framework, developing-country governments had to slash imports, cut public spending, reduce subsidies on food prices, increase interest rates, devalue their exchange rate, and increase exports. They also had to open previously protected markets to competition. As coordination among donors increased, it became impossible to raise bilateral or commercial loans without the imprimatur of the IFIs. Aid to Africa from the European Community under the Lomé Convention became similarly tied to conditionality.

World Bank structural adjustment lending complemented IMF conditionality, primarily concentrating on a reduction in the state sector through privatization and a shift in resources to agriculture. The bank moved to structural adjustment lending in the 1980s as debt prevented developing countries from absorbing the West's capital in project loans. Structural adjustment programs were designed to ensure that capital continued to be exported and that the economies of the developing countries were opened to the exports of the West and to the investment of multinational companies.

For Africa, World Bank thinking was set out in the Berg Report of 1981, which played down the impact of external factors and laid the blame for Africa's poverty on internal factors. "The main cause of rising current account deficits and shortages of foreign exchange in the 1970s was not the terms of trade, but the slow growth of exports." The report highlighted three domestic policy inadequacies: "Trade and exchange rate policies have overprotected industry. . . ; public sectors frequently become overextended; there has been a consistent bias against agriculture."[49]

Over the following decade the bank argued in favor of privatization based on an American understanding of a rational-legal state that constructed a liberal dichotomy between a *public* and *private* sector, despite the fact that this concept was alien to African postindependence history and practice. Structural adjustment undermined states' fiscal capacity, their legitimacy, and their bureaucracy.[50]

Only in 1993 did Edward Jaycox, the bank's vicepresident for Africa, acknowledge that a reduction in the role of the state had left a vacuum filled not by the market, as the bank had forecast, but by development agencies. Although development agencies are themselves caught in the dilemma of how far they should undertake services previously provided by the state, the president of the World Bank nevertheless commented:

> Donors cannot be satisfied that external technical assistance to sub-Saharan Africa has increased over the last decade and now stands at $4 billion a year. Nor can they be satisfied that an estimated 100,000 *expatriate* advisers are at work in Africa today, a larger number than at independence.[51]

Again one sees the off-loading of responsibility.

After the 1980s, in accordance with the policy of distributing resources in favor of agriculture, the IFIs supported the abolition of all food subsidies and the increase of prices to producers. However, the purpose of a shift in resources to agriculture was to increase exports, not food self-sufficiency. In Africa's case increased exports meant increasing sales of commodities. The IFIs' view was based on the neoclassical theory of comparative advantage in world trade—that countries specialize in those products for which they hold particular advantages—combined with an export-oriented development theory. But as Woodward pointed out, no other countries have attempted export orientation in commodities. The newly industrializing countries of Asia have grown by the export of manufactures.[52] Such a policy returned Africa to colonial days when its resources were consumed and processed in the West and not in the continent.

Devaluation of exchange rates may have lowered the prices of exports, but it also increased the costs of necessary inputs to African industry and agriculture. Thus, for the period 1986–1990, compared with 1981–1985, sub-Saharan Africa's imports fell from an annual average of $69.1 billion to $62.3 billion. During the past decade investment has slumped by 20 percent.[53]

Nor has overseas investment been attracted by the devaluation of currencies. In the 1990s, just as foreign direct investment (FDI) is increasing worldwide, so in Africa it is falling. From 7 percent of worldwide FDI into developing countries in the 1980s, in 1991 Africa's share totaled 5 percent of such FDI and 0.7 percent of worldwide FDI. Most went to Nigeria, Zimbabwe, Gabon, Liberia, and Cote d'Ivoire, and most was into the oil sector.[54] Lack of education and infrastructure, political instability, and poor returns deter investors. At the same time, whereas many middle-income developing countries are benefiting from the investment of equity into their emerging markets, the poorest countries in Africa are in fact suffering from disinvestment. Hence the outward repatriation of profits is not balanced by new inward investment.

The Social Impact of Structural Adjustment

Africa is the only region in the world where the World Bank itself estimates that poverty grew between 1985 and 1990 and will increase from the 47.8 percent of the population in 1990 to 49.7 percent in the year 2000.[55] Real per capita income in sub-Saharan Africa declined by 0.9 percent between 1980 and 1990 and declined by a further 2 percent in 1990 and 1 percent in 1991.[56] The World Bank estimates real growth in per capita income will be only 0.3 percent until the year 2000. Unemployment affects 100 million people (four times as many as in 1979). In general, Africans are now 20 percent poorer than ten years ago, and over 200 million people are unable to meet even their basic needs.

African infant mortality is set to increase to 39 percent of infant deaths worldwide in the year 2000 compared with 29 percent in the 1980s.[57] In 1990 more than 4 million children under the age of five died from malnutrition. According to UNICEF, African countries now spend four times as much on servicing debt as on health care. Dorothy Mutemba reported that in Zambia malnutrition is now the major cause of death among children between ages one and fourteen; dysentery, enteritis, and diarrhea, all diseases resulting from lack of access to clean water, rank second.[58] In addition, by 1990 two-thirds of African governments were spending less per capita on health care than in 1980. On a continent where AIDS is estimated to have already killed 1.5 million people and infected millions more and where malaria and tuberculosis are on the increase, expenditure on health has been reduced.

In Nigeria, diseases such as smallpox, yellow fever, and guinea-worm infestation have reappeared, as have waterborne diseases such as cholera. Measles and tuberculosis are increasing, as is kwashiorkor. Deji Popoola quoted a 1988–1989 study of Lagos children that found stunted growth in 51 percent.[59] Similarly, in Zaire a study of mortality at the pediatric hospital in Kinsasha found 44 percent of deaths to be from malnutrition in 1986. World Bank *user-pays* policies have discriminated against the poor. Imported drugs are expensive or unavailable. Nil Kwaku Sowa found that in Ghana the World Bank's imposition of charges for treatment has caused a 50 percent drop in attendances at clinics in rural areas. But urban facilities have also suffered. In Zambia, after becoming a health hazard to staff and patients in 1991, all the operating theaters in the country's largest hospital were closed down.[60]

In education, structural adjustment has resulted in falling enrollment in primary school, down from 78 percent in the 1970s to 68 percent in the 1980s. Less than 80 percent of boys and 60 percent of girls enroll for primary school. Only 20 percent of boys and 10 percent of girls go on to secondary school. These figures are overestimates because as families find that they cannot afford books and equipment, dropout rates have increased. User fees have also increased the gender imbalance in education. Families already struggling to survive educate sons in preference to daughters. User fees are levied despite recognition that the education of girls is crucial to a reduction in population growth and to a reduction in infant mortality.[61] Such policies reflect the short-term financial targets of structural adjustment designed to ensure debt servicing, not long-term development concerns.

The World Bank's prescriptions for Africa were predicated on public choice theory, advocates of which argued that the root cause of the lack of economic success lay with the coalition built up between rulers and urban dwellers at the expense of the rural and agricultural sector.[62] What was required was a political transformation of the state itself. New coalitions could be formed using economic incentives. In particular, by substituting the market for the state, a *free* market would herald the rise of a bourgeois class in opposition to the state.

Yet one of the common conclusions of a number of African writers reporting on a sample of countries is that the beneficiaries of structural adjustment have been those with links into the state, who have been able to exploit access to capital to set up in business or to expand their business. If anything, patronage networks linked to the state have been reinforced by their declining resource base.

In general, structural adjustment redistributes resources away from the poorest stratas of society to those who can pay. Hence, the urban *rent-seekers* who lose out are those with little power—workers, the urban poor, and the increasingly impoverished middle classes. Although in some countries, such as Nigeria, agribusinesses and transnational corporations have benefited in general by justifying preferential allocation to those who can demonstrate existing productivity, in rural areas structural adjustment has an inbuilt bias against the poor.[63] Overall, the weight of evidence is that programs intensify inequalities, and on a continent where women are already disadvantaged they are disadvantaged more.

The debt war on Africa is waged against a continent where climate and earth are fragile, where drought is common and population increasing. Intensified cultivation reduces land fertility and increases deforestation and soil erosion. The U.N. Food and Agriculture Organization estimates that 3.2 million hectares of land each year are lost in Africa to desertification. Less land must support more people and cash crops. Cash crops have taken the best land. Increasingly, land devoted to production for the family or for local sale has been pushed into marginal land, and the rural poor have been forced to overcultivate. Land degradation and erosion from the cutting down of trees for firewood have contributed to lower yields. Imported fertilizer is in short supply and expensive, yet in half the non-desert areas of Africa there is no natural fertilizer. Climate and the tsetse fly prevent the integration of livestock and arable farming. A fragile rural environment, where the difference between life and death can be rain at a certain time, has been placed under increased pressure by the debt war.[64]

Where prices for cash crops have fallen, it becomes uneconomic to produce them. Yet rural households must do so to pay for education and health care. Such payments are the equivalent of the old British poll tax that forced the indigenous population to work for the benefit of Western companies. Even where cash crop prices have increased, the increase is eaten up by the additional costs of basic goods, such as cooking oil, clothing, and soap.[65]

As Diane Elson noted, cash crops are grown mainly under the control of men, and income goes to husbands. Women lose access to better land diverted to cash crop production. Export crops are allocated better seeds, fertilizer, credit, and extension services.[66] In Ghana, Kenya, and Malawi evidence indicates that women have less access to credit and extension services.[67] Pushed onto marginal land, they must spend more time raising food crops, seeking firewood, and fetching water. One study of women in the south of Guinea-Bissau reported eighteen- or nineteen-hour working days for women.[68] As mothers increasingly struggle to keep the family fed, daughters are expected to contribute both paid and unpaid labor to the household and are denied education.

About one in five households in Africa is headed by a woman. Responsible as they are for feeding the family, women have had to increase their income earning or food production activities, whether in the informal sector or by raising vegetables in the urban areas or by producing handicrafts in the rural. In urban areas, low-paid women workers in the formal sector are the first to be laid off, and because of low education, they are unlikely to find work. Work in the informal sector involves long hours and exploitation. Women must often work two jobs, care for children, find or grow food, and undertake household tasks. Inflation has made the satisfaction of basic needs difficult. Banugire reported a widening gap between formal wages and basic-needs requirements in Uganda for both lower- and middle-income workers and found that workers in both groups could not fill a third of this basic-needs deficit.[69]

People in urban areas who have suffered are those previously employed in the public sector or those still employed whose wages are now so low that they must work two or more jobs. In Nigeria, civil servants and other professionals now grow their own food, use their cars and motorbikes as taxis, organize sweatshops and small-scale manufacturing, and indulge in corruption; in general, the urban poor turn their hands to anything from petty trading to drugs and prostitution. Almost everywhere, survival strategies involve a multiple-mode existence—finding money and food for subsistence from different sources, including migration and remittances in cash or kind from relatives in rural areas and overseas.

When large proportions of populations must devote their energy to basic needs and survival, societies begin to break down. Without money to maintain it public infrastructure crumbles; bureaucrats have second jobs; teachers teach without books, blackboards, and slates (and often without pay); doctors practice without drugs; roads become dirt tracks; power fails; water is dirty; sanitation breaks down; disease spreads quickly. And in rural areas land becomes exhausted.

The International Response

After a decade of structural adjustment, Africa is worse off than it was in 1984. Africa now owes $199 billion, an increase of 2.5 percent over 1992 and more than three times the debt in 1990. For the twenty-nine severely indebted, low-income countries, mainly in sub-Saharan Africa, debt averaged four times the annual value of their exports of goods and services and more than 120 percent of their GDP. Their arrears of interest and principal have more than doubled since 1986 to $38 billion; in the same period, they have repaid over $11 billion to commercial banks.[70] Africa's share of world trade has fallen to 4 percent, and even the World Bank now agrees that there is no hope that the poorest countries can ever repay their debt.

Faced with such evidence of the impact of its policies, the IMF has refused to countenance any alternative, arguing that social matters are for the World Bank. In turn, the bank began in 1992 to focus on poverty and to target lending where it would alleviate such poverty. Yet in 1993, it acknowledged that half of its loans were still not fulfilling *poverty* criteria.

Such a current focus, however welcome it might be, cannot alter the major responsibility of the IFIs and Western governments for African decline. Although alternative development strategies are required that emphasize self-sufficiency in food, people-led development involving women, and a restoration of public infrastructure,[71] there are such extensive interlinkages among debt, trade, environment, poverty, and death that nothing less than the wholesale write-off of outstanding debt can hope to turn the disaster around in the poorest countries of sub-Saharan Africa. The Baker plan, the Brady plan on commercial debt, the Trinidad terms, and the enhanced Toronto terms have all had very limited impact in reducing African debt. To sweeten the 50 percent devaluation of the CFA for the ten poorest Francophone countries, France is writing off 100 percent of its bilateral debt and 50 percent of that of middle-income countries.[72] However, the CFA countries will still be left with considerable debt. As Oxfam noted, Western leadership and political will are needed to solve the debt overhang.[73]

Conclusion

If the knowledge of what the West is doing to the poor in Africa were unknown to politicians, it might be considered accidental, an unfortunate mistake. Yet that is not the case. The evidence has been growing in volume since the mid-1980s. Aid agencies have not been silent.

In view of the catalog of Western policies described here on the part of governments, their agents, the IFIs, and multinationals, the West can hardly deny overwhelming responsibility for the current African suffering. However, each government can point to another government or agency as being at fault. These governments can also argue that they have no control over trade regimes. The United States can argue that a write-off of debt will increase its own budget deficit and that the Japanese are equally unwilling to write off debt. It can argue that the constitution of the IFIs precludes debt forgiveness and that commodity prices are a matter for the free market. The multinationals that control the commodity markets can argue that they are simply making the best profit for their shareholders—that they are not the *gangleaders* in the new international division of labor. All can deny major responsibility.

The lack of a policy is also a policy. In that sense, the collective nondecision that causes mass deaths and starvation is a decision for war and genocide. This approach—the exclusion of black leaders from international economic affairs, the forcing of black people to work for almost nothing for whites located in another country, the denial of basic education and health, the denial of any right of movement of labor from Africa to the West, the denial of hope—is a denial of the human rights of one-eighth of the population of the world. In remaining silent on the linkages among trade, debt, poverty, environment, and death, the Western media also take part in the debt war on Africa.

NOTES

I would like to thank Iheoma Obibi, Philip Fergusson, and all my past and present African students for their direct and indirect help with this chapter.

1. Bade Onimode, *A Future for Africa: Beyond the Politics of Adjustment* (London: Earthscan Publications, 1992).

2. Quoted in *The Guardian,* January 13, 1994.

3. John Harbeson and Donald Rothschild, eds., *Africa in World Politics* (Boulder: Westview Press, 1991).

4. Michael Meacher, "We Need a New Ministry to Tackle the Problems Developing Countries Face," *Independent,* October 26, 1993.

5. Reuters, October 1, 1993.

6. The British media giving most coverage to Africa are the *Financial Times,* the *Guardian,* the *Independent* (newspapers), and *The Economist* (weekly magazine).

7. Kevin Watkins, "IMF's Russian Medicine Harms Africa Too," the *Guardian,* December 29, 1993.

8. Carol Lancaster, "Governance and Development: The Views from Washington," *IDS Bulletin,* January 24, 1993, pp. 9–15.

9. Deepak Lal, *The Poverty of "Development Economics"* (London: IEA, 1983).

10. Nicholas Hopkinson, *Good Government in Africa,* Wilton Park Paper no. 54 (London: HMSO, 1992), pp. 33–34.

11. Hopkinson, *Good Government,* p. 36.

12. Quoted in ibid., p. 33.

13. Samuel Brittan, "Where Gatt's $200 Billion Really Comes From," *Financial Times,* October 4, 1993.

14. *The Economist,* October 10, 1993.

15. Lawrence Harris, "The Bretton Woods System and Africa," in Bade Onimode, ed., *The IMF, the World Bank, and African Debt: The Social and Economic Impact* (London: Zed Books, 1989); Onimode, *A Future for Africa.*

16. Paul Harrison, *The Greening of Africa* (London: Paladin, 1987), p. 50.

17. Ibid., p. 23.

18. Onimode, *A Future for Africa,* p. 32.

19. Bolton, 1987, quoted in Paul Vallely, *Bad Samaritans: First World Ethics and Third World Debt* (London: Hodder and Stoughton, 1990), p. 111.

20. Vallely, *Bad Samaritans,* p. 116.

21. Ben Jackson, *Poverty and the Planet: A Question of Survival* (London: Penguin, 1993), p. 42.

22. Onimode, *A Future for Africa,* p. 40.

23. Ibid., p. 32.

24. Vallely, *Bad Samaritans,* pp. 95–98.

25. In 1988, the Bank of France was said to have purchased $1.8 billion of CFA banknotes transferred to Europe in suitcases and diplomatic bags. John-Jean B. Barya, "The New Political Conditionality of Aid: An Independent View from Africa," *IDS Bulletin,* January 24, 1993, p. 22.

26. Cheryl Payer, *Lent and Lost: Foreign Credit and Third World Development* (London: Zed Books, 1991), pp. 10–19.

27. Eboe Hutchful, ed., *The IMF and Ghana: The Confidential Record* (London: Zed Books, 1987).

28. Payer, *Lent and Lost,* pp. 20–22.

29. Harold Lever and Christopher Hulne, *Debt and Danger: The World Financial Crisis* (London: Penguin, 1985), p. 14.

30. Belinda Coote, *The Trade Trap: Poverty and the Global Commodity Markets* (Oxford: Oxfam, 1992), pp. 3–5.

31. Avery, 1990, p. 509.

32. Avery, 1990, p. 57, quoting Khan and Knight, 1983, p. 821.

33. Lever and Hulne, *Debt and Danger,* p. 56, quoting U.S. Secretary of Treasury.

34. Vallely, *Bad Samaritans,* p. 141.

35. Ibid., p. 161.

36. Chanu, 1989, 23.

37. Onimode, *A Future for Africa,* p. 27.

38. Ibid., p. 27.

39. Chanu, 1989, p. 25.

40. Payer, *Lent and Lost*, p. 14.

41. Stuart Corbridge, *Debt and Development* (Oxford: Blackwell, 1993), p. 48.

42. "Third World Finance Survey," *The Economist*, September 25, 1993, p. 32.

43. David Buchan and Leslie Crawford, "IMF Persuades French Africa to Go for Growth," *Financial Times*, January 13, 1993.

44. Onimode, *A Future for Africa*, p. 11.

45. Lever and Hulne, *Debt and Danger*, p. 45.

46. Blaine Harden, *Africa: Dispatches from a Fragile Continent* (London: Fontana, 1992), pp. 208–211.

47. Alex Brummer, "Cold War's Ending Leaves Spotlight on Wobbly World Bank," *The Guardian*, September 25, 1993.

48. Harrison, *The Greening of Africa*, p. 47.

49. World Bank, 1981, p. 4.

50. Richard Sandbrook, "Economic Crisis, Structural Adjustment, and the State in Sub-Saharan Africa," in Dharam Ghai, ed., *The IMF and the South: The Social Impact of Crisis and Adjustment* (London: Zed Books, 1991), pp. 91–114.

51. Lewis T. Preston, "Private Sector Key to Africa's Future," *Financial Times*, September 27, 1993.

52. David Woodward, *Debt, Adjustment, and Poverty in Developing Countries* (London: Pinter and Save the Children Fund, 1992), pp. 168–169.

53. Watkins, "IMF's Russian Medicine," p. 15.

54. Tony Hawkins, "At the Edge of Prosperity," *Financial Times*, September 1, 1993.

55. World Bank, 1992.

56. Oxfam, *Africa Make or Break: Action for Recovery* (Oxford: Oxfam, 1993), p. 4.

57. Ibid., p. 3.

58. Dorothy Mutemba, "The Impact of IMF–World Bank Programs on Women and Children in Zambia," in Onimode, *The IMF, The World Bank, and the African Debt*, p. 122.

59. D. Popoola, "Nigeria: Consequences for Health," in Aderanti Adepoju, ed., *The Impact of Structural Adjustment on the Population of Africa* (London: James Currey, 1993), p. 96.

60. A. Mwanawina, "Zambia," in Onimode, *The IMF, the World Bank and the African Debt*, p. 75.

61. Rosemary Bellew, Laura Raney, and K. Subbarao, "Educating Girls," *Finance and Development*, March 1992, pp. 54–56.

62. Peter Gibbon, "Structural Adjustments and Pressures Toward Multipartyism in Sub-Saharan Africa," in Peter Gibbon, Yusuf Bangura, and Ave Ofstad, *Authoritarianism, Democracy, and Adjustment: The Politics of Economic Reform in Africa* (Uppsala: Nordiska Afrikainstituet, 1992), p. 140.

63. Bonat Zuwaqhu and Yahaya A. Abdullahi, "The World Bank, IMF, and Nigeria's Agricultural and Rural Economy," in Onimode, *The IMF, The World Bank, and the African Debt*, p. 171; Reginald Herbold Green, "The Broken Pot: The Social Fabric, Economic Disaster, and Adjustment in Africa," in Onimode, *The IMF, the World Bank and the African Debt*, p. 41.

64. Harrison, *The Greening of Africa*.

65. Rosemary Galli and Ursula Frank, "Structural Adjustment and Gender in Guinea-Bissau" (n.p., n.d.).

66. Diane Elson, "The Impact of Structural Adjustment on Women: Concepts and Issues," in Onimode, *The IMF, the World Bank and the African Debt,* p. 73.

67. Mary Chinery-Hesse et al., *Engendering Adjustment for the 1990s* (London: Commonwealth Secretariat, 1989).

68. Galli and Frank, "Structural Adjustment."

69. Firmooni R. Banugire, "Employment, Incomes, Basic Needs, and Structural Adjustment Policy in Uganda, 1980–87," in Onimode, *The IMF, the World Bank and the African Debt,* p. 98.

70. World Bank, 1994.

71. Frances Stewart, ed., *Alternative Development Strategies in Sub-Saharan Africa* (Basingstoke: Macmillan, 1993).

72. Will Hutton, "The New World Order Leaves a Continent Sunk in Debt," *The Guardian,* January 13, 1993.

73. Oxfam, *Africa Make or Break,* p. iii.

17

Global Drug Scourge: The Hidden Story

STEPHEN E. FLYNN

Illicit drug production, trafficking, and consumption are growing and spreading at an alarming rate. What has been long labeled the "American disease" is now a global epidemic. Today, drugs are a burgeoning $250–300 billion a year global business,[1] making it at least three-quarters the size of the world petroleum industry. It is a business that owes much of its recent success to dramatic changes in the international system that have fueled the incentives and undermined the barriers to cultivating, refining, distributing, and consuming drugs. Its success, in turn, has ominous implications for the peaceful evolution of the post–Cold War international system, and yet few policymakers consider the challenge of illicit drugs a priority.

Does the drug issue represent one of the array of invisible crises that threaten global society? Answering this question in the affirmative mandates that two requirements be satisfied. First, we must demonstrate that drugs are a global and dynamic phenomenon that increasingly place at risk our political, economic, and social well-being. Second, we must identify why governments and pundits are wont to conceive of drugs as no more than conventional law enforcement or public health issues. That means presenting evidence that they jeopardize important interests and explaining why such evidence has stayed largely out of view.

Defining Crisis

Pinning down a universally accepted meaning of *crisis* is an elusive exercise. The word has become so much a part of popular parlance that on any given day we are likely to hear people speaking of their identity crises, midlife crises, and crises in their families. In the media and in our conversations, we are confronted with discussions of an environmental crisis, a budget crisis, a foreign debt crisis, and even a crisis of confidence. It seems that we have found in the term *crisis* a way to say that we have many problems, each of which is important and deserves attention.

The everyday use of *crisis* may help us to articulate our anxiety about the future, but this usage comes at a cost—it makes it hard to establish real priorities. National leaders and the general public must sort through the myriad of daily problems that confront society and determine which ones most deserve attention. If all problems are labeled as *crises,* our leaders are likely to become inured to claims of urgency. Hearing too many special pleaders cry wolf, they become deaf to genuine alarms with the result that time-critical opportunities to prevent harm or to promote the common good are lost.

At the same time, an open-ended definition of crisis leaves citizens vulnerable to manipulation by their leaders. Crises bring with them the imperative to act quickly, therefore justifying centralized decisionmaking. This ability to limit the number of participants, in turn, provides policymakers with the opportunity to limit the debate over how a threat is defined and what the appropriate response should be. As a result, leaders intent on achieving certain outcomes might be tempted to label a problem a *crisis* so that they can take immediate unilateral actions that would normally not be permitted in noncrisis circumstances.[2] Likewise, there may be important threats that are simply overlooked or actively downplayed, perhaps because their implications for the existing power structure or the societal norms and values are too great.

Similarly, the power of modern communications technology to capture images and transmit them immediately and repetitively gives the media considerable power to identify, substantiate, bypass, or create crises. Through the stories they tell, the media filter for us the events and challenges that exist beyond our national borders. Stories of unfamiliar situations become new developments whether they are old problems newly discovered or new circumstances just unfolding. Editorial practices can also have the effect of allowing situations that present legitimate threats to important interests to go unreported. If a new development is judged too difficult to communicate to a mass audience—perhaps because it is a very complicated story or because it is hard to capture visually—it may be cast aside for a story that is perceived to have wider appeal.

In short, the lack of definitional clarity connected with the term *crisis* provides ample opportunity for the subjective to be mixed with the objective when it comes to establishing what is and is not a crisis. As the authors of one treatise on political crisis observed nearly twenty years ago: "In a sense, crises are unto the beholder. What is a crisis to one individual or group may not be to another."[3] But this state of affairs is unsatisfactory from both an analytic and a prescriptive standpoint. Accordingly, although it may never be possible to define *crisis* in a way that eliminates its subjective elements, I do believe it is possible to make these elements more transparent by classifying crises as *visible, contrived,* and *invisible* and defining each as follows:

- A visible crisis is a situation in which (1) there is an objective change in a pattern of interactions that has important implications for the stability of a system or subsystem, and (2) this change takes policymakers by surprise and compels them to choose quickly among options that will reduce the risk to the vital interests they believe to be at stake.
- A contrived crisis is one in which policymakers or the media manipulate images so as to suggest that a change in a pattern of interactions has taken place that has important implications for the stability of a system or subsystem and that mandates an immediate policy response, when in fact no such change has occurred.
- An invisible crisis is one in which the first criterion of a visible crisis is present but not the second. The objective reality that new developments are undermining the stability of a system or subsystem is ignored or denied and no new initiatives are considered in response.

As will now be illustrated, the emerging global drug scourge is a prominent example of an invisible crisis.

The Global Drug Market in Transition

Inherent in any description of a crisis—*visible, contrived,* or *invisible*—is the notion that a relationship or a system has moved from a static status to a transitional one. It is the very uncertainty as to the ultimate outcome of this transitional stage that gives crises their poignancy. Therefore, to aver that the drug issue represents a crisis for the global community, we must first demonstrate that it is undergoing some form of transformation. Examination of the three essential features of the drug trade—production, trafficking, and consumption—will show that this is indeed the case.

We begin with the baseline. For most of the post–World War II period, the international drug market could be largely characterized as one in which criminals sought to link distant producers with consumers in the United States and western Europe by developing essentially episodic schemes to evade customs and law enforcement agents. Understandably, therefore, the focus of U.S. and European drug control exertions has been on stopping foreign suppliers from feeding the habits of their addicts and on reducing the crime and public health consequences of drug use in their communities.

By the late 1980s, however, three important developments converged to transform the global drug market. First among these developments was that the demand for cocaine in the United States and heroin in western Europe began to level off while production of illicit coca and opium poppies reached unprecedented levels and began to spill over into new areas in the developing and postcommunist worlds. Second, the most successful drug traffickers developed sophisticated organizations capable of evading even the more aggressive and advanced interdiction efforts designed to combat them. The traffickers accomplished this largely by developing the capacity to immerse their illicit activities in the international transportation, banking, and commercial sectors that service the burgeoning legitimate global economy. Third, the political, economic, and social changes connected with the collapse of the postcommunist world and the end of the Cold War generated new incentives and opportunities for creating new drug markets within and outside the traditional consumer nations.

In short, rising supplies generated new incentives to seek new markets, the evolution of the modern drug cartel provided new means to distribute globally, and the fundamental transformations under way in the international system created new opportunities to develop new markets. We shall examine each of these developments in turn.

Drug Production in the 1990s

U.S. drug use survey data in the mid-1980s indicate that after years of significant rise, casual consumption of cocaine, particularly among middle-class and upper-middle-class Americans, began to level off.[4] Similarly, heroin consumption in western Europe began to stabilize if not decline in certain areas. Against this backdrop has been a persistent rise in drug production.

Evidence of trends in cocaine production indicates that coca cultivation is no longer strictly concentrated in the upper Huallaga valley in Peru or the Chapare in Bolivia. Cultivation has spread to virtually every region in Peru, to northwestern Brazil, to southern Venezuela, and reportedly, even into remote regions in Nigeria.[5] Refinement of coca paste into cocaine hydrochloride—once almost an exclusively Colombian activity—now takes place in the primary coca source countries of Peru and Bolivia as well as the adjacent countries of Venezuela, Ecuador, Brazil, and Panama. Finally, recent seizures of coca paste in Lebanon and Italy indicate that cocaine refinement is no longer confined to the Western Hemisphere.

The practice of cultivating opium poppies has consistently demonstrated its geographical mobility. Illicit poppy cultivation that was once associated with the Golden Crescent countries of Iran, Afghanistan, and Pakistan and the Golden Triangle countries of Laos, Thailand, and Burma is now spreading to other areas. Since 1990, Colombia, China, Vietnam, Cambodia, the Central Asian republics of the former Soviet Union, Ukraine, Bulgaria, and Romania have all joined the ranks of opium-producing nations. Refinement of opium into heroin, once limited to advanced industrialized societies, now is accomplished more often in the developing world than in the developed world.

Cannabis, the most ubiquitous of drugs, is now being produced in new areas including Central Asia and sub-Saharan Africa. The Central Asian republic of Kazakhstan with an estimated 138,000 hectares of wild-growing cannabis—approximately five times the recorded cannabis cultivation in Mexico and Colombia combined—gives some idea of the potential productive capacity of the region.[6] In Africa, cannabis is being grown in the Saloum Islands and Casamance in Senegal, the San Pedro Forest in Ivory Coast, the banks of the Gambia River, the Black Volta littoral in Ghana, the Nyungew region in Rwanda, and various regions in Togo, Benin, Nigeria, and Zaire.[7] There has been also a recent resurgence in marijuana cultivation in Colombia. Even in the United States, large tracts of national forest and national park land are being used by illicit cultivators, potent new strains are being developed and grown in state-of-the-art greenhouses, and by some estimates, marijuana has become one of the leading cash crops in the states of Kentucky and California.[8]

The production of synthetic narcotics, such as methamphetamine, amphetamine, LSD, methaqualone, and methcathinone, appears to be spreading. Laboratories in Taiwan and South Korea are the major source of *ice,* a high-purity methamphetamine developed in the mid–1980s.[9] Poland recently emerged as one of the largest producers of amphetamines for the European market, with police lab analyses indicating that nearly one-quarter of the amphetamines seized in western Europe originate in Poland. Underground laboratories for synthetic drugs have been discovered in Moscow, St. Petersburg, Sverdlovsk, and many of the other major cities in the former Soviet Union. Methaqualone (mandrax) is produced in laboratories throughout India primarily for the large market in southern Africa.[10]

Drug Trafficking in the 1990s

Since the major markets for drugs have traditionally been at some distance from production areas, linking suppliers with consumers presents a significant logistical challenge. In recent years, the tasks of acquiring chemicals for the refinement of illicit drugs, transporting and distributing the finished contraband, and managing the enormous sums of cash involved have been conducted against a backdrop of an increasingly vigorous law enforcement regime designed to curb them. The result has been to create something of a Darwinian evolution in the drug trade: The unskilled and unlucky drug traffickers fill prisons, and the survivors have become sophisticated, highly adaptive, and opportunistic organizations.

The Colombian organizations represent the prototype of the contemporary trafficking organization, having developed the capacity to conduct research and development; to manage large-scale refinement, transportation, distribution, and financial operations; to collect intelligence; and to ensure operational and organizational security. Today, Colombian operatives can be found working outside the Western Hemisphere in Japan, Russia, Bulgaria, Algeria, Morocco, Tunisia, Australia, and throughout western Europe.[11]

A brief overview of how the Cali organization services the U.S. cocaine market provides a sobering insight into the trafficking challenge that confronts the international community. Contrary to popular belief, most drugs do not cross American borders on low-flying Cessnas, aboard fast-moving "cigarette" boats, or among the belongings of illegal Mexican immigrants. Most reach their markets by way of commercial conveyances. Containerized shipments, bulk cargo, false documentation, and front companies conceal the movement of cocaine by water. By land, most cocaine crosses the U.S.-Mexican border in hidden compartments of tractor trailers and other vehicles or in commercial cargo itself.

The Cali organization uses international shipping centers in Central and South America, particularly in Brazil, Venezuela, Surinam, and Panama, to ship cocaine by sea to Europe and to the eastern United States. When commercial airlines are used, the drug is hidden on the plane itself, among perishable cargoes such as cut flowers or fruit pulp or among passengers who conceal it by placing it in luggage with false bottoms or in hollowed-out sneakers, by taping it to their bodies, or by swallowing condoms filled with cocaine. Sometimes it is converted to liquid and smuggled in bottles of shampoo, mouthwash, and liquor.

Once the drug arrives, it is distributed by one of the dozens of Cali distribution cells throughout the country. Each cell, made up of ten to fifteen Colombian employees who earn monthly salaries ranging from $2,000 to $7,500, conducts as much as $25 million of business a month. Each cell is self-contained, with information tightly compartmentalized. Only a few managers know all the operatives. The cell typically has a head, bookkeeper, money handler, cocaine handler, motor pool, and ten to fifteen apartments serving as stash houses.

Communications are conducted in code over facsimile machines, cellular phones, and pay phones. To eliminate any risk of interception, cellular phones are purchased and discarded, often weekly. When a wholesale customer wants to make a purchase, a cell member is notified by a pager system. That cell member proceeds to a public phone and arranges a rendezvous site. He then gets, from the motor pool, a rental car that is returned to the rental agency after the transaction. The transaction itself, including travel receipts, is logged by the bookkeeper, and the money is turned over to the money handler to be shipped to the financial network set up by the cartel to hide and invest it. A favorite way to ship within the United States is the U.S. Postal Service's Express Mail.

Once the cartel has received the money for its drug sales, it moves the funds into and through the legal financial system to conceal the origin. If a Cali cell broken up by federal authorities in December 1991 is representative, the Cali financial network must launder about $200 million each year per cell. Money laundering typically involves three independent phases. First, drug proceeds are *placed*—that is, deposited—in banks or used to purchase monetary instruments or securities that can be converted to cash elsewhere. This is often done by hiring individuals known as *smurfs* to deposit the money in small denominations in as many banks and financial institutions as possible so as to defeat currency-reporting requirements. Second, the money is *layered*, or sent through multiple electronic transfers or other transactions to make it difficult to track and blur its illicit origin. Finally, the source of the money disappears as it is *integrated*, that is, invested into seemingly legitimate accounts and enterprises. To lower their exposure to law enforcement yet further, the Cali families increasingly have contracted out these last two phases, requiring money handlers in Colombia to provide them the money up front, less a 10 to 15 percent commission, in return for providing these handlers the opportunity to launder and keep the full amount.[12]

Despite their clear domination of the cocaine market, the Colombians are finding the drug trafficking field increasingly crowded. They now fight for market share with Chinese, Azeri, Chechen, Italian, Lebanese, Nigerian, Pakistani, Polish, Russian, Turkish, and Vietnamese crime syndicates. Happily for these organizations and unfortunately for civil society, there are more drug spoils to compete for. New markets are emerging throughout the postcommunist and developing worlds.

Access to these new markets has been facilitated in part by the tumultuous political changes connected with the passing of the Cold War era. Among the republics of the former Soviet Union and the countries of eastern Europe, the once formidable border controls have virtually disappeared, and few resources are available to support criminal investigations and law enforcement activities. Further, the disturbing rise in ethnic conflicts and civil wars is creating new trafficking hubs where drugs and arms can be bought and sold with little risk of interference by governmental authorities.

As with global economic activity in general, trafficking organizations also have benefited from the technological and liberalization trends that have fueled the development of an increasingly open and vibrant global economy. The dramatic rise in international trade, facilitated by the development of a robust transportation infrastructure and the voluntary easing of border controls, has created unparalleled challenges for national customs authorities. In 1991, for instance, the world's top ten ports handled 33.6 million containers. If just two dozen of these containers were filled with cocaine, the world's cocaine habit could be satisfied for one year. Likewise, the deregulation of financial markets and the privatization revolution in the postcommunist and developing worlds are overwhelming the abilities of government regulators to police commercial activities within, across, and beyond their borders. The daily turnover of foreign exchange markets is close to $1 trillion. Annual international capital flows account for about seventy times the value of world trade. In light of these developments, identifying good money from bad money once it has gained access to the legitimate financial markets is worse then searching for the proverbial needle in the haystack.

Drug Consumption in the 1990s

As the production of illicit drugs surges and the means for traffickers to make these drugs more widely available improves, will there in fact be a market for them? Predicting with any precision the character and dimension of the global drug market is difficult. Most drug abuse research has been done on population groups within advanced societies, and epidemiologists are understandably hesitant to apply these findings to the developing world. Too, drug epidemics typically refuse to stay within tidy political, cultural, or geographical boundaries. Islamic fundamentalism, for instance, may help to explain why drug abuse is uncommon in Saudi Arabia, but not why there are a half million addicts in greater Teheran, Iran,[13] and why nearly 2 million Pakistanis use drugs.[14]

But although it may not be possible to anticipate precisely which specific locations are likely to suffer from widespread abuse and when, forecasting the overall trend in global drug consumption is less problematic. The prospect for growing drug abuse worldwide can be correlated with the prevalence of its three requisite ingredients: an awareness of drugs, access to them, and the motivation to use them.[15]

The awareness of drugs has become almost universal. In the Third World, demographic pressures are forcing millions of people out of their isolation in remote villages and into large cities, where it is impossible not to know about drugs. And the collapse of the communist regimes in the former Soviet bloc has ended the state's monopoly on information and has made it possible for people to travel freely both at home and abroad. Word of a drug that has acquired popularity somewhere can spread quickly almost anywhere.

Access to drugs is also increasing with production soaring and traffickers aggressively marketing drugs throughout the global community. Further, if democratization and economic liberalization trends persist, individuals will have greater personal freedom, mobility, and control over their personal incomes, and these factors will facilitate contacts with drug distributors and their purchases.

Many of the risk factors that motivate drug use are becoming more prevalent in most Third World societies while long-standing preventative factors are being simultaneously undermined. For one thing, the population of the developing world is becoming younger. More than half the people in Nigeria and Kenya and more than 40 percent in the developing world are under the age of fifteen. Regardless of culture, teenagers are known for risk-taking behavior and the willingness to challenge social conventions. In addition, rapid population growth rates are causing people, particularly young men, to move to big cities. Separated from their families, often unemployed or underemployed, and with little opportunity for schooling, more and more of these disillusioned young people are at great risk of taking up drugs.

Peer pressure and the mass media can also motivate young people to use drugs. Most drug experimentation begins in intimate social settings where friends introduce friends to drugs. The prod by one's peers to use drugs is reinforced by mass media messages of instant gratification and fast-paced consumerism in general and by pro-drug messages that strongly favor the widespread purchase and use of legal drugs in particular. Many European and American movies and television programs portray drugs as luxury goods consumed by wealthy Westerners. As such, drugs end up serving as status symbols, or as one Nigerian addict recently put it, as a way to "become like an American."[16]

Finally, the dislocations associated with the end of the socialist experiment and the desperate economic plight of much of the developing world are increasing the willingness of people, young and old, to violate the law.

What evidence is there that global drug consumption is in fact on the rise? In addition to widespread use in Pakistan and Iran, India has 1–5 million opium users and 1 million heroin addicts.[17] In China, after virtual eradication of drugs in the early 1950s, today there are at least 1–2 million drug users with public security officials reporting 500,000–600,000 in the Guangdong province alone.[18] Russian authorities estimate there are now 1.5 million users, and the consumption is growing at an alarming rate.[19] Poland has more than 200,000 drug users, many of whom use a homegrown heroin derivative known as *kompot*.[20] In the Western Hemisphere, virtually every Latin American and Caribbean country has reported a rise in drug consumption.

The Implications of the Global Drug Trade

The crisis stemming from the recent and dramatic global spread of drug production, trafficking, and consumption primarily grows out of the ability of this multibillion-dollar industry to fuel a host of developments inimical to the peaceful evolution of twenty-first-century societies.

It has become almost a cliché to assert that we are living in revolutionary times. When technological developments are combined with such epochal events as the collapse of the Soviet bloc, the Israeli and PLO peace process, the end of apartheid in South Africa, the opening of borders between European Community nations, the passage of the North American Free Trade Agreement, the conclusion of the Uruguay Round of the General Agreement on Tariffs and Trade, and the privatization revolution in the developing world, few would contest the notion that we are entering a new era. Yet the war in Bosnia, the chaos in Africa, the rampant crime in Russia, and the resurgence of neo-Nazism and fascism remind us that times of transition are rarely tidy. As we approach the end of the millennium, every society appears to be in a state of transition. Developing countries are attempting to modernize. Communist societies are moving from centrally planned to market economies. Even developed countries are in flux as they are confronted with the collapse of traditional industries, rising unemployment, weakened social safety nets, and urban decay.

Central to the transition process in Third World and postcommunist countries is the development of competent political institutions. The money and the violence connected with the drug trade undermine this development. Profit from the sales in drugs provides the means to ravage the legitimacy of political institutions, either by corruption from within or attacks from without. When traffickers have access to executive, legislative, or judicial levels of government, they can tempt officials with spectacular bribes in return for influence and protection.[21] If they lack this access, in many cases they can buy protection from a menu of antigovernment groups that are willing to use force to defeat or to keep at bay central governmental authorities. When governments fight back, human rights are among the first casualties.

Drug profits also give rise to powerful underground economies, weakening the ability of national and international financial institutions to influence the economic destinies of the affected nations. Carrying out effective macro- and microeconomic policies in developing countries is difficult under the best of circumstances. But when the informal economy becomes powerful enough to distort investment, employment, and consumption patterns significantly, enacting such policies rarely achieves the intended consequences. Such is the case with the unstable economy in Bolivia, where approximately 300,000 people are involved in illicit coca production and the cocaine industry generates annual revenues of $490 million, or almost 12 percent of gross domestic product.[22]

The problems attendant with widespread drug use—crime, lower levels of worker productivity, and health consequences that include the spread of HIV infection through intravenous drug use—add painful new burdens on all societies. For developing and postcommunist countries, the inability to meet these burdens can have a particularly deleterious effect. Rampant crime fuels public apathy and provides a rallying point for reactionary forces. The December 1993 elections in Russia offers a case in point: The searing anticrime rhetoric of extreme nationalist Vladimir Zhirinovsky was met with considerable sympathy at the polls.[23] In impoverished underdeveloped countries, such as in Western and Central Africa, many of which are already sliding toward anarchy, the inability of authorities to respond to drug-related crime and health problems is but another stark demonstration of governmental impotence.[24] For advanced societies, drug-related crime is threatening to overwhelm many urban areas already reeling from the collapse of manufacturing jobs and urban flight. In addition, basic civil liberties have consistently been endangered by zealous law enforcement responses to this crime. The health consequences of drug use, particularly HIV infection by way of shared hypodermic needles, contribute to skyrocketing health care costs and siphon limited resources away from other public health and social welfare challenges.[25]

The global drug trade also adversely affects an array of other important challenges confronting the international system. Consider the explosion of ethnic conflicts and civil wars that have multiplied so dramatically in recent years. Many ethnic and insurgent groups have seen the collapse of the Soviet bloc as an opportunity to pursue revanchist causes, but they must do so without the benefit of a superpower benefactor. By either directly participating in or providing protection for the production and trafficking of drugs, these groups can raise the requisite hard currency to pursue their political aims. Examples include the Croats and Serbs, both of whom have been linked to the flow of heroin destined for western Europe via the Balkan route; General Aidid in Somalia, who has for some time been a dominant player in the Horn of Africa khat trade; the military dictators in Haiti whose ability to withstand the U.N. economic embargo has been strengthened by the money generated from allowing cocaine shipments to pass through their country; and the warring parties in the conflict-ridden former Soviet republics of Azerbaijan, Georgia, and Tajikistan, all of whom have been implicated in the heroin trade that originates in the Golden Crescent region.

Closely related to the drug trade's connection with ethnic conflict and civil war is its link to weapons proliferation. Weapons often make their way to underground arms markets via the same routes and by the same traffickers used to move drugs. The arms-drugs nexus is not a new one, as demonstrated by the Iran-Contra connection in the United States and by conflicts in Southeast Asia, Central America, and Afghanistan during the 1970s and 1980s. Wars in the conflict areas created virtual no-man's lands through which drugs and arms passed unhindered. But the disintegration of the Soviet Union represents a troubling new chapter in the proliferation story.

Russia is now a burgeoning transshipment point for heroin and hashish from the Golden Crescent region and is becoming an important drug market in its own right. These developments have been facilitated by the explosive growth of organized criminal networks, many of which have links with Russian military units. According to Russian military sources, in 1993 there were 6,430 cases of thefts of weapons from military depots, an increase of 60 percent from the year before. As Russia has at least 30,000 nuclear warheads, 500 to 600 tons of highly enriched uranium, 100 to 200 tons of plutonium, and a cornucopia of sophisticated and deadly conventional and chemical weapons, it would appear that Western security experts are properly quite concerned by lax security and the linkage between Russian military and criminal elements.[26]

Drug cultivation and refinement are also linked to another issue preoccupying the American public and the global community: the environment. According to a U.N. report entitled *Illicit Narcotics Cultivation and Processing: The Ignored Environmental Drama,* the cultivation of cannabis, coca, and opium accounts for a growing share of the loss of tropical forest resources and the pollution of important waterways. In the upper Amazon basin and in the high mountain forests of Southeast Asia, each year thousands of hectares are cleared for cultivation and the construction of illicit airstrips. As refinement now takes place closer to production areas, hundreds of thousands of metric tons of chemicals find their way into these delicate ecosystems. On average, two tons of waste by-products are generated for each hectare of illicit coca cultivation. In the process of maceration and washing coca leaf to make coca paste, enormous amounts of gasoline, kerosene, sulfuric acid, ammonia, sodium carbonate, potassium carbonate, and lime are dumped onto the ground and into nearby waterways, poisoning water supplies and destroying fisheries. Likewise, heroin refiners wreak havoc in their producing areas by aimlessly discarding lime, ammonia, tartaric acid, ammonium chloride, alcohol, acetone, acetic anhydride, and hydrochloric acid. What the net result of all this will be is difficult to calculate. At a minimum, the surge in the supply of illicit drugs will add to the depletion of valuable and vulnerable lands, accelerate the loss and extinction of flora and fauna in genetically rich tropical regions, contribute to the loss of watershed and thus further compound socioeconomic imbalances, and add to global atmospheric concerns as a result of the wholesale clearing of rain forest reserves.[27]

Impotence, Incompetence, Complicity

The drug crisis remains invisible because there is widespread reluctance both to acknowledging new developments connected with the drug issue and to considering the resultant implications for drug control policy. For instance, governments responsible for the territory where new cultivation or refinement of illicit drugs is taking place generally find these activities a source of embarrassment, since widespread production would appear to be prima facie evidence of either governmental impotence or of governmental complicity. The result is that governments often ignore or try to deflect accusations that large-scale production is taking place within their borders. If the production moves into areas embroiled in ethnic conflict or civil war, the rationale of higher national security interests can lead governments or allies to downplay or deny this activity or to counter claims of impropriety by disparaging the source as biased in favor of an adversary. Even among agencies and individuals responsible for drug control programs there is often a reluctance to look too hard to find evidence of the displacement of production to new areas, since such an admission could be used by critics to challenge existing programs as being too narrowly focused or as being largely ineffective.

Acknowledging the growth and diffusion of drug production not only raises questions about the efficacy of existing drug control programs but also forces the observer to examine the underlying motives for participating in this activity. The conclusions from such an examination are almost self-evident but by no means very palatable for policymakers in advanced societies.

There is no shortage of new incentives to participate in the drug trade. The debt crisis of the 1970s forced many developing countries to curtail severely their funding of social programs and development projects as a condition for debt forgiveness and new International Monetary Fund and World Bank loans. The hardships resulting from these austerity programs and from the precipitous drop in primary commodity prices in the 1980s have been inequitably shouldered by impoverished farmers and workers. The resultant social dislocations have created no shortage of desperate people willing to do almost anything to assure their economic survival. In Bolivia, for instance, the collapse of tin prices in the mid-1980s, the subsequent closing of the mines, and the imposition of a draconian national economic plan motivated large numbers of unemployed workers to migrate to the remote Chapare region to cultivate coca.[28] In other producing areas such as Peru and Afghanistan, not only is there a shortage of meaningful alternatives for the growers, but widespread and persistent political violence virtually eliminates the opportunity to access legitimate national or international commercial markets. In the former Central Asian republics, the loss of billions of dollars from Moscow to subsidize agricultural production has made opium and cannabis very attractive sources for hard currency.

But these linkages between rising drug production and such problems as the widening gap between advanced and developing countries, the challenge of transition in the postcommunist world, ethnic conflict and civil war, and the debt-restructuring policies of international financial institutions are extremely unsettling for most policymakers in the developed world. Since there is a general unwillingness to tackle these larger problems, there is a great reluctance to seeing the issue of illicit drug production tied to them. Rather than confront these implications, policymakers instead persist in seeing the issue as essentially a static law enforcement problem; that is, growing these drugs is illegal and the responsible governments should enforce the law.

Acknowledging the growth of drug trafficking activities creates problems for the affected countries similar to those connected with new drug production. Again, the existence of such activities tends to illustrate that governments are unable to regulate criminal activities within or across their borders either because of widespread corruption or because of an embarrassing gap in their resources and capabilities to enforce the law. Similarly, an analysis of why drug trafficking has grown so dramatically in recent years brings policymakers face-to-face with very sobering implications. As discussed previously, the drug trade has successfully penetrated legitimate commercial, transportation, and financial institutions. This has been made possible in large part because there are powerful interests that promote and defend sanctuaries within the global economy that allow businesses to evade the ability of governments to monitor, regulate, and tax the private sector. As an astute observer of drug money laundering activities has pointed out, there is a very fine line between "illicit illicit" activity and "illicit licit" activity.[29] That is, the same instrumentalities that allow the private sector to evade taxes and skirt regulations are the same procedures that allow illicit enterprises like drug organizations to move their money and merchandise within the legitimate global economy with little risk of detection.

Directing a light at these practices that have allowed the drug trade to become a global enterprise of the first order also casts an embarrassing light on legitimate enterprises that are trying to maximize profits by minimizing their obligation to play by the formal rules set by governments. Obviously, solutions designed to close these kinds of loopholes—for instance, adopting regulations that would ensure virtual transparency in the transportation industry and within global financial markets—would be met with strong resistance. Few policymakers are willing to take on these issues; most instead persist in viewing drug trafficking as a long-standing law enforcement problem of finding criminals and bringing them to justice.

Finally, there are the disincentives connected with acknowledging a rise in consumption. For years communist and non-Western countries have pointed to widespread drug abuse as a prominent example of Western decadence. Having stigmatized drugs as essentially an *American disease,* these countries find themselves too embarrassed to admit that the disease can be contagious. Lack of resources or the political will to conduct epidemiological studies or to fund drug treatment, has led to drug abuse becoming one of the most poorly monitored public health problems of our time.

As in the case of production and trafficking, an analysis of why drug consumption is spreading exposes its relationship to some very vexing and complicated issues. The demographic trends that are producing such enormous social dislocations in the developing world, the shortage of meaningful employment or educational opportunities particularly for young people, and the widening mesh of the social safety nets in postcommunist countries are clearly all contributing factors. These are also problems that policymakers in advanced societies would generally prefer to sidestep.

Another contributing factor to the growth in global consumption is the widening reach of what George Gerbner has called "messages that hurt."[30] Tobacco, alcohol, and pharmaceutical companies have taken to the global airwaves to promote their products with reckless abandon. Billions of dollars are spent on advertising to promote drug use with only the tiniest percentage of those advertising dollars cautioning against misuse. As one tobacco industry analyst stated in commenting on the success of American cigarette companies in capturing the Asian market: "As poor countries get richer they smoke more American cigarettes. That doesn't change until they get rich enough to worry about their health."[31] The specific content of these messages is reinforced more generally by the consumer-oriented thrill-seeking messages so pervasive in Western television programming, movies, musical recordings, and other media. Policymakers and substantial media and commercial interests are extremely reluctant to acknowledge the relationship of drug demand to its underlying cultural-environmental supports. Rather than address the daily cultivation of appeals and associations that make drug use so attractive, they prefer to see illicit drug consumption as deviant social behavior that resembles other forms of criminal activity.

The global drug crisis will remain largely invisible because policymakers will be unwilling to acknowledge the relationship of drug production, trafficking, and consumption to wider systemic forces within the international system. The turbulence in world politics that is characterized by the transitional challenges confronting developing, postcommunist, and advanced societies is playing a role in fueling the global drug scourge. Similarly, the liberalization and privatization trends in the global economy when combined with the cascading effects of the communications revolution have created a fertile global environment for all commercial activities—illicit as well as licit. Indeed, as the international economy increasingly is guided by laissez-faire, distinctions between licit and illicit become analytically meaningless.

By persisting in seeing the drug issue as primarily a law enforcement challenge, societies imbue it with domestic, static, and reactive qualities. Law enforcement authorities are charged with enforcing their own national laws, not those of others. By training and inclination, police officials and government regulators tend to steer clear of issues outside their jurisdictional reach. As *crimes,* the production, refinement, distribution, and consumption of illicit drugs end up joining the ranks of age-old vices such as prostitution and gambling. When the issue is placed within this context, it is easy to be seduced into believing that there is nothing new under the sun. Also, as crimes these activities must manifest themselves before law enforcement is authorized, since the very notion of *preventative law enforcement* strikes at the heart of our basic civil liberties.

By overlooking this crisis we overlook both a threat and an opportunity. Unreceptive to the possibility that the drug phenomenon is subject to qualitative changes in the wider global environment in which it exists, we end up seeing only the proverbial tip of the iceberg as we steam at flank speed into the unfamiliar waters of the next millennium. At risk is an array of policies designed to smooth the international system's transition into the post–Cold War era. The drug issue inevitably complicates the process of modernization in the developing world; the painful political, economic, and social adjustments now under way in the postcommunist world; and the difficult postindustrial transition in the developed world. The drug issue also contributes to the challenges of ethnic conflict and civil war, weapons proliferation, and environmental devastation.

The opportunity is to link many direct or indirect relationships through the burgeoning global drug trade, to help mobilize the general public to tackle a host of global challenges. That is, to the extent that there is a growing consensus that drugs produce unacceptable levels of societal harm and human misery, then there is a natural constituency for supporting programs that address the core causes of the problem that exist beyond one's national borders. The dynamic and global qualities of the drug issue make clear that a purely national response to the drug problem makes as much sense as a national response to ozone depletion. As with the rise in greenhouse emissions, a comprehensive and coordinated global response to its contributing causes is needed to spare the planet from the far-reaching outcomes of an explosive growth in illicit drugs worldwide.

NOTES

1. The $250–300 billion figure is an average of estimates that range from a low of $100 billion to a high of $500 billion. See LaMond Tullis, *Handbook of Research on the Illicit Drug Traffic: Socioeconomic Consequences* (New York: Greenwood Press, 1991), p. xvii; and *Latin America and the Caribbean Section,* a United Nations Drug Control Program Report, Vienna, October 1993.

2. Stephen E. Flynn, *Grenada as a "Reactive" and a "Proactive" Crisis: New Models of Crisis Decision Making* (Ann Arbor, MI: UMI Dissertation Information Service, 1992), pp. 14–15.

3. R. H. Kupperman, R. H. Eilcox, and H. A. Smith, "Crisis Management: Some Opportunities," *Science* 182 (February 7, 1975):404.

4. Susan Schober and Charles Schade, eds., *The Epidemiology of Cocaine Use and Abuse* (Rockville, MD: NIDA Research Monograph 110, 1991), pp. 19–44.

5. Alain Labrousse, "Regional Outlook: Africa," presentation at workshop "The Global Drug Phenomenon," Brookings Institution, Washington, DC, January 22, 1994.

6. Rensselaer W. Lee III, "Post-Soviet Organized Crime and Western Security Interests," testimony submitted to the Subcommittee on Terrorism, Narcotics, and International Operations, Senate Committee on Foreign Relations, April 21, 1994.

7. The spread of cannabis production in Africa is documented in a series of articles in the *Geopolitical Drug Dispatch,* a monthly newsletter published by Alain Labrousse in Paris, France.

8. Details on U.S. cannabis production can be found in *1990 Domestic Cannabis Eradication/Suppression Program,* report prepared by the Cannabis Investigations Section, Drug Enforcement Administration, Washington, DC, December 1990.

9. National Narcotics Intelligence Consumers Committee (NNICC), *The NNICC Report 1992: The Supply of Illicit Drugs to the United States* (Washington, DC: Drug Enforcement Administration, September 1993), pp. 40–45.

10. Stephen Flynn, "The Worldwide Drug Scourge: The Expanding Trade in Illicit Drugs," *Brookings Review* 11, no. 1 (Winter 1993):8.

11. NNICC, *The NNICC Report 1992,* pp. 15–17.

12. I was given details on the organization and operation of the Cali distribution cells during a personal briefing at U.S. Drug Enforcement Administration (DEA) headquarters in February 1992 and a subsequent briefing in May 1994. These details were discovered after the arrest of an entire cell in New York City and seizure of its records in December 1991.

13. "Iran: The Great Wall," *Geopolitical Drug Dispatch,* April 30, 1994, p. 4.

14. *International Narcotics Control Strategy Report* (Washington, DC: U.S. Department of State, April 1993), p. 246.

15. Research to develop macrolevel risk factors that can be used to anticipate the likely prevalence of drug use within a society is very rudimentary. All the proposed frameworks within the epidemiological community appear to have these three ingredients in common. Richard Clayton, director of the Center for Prevention Research, Lexington, Kentucky, has proposed another two: reassurance and a willingness to violate the law and predominant norms. Richard Clayton, "Assessing the Risk of a Global Drug Epidemic," paper presented at workshop "International Implications of the Transnational Drug Phenomenon," Annenberg Public Policy Center, Philadelphia, PA, April 19, 1994.

16. This comment was related to me in June 1992 by the addict's physician, Isador Obot, professor of psychology, University of Jos, Jos, Nigeria.

17. *International Narcotics Control Strategy Report,* p. 232.

18. Dale L. Yang, "Illegal Drugs, Policy Change, and State Power: The Case of Contemporary China," *Journal of Contemporary China* 4 (Fall 1993):17–18.

19. *International Narcotics Control Strategy Report,* p. 367.

20. Ibid., p. 359.

21. In Latin America, these bribes frequently are combined with threats. Government authorities are told they must choose between the "*plata o plomo*"—the silver or the lead (bullet). For a discussion of drug-related corruption, see Ethan A. Nadelmann, *Cops Across Borders: The Internationalization of U.S. Criminal Law Enforcement* (University Park: Pennsylvania State University Press, 1993), pp. 251–310.

22. Eduardo Gamarra, "Bolivia," in Scott B. MacDonald and Bruce Zagaris, eds., *International Handbook on Drug Control* (Westport, CT: Greenwood Press, 1992), pp. 101, 110.

23. Stephen Handelman, "The Russian 'Mafiya,'" *Foreign Affairs* 73, no. 2 (March/April 1994):92.

24. Robert D. Kaplan, "The Coming Anarchy," *Atlantic Monthly*, February 1994, pp. 44–76.

25. According to Ernest Drucker, professor of epidemiology at the Montefiore Medical Center in the Bronx, every new HIV infection costs $100,000–$200,000 to treat over the lifetime of the patient. "Drugs and the Future of the AIDS Epidemic," paper presented workshop "International Implications of the Transnational Drug Phenomenon," Annenberg Public Policy Center, Philadelphia, PA, April 19, 1994.

26. The data and these observations on the proliferation risks connected with the rise of Russian organized crime are drawn from Lee, "Post-Soviet Organized Crime and Western Security Interests."

27. *Illicit Narcotics Cultivation and Processing: The Ignored Environmental Drama*, a United Nations Drug Control Program informational publication, Vienna, 1993.

28. Eduardo Gamarra, "Bolivia," p. 102.

29. Jack Blum, "The Impact of Money Laundering on the International Financial System," paper presented at workshop "International Implications of the Transnational Drug Phenomenon," Annenberg Public Policy Center, Philadelphia, PA, April 19, 1994.

30. George Gerbner, "Stories That Hurt: Tobacco, Alcohol, and Other Drugs in the Mass Media," in Hank Resnik, ed., *Youth and Drugs: Society's Mixed Messages* (Rockville, MD: OSAP Prevention Monograph 6, 1990), pp. 53–128.

31. Nancy Hass and Steven Strasser, "Fighting and Switching," *Newsweek*, March 21, 1994, p. 53.

Selected Bibliography

Adepoju, Aderanti, ed. (1993). *The impact of structural adjustment on the population of Africa*. London and Portsmouth: James Currey and Heinemann.

Africa: A continent at stake. (1993, September 1). *Financial Times*.

Ahmad, Mumtaz, ed. (1986). *State politics and Islam*. Washington, DC: American Trust Publications.

al Farugi, Isma'il Raji. (1983). *Tawhid: Its relevance for thought and life*. Kuwait: International Islamic Federation.

Algar, Hamid. (1969). *Religion and state in Iran: 1785–1906*. Berkeley: University of California Press.

al-Turabi, H. (1992, June 15). A gathering force. *Newsweek*, p. 48.

American Library Association. (1992). Less access to less information by and about the government. Washington, DC.

Applebome, Peter. (1993, February 9). Adman in Atlanta tries to sell city. *New York Times*, p. A8.

Aronson, J. (1992). Telecommunications infrastructure and U.S. international competitiveness. In *A national information network: Changing our lives in the twenty-first century*. Falls Church, VA: Institute for Information Studies.

Attenborough, P. (1992). The rebirth of European publishing. In F. Kobrak and B. Luey, eds., *The structure of international publishing in the 1990s*. New Brunswick: Transaction Publishers.

Baensch, R. E. (1992). Consolidation in publishing and allied industries. In F. Kobrak and B. Luey, eds., *The structure of international publishing in the 1990s*. New Brunswick: Transaction Publishers, pp. 141–148.

Bagdikian, Ben. (1993). *The media monopoly*. 4th ed. Boston: Beacon.

Balls, Edward, and Tony Hawkins. (1993, September 1). Wanted: Bigger carrot, more stick. *Financial Times*.

Bamford, J. (1982). *The puzzle palace*. Boston: Houghton Mifflin.

Bangura, Yusuf. (1989). Crisis and adjustment: The experience of Nigerian workers. In Bade Onimode, ed., *The IMF, the World Bank, and the African debt*. London: Zed Books, pp. 177–190.

Bangura, Yusuf, and Bjorn Beckman. (1991). African workers and structural adjustment: The Nigerian case. In Dharam Ghai, ed., *The IMF and the South: The social impact of crisis and adjustment*. London: Zed Books.

Banugire, Firmooni R. (1989). Employment, incomes, basic needs, and structural adjustment policy in Uganda, 1980–87. In Bade Onimode, ed., *The IMF, the World Bank, and the African debt*. London: Zed Books.

Barinaga, Marcia. (1992, July 31). Confusion on the cutting edge. *Science* 257 (31):616–619.

———. (1993, February 12). Hughes' tough stand on industry ties. *Science* 259:884–889.

Barlow, John Perry. (1993, November). A plain text on crypto policy. *Communications of the ACM* 36 (11):21–26.

Barthes, Roland. (1975). *Mythologies.* New York: Hill and Wang.

Barya, John-Jean B. (1993, January 24). The new political conditionality of aid: An independent view from Africa. *IDS Bulletin.*

Bell, Daniel. (1960). *The end of ideology: On the exhaustion of political ideas in the fifties.* Glencoe: Free Press.

Bellew, Rosemary, Laura Raney, and K. Subbarao. (1992, March). Educating girls. *Finance and Development,* pp. 54–56.

Bentham, J. (1791). *Panopticon; or, the Inspection House.*

Bernstein, Richard. (1993, July 25). U.N. flight from Bosnia's reality. *New York Times,* p. 8.

Bill, James A. (1988). *The eagle and the lion.* New Haven: Yale University Press.

Blum, Jack. (1994, April 19). The impact of money laundering on the international financial system. Paper presented at workshop International Implications of the Transnational Drug Phenomenon. Philadelphia, PA, Annenberg Public Policy Center.

Bolton, Brian. (1987). *The common agricultural policy, African food, and international trade.* London: Catholic Institute for International Relations.

Bonat, Zuwaqhu A., and Yahaya A. Abdullahi. (1989). The World Bank, IMF, and Nigeria's agricultural and rural economy. In Bade Onimode, ed., *The IMF, the World Bank, and the African debt: The social and economic impact.* London: Zed Books. pp. 153–176.

Book conglomerates. (1990, June). *World Press Review* 37 (3):63.

Bowers, C. A. (1988). *The cultural dimensions of educational computing: Understanding the non-neutrality of technology.* New York: Teachers College Press.

Brandt, Willy. (1987). *Arms and hunger.* Cambridge, MA: MIT Press.

Brittan, Samuel. (1993, October 4). Where Gatt's $200 billion really comes from. *Financial Times.*

Brooks, Gwendolyn. (1981). *Building the dream.* New York: Pantheon.

Brown, Michael, and Steven Erie. (1981, Summer). Blacks and the legacy of the great society: The economic and political impact of federal social policy. *Public Policy* 29, no. 3.

Brownmiller, Susan. (1975). *Against our will: Men, women, and rape.* New York: Simon and Schuster.

Brownowski, Jacob. (1973). *The ascent of man.* Boston: Little Brown.

Brummer, Alex. (1993, September 25). Cold War's ending leaves spotlight on wobbly World Bank. *The Guardian.*

Buchan, David, and Leslie Crawford. (1994, January 13). IMF persuades French Africa to go for growth. *Financial Times.*

Bullard, Robert Bullard. (1992, June). The politics of race and pollution: An interview with Robert Bullard. *Multinational Monitor* 13 (6):21–22.

Cairncross, Frances. (1991). *Costing the earth.* London: Economist Books.

Caldicott, Helen. (1992). *If you love this planet.* New York: W. W. Norton.

———. (1984). *Missile envy: The arms race and nuclear war.* New York: Morrow.

Carey, James. (1969). The communications revolution and the professional communicator. In Paul Halmos, ed., Sociology of mass media communicators. *Sociological Review,* Monograph 13:23–38.

Castellon, Lucia, and Alejandro Guillier. (1993, Winter-Spring). Chile: The emerging influence of women in journalism. *Media Studies Journal* (New York, Freedom Forum Media Studies Center), pp. 231–239.

The challenge to the South: The report of the South Commission. (1990). Oxford: Oxford University Press.

Chandler, Alfred D., Jr. (1977). *The visible hand: The managerial revolution in American business.* Cambridge, MA: Belknap Press.

Chanu, Fantu. (1989). *The silent revolution in Africa: Debt, development, and democracy.* London: Zed Books.

Chinery-Hesse, Mary, et al. (1989). *Engendering adjustment for the 1990s.* London: Commonwealth Secretariat.

Chomsky, Noam. (1972). On changing the world. In *Problems of freedom and knowledge.* London: Fontana.

Clarke, Roger. (1988, May). Information technology and dataveillance. *Communications of the ACM* 31(5):498–512.

Clayton, Richard. (1994, April 19). Assessing the risk of a global drug epidemic. Paper presented at workshop International Implications of the Transnational Drug Phenomenon. Annenberg Public Policy Center, Philadelphia, PA.

Cline, William R. (1992). *The economics of global warming.* Washington, DC: Institute for International Economics.

Cohen, Claude. (1970). Economy, society, and institutions. In P. M. Holt, H. Fisher, A. Lambton, and B. Lewis, eds., *The Cambridge History of Islam.* Vol. 2. Cambridge: Cambridge University Press.

Cohen, Roger. (1993, October 5). World's tallest minaret, but short on popularity. *New York Times.*

Cohn, Carol. (1987). Sex and death in the rational world of defense intellectuals. *Signs 12* (4):687–718.

Commager, Henry Steele, ed. (1945). *Documents of American history.* New York: Crofts.

Commission of the European Communities. (No date). *Equal opportunities in European broadcasting: A guide to good practice.* N.p.: Commission of the European Communities Directorate—General Employment, Industrial Relations, and Social Affairs.

Commoner, Barry. (1992). *Making peace with the planet.* New York: New Press.

Congress of the United States. (1987). *The GATT negotiations and U.S. trade policy.* Washington, DC: Congressional Budget Office and Government Printing Office.

Connell, R. W. (1987). *Gender and power.* Stanford: Stanford University Press.

Connors, L., S. L. Henry, and J. W. Reader. (1992). From art to corporation: Harry N. Abrams, Inc., and the cultural effects of merger. In F. Kobrak and B. Luey, eds., *The structure of international publishing in the 1990s.* New Brunswick: Transaction Publishers, pp. 39–70.

Cooper, Anne M. (1988). Television's invisible women: A five-nation study of anchors, reporters, and correspondents. Paper presented at the annual convention of the Association for Education in Journalism and Mass Communication, Portland, OR.

Coote, Belinda. (1992). *The trade trap: Poverty and the global commodity markets.* Oxford: Oxfam.

Corbridge, Stuart. (1993). *Debt and development.* Oxford: Blackwell.

Coser, L. A., C. Kadushin, and W. W. Powell. (1982). *Books, culture, and the commerce of publishing.* New York: Basic Books.

Court says Nixon must be compensated for tapes. (1992, November 18). *New York Times.*

Cowen, Joseph. (1929). Speaking in the House of Commons, November 10, 1882. In Edgar R. Jones, ed., *Selected English speeches.* New York: Oxford University Press.

Davis, Mike. (1992, Summer). Interview. *CovertAction.* Info Bulletin.

Dean, John. (1947, November). "None other than Caucasians." *Journal of Land and Public Utility Economics* (University of Wisconsin).

Decornoy, Jacques. (1991, May). "Aux ordres du Nord, l'ordre de l'information." *Le Monde Diplomatique.*

De Palma, Anthony. (1993, March 17). Universities' reliance on companies raises vexing questions in research. *New York Times,* p. B8.

Dessauer, J. P. (1992). Coming full circle at Macmillan: A publishing merger in economic perspective. In F. Kobrak and B. Luey, eds., *The structure of international publishing in the 1990s.* New Brunswick: Transaction Publishers, pp. 25–37.

Dionne, E. J., Jr. (1990, May 29). "Defense intellectuals" in a new world order: Rand analysts rethink the study of conflict. *Washington Post.*

Drozdiak, William. (1993, February 6). Morocco building ties with Europe by opposing Islamic militancy. *Washington Post,* p. A17.

Easlea, Brian. (1983). *Fathering the unthinkable: Masculinity, scientists, and the nuclear arms race.* London: Pluto Press.

Edsall, Thomas, and Mary Edsall. (1991). *Chain reaction: The impact of race, rights, and taxes on American politics.* New York: W. W. Norton.

Ehrlich, Paul R., and Anne H. Ehrlich. (1991). *Healing the planet.* New York: Addison-Wesley.

Eichel, Larry. (1989, September 11). Wall kept things simple. *Philadelphia Inquirer.*

Elson, Diane. (1989). The impact of structural adjustment on women: Concepts and issues. In Bade Onimode, ed., *The IMF, the World Bank, and the African debt.* London: Zed Books, pp. 56–74.

Enayat, Hamid. (1982). *Modern Islamic political thought.* Austin: University of Texas Press.

Engelberg, Stephen, Jeff Gerth, and Tim Wiener. (1993, August 22). Saudis' stability is hit hard by heavy spending over the last decade. *New York Times,* pp. A1, A12.

Enloe, Cynthia. (1989). *Bananas, beaches, and bases: Making feminist sense of international politics.* Berkeley: University of California Press.

Faison, Seth. (1993, July 25). Bosnian in U.S.: Horror behind and new life ahead. *New York Times,* p. 8.

Faris, Nabih Amin, ed. (1944). *The Arab heritage.* Princeton: University Press.

Farmanfarmaian, Abouali. (1992, Spring). Sexuality in the Gulf War: Did you measure up? *Genders* 13:1–29.

Farrah, B., and D. Maxwell. (1992, April 20). Building America's infostructure: Public policy in the information age. *Telephony.*

Fijalkowski, Jurgen. (No date). Aggressive nationalism, immigration pressure, and asylum policy disputes in contemporary Germany. *International Migration Review* 27 (4):850–869.

Fisher, Humphrey. (1970). "The Western and Central Sudan." In P. M. Holt, H. Fisher, A. Lambton, and B. Lewis, eds., *The Cambridge history of Islam.* Vol. 2. Cambridge: Cambridge University Press.

Flynn, Stephen E. (1992). Grenada as a *"reactive"* and a *"proactive" crisis: New models of crisis decision making.* Ann Arbor, MI: UMI Dissertation Information Service.

_____. (1993, Winter). The worldwide drug scourge: The expanding trade in illicit drugs. *Brookings Review* 11 (1):6–11.

Foucault, M. (1977). *Discipline and punish: The birth of the prison.* New York: Pantheon.

Freedom Forum. (1993, May). Mistreated by the media? Or not at all. In *Covering today's women.* Arlington, VA: Freedom Forum.

_____. (1993, Winter/Spring). Who's covering what in the year of the woman? *Media Studies Journal* (New York, Freedom Forum Media Studies Center), pp. 134–140.

Fukuyama, Francis. (1989, Summer). The end of history? *National Interest,* pp. 3–18.

_____. (1992). *The end of history and the last man.* New York: Free Press.

Gallagher, Margaret. (1981). *Unequal opportunities: The case of women and the media.* Paris: UNESCO.

Galli, Rosemary E., and Ursula Frank. (Undated paper). Structural adjustment and gender in Guinea-Bissau.

Galtung, Johan. (1992). The emerging conflict formations. In K. Tehrenian and M. Tehrenian, eds., *Restructuring for world peace on the threshold of the twenty-first century.* Cresskill, NJ: Hampton Press.

_____. (1993). Geopolitical transformations and the 21st century world economy. In K. Nordenstreng and H. Shiller, eds., *Beyond national sovereignty: International communication in the 1990s.* Norwood, NJ: Ablex.

_____. (1988). Intellectual styles: Saxonic, Teutonic, Gallic, Nipponic. In Galtung, *Methodology and development.* Copenhagen: Eljers.

_____. (1967). *Theory and methods of social research.* New York: Columbia University Press.

_____. (1987). *United States foreign policy as manifest theology.* San Diego: University of California Press.

Galtung, Johan, et al. (1979). On the last 2,500 years in western history and some remarks on the coming 500. In Peter Burke, ed., *The new Cambridge modern history.* Vol. 13 (companion volume). Cambridge: Cambridge University Press.

Galtung, Johan, and Fumiko Nishimura. (1983). Structure, culture, and Japanese languages. *Social Science Information:* 885–925.

Gamarra, Eduardo. (1992). Bolivia. In Scott B. MacDonald and Bruce Zagaris, eds., *International handbook on drug control.* Westport, CT: Greenwood Press.

Gandy, Oscar, Jr. (1982) *Beyond agenda setting: Information subsidies and public policy.* Norwood, NJ: Ablex.

_____. (1993). *The panoptic sort: A political economy of personal information.* Boulder: Westview Press.

_____. (1988). Political economy of communications competence. In Vincent Mosco and Janet Wasko, eds., *The political economy of information.* Madison: University of Wisconsin Press.

George, Susan. (1988). *A fate worse than debt.* London: Penguin.

Georges, Christopher. (1993, July/August). Bad news bearers. *Washington Monthly,* pp. 28–35.

Gerbner, George. (1993, Spring). Instant history: The case of the Moscow coup. *Political Communication* 10:185–194.

_____. (1993). Miracles of communication technology: Powerful audiences, diverse choices, and other fairy tales. In Janet Wasko, ed., *Illuminating the blind spots.* New York: Ablex.

_____. (1990). Stories that hurt: Tobacco, alcohol, and other drugs in the mass media. In Hank Resnik, ed., *Youth and drugs: Society's mixed message.* Rockville, MD: OSAP Prevention Monograph 6, pp. 53–128.

_____. (1995). Television violence: The power and the peril. In Gail Dines and Jean M. Humez, eds., *Gender, race, and class in media: A critical text reader.* Newbury Park: Sage Publications.

Gerth, Jeff. (1993, August 22). Saudi stability hit by heavy spending over the last decade. *New York Times,* p. A14.

Gibbon, Edward. (1777). *Decline and fall of the Roman Empire.* Oxford: Bury, ch. 52.

Gibbon, Peter. (1992). Structural adjustment and pressures toward multipartyism in sub-Saharan Africa. In Peter Gibbon, Yusuf Bangura, and Ave Ofstad, eds., *Authoritarianism, democracy, and adjustment: The politics of economic reform in Africa.* Uppsala: Nordiska Afrikainstituet.

Gittings, John. (1993, August 5). Communists have parents too. *London Review of Books,* pp. 3–4.

Golden, Tim. (1994, January 4). News. *New York Times.*

Goldsmith, Edward, et al. (1990). *The imperiled planet.* Cambridge, MA: MIT Press.

Government records are public property. (1992, June 2). *New York Times,* p. A13.

Green, Reginald Herbold. (1989). The broken pot: The social fabric, economic disaster, and adjustment in Africa. In Bade Onimode, ed., *The IMF, the World Bank, and the African debt.* London: Zed Books, pp. 31–55.

Guahar, Altaf. (1978). Islam and secularism. In Altaf Guahar, ed., *The Challenge of Islam.* London: Islamic Council of Europe.

Gulhati, Ralph. (1988). *The political economy of reform in sub-Saharan Africa.* EDI Policy Seminar Report no. 8. Washington, DC: World Bank.

Hakovirta, Harto. (1993). The global refugee problem: A model and its application. *International Political Science Review* 14 (1):35–57.

Hall, Stuart. (1988, October). Brave new world. *Marxism Today,* pp. 24–29.

Handelman, Stephen. (1994, March/April). The Russian "Mafiya." *Foreign Affairs* 73 (2).

Harbeson, John W., and Donald Rothchild, eds. (1991). *Africa in world politics.* Boulder: Westview Press.

Harden, Blaine. (1992). *Africa: Dispatches from a fragile continent.* London: Fontana.

Harris, Lawrence. (1989). The Bretton Woods system and Africa. In Bade Onimode, ed., *The IMF, the World Bank, and African debt.* London: Zed Books, pp. 19–24.

Harrison, Paul. (1987). *The greening of Africa.* London: Paladin.

Hart, George W. (1990, September). Reaching out with 2-way communications. *EPRI Journal.*

_____. (1989, June). Residential energy monitoring and computerized surveillance via utility power flows. *IEEE Technology and Society Magazine,* pp. 12–16.

Hasan, Ahmad. (1978). *The doctrine of Ijma in Islam.* Islamabad, Pakistan: Islamic Research Institute.

Hass, Nancy, and Steven Strasser. (1994, March 21). Fighting and switching. *Newsweek,* p. 53.

Havel, Vaclav. (1992, March 1). The end of the modern era. *New York Times,* p. E15.

Hawkins, Tony. (1993, September 1). At the edge of prosperity. *Financial Times.*

Hedges, Chris. (1993, October 4). As Egypt votes on Mubarak, he faces rising peril. *New York Times,* p. A8.

_____. (1993, October 12). Mubarak promising democracy, and law and order. *New York Times,* p. A3.

Henderson, H. (1992, Fall). Perfecting democracy's tools. In After the nation-state: Reinventing democracy. *New Perspectives Quarterly.*

Hersch, Seymour M. (1993, November 1). *New Yorker.*

Hillman, James. (1972). *The myth of analysis.* New York: Harper and Row.

Hitti, P. K. (1944). *History of the Arabs.* London: Macmillan.

Hopkinson, Nicholas. (1992). *Good government in Africa.* Wilton Park Paper no. 54. London: HMSO.

Huenefeld, J. (1992). Can small publishers survive . . . and who cares? In F. Kobrak and B. Luey, eds., *The structure of international publishing in the 1990s.* New Brunswick: Transaction Publishers.

Huntington, Samuel P. (1993, Summer). The clash of civilizations. *Foreign Affairs* 72 (3):22–49.

Hutchful, Eboe, ed. (1987). *The IMF and Ghana: The confidential record.* London: Zed Books.

Hutton, Will. (1993, January 13). The new world order leaves a continent sunk in debt. *The Guardian.*

Intergovernmental Panel on Climate Change. (1990). *Climate change.* New York: Cambridge University Press.

International Narcotics Control Strategy Report. (1993, April). U.S. Department of State.

Iran: The great wall. (1994, April 30). *Geopolitical Drug Dispatch.*

Isaacs, Harold R. (1958). *Scratches on our minds.* New York: John Day.

Jackson, Ben. (1990). *Poverty and the planet: A question of survival.* London: Penguin.

Jansen, Sue Curry, Julian Halliday, and James Schneider. (1992). *Framing the crisis in eastern Europe.* London: Sage Publications.

Jansen, Sue Curry, and Donald F. Sabo (1992). Sport/war: The gender order, the Persian Gulf War, and the new world order. Paper presented at International Communication Association Meeting, Miami.

Jones, Edgar R., ed. (1929). *Selected English speeches.* New York: Oxford University Press.

Judge calls administration lax on predecessors' computer records. (1993, June 9). *New York Times,* p. 8.

Kaplan, Robert D. (1994, February). The coming anarchy. *Atlantic Monthly,* pp. 44–76.

Keller, Evelyn Fox. (1985). *Reflections on gender and science.* New Haven: Yale University Press.

Kelly, Michael. (1993, June 6). Clinton myth of nonideological politics stumbles. *New York Times,* p. 26.

Kennan, George. (1993). *Around the cragged hill.* New York: W. W. Norton.

Kennedy, Paul. (1993). *Preparing for the twenty-first century.* New York: Random House.

Kennedy, Paul, and Matthew Connelly. (1994, December). *Atlantic Monthly* 274 (6):61–91.

Khaldun, I. (1967). *The Muqaddimah: An introduction to history.* London: Routledge & Kegan Paul.

Khan, Mohsin, and Malcolm Knight. (1983). *Determinants of current account balances of non-oil developing countries in the 1970s.* IMF Staff Papers no. 31. Washington, DC: IMF.

Khan, Q. (1973). *The political thoughts of Ibn Taymiyah.* Islamabad, Pakistan: Islamic Research Institute.

Khomeini, Ayatollah Imam Ruhollah. (1981). *Islam and revolution: Writings and declarations of Imam Khomeini.* Trans. Hamid Algar. Berkeley, CA: Mizan Press.

_____. (1988). *Islamic government.* Trans. and annot. Hamid Algar. Kerala, India: Islamic Foundation Press, Malappuram District.

Kirn, Walter. (1993, March 7). The editor as gap model. *New York Times Magazine,* pp. 26–27, 35, 55–56.

Kupperman, R. H., R. H. Eilox, and H. A. Smith. (1975, February 7). Crisis management: Some opportunities. *Science* 182:404.

Labrousse, Alain. (1994, January 22). Regional outlook: Africa. Presentation at workshop The Global Drug Phenomenon, Brookings Institution, Washington, DC.

Lal, Deepak. (1983). *The poverty of "development economics."* London: IEA.

Lancaster, Carol. (1993). Governance and development: The views from Washington. *IDS Bulletin* 24 (1):9–15.

Lee, Rensselaer W., III. (1994, April 21). Post-Soviet organized crime and western security interests. Testimony submitted to the Subcommittee on Terrorism, Narcotics, and International Operations, Senate Committee on Foreign Relations.

Lehman, Nicholas. (1991). *The great black migration and how it changed America.* New York: Alfred Knopf.

Lenczowski, George. (1990). *The Middle East in world affairs.* 4th ed. Ithaca: Cornell University Press.

Lenk, K. (1982). Information technology and society. In A. Schaff and G. Griedrichs, eds., *Microelectronics and society, for better or for worse: A report to the Club of Rome.* Elmsford, NY: Pergamon.

Lever, Harold, and Christopher Hulne. (1985). *Debt and danger: The world financial crisis.* London: Penguin.

Levine, Hillel, and Lawrence Harmon. (1992). *The death of an American Jewish community: A tragedy of good intentions.* New York: Free Press.

Levitt, William. (1976). Cited in Michael Danielson, *The politics of exclusion.* New York: Columbia University Press.

Lewis, Neil A. (1993, August 14). Government told to save messages sent by computer. *New York Times*, p. 1.

Licklider, J. (1979). Computers and government. In M. Dertouzos and J. Moses, eds., *The computer age.* Cambridge, MA: MIT Press.

Long, E. (1992). The cultural meaning of concentration in publishing. In F. Kobrak and B. Luey, eds., *The structure of international publishing in the 1990s.* New Brunswick: Transaction Publishers, pp. 39–70.

Luey, B. (1992). Introduction. In F. Kobrak and B. Luey, eds., *The structure of international publishing in the 1990s.* New Brunswick: Transaction Publishers, pp. 1–19.

MacKinnon, Catherine A. (1993, July/August). Turning rape into pornography: Postmodern genocide. *Ms.*, pp. 24–30.

MacNeill, Jim, et al. (1991). *Beyond interdependence.* New York: Oxford University Press.

Madden, Peter, and John Madeley. (1993). *Winners and losers: The impact of the GATT Uruguay Round on developing countries.* London: Christian Aid.

Magrass, Y., and R. Upchurch. (1988, April). Computer literacy: People adapted for technology. *Computers and Society* 18 (2).

Mander, Jerry. (1991). *In the absence of the sacred: The failure of technology and the survival of the Indian nations.* San Francisco: Sierra Club Books.

Marcuse, Herbert. (1969). *An essay on liberation.* Boston: Beacon Press.

Mboya, Tom. (1963). *Freedom and after.* London: Deutsch.

McKibben, Bill. (1992). *The age of missing information.* New York: Random House.

McMillen, Liz. (1992, April 24). Quest for profits may damage basic values of universities, Harvard's Bok warns. *Chronicle of Higher Education* 37 (32):1.

Meacher, Michael. (1993, October 26). We need a new ministry to tackle the problems developing countries face. *Independent.*

Meadows, Donella, et al. (1992). *Beyond the limits*. London: Earthscan.

Meena, Ruth. (Undated paper). Women and debt: The Tanzanian experience.

Miller, Susan. (1993, Winter/Spring). Opportunity squandered: Newspapers and women's news. *Media Studies Journal*. (New York, Freedom Forum Media Studies Center), pp. 167–182.

Mills, C. Wright. (1959). *The sociological imagination*. New York: Oxford University Press.

Mills, Kay. (1993, Winter/Spring). The media and the year of the woman. *Media Studies Journal* (New York, Freedom Forum Media Studies Center), pp. 19–32.

Moore, Charles A. (1967). *The Chinese mind*. Honolulu: University of Hawaii Press.

Morgan, Edward S. (1981, February 22). *New York Times*.

Morgan, M., and J. Shanahan. (1991). Do VCRs change the TV picture? VCR's and the cultivation process. *American Behavioral Scientist* 35 (2):122–135.

Morgan, M., and N. Signorielli. (1990). "Cultivation analysis: Conceptualization and methodology." In M. Morgan and N. Signorielli, eds., *Cultivation analysis: New directions in media effects research*. Newbury Park: Sage.

Morita, Akio. (1993, June). Toward a new world economic order. *Atlantic Monthly*.

Mosco, Vincent, and Janet Wasko, eds. (1988). *The political economy of information*. Madison: University of Wisconsin Press.

Mowlana, Hamid Mowlana. (1993). The new global order and cultural ecology. *Media, culture, and society* (special issue of *Islam and Communication*) 15 (4):9–27.

_____. (1979, Summer). Technology versus tradition: Communication in the Iranian revolution. *Journal of Communication* 29 (3):107–112.

Mowlana, Hamid, and Laurie J. Wilson. (1990). *The passing of modernity: Communication and transformation in society*. White Plains, NY: Longman.

Moyers, Bill, and Center for Investigative Reporting. (1991). *Global dumping ground*. Cambridge: Lutterworth Press.

Mutemba, Dorothy. (1989). The impact of IMF–World Bank programs on women and children in Zambia. In Bade Onimode, ed., *The IMF, the World Bank, and the African debt*. London: Zed Books, pp. 111–124.

Mwanawina, A. (1993). Zambia. In Aderanti Adepojou, ed., *The impact of structural adjustment on the population of Africa*. London and Northampton: James Currey and Heinemann, pp. 69–77.

Nadelmann, Ethan A. (1993). *Cops across borders: The internationalization of U.S. criminal law enforcement*. University Park: Pennsylvania State University Press, pp. 251–310.

National Academy of Sciences. (1990). *One earth, one future*. Washington, DC: National Academy Press.

National Narcotics Intelligence Consumers Committee (NNICC). (1993, September). *The NNICC report 1992: The supply of illicit drugs to the United States*. Washington, DC: Drug Enforcement Administration.

New Nielsen system is turning heads: Peoplemeter that reads faces, and where they're looking, raises specter of Big Brother. (1992, May 18). *Broadcasting* 122 (21).

Nimtz, A. H., Jr. (1980). *Islam and politics in East Africa*. Minneapolis: University of Minnesota Press.

Nixon, Richard. (1971, January 14). *Federal policies relative to equal housing opportunity statement by the President*. 7 Weekly Compilation of Presidential Documents.

Noble, Kenneth B. (1993, October 31). *New York Times*.

O'Neil, John. (1993, March 14). Bush tapes lost, U.S. archivists say. *New York Times*, p. 16.

Onimode, Bade. (1992). *A future for Africa: Beyond the politics of adjustment.* London: Earthscan Publications.

Ottoway, David B. (1994, January 10). Ethnic Hungarians in Slovakia are demanding self-government. *Washington Post,* p. A12.

Oxfam. (1993). *Africa make or break: Action for recovery.* Oxford: Oxfam.

Parsons, Talcott, ed. (1966). *Societies: Evolutionary and comparative perspectives.* Englewood Cliffs: Prentice-Hall.

Patai, Raphael. (1973). *The Arab mind.* New York: Scribner's.

_____. (1977). *The Jewish mind.* New York: Scribner's.

Payer, Cheryl. (1975). *The debt trap: The IMF and the Third World.* Harmondsworth: Penguin.

_____. (1991). *Lent and lost: Foreign credit and Third World development.* London: Zed Books.

Pear, Robert. (1993, March 1). Health data sought by Clinton is no longer collected. *New York Times,* p. A13.

Piller, Charles. (1993, July). Bosses with X-ray eyes. *Macworld.*

Popoola, D. (1993). Nigeria: Consequences for health. In Aderanti Adepoju, ed., *The impact of structural adjustment on the population of Africa.* London: James Currey, pp. 79–92.

Potter, C. N. (1990). *Who does what and why in book publishing.* New York: Birch Lane Press.

Preston, Lewis T. (1993, September 27). Private sector key to Africa's future. Letter to *Financial Times.*

Privacy concern raised over Lotus marketplace. (1990, Fall). *CPSR Newsletter* 8 (4):24–25.

Prowse, Michael. (1993, April 29). Economists faith in "new consensus" raises old concerns. *Financial Times.*

Quindlen, Anna. (1993, March 10). Gynocide. *New York Times,* p. A15.

Rafi-ud-din, Mohammad. (1946). *Ideology of the future.* Lahore, Pakistan: Muhammad Ashraf Publishers.

Rakow, Lana, and K. Kranich. (1991, Winter). Woman as sign in television news. *Journal of Communication* 41 (1):8–23.

Richard Nixon's unjust demand. (1992, November 19). *New York Times,* editorial.

Richburg, K. (1992, December 21). Somali Muslims warily eye GIs. *Washington Post,* p. A1.

Rivkin, S. (1993, September 26). While the cable and phone companies fight . . . look who's wiring the home now. *New York Times Magazine.*

Robins, K., and F. Webster. (1988). Cybernetic capitalism: Information, technology, everyday life. In V. Mosco and J. Wasco, eds., *The political economy of information.*

Rostow, W. W. (1960). *The stages of economic growth: A non-communist manifesto.* Cambridge: Cambridge University Press.

Rubin, Gayle. (1975). The traffic in women: Notes on the political economy of sex. In *Toward an anthropology of women.* New York: Monthly Review Press, pp. 157–210.

Said, Edward. (1979). *Orientalism.* New York: Vintage.

Sandbrook, Richard. (1991). Economic crisis, structural adjustment, and the state in sub-Saharan Africa. In Dharam Ghai, ed., *The IMF and the South: The social impact of crisis and adjustment.* London: Zed Books, pp. 95–114.

Sardar, Ziauddin. (1987). *The future of Muslim civilization.* London and New York: Mansell Publishing, pp. 53–76.

_____. (1985). *Islamic futures: The shape of ideas to come.* London and New York: Mansell Publishing, pp. 126–156.

Saudis without dollars. (1993, August 25). *New York Times,* p. A14.

Saunders, Harold H. (1993, November 9). Enlarging U.S. policy toward "ethnic" conflict: Rethinking intervention. Paper prepared for symposium Ethnic Conflicts: Threat to Domestic and International Peace. Jointly sponsored by the National Defense University and the Joint Center for Political and Economic Studies of Washington, DC.

Schiller, Dan. (1981). *Objectivity and the news: The public and the rise of commercial journalism.* Philadelphia: University of Pennsylvania Press.

Schneider, Keith. (1992, December 2). U.S. lack of supervision encouraged waste in contracts. *New York Times,* p. 1.

Schober, Susan, and Charles Schade, eds. (1991). *The epidemiology of cocaine use and abuse.* Rockville, MD: NIDA Research Monograph, pp. 19–44.

Schrage, Michael. (1993, May 6). High-tech programs are no substitute for quality education. *Los Angeles Times,* p. D1.

Schudson, Michael. (1978). *Discovering the news.* New York: Basic Books.

Schwartz, M., and D. Wood. (1993, August). Discovering shared interests using graph analysis. *Communications of the ACM* 36 (8):78–79.

Segal, David. (1993, July/August). The shell game. *Washington Monthly,* pp. 36–44.

Shilts, Randy. (1987). *And the band played on: Politics, people, and the AIDS epidemic.* New York: St. Martin's Press.

Simons, Marlise. (1993, April 9). The sex market: Scourge on the world's children. *New York Times,* p. A3.

Sisterhood is global: International news. (1993, July/August). Ms., pp. 14–15.

Smith, R. (1993, February 3). Administration to consider giving spy data to business. *Washington Post.*

Solotaroff, T. (1991, October 7). The paperbacking of publishing. *The Nation* 253 (11):300.

Sorokin, Pitirim. (1957). *Social and cultural dynamics.* Boston: Porter and Sargent.

South Center, The. (1993). *Facing the challenge: Responses to the Report of the South Commission.* London: The South Center.

Southern, Richard. (1980). *Western views of Islam in the Middle Ages.* Cambridge: Cambridge University Press.

Stanford, James. (1993, March). Continental economic integration: Modeling the impact on labor. *Annals of the American Academy of Political and Social Science* 526:92–110.

Steeves, H. Leslie. (1989). Gender and mass communication in a global context. In Pamela J. Creedon, ed., *Women in mass communication: Challenging gender values.* Newbury Park: Sage Publications, pp. 83–111.

Stewart, Frances, ed. (1993). *Alternative development strategies in sub-Saharan Africa.* Basingstoke: Macmillan.

Sun, L. (1989). Limits of selective viewing: An analysis of "diversity" in dramatic programming. Master's thesis, University of Pennsylvania.

Sweenzy, Paul M. (1989, June). Capitalism and the environment. *Monthly Review* 41 (2):6.

Technology and terrorism: Privatizing public violence. (1991, Summer). *IEEE Technology and Society Magazine* 10 (2).

Third world finance survey. (1993, September 23, 25). *The Economist.*

Thompson, E. P. (1990, January 28). End and the beginning: History turns on a new hinge. *The Nation,* pp. 117–118, 120–122.

Tofani, Loretta. (1993, August 2). "Comfort women" seek confession from Japan. *Philadelphia Inquirer,* pp. 1 and A10.

Tolba, Mostafa K. (1992). *Saving our planet.* New York: Chapman and Hall.

Tolchin, Susan, and Martin Tolchin. (1983). *Dismantling America.* Boston: Houghton Mifflin.

Tonelson, Alan. (1993/94, Winter). Beyond left and right. *National Interest,* pp. 3–18.

_____. (1978). Objectivity as strategic ritual: An examination of newsmen's notions of objectivity. *American Journal of Sociology* 77 (4):660–679.

Tuchman, Gaye, Arlene Kaplan Daniels, and James Benet, eds. (1978). *Hearth and home: Images of women in mass media.* New York: Oxford University Press.

Tullus, LaMond. (1991). *Handbook of research on the illicit drug traffic: Socioeconomic consequences.* New York: Greenwood Press.

Tunstall, Jeremy. (1986). *Communication deregulation.* Oxford: Basil Blackwell.

Turow, J. (1983, Fall). A mass communication perspective on book publishing. *Journal of Popular Culture* 17.

Twain, Mark. (1881). *Innocents Abroad.* London: Chatto & Windus.

ul-Haq, Mahbub. (1993, September 1–3). U.N. Development Program, paper presented at the North-South Roundtable, Bretton Woods, NH.

Umar-ud-din, M. (1962). *The ethical philosophy of Al-Ghazzali.* Lahore: Muhammad Ashraf Publishers.

United Nations. (1947). Document A/311.

_____. (1993, June 24). Report of the Secretary-General on the Financial Situation. U.N. Document A/C.5/47/13/Add.1.

_____. (1991). U.N. Development Program Human Development Report. New York.

United Nations Drug Control Program. (1993). *Illicit narcotics cultivation and processing: The ignored environmental drama.* Vienna.

_____. (1993, October). *Latin American and the Caribbean Section.* United Nations Drug Control Program Report. Vienna.

U.S. Congress. (1993, November 1). Report of the U.S. Congressional Research Service.

U.S. Department of Commerce, International Trade Administration. (1989). *1989 U.S. Industrial Outlook.* Washington, DC: GPO.

U.S. Drug Enforcement Administration. (1990, December). *1990 Domestic Cannabis Eradication/Suppression Program.* Washington, DC: DEA.

U.S. House Committee on Energy and Commerce. (1992, December 3). GAO Report. *Federal Contracting.* GAO/TRCED-93-2.

U.S. State Department. (1993, April). *International Narcotics Control Strategy Report.* Washington, DC.

Utim, Ekei U. (1992, October 30–31). Debt and structural adjustment programs: Mixed blessings for the women of Africa. Paper presented to Akina mama wa Afrika Conference, London.

_____. (1992, June 4–14). Women and development in Nigeria: Problems and prospects. Paper presented to seminar Women and Development: Crisis and Alternative Visions. Bossey, Switzerland, Ecumenical Institute.

Vallely, Paul. (1990). *Bad samaritans: First World ethics and Third World debt.* London: Hodder and Stoughton.

Victims of the flesh trade: Thailand's child slavery. (1993, March 8). *Miami Herald,* p. 8A.

Vitousik, Peter M., et al. (1986, June). Human appropriation of the products of photosynthesis. *Bioscience* 36 (6).

Volga Germans seek lost homeland. (1993, September 8). *Christian Science Monitor*, p. 8.

Watkins, Kevin. (1992). *Fixing the rules: North-South issues in international trade and the GATT Uruguay Round.* London: Catholic Institute for International Relations.

_____. (1993, December 19). IMF's Russian medicine harms Africa, too. Letter to *The Guardian*.

Weinberg, Bill. (1991). *War on land.* London: Zed Books.

Weisberg, J. (1991, June 17). Rough trade: The sad decline of American publishing. *New Republic* 204 (24):16.

Weizenbaum, Joseph. (1976). *Computer power and human reason: From judgment to calculation.* San Francisco: W. H. Freeman.

Whalen, Christopher. (1993, August 29). The Saudi well runs dry. *Washington Post*, p. C2.

What the world's women want. (1993, May 16). *New York Times*, p. 16.

Whiteside, T. (1981). *The blockbuster complex: Conglomerates, show business, and book publishing.* Middletown, CT: Wesleyan.

Wiesner, Louis A., and Steve Edminster. (1993). Asylum seekers, other foreigners, and neo-Nazi violence in Germany. *World Refugee Survey*, pp. 121–125.

Williams, Carol J. (1994, January 7). Ethnic tension poses threat to Hungarians. *Los Angeles Times*, Washington ed., p. A12.

Winner, L. (1986). *The whale and the reactor.* Chicago: University of Chicago Press.

Women breaking the silence. (1990, October). *Index on Censorship* 19 (9):2, 7–36.

Wood, R. (1986). *Marshall Plan to debt crisis.* Berkeley: University of California Press.

Woodward, David. (1992). *Debt, adjustment, and poverty in developing countries.* London: Pinter and Save the Children Fund.

World Bank. (1981). *Accelerated development in sub-Saharan Africa.* Washington, DC: World Bank.

_____. (1992). *Good governance and development.* Washington, DC: World Bank.

_____. (1994). *World Debt Tables 1993–4.* Washington, DC: World Bank.

_____. (1992). *World Development Report.* Washington, DC: World Bank.

Wright, Robin. (1993, May 16). Equality elusive, U.N. reports. From *Los Angeles Times*, reprinted in *Morning Call* (Allentown, PA), p. A3.

Yang, Dali L. (1993, Fall). Illegal drugs, policy change, and state power: The case of contemporary China. *Journal of Contemporary China* 4:17–18.

Yuppie lit: Publicize or perish. (1987, October 19). *Time*, pp. 77–79.

Zuwaqhu, Bonat, and Yahaya A. Abdullahi. (1989). The World Bank, IMF, and Nigeria's agricultural and rural economy. In Bade Onimode, ed., *The IMF, the World Bank, and the African debt: The social and economic impact.* London: Zed Books.

About the Book and Editors

Hidden from public sight and mind today are invisible crises that threaten our democracy and existence even more than the crises we know about—or think we know about. These invisible crises include the promotion of practices that drug, hurt, poison, and kill thousands every day; cults of violence that desensitize, terrorize, and brutalize; the growing siege mentality of our cities; widening resource gaps and the most glaring inequalities in the industrial world; the costly neglect of vital institutions such as public education and the arts; and media-assisted make-believe image politics corrupting the electoral process.

Deprived of sustained attention but bombarded by eruptions of surface consequences (often presented as unique events stripped of historical context), people are bewildered, fearful, angry, and cynical.

The contributors to this volume—exploring such unattended crises, analyzing why they are hidden, and focusing on the increasing concentration of culture-power that keeps them from view—maintain that a profound general crisis of social vision, public communication, and representative government underlies all of the invisible crises.

George Gerbner is professor emeritus at the Annenberg School for Communication at the University of Pennsylvania. **Hamid Mowlana** is professor of communication at American University and president of the International Association of Media Research. **Herbert I. Schiller** is professor emeritus of communication at the University of California at San Diego.

Index